ETHICAL PRACTICE IN PSYCHIATRY AND THE LAW

CRITICAL ISSUES IN AMERICAN PSYCHIATRY AND THE LAW

was edited for

THE AMERICAN ACADEMY OF PSYCHIATRY AND THE LAW (TRI-STATE CHAPTER)

Volume 1 Edited by Richard Rosner, M.D.

Volume 2 Edited by Richard Rosner, M.D.

Volume 3 GERIATRIC PSYCHIATRY AND THE LAW
Edited by Richard Rosner, M.D., and Harold I. Schwartz, M.D.

Volume 4 JUVENILE PSYCHIATRY AND THE LAW
Edited by Richard Rosner, M.D., and Harold I. Schwartz, M.D.

Volume 5 CRIMINAL COURT CONSULTATION
Edited by Richard Rosner, M.D., and Ronnie B. Harmon, M.A.

Volume 6 CORRECTIONAL PSYCHIATRY
Edited by Richard Rosner, M.D., and Ronnie B. Harmon, M.A.

Volume 7 ETHICAL PRACTICE IN PSYCHIATRY AND THE LAW
Edited by Richard Rosner, M.D., and Robert Weinstock, M.D.

A Continuation Order Plan is available for this series. A continuation order will bring delivery of each new volume immediately upon publication. Volumes are billed only upon actual shipment. For further information please contact the publisher.

ETHICAL PRACTICE IN PSYCHIATRY AND THE LAW

Edited by

RICHARD ROSNER, M.D.

Clinical Professor, Department of Psychiatry
New York University School of Medicine
Diplomate, American Board of Forensic Psychiatry
and Medical Director, Forensic Psychiatry Clinic for the
New York Criminal and Supreme Courts (First Judicial Department),
Department of Mental Health, Mental Retardation, and
Alcoholism Services of the City of New York
New York, New York

and

ROBERT WEINSTOCK, M.D.

Associate Clinical Professor, Department of Psychiatry and Biobehavioral
Sciences, University of California, Los Angeles, School of Medicine
Director, Forensic and Ethical Consultation, Psychiatry Service,
West Los Angeles Veterans Administration Medical Center,
Los Angeles, California
Director, Psychiatric Training, Student Psychological Services,
University of California, Los Angeles
Diplomate, American Board of Forensic Psychiatry

PLENUM PRESS • NEW YORK AND LONDON

To our teachers, our students,

and our patients

Library of Congress Catalog Card Number 88-657025

ISBN 0-306-43476-8

A Division of Plenum Publishing Corporation
233 Spring Street, New York, N.Y. 10013

Printed in the United States of America

Contributors

Baruch A. Brody • Center for Ethics, Medicine, and Public Issues, Baylor College of Medicine, Houston, Texas 77030

Cynthia B. Cohen • Department of Philosophy, Villanova University, Villanova, Pennsylvania 19085, and the Hastings Center, 255 Elm Road, Briarcliff Manor, New York 10510

Bernard L. Diamond • School of Law, University of California at Berkeley, Berkeley, California 94720

Spencer Eth • Veterans Administration Medical Center, Los Angeles, California 90073; Department of Psychiatry and Biobehavioral Sciences, University of California at Los Angeles, Los Angeles, California 90024; and Department of Psychiatry, University of Southern California School of Medicine, Los Angeles, California 90033

Philippa Foot • Department of Philosophy, University of California at Los Angeles, Los Angeles, California 90024

Harold M. Ginzburg • Bureau of Health Care Delivery and Assistance, Health Resources and Services Administration, United States Public Health Service, 5600 Fishers Lane, Rockville, Maryland 20857

Robert Lloyd Goldstein • Department of Psychiatry, College of Physicians and Surgeons of Columbia University, New York, New York 10032

Abraham L. Halpern • Department of Psychiatry, New York Medical College, Valhalla, New York 10595, and Department of Psychiatry, United Hospital Medical Center, Port Chester, New York 10573

Edward M. Hundert • McLean Hospital, 115 Mill Street, Belmont, Massachusetts 02178

Stanley R. Kern • New Jersey Medical School, South Orange, New Jersey 07079

Gregory B. Leong • Department of Psychiatry and Biobehavioral Sciences, School of Medicine, University of California at Los Angeles, Los Angeles,

California 90024, and the Psychiatry Service, West Los Angeles Veterans Administration Medical Center, Los Angeles, California 90073

Ruth Macklin • Department of Epidemiology and Social Medicine, Albert Einstein College of Medicine, Yeshiva University, Bronx, New York 10461

Robert D. Miller • Forensic Center, Mendota Mental Health Institute, 301 Troy Drive, Madison, Wisconsin 53704; Department of Psychiatry and Law School, University of Wisconsin–Madison, Madison, Wisconsin 53706; and Department of Psychiatry, Medical College of Wisconsin, Milwaukee, Wisconsin 53226

Mark J. Mills • Department of Psychiatry and Biobehavioral Sciences and Program in Psychiatry and Law, University of California at Los Angeles, Los Angeles, California 90024

Richard Rosner • Department of Psychiatry, New York University School of Medicine, New York, New York 10016, and Forensic Psychiatry Clinic of the New York Criminal and Supreme Courts, 100 Centre Street, New York, New York 10013

Robert L. Sadoff • Department of Psychiatry and Center for Studies of Social-Legal Psychiatry, University of Pennsylvania School of Medicine, Jenkintown, Pennsylvania 19046

J. Arturo Silva • Department of Psychiatry and Biobehavioral Sciences, School of Medicine, University of California at Los Angeles, Los Angeles, California 90024, and the Psychiatry Service, West Los Angeles Veterans Administration Medical Center, Los Angeles, California 90073

Ralph Slovenko • Wayne State University School of Law, Detroit, Michigan 48202

Alan A. Stone • Faculty of Law and Faculty of Medicine, Harvard Law School, Harvard University, Cambridge, Massachusetts 02138

Sheldon Travin • Department of Psychiatry, Bronx-Lebanon Hospital Center, 1285 Fulton Avenue, Bronx, New York 10456, and Department of Psychiatry, Albert Einstein College of Medicine, Bronx, New York 10461

Henry C. Weinstein • Forensic Psychiatry Service, New York University Medical Center/Bellevue Hospital Center, 550 First Avenue, New York, New York 10016

Robert Weinstock • Department of Psychiatry and Biobehavioral Sciences, School of Medicine, University of California at Los Angeles, Los Angeles, California 90024, and the Psychiatry Service, West Los Angeles Veterans Administration Medical Center, Los Angeles, California 90073

Joan G. Wexler • Brooklyn Law School, 250 Joralemon Street, Brooklyn, New York 11201

Foreword

We would expect a successful series such as *Critical Issues in American Psychiatry and the Law* to present timely, relevant issues in a high-quality manner, and such is the hallmark of this outstanding series. But we might not expect the editors to dive into the especially controversial issues, e.g., ethics, and I applaud them for doing so and in such a comprehensive and thorough fashion.

Public and professional concern about ethical aspects of psychiatrists' behavior and practice is growing, and exponentially. Concern about the ethical practice of modern forensic psychiatry is paralleled by deep-seated apprehension not only about the ethical dilemmas of psychiatry and medicine (e.g., societal versus individual patient values, the corporatization of medicine, access to versus cost of medicine) but also about the widely publicized ethical transgressions of religious and political leaders. That's why this volume is so timely and important.

Ethics—the principles and rules of right conduct. Sounds simple. We know it is not. When I'm asked by colleagues to consider the perceived unethical behavior of a fellow professional, I often find that, like obscenity, they can't always define it but they are definite that they know it when they see it. The perception of ethical conduct often appears to be in the eyes of the beholder. Well, that's why you will want to read this volume. It may not always please you, it may upset you and even offend you, but it will definitely inform you.

On behalf of the officers and members of the American Academy of Psychiatry and the Law, congratulations to Richard Rosner and his co-editor Robert Weinstock for this outstanding contribution to the forensic literature.

RICHARD T. RADA, M.D.
President-Elect
American Academy of Psychiatry and the Law
Baltimore, Maryland

Introduction

This volume is intended to stimulate thought and discussion of ethical issues relevant to the practice of forensic psychiatry as well as consideration of ethical dilemmas occurring when the law impacts upon psychiatric practice. Though this volume is directed toward forensic psychiatrists, it has relevance for all mental health practitioners, administrators, attorneys in medical jurisprudence, and those with an interest in professional ethics.

The genesis of this volume has proceeded over a five-year period. The contents are work products of the committees on ethics of the Psychiatry and Behavioral Science Section of the American Academy of Forensic Sciences (AAFS), and of the American Academy of Psychiatry and the Law (AAPL). Contributions are derived in part from highlights of two meetings of the Tri-State AAPL chapter, annual meetings of AAPL and AAFS, and a meeting of the Southern California chapter of AAPL. Other book chapters were written especially for this volume. Opinions expressed are those of the individual authors and are not necessarily the position of any organization, or of the editors. The purpose of this volume is to encourage interchange between the authors and the minds of the readers rather than presenting arbitrary answers to problems that have no simple solutions.

This volume's first part, "Issues and Approaches," begins with a chapter by Alan Stone, Professor of Law and Psychiatry, Faculties of Law and Medicine, Harvard University, who examines ethical problems and issues. His important though sometimes disturbing contribution has stimulated discussion of ethical complexities. He sets forth an intellectually provocative challenge to forensic psychiatrists. Next is presented Richard Rosner's presidential address to the AAPL October 1988 meeting in which he attempts to respond to some of Stone's challenges. He also sets forth a rationale for forensic psychiatry as a subspecialty. Following this, Robert Weinstock, Gregory Leong, and J. Arturo Silva suggest that traditional Hippocratic medical ethics do and should continue to play an important role as one consideration in the functioning of a forensic psychiatrist, as indicated by surveys of members of the Psychiatry and Behavioral Science Section of AAFS and of Tri-State AAPL. In their opinion, forensic psychiatrists are not and should not remain ethically neutral. Edward

Hundert, hospital ethicist from McLean Hospital, presents an approach to ethical problems that involves the balancing of conflicting values. The forensic psychiatrist is required to perform the sometimes difficult task of balancing the conflicting ethical demands of the legal and medical professions.

In the second part, "Models and Guidelines for Ethical Practice," the role of the forensic psychiatrist is considered first. In a survey of AAFS Psychiatry and Behavioral Science members, the "hired gun" was the ethical problem of most concern to respondents. In his chapter, Bernard Diamond considers the role of the honest advocate and distinguishes it from the dishonest advocate or "hired gun." An honest advocate presents his unavoidably partial and subjective opinion honestly, regardless of his admitted biases. He does not claim impossible impartiality or objectivity, and refuses to participate when he cannot do so truthfully and honestly, yet remain true to his values and personal ethics. Ralph Slovenko, in his chapter, considers many differing aspects of the role of forensic psychiatrists and the resulting ethical problems and dilemmas, and agrees with Diamond on the impossibility of impartiality. Slovenko believes the crucial issue in the role of the forensic expert is "helpfulness." In his opinion, the revised rule 704(b) of the federal law on opinion evidence limits this helpfulness by precluding testimony on the ultimate legal issue. Henry Weinstein, previous chairman of AAPL's Committee on Ethics, was instrumental in the development of AAPL's ethical guidelines. His chapter defends those aspects of the earlier version of the ethical guidelines directed to the issue of impartiality. He argues for its retention at least as an ideal and explains his reasons for its original inclusion.

During October, 1989, AAPL changed the "impartiality and objectivity" section of its ethical guidelines to read, "honesty and striving for objectivity"—a compromise recommended by the AAPL Committee on Ethics, presently chaired by one of this volume's co-editors, Robert Weinstock. This compromise was made after intense debate because of the conclusion that bias is unavoidable and is permissible if acknowledged honestly. If faced directly, bias does not preclude an honest opinion and is not necessarily undesirable. It can motivate a search for other data as well as for alternative interpretations of the legal criteria. Moreover, as Diamond notes, it is not unethical to participate only in such cases which conform to the expert's personal or professional philosophy or social agenda. What is necessary is that the expert is scrupulously honest and does not knowingly leave a false impression. Claiming impartiality, however, is misleading since the adversary process will result in bias even if the expert truly was relatively unbiased before agreeing to participate in the case. AAFS also removed "impartiality" from its Code of Ethics several years ago, so both groups no longer require the impossible.

However, even though true objectivity also is impossible, "striving for objectivity" was included in the revised AAPL guidelines because of the belief that a forensic psychiatrist should not reach a subjective opinion consistent with his biases too readily. He should strive for an honest opinion reflective of all the relevant data. He also should strive to prevent unavoidable bias from limiting his exploration of alternative possibilities different from his initial impressions.

Although experts honestly may differ in their opinions, the revised guidelines suggest that they should strive for objectivity after considering the pertinent data and base their opinions, insofar as possible, on scientific fact and the literature, and not on speculation. The chapters by Diamond, Slovenko, and Weinstein discuss these issues from differing perspectives. The current revised AAPL Ethical Guidelines are included in the Appendix of this volume.

Robert Miller considers the problem of the treating psychiatrist as forensic evaluator, and the strong discouragement of assuming both roles set forth in AAPL's current ethical guidelines. He comments on the necessity for state psychiatrists to function frequently in both roles simultaneously. This issue is being reviewed by AAPL's Committee on Ethics. Gregory Leong, J. Arturo Silva, and Robert Weinstock next discuss various ethical aspects and ramifications of giving Miranda warnings in criminal evaluations. In his chapter, Robert Sadoff reviews and summarizes the fundamental ethical issues included in AAPL's current ethical guidelines (see Appendix). Presently, the APA has the only enforcement mechanism for ethical violations in forensic psychiatry, except for a few facets (i.e., not distorting data or credentials) currently enforced by AAFS. The APA can only enforce ethical guidelines that fall within their format. At this writing, AAPL's Committee on Ethics is working on translating AAPL's guidelines into the APA format. Abraham Halpern next presents a proposal that AAPL hold its own ethics hearings to enforce its own guidelines, rather than rely solely upon the APA. Spencer Eth, past Chairman, Ethics Committee, Southern California District Branch, American Psychiatric Association (APA), in the last chapter of this section considers the ethical problems of sex between therapist and patient. He discusses the role of district branches of the APA in the enforcement process for violations of ethical guidelines, and gives an illustrative example.

The final part, "Applications," addresses some of the areas of practice in which special ethical problems can arise. Baruch Brody, Leon Jaworski Professor of Medical Ethics, and Director, Center for Ethics, Medicine, and Public Issues at Baylor University, reviews the literature on the controversial subject of dangerousness prediction, including recent studies and developments. He raises questions about the reasons for psychiatrists sometimes having differing opinions about their ability to predict dangerousness in diverse situations. Spencer Eth and Mark Mills next present the view that laws involving the treatment of dangerous persons in fact do not interfere seriously with treatment, and are less unreasonable and restrictive and less likely to subject therapists to liability than many psychiatrists believe.

Philippa Foot, Griffin Professor of Philosophy, University of California, Los Angeles, and Faculty, Oxford University, England, reflects on the problem of ethics and the death penalty and, specifically, the participation of forensic psychiatrists in capital trials. She presents an argument for the relevance of this issue for the forensic psychiatrist, and suggests that those who oppose the death penalty should not withdraw from this area. They should participate by performing honest forensic evaluations. They should strive to become involved only when a truthful evaluation may be helpful in avoiding a death penalty.

Even if forced on occasion to testify for the opposite side, she believes that participation is virtuous if the forensic psychiatrist tries to perform ethically regardless of any unintended consequences. In Professor Foot's opinion, ethical aspects are relevant for the forensic psychiatrist as a consequence of his belonging to a profession that places him in a position to be asked to participate in aspects of the death penalty process. Harold Ginzburg, formerly Chief, Epidemiology, AIDS Program, National Institute of Health, and presently Senior Medical Consultant, Bureau of Health Care Delivery and Assistance, United States Public Health Service, addresses many facets of HIV testing and AIDS, emphasizing ethical aspects. The topic of HIV testing and AIDS unavoidably is becoming increasingly important for all practitioners and administrators.

Sexual issues can involve passionately felt, strongly held viewpoints. Ruth Macklin, Joan Wexler, Sheldon Travin, and Robert Goldstein consider ethical aspects of sexual issues that affect forensic practice. Ruth Macklin, Professor of Bioethics, Department of Epidemiology and Social Medicine, Albert Einstein College of Medicine, New York, humorously demonstrates the ethical and legal complexities of the newer sexual reproductive technologies. Joan Wexler, Professor of Law, Associate Dean, Brooklyn Law School, discusses current law in this area of sexual reproductive technologies. She makes several proposals for change that would involve active participation by mental health professionals. Increasingly, forensic psychiatrists and psychologists may be called upon to function in various capacities in this complex and controversial context. Sheldon Travin then discusses the ethical problems involved in treating and evaluating sex offenders. Robert Goldstein presents ethical aspects of the APA decision not to designate homosexuality as an illness. He contrasts this development with recent legal developments in this area. Stanley Kern next discusses, with illustrative case examples, the ethical need to protect the rights of the elderly, even if such problems were not the reason for the consultation. According to Kern, the forensic psychiatrist may be knowledgeable about relevant areas of which others may be unaware. Such rights violations are likely to escalate in importance if society's commitment to the elderly continues to diminish and if limiting expenditures continues to receive highest priority.

In the final chapter, Cynthia Cohen, Professor of Philosophy, Villanova University and the Hastings Center, analyzes the many complex ethical aspects of mandatory drug testing. At this writing, the United States Supreme Court has not fully resolved this issue. Psychiatrists are likely to become increasingly involved in the treatment of individuals who test positive on mandatory drug screens, as well as in legal challenges in which employment has been terminated as a result of such testing. Recent Supreme Court decisions have allowed routine mandatory drug testing in the workplace for certain occupations and seem to be expanding the permissible indications. Knowledge of the ethical issues thus can become increasingly relevant for ethical practice.

Each of the volumes in this series, Critical Issues in American Psychiatry and the Law, including the present volume on Ethical Practice in Psychiatry and the Law, may be read independently. Nonetheless, an appreciation of ethical problems will be enhanced by reading other volumes in this series. As a convenience to the reader, each chapter may be read as an independent unit. As a consequence, some matters may be repeated in more than one chapter, but from a different perspective.

With the current emphasis and concern about ethics, it is hoped that this volume will prove valuable in increasing awareness of diverse issues, as well as skills in coping with them. It also is designed to heighten appreciation of ethical complexities relevant to forensic practice.

The editors hope that the reader will find the contents a challenge to develop his/her own thoughts on the issues. Not all views can be included, as our goal is to present ways of thinking about and analyzing current and future ethical problems. Our goal is best served if discussion and constructive thought are stimulated so that readers can reach their own carefully considered conclusions rather than merely accept opinions of others as definitive.

RICHARD ROSNER
ROBERT WEINSTOCK

Contents

PART I. ISSUES AND APPROACHES

Chapter 1. *The Ethics of Forensic Psychiatry: A View from the Ivory Tower* 3
Alan A. Stone

Chapter 2. *Forensic Psychiatry: A Subspeciality* 19
Richard Rosner

Chapter 3. *The Role of Traditional Medical Ethics in Forensic Psychiatry* 31
Robert Weinstock, Gregory B. Leong, and J. Arturo Silva

Chapter 4. *Competing Medical and Legal Ethical Values: Balancing Problems of the Forensic Psychiatrist* 53
Edward M. Hundert

PART II. MODELS AND GUIDELINES FOR ETHICAL PRACTICE

Chapter 5. *The Psychiatric Expert Witness: Honest Advocate or "Hired Gun"?* 75
Bernard L. Diamond

Chapter 6. *The Role of the (Psychiatric) Expert in the Judicial Process* 85
Ralph Slovenko

Chapter 7. *The Impartial Expert: Myth or Reality?* 117
Henry C. Weinstein

Chapter 8. *Ethical Issues Involved in the Dual Role of Treater and Evaluator* 129
Robert D. Miller

Chapter 9. *Ethical Considerations of Giving* Miranda-*Type Warnings in Psychiatric Evaluations in Criminal Cases* 151
Gregory B. Leong, J. Arturo Silva, and Robert Weinstock

Chapter 10. *Ethical Issues in Forensic Psychiatry* 163
Robert L. Sadoff

Chapter 11. *Adjudication of AAPL Ethical Complaints: A Proposal* 171
Abraham L. Halpern

Chapter 12. *Ethical Problems Regarding Sex between Therapist and Patient* .. 175
Spencer Eth

PART III. APPLICATIONS

Chapter 13. *Prediction of Dangerousness in Different Contexts* 185
Baruch A. Brody

Chapter 14. *Treating Patients Who Threaten Violence: Ethical Concerns* 197
Spencer Eth and Mark J. Mills

Chapter 15. *Ethics and the Death Penalty: Participation by Forensic Psychiatrists in Capital Trials* 207
Philippa Foot

Chapter 16. *HIV Infections and AIDS: Neuropsychiatric, Psychosocial, and Legal Issues* 219
Harold M. Ginzburg

Chapter 17. *The New Sexual Issues: Public Policy Implications* 243
Ruth Macklin

Chapter 18. *Surrogate Parenting: Some Guiding Principles for a Legislative Response* 257
Joan G. Wexler

Chapter 19. *The Use of Psychiatric Expertise in Sex Offender Cases* 269
Sheldon Travin

Chapter 20. *Clinical Judgment and Value Judgment: Moral Foundations of Psychiatric and Legal Determinations of the Status of Homosexuality* 293
Robert Lloyd Goldstein

Chapter 21. *Protecting the Rights of the Elderly* 307
Stanley R. Kern

Chapter 22. *Ethical Issues in Mandatory Drug Testing* 313
Cynthia B. Cohen

Appendix: AAPL Ethical Guidelines for the Practice of Forensic Psychiatry 327

Index 333

I

Issues and Approaches

1

The Ethics of Forensic Psychiatry

A View from the Ivory Tower

ALAN A. STONE

At a recent meeting of 60 federal judges from around the country, one of the trial judges defined the essence of the distinction between trial and appellate judges. "Trial judges," he said, "are in the front lines of legal warfare; they are foot soldiers involved in bloody hand-to-hand combat. Appellate judges, in contrast, sit on a safe hill overlooking the battlefield. When the fighting is over, the appellate judge comes down from his position of safety and goes about shooting the wounded." Similarly one could describe forensic psychiatry as a kind of hand-to-hand combat, and now as never before, the troops are wounded and bloody. Scholarly criticism has been blistering,[1] and after the trial of John Hinckley, the media have been unrelenting in their attacks. Now, when forensic psychiatrists need encouragement, healing balms, and soothing treatment, I have come down from my ivory tower to "shoot the wounded."

But forensic psychiatrists need not be afraid: like the trial judges, they will survive to fight again. In fact, though wounded and bloody, they are paradoxically stronger than ever before. The legal assault on psychiatry of the past two decades had one consistent result. It took discretionary authority away from the psychiatrist and handed it over to the courts. But the courts, in order to take on this burden responsibly, require more, not less psychiatric testimony. The more they distrust forensic psychiatrists, the more they need them. Whatever the

From "The Ethics of Forensic Psychiatry," Chap. III, *Law, Psychiatry, and Morality,* Alan A. Stone. Washington, D.C. American Psychiatric Press, 1984. Reprinted by permission of the author.

ALAN A. STONE • Faculty of Law and Faculty of Medicine, Harvard Law School, Harvard University, Cambridge, Massachusetts 02138.

reasons, forensic psychiatry, though condemned and repudiated, seems nonetheless to be flourishing. There is an array of related journals,* new organizations and subspecialty boards, a remarkable number of well-trained competent practitioners, and an increasingly sophisticated intellectual dialogue. In a stagnant psychiatric economy, forensic psychiatry is one of the few growth stocks. The sudden boom in forensic psychology gives further evidence of the strength and attractiveness of the market.

Although I have spent the past 20 years teaching, studying, and writing about Law and Psychiatry, I am not a forensic psychiatrist. The reasons why I am not are in fact what I shall here discuss. What has kept me out of the courtroom is my concern about the ambiguity of the intellectual and ethical boundaries of forensic psychiatry. At the outset, let me state what I think the boundary problems are.

First, there is the basic boundary question. Does psychiatry have anything true to say to which the courts should listen?

Second, there is the risk that the forensic psychiatrist will go too far and twist the rules of justice and fairness to help the patient.

Third, there is the opposite risk that the forensic psychiatrist will deceive the patient in order to serve justice and fairness.

Fourth, there is the danger that forensic psychiatrists will prostitute the profession, as they are alternately seduced and assaulted by the power of the adversarial system.†

Finally, as one struggles with these four issues (Does one have something true to say? Is one twisting justice? Is one deceiving the patient? Is one prostituting the profession?), there is the additional problem that forensic psychiatrists seem to be without any clear guidelines as to what is proper and ethical. In this regard I shall be commenting on (1) the good clinical practice standard; (2) the scientific standard; (3) the truth and honesty standard; and (4) the adversary standard. For now I shall simply assert that the American Medical Association's *Principles of Ethics with Annotations for Psychiatrists*[2] are irrelevant as guidelines for forensic psychiatrists. Eventually, I shall test this proposition by examining the ethical complaints that have been voiced against forensic testimony for the prosecution as considered by the Supreme Court in the *Barefoot v. Estelle*[3] case. I will argue that there is no neutral general principle by which such testimony can be called unethical.

***Bulletin of the American Academy of Psychiatry and the Law; Criminal Justice and Behavior; International Journal of Law and Psychiatry; International Journal of Offender Therapy and Comparative Criminology; Journal of Forensic Sciences; Journal of the Forensic Science Society; Journal of Psychiatry and Law; Law and Human Behavior; Law and Psychology Review; Mental Disability Law Reporter.*

†Different problems arise when the psychiatrist testifies as *amicus* to the court. Although many psychiatrists prefer this role, it is, from the point of view of Anglo-American law, employing the procedures of the inquisitional process. The difficulties in making inquisitional exceptions to the adversarial process go far beyond the scope of this essay, and indeed of psychiatric testimony.

PSYCHIATRY AND TRUTH

The most basic question is whether psychiatrists have true answers to the legal and moral questions posed by the law. Immanuel Kant, who after two centuries is still a dominant figure in the landscape of moral philosophy, had strong opinions about this question. He wrote, "concerning the question whether the mental condition of the agent was one of derangement or of a fixed purpose held with a sound understanding, forensic medicine is meddling with alien business."[4] Kant would give a different meaning to the ancient designation of the forensic psychiatrist as an *alienist*. Kant also wrote, "physicians are generally still not advanced enough to see deeply into the mechanisms inside a human being in order to determine the cause of an unnatural transgression of the moral law."[5]

Kant's opinion was both that our science was inadequate and that, as to moral questions, alienists were meddling in alien business. A century later, Freud echoed Kant's sentiments in a new vocabulary: "[T]he physician will leave it to the jurist to construct for social purposes a responsibility that is artificially limited to the metapsychological ego."[6] Since Freud's time some psychoanalysts have attempted to generate a theory of moral responsibility not limited to the metapsychological ego. But Freud's most authoritative interpreter—certainly his most orthodox—Heinz Hartmann, in his monograph *Psychoanalysis and Moral Values,*[7] drew a sharp clear line: psychoanalysis could say something about why people come to hold the values and morality they hold but could say nothing substantive about those values and morals.

This purist position of Kant-Freud-Hartmann would suggest that even today the forensic psychiatrist outside the therapeutic context is meddling in alien business. Given the basic premise of these purists, the attempt to delineate the ethical boundaries of forensic psychiatry is vacuous. Psychiatrists are immediately over the boundary when they go from psychiatry to law. To ask what are the ethical boundaries for this practice would be rather like asking what are the ethical boundaries for an imposter. From this purist perspective the problem with forensic psychiatry is not the adversarial process and its use of adversarial experts, which distorts the "science." Rather, purists think it is as absurd for psychiatrists to decide legal-moral questions and questions of social justice as neutral scientific friends of the court as it is for them to be adversarial witnesses.

The purist position can be reached by different kinds of reasoning. Intellectually, there seem to be five strands that make up the purist position. I shall briefly allude to them and suggest their relevance to forensic psychiatry.

THE INTELLECTUAL CHASM

First, there is the problem of the fact–value distinction. This is the philosophical line followed by Hartmann. It assumes that there is a sharp distinction between facts in the objective sphere of science and values in the subjective sphere of morality and law and that the gap between them is unbridgeable. The purist sees forensic psychiatrists as simply confusing the two spheres or as failing to recognize their distinctions. Forensic psychiatrists present their values as though they were scientific facts.

Two lines have been taken here. One is Hartmann's, and according to it the psychoanalyst has nothing to say about moral questions, except possibly to explain how people come to hold their particular moral values, and that is the end of the matter. The second line says that psychoanalysts should acknowledge their own value preferences—for example, a belief that our society should place the interests of children above those of adults—and then in light of the psychoanalytic facts develop particular legal policies. This is the familiar strategy adopted by Goldstein, Freud, and Solnit in formulating a variety of legal rules having to do with the interests of children.[8] Since such views have had considerable acceptance and influence, they merit more detailed, though still too brief, considerations among the five strands of the purist position.

When one looks at what these authors offer as psychoanalytic facts, one must question whether the purported facts are not themselves tainted by value judgments. Goldstein, Freud, and Solnit offer as a psychoanalytic fact the claim that events affecting young children are more important than those affecting older children.

Children, in this conception, are like a biological system. When exposed to a trauma at an early point they are more apt to be harmed than when trauma happens at a later date. This is the implicit assumption behind the authors' psychoanalytic "fact," and although the analogy is intuitively appealing, it is in essence unwarranted biological reductionism—unwarranted by empirical observation and by psychoanalytic theory itself. This implicit biological reductionism creates the illusion that the authors are talking about facts rather than values.

They argue, for example, that given their explicit value preference for children over adults and given these psychoanalytic facts, the law should keep a small child with his psychological parents rather than make him suffer the separation trauma inherent in handing him over to his biological parents-even if at a later time the decision to deprive him of his biological parents may be troubling. But in fact the empirical studies of separation trauma have to do with the unreplaced loss of the psychological parent, not transfer to a biological parent who is eager to become a psychological parent—a transfer in which the psychological parent could assist under the best circumstances.

Even if there were empirical evidence that the trauma of such transfer is apparent in the short run, there is no evidence that in the long run the trauma of transfer is worse than the trauma of deprivation of one's biological parents. The latter depends on a multitude of variables, including the meaning of the transfer and the meaning of having biological parents.[9] The issue of meaning suggests the fallacy in their reductionistic concept of trauma.

Trauma in psychoanalysis is psychic trauma. Psychic trauma involves an interactive event plus its meaning and its conscious and unconscious significance. Indeed, the meaning and significance of an observable event over time may well determine whether that event was a trauma or a helpful emotional experience. Whether or not these criticisms are entirely correct, they show the perils of trying to separate facts and values, even when those making the claim are acutely aware of the difficulty. Indeed, it is possible to argue that Goldstein, Freud, and Solnit can best be understood as having a value preference not for children, but for adults who devote themselves to children, that is, psychological parents. One can argue about the pros and cons of such a value preference, but one should not claim it is an argument about psychoanalytic facts.

The second problem area is that of free will vs. determinism. The debate has never been resolved by psychiatrists. It is relevant to every question of volition and responsibility. It is a principal theme in Professor Morse's lengthy and detailed attack of the fallacies of psychodynamic testimony in criminal trials.[10] Without a resolution of the problem it is impossible to evaluate the significance of the psychiatrist's testimony. If his account of a party's condition is presented in terms of deterministic causal forces which preclude the party's being responsible for his own actions, then we may draw one conclusion.

If the account is one which outlines deterministic causes which somehow leave untouched a sphere of free will (as Kant might have said), one need not draw the same conclusion. If the psychiatric account should be understood as something other than a deterministic causal account, its implications could again be different.

A third area is the deconstruction of the self: without the unity of the self, moral reasoning becomes impossible. It is the deepest, most basic theoretical dilemma of modern psychiatry, and it is not just the work of psychoanalysis and the metapsychological ego. It is an issue in behavioral and biological psychiatry. It is specifically relevant to claims about how the criminal law should deal with multiple personality, dissociative reactions, and unconscious forces in general.

Without an understanding of when the self retains its unity and how that unity is essential to moral conduct, we cannot assess the relevance of psychiatric accounts for moral-legal questions concerning how the law should deal with the party to whom the psychiatric accounts apply. Freud implicitly acknowledged this problem when he wrote about "a responsibility that is artificially limited to the metapsychological ego." The moral theorist would argue that Freud "artificially" divided the self into the ego, the superego, and the id. But this deconstruction of the self is characteristic of modern thought. The self, like Humpty Dumpty, has been shattered, and all the king's philosophers and all the king's lawyers cannot put Humpty Dumpty together again.

The fourth area is the mind-brain problem.[11] The mind-brain problem plagues all our endeavors to account for human actions. It is particularly pertinent to alcoholism, to drug abuse, and to recent theories of violence. Whatever understanding science may offer of the nature and functions of the brain, we cannot assess its relevance to the law's proper disposition of a particular party's case without taking a position on the mind-brain problem. If mental states are somehow reducible to brain states, then scientific accounts of the brain could in principle provide full accounts of human psychology. But on any other hypothesis about the mind-brain problem, the very relevance of information about the brain is less clear. If there is somehow a mind-brain interaction, its relevance depends on the nature of that interaction; if there is minimal or no mind-brain interaction, its relevance is minimal or nonexistent. If this is too abstract, think of the *Torsney*[12] case in which a white police officer's unprovoked killing of a black youth was attributed to temporal lobe epilepsy resulting in a verdict of not guilty by reason of insanity. A chapter in my book *Law, Psychiatry, and Morality* offers examples from the Hinckley trial, and the reader will see how important the mind-brain problem is to forensic psychiatry. Professor Michael Moore has demonstrated, to my satisfaction, that America's most influential forensic psychiatrist, Isaac Ray, got lost in the mind-brain trap and never got out.[13]

Last, there is the chasm that has opened up between what Kuhn[14] would call "normal science," and morality—a chasm which characterizes almost all of modern thought and, particularly, behavioral sciences. The chasm can be seen in terms of some of the preceding strands. Science is the realm of fact, while morality is the realm of value, so that the gap between fact and value contributes to the distance between science and morality. Similarly, science is the attempt to discover causal explanations of behavior, while morality may seem to presuppose the absence of such explanations of behavior.

The apparent incompatibility of free will and determinism thus further splits science and morality. Finally, science, particularly "bench science," seems to be well equipped to study the brain, but it cannot apply its methods directly to the study of the mind. The mind is an essential aspect of the domain where morality has its more ready application. The mind-brain question thus also contributes to the chasm between morality and normal science. It is that chasm which forensic psychiatry tries to bridge. I shall touch on some of these strands, but here let me say only that the purist position is not easily dismissed—it raises serious questions about the basic legitimacy of forensic psychiatry.

Each forensic psychiatrist may have resolved the five intellectual problems in his or her own mind, but I doubt that any of us would claim that forensic psychiatry has achieved a consensus on these issues. Philosophers[15] and lawyers[16] might also claim to have resolved these questions, but it seems that they have no more consensus as to these problems than do psychiatrists. The conceptual problems which have been outlined are not limited to psychodynamic testimony. They apply equally to behavioral, biological, and social psychiatry. They apply even to what many would consider the hard science part of psychiatry.

THE GOOD CLINICAL PRACTICE STANDARD

Now it can be argued against my position that all that I have said is applicable to everything psychiatrists do and not just to forensic psychiatry. This counterargument leads to the good clinical practice standard, the argument made by my colleague and friend, Andrew Watson. He believes that psychiatrists are constantly making value judgments and expressing moral convictions implicitly, if not explicitly. He would acknowledge all of the difficult intellectual problems I have enumerated, but he would say they are just as relevant to clinical practice as to forensic psychiatry. Finally, he would say, if we do it in our office why can't we do it in the courtroom? We even make predictions about future dangerousness in our office. Do we believe in the practice of psychiatry or don't we? I shall accept Doctor Watson's "good clinical practice" argument so that we can cross the first boundary into the law.

But I shall first take you back almost two centuries to enter the courtroom. From this safe vantage point we can consider twisting justice, deceiving the patient, and prostituting the profession. Let me quote the interrogation of a "forensic" psychiatrist that took place in 1801. It is reported by Nigel Walker in his treatise on crime and insanity in England.[17] The trial involved a Jew who had been caught stealing spoons.

The Jews of the London community had set up a society for visiting the sick and doing charitable deeds. The society employed a Doctor Leo, who three times testified at the Old Bailey on behalf of his Jewish patients. On all three occasions, his patients had been accused of shoplifting. This was his third appearance. First Doctor Leo was questioned by the court.

> *Court:* Are you particularly versed in this disorder of the human mind?
> *Leo:* I am.
> *Court:* Then you are what is called a mad doctor? [Walker adds, "no doubt there was laughter in the court at this sally."]
> Then he was cross examined by the prosecutor.
> *The Prosecutor:* Have you ever given evidence before?
> *Leo:* [Walker adds, "almost losing his temper."] I believe that I have. Is that any matter of consequence?
> *The Prosecutor:* Upon your oath, have you or have you not been examined as a witness here before?
> *Leo:* I never took any notice.
> *The Prosecutor:* Have you not been here twice?
> *Leo:* Yes.
> *Prosecutor:* Have you not been here more than three times?
> *Leo:* I cannot say.
> *Prosecutor:* Have you not been here before as a witness and a Jew physician, to give an account of a prisoner as a madman, to get him off upon the ground of insanity?

The nastiness with which Doctor Leo was treated by these English contemporaries of Immanuel Kant (who shared their anti-Semitism) cannot be attributed to their intellectual position, but their examination of the witness strikes two notes which resonate even today in the halls of Congress and our state legislatures—namely, that the psychiatrist is a bad joke in the courtroom, and that forensic psychiatrists are there to get defendants off.[18]

The question I would pose to Doctor Watson is, what could he say today in defense of Doctor Leo's testimony? He could tell the prosecutor, as I would, that anti-Semitism is vile and repugnant, particularly so in an officer of the court. But could he argue, given the primitive state of psychiatry in 1801, that Doctor Leo had a good clinical understanding of what he called "the mania" of his patient for stealing spoons? Could he say that his purpose in testifying was other than to help a fellow Jew escape what the law of the day considered just punishment? Was he not twisting justice and fairness to help his patient and prostituting his profession to do so?

Doctor Watson might say that my example is ridiculous and far-fetched, but I ask him and those who share his view to imagine some psychiatric historian 200 years from now examining the good clinical practice and the clinical diagnostic concepts advanced by the psychiatrists on either side of the Hinckley trial. Is there much chance that the historian of our profession would conclude that those psychiatrists, to use Kant's language, "saw deeply into the mechanisms inside the human being in order to determine the cause of an unnatural transgression of the moral law?"[19] Or would the historian more likely comment on the primitive state of clinical psychiatry in 1982: its incomplete understanding of the brain and the mind and its bizarre diagnostic categories as set out in DSM-III?

THE SCIENTIFIC STANDARD

Another of my friends and colleagues, Loren Roth, is of the view that what should guide ethical forensic psychiatrists is their commitment to the standards of science. As I understand his view, he wants to set a higher standard than Andrew Watson's "good clinical judgment." I think Loren Roth shares my view that "good clinical judgment" is a precariously egocentric standard.

I once assisted in some empirical research on humor. It turned out that every subject I gave the "Mirth Response Test" to thought he or she had a very good sense of humor.[20] Similarly, it seems to me that every psychiatrist thinks he has very good clinical judgment. Doctor Roth wants to find a brighter line. He would limit his testimony to what he knows to be scientific. Based on that standard, he would not allow forensic psychiatrists to answer ultimate legal questions which have no scientific answers. But I would claim that if forensic psychiatrists limited themselves to the standards of bench scientists, not only would they not testify about ultimate legal questions; their lips would be sealed in the courtroom.

Psychiatry is still closer to social science than to physical science, and Max Weber's statement about social science applies to us. We must expect that what we believe to be right will soon be proved wrong.[21] It is no disgrace to work at a primitive science. As Jonas Rappeport asks, "Are we embarrassed to let the public know that the state of our art is such that we do not know everything and that there are different schools and theories in psychiatry?"[22] The hubris in psychiatry has come from passing it off as scientific certainty or claiming that we know things beyond a reasonable doubt. But if psychiatry is an art, as Rappeport's candor suggests, how do we adhere to Roth's standards of science?

The relevant difference between clinical practice and forensic practice has sometimes been discussed under the heading of the psychiatrist as double agent. I do not want to rehearse that discussion, although it is a valuable way to analyze these problems. A forensic examination for the other side confronts the psychiatrist with problems of being a double agent—problems which otherwise often go unnoticed.

Rappeport's solution to the thorny dilemma of examining a patient for the other side is for the interviewer to recognize the potential for abuses of confidentiality and always to inform the patient which side he or she is serving.[23] But I agree with Seymour Halleck that informing the examinee of the fact that you are a double agent is necessary but not sufficient to resolve the conflict of interests. There are two reasons for this conclusion; I put off one until my discussion of testimony in capital punishment. Skilled interviewers like Doctors Halleck, Roth, and Watson will create a relationship in which the examinee can readily forget that he has been warned. It is no accident that good clinicians are often emotionally seductive human beings who inspire personal trust. Emotionally seducing a schizophrenic to reach him in his autistic withdrawal may or may not be bad technique, but it is certainly easier to justify as a parameter of treatment than as a method of obtaining information to determine whether he should have visitation rights with his children.

THE ETHICAL DIALECTIC OF PSYCHIATRY

The crucial word for me in what I have just said is "justify": when our goal as psychiatrists is to do our best to ease a patient's suffering, we have a powerful justification. It is the justification for every physician who did not wait for science and theory to be perfected. Do whatever you can to help your patient and *primum nil nocere,* first of all do no harm.[24] These contradictory claims constitute the ethical dialectic of the physician's practice. We have not yet found the synthesis of this thesis and antithesis; our fate is to struggle within this contradiction. But as physicians treating patients, we know what the ethical struggle is. We know the boundaries of the ethical debate. When we turn our skills to forensic psychiatry, when we serve the system of justice, we can no longer agree on the boundaries of the debate.

A few words about the adversary system and how it bears on this ethical dialectic. Let me return to Doctor Leo at the Old Bailey in 1801. Doctor Leo is typical of a certain kind of psychiatrist who goes to court: the psychiatrist who knows very little about the law but who goes to court out of sympathy for a client or for a cause. To some forensic psychiatrists these are the real villains, and amateurs who do not recognize that forensic psychiatry is a professional subspecialty.

But it is not the amateur's naïveté about the law which interests me; rather, it is his impulse to help the patient or to serve some cause which the patient represents. The amateur, it seems to me, is still trying to act according to the basic ethical calling of the physician—he is trying to relieve suffering, he is still struggling within the ethical dialectic of the healer.

It is my impression that this impulse has not been limited to amateurs. Many distinguished forensic psychiatrists have felt more comfortable acting on behalf of criminal defendants than on behalf of the prosecution. The current professional attitude of forensic psychiatry is to provide testimony for both sides, in part because otherwise the forensic psychiatrist runs the risk of being pilloried by the prosecution as a defense-biased witness. But it seems to me there has long been a very comfortable ideological fit between being a forensic psychiatrist and being against capital punishment, being therapeutic rather than punitive, being against the prosecution and what was seen as the harsh status quo in criminal law. This ideological fit has begun to come apart in recent history. But during the days when Judge David Bazelon and American psychiatry had their love affair the fit was real. Those were the halcyon days when the concept of treatment and the concept of social justice were virtually indistinguishable.

Here we confront what I believe is still a lingering confusion in the enterprise of forensic psychiatry. The problem is that helping the patient—which is the ethical thesis of the practitioner—becomes the ethical temptation in the legal context. What principle does the forensic psychiatrist have to restrain himself against this temptation? What is his equivalent to the therapist's antithesis of do no harm, particularly when he is cajoled by the lawyers, dazzled by the media spotlight, and paid more than Blue Cross/Blue Shield? I have already suggested that I believe Doctor Watson's good clinical practice is a precariously egocentric standard for self-administered ethical restraints. One only needs to hear forensic psychiatrists criticizing each other's ethics to see how precarious it is. Doctor Roth's scientific standard would, in my opinion, lead to a vow of silence.

THE STANDARD OF TRUTH

My colleague and friend, Paul Appelbaum, has suggested that the standard of truth should govern the forensic psychiatrist. In a moral dialogue it seems to me that this is a very appealing standard, but like Kant's categorical imperative it is much more convincing as an abstract statement than it is useful as a practical guide to conduct. I assume that Paul Appelbaum's standard of the truth is not the same as the one I raised at the beginning of this chapter—the truth in some absolute sense. That kind of absolute truth keeps the psychiatrist out of the courtroom. What Doctor Appelbaum means, I think, is closer to honesty; the forensic psychiatrist must honestly believe what he says and should not allow his views to be distorted by the media spotlight, by the lawyers, or by the money. He should be an honest, good clinical practitioner. Let us consider how this standard fares in the adversarial context.*

The adversarial system, of course, requires psychiatrists for both sides. That was one of the complaints against the old lineup of concerned psychiatrists for the defense: psychiatry was not being fair to the adversarial system.

*But, *see* Rappeport, *op cit,* pp 258–259. Rappeport believes it is possible to testify honestly and effectively. He argues that the limits of our knowledge will be made evident, so long as we do not try to confuse the issues or suggest that we have knowledge which we in fact lack.

My late friend and colleague Seymour Pollack was particularly concerned about this issue,[25] and even Judge Bazelon lamented the lack of competent psychiatrists on both sides. Bazelon wanted psychiatrists to recognize and accede to the higher ethical framework of the adversarial system's search for justice.[26] The problem he failed to consider was how the psychiatrists would square the ethical imperative of the healing profession with the adversarial goals of criminal prosecution.

TESTIFYING FOR THE PROSECUTION IN CAPITAL PUNISHMENT

To illuminate that problem I want to examine what I take to be the most challenging case—Doctor Grigson's practice of testifying for the prosecution in capital punishment cases, such as *Barefoot v. Estelle*. At the outset, let me say that I disagree with those who would claim that such testimony is unethical.* By that I mean that it does not violate the American Psychiatric Association's canons of ethics as I would interpret them, it does not violate the good clinical practice standard, and it does not violate the truth as honesty standard. It may violate Doctor Roth's scientific standard, but again I claim that almost everything but a vow of silence would violate his standard.

The practice in question is as follows. The defendant had been found guilty of a capital offense. The court then heard testimony from Doctor Grigson, who had never personally examined the defendant. (A prior decision by the Supreme Court had dealt with an earlier practice in which psychiatrists who had examined defendants for some other purpose then testified against them at this capital punishment stage.[27] This decision is discussed at length in other chapters.) Here, there had been no prior professional contact and therefore no possible allegation could be made that Doctor Grigson had violated the rights of the defendant. Doctor Grigson was asked a series of hypothetical questions relevant to the defendant's history and criminal behavior. His answers, expressed with almost absolute clinical conviction, were that such persons are sociopaths: they are and will be very dangerous, and they do not experience remorse. Dangerousness and lack of remorse are two of the criteria which are relevant to the death penalty.

Now what is unethical about such testimony? I assume that Doctor Grigson believes what he is saying. One certainly has no basis to assume otherwise just because he almost always testifies for the prosecution, and in favor of the death penalty. I assume he is as honest and sincere and as much committed to the good clinical practice standard as the forensic psychiatrists who almost always testify against the death penalty or who go around the country urging verdicts of not guilty by reason of insanity.

After all, Doctor Grigson and the other psychiatrists testify under oath; they are sworn to tell the truth. "You do solemnly swear to testify to the truth,

*Nor did the Court in *Barefoot* state that such testimony was unethical. Rather, it upheld the practice of allowing psychiatrists to respond to hypothetical questions about a person they had never examined.

the whole truth, and nothing but the truth. So help you God."[28] I may not have done justice to Doctor Appelbaum's standard—he may have been thinking along different lines (I shall return to this matter of sworn testimony). But if I have made my friends into strawmen, it was to make clear to you that my ideas are part of an intellectual dialogue with them.

Let me turn briefly and finally to examine Doctor Grigson's testimony in light of the APA's own Principles of Ethics. Here the language is specific. What annotations could one cite if one wished to make an ethical complaint against such testimony in capital punishment cases? One might allege that he gave diagnostic opinions about a patient he never examined.

The relevant annotation, annotation 3 of section 7, clearly is not aimed at courtroom testimony. It was added by the APA after the Goldwater fiasco.[29] Hundreds of psychiatrists were willing to fill out questionnaires and diagnose Barry Goldwater as mentally ill during the Presidential elections of 1964. The incident, which says something about the fact-value problem in psychiatry, embarrassed the psychiatric establishment, resulting in the addition of this annotation. I opposed this change at the time as a denial of free speech and of every psychiatrist's God-given right to make a fool of himself. If the psychiatric establishment banned everything that embarrassed them, they would ban forensic psychiatry. And if annotation 3 of section 7 were strictly enforced, forensic psychiatrists could never write or lecture relying on decided case law and the trial transcripts which present relevant clinical aspects of "patients" like Hinckley, Sirhan, Poddar, Torsney, etcetera. Parts of this book would be unethical.

Furthermore, if Doctor Grigson violated annotation 3 then it is also regularly violated when forensic psychiatrists routinely answer hypothetical questions about testamentary capacity long after a person they never examined has died.

Testifying to hypothetical questions in court is not unethical, at least as I interpret the language and the history of annotation 3 of section 7. The procedure is used by Doctor Grigson, of course, to escape the double-agent conflict I mentioned earlier. Never having examined the patient, there is no doctor-patient relation, no false expectation, no deception, and no conflict of interest.

To object to Doctor Grigson's procedure is to attempt to deprive the prosecution of a legitimate adversarial witness. Forensic psychiatry has no general neutral principle for doing that. We have the intuition that such testimony in death penalty cases is unethical because of our basic practical ethical guideline to do all we can to ease the suffering of our patients. Ironically, this basic guideline is no longer part of the American Medical Association's ethical guidelines—nor is "first of all do no harm." If we were to take this basic guideline very seriously, how could we ever be zealous advocates for the prosecution in death penalty cases? And if the legal system thought we were bound by this practical ethical guideline, how could we serve the adversarial system of criminal justice? The Supreme Court seems to share these views. It upheld the constitutionality of Doctor Grigson's hypothetical testimony despite a dissenting opinion that raised the ethical questions.[30] If there are problems with Doctor Grigson's testimony, as I believe there are and as I try to demonstrate in my book *Law, Psychiatry, and Morality,* the fault lies not in his professional integrity but in forensic psychiatry.

THE APPEAL TO NONMEDICAL VALUES

When we object to the ethical conduct of Doctor Grigson as the prosecution's expert, it is because we want to have our cake and eat it too. We want to be doctors who are healers and we want to serve the adversary system. My colleague and friend, Laurence Tancredi, has commented that to many moral philosophers, justice is itself a beneficence. He is certainly correct, but justice is a beneficence to a society of unidentified persons—that is, to the general good. In contrast, the doctor's practical ethical duty is to ease the suffering of particular identified patients. Medicine has not yet solved the problem of how to balance the particular good of the identified patient against the general good of the unidentified masses. We lose our practical ethical guidelines when we try to serve such greater good in the courtroom.

Consider in this regard the Soviet psychiatrists whom we have condemned for the unethical political abuse of psychiatry. If one has a dialogue with these Soviet forensic psychiatrists, one of the first points they make is that for them, the revolution is the greatest good for the greatest number. The greatest piece of social justice in the twentieth century is the greatest beneficence imaginable. It is when these psychiatrists act in the service of that beneficence that we believe their ethical compass as psychiatrists begins to wander. The scandals in medical research in this country demonstrate the same theme.* The advancement of science is a noble goal; you may prefer it to the revolution, or to the American system of justice, but when doctors give it greater weight than helping their patients or doing no harm they lose their ethical boundaries.

THE ADVERSARIAL STANDARD

It is sometimes said by forensic psychiatrists that all of the supposed ethical problems which have been rehearsed here do not exist because I have failed to recognize the avowedly adversarial nature of forensic testimony. These forensic psychiatrists would argue that they openly accept the fact that they have been selected in a biased fashion to be partisan expert witnesses. They have no ethical problems because they openly accept the responsibility of putting forward the best possible case for their side. Furthermore, they could argue that the ethics and value of such adversarial testimony is in fact as intelligible as it is for lawyers. But their assumption must be that this practice is ethical because,

**See, e.g.,* discussion of cancer research in Katz, J: *Experimentation with Human Beings: The Authority of the Investigator, Subject, Profession and State in the Human Experimentation Process,* Russell Sage, 1972.

just as is the case with lawyers, it is understood by all of the participants in the system of Justice and no one is misled.

But does the jury clearly understand this partisan role of the forensic psychiatrist? After all, they watch as the forensic psychiatrist takes an oath to tell the truth, the whole truth, and not the partisan truth. The psychiatrist does not begin by revealing to the jury that he or she has been retained to make the best case possible. Rather, he or she is introduced to the jury with an impressive presentation of distinguished credentials to establish expertise, not partisanship or bias.

Nor does the judge instruct the jury that they should keep in mind, in weighing the expert testimony, that the forensic psychiatrists have an "ethical" responsibility to be biased. The jury is not told that even the most prestigious and convincing expert should be understood as having attempted to present the best case possible. Until there is this kind of candor in the courtroom, it will be impossible to sweep the ethical problems of psychiatry under the rug of intelligible adversarial ethics. And if the forensic psychiatrist is an explicit adversarial witness, think of how the intellectual problems will be solved! This may be an intelligible solution of the ethical boundaries, but it will certainly expose the limitations of our scientific and intellectual boundaries.

None of these are simple matters and I do not mean to suggest that they are or that I have any answers. What I have tried to do in this chapter is to suggest that from the vantage point of the ivory tower, the intellectual and the ethical problems are inescapably linked.

Forensic psychiatry is caught on the horns of an ethical dilemma. It is a painful position to be in, but the greater danger is to think that one has found a more comfortable position: that one can simply adjust to the adversarial system or remain true to one's calling as a physician. The philosophers say life is a moral adventure; I would add that to choose a career in forensic psychiatry is to choose to increase the risks of that moral adventure.

REFERENCES

1. Morse: Failed Explanations and Criminal Responsibility. *Va Law Rev* 1982; 68:971–1084.
2. American Psychiatric Association: *The Principles of Medical Ethics with Annotations Especially Applicable to Psychiatry.* Washington, DC, APA, 1981.
3. Barefoot v Estelle, 103 S. Ct. 3383, 1983.
4. Kant I: *Anthropology from a Pragmatic Point of View,* Dowdell, VL (trans), Southern Illinois University Press, 1978, p 111.
5. *Id.*
6. Freud, S: Moral Responsibility for the Content of Dreams, cited in Katz, Goldstein and Dershowitz: *Psychoanalysis, Psychiatry and Law.* New York, Free Press, 1967, p 127.
7. Hartmann H: *Psychoanalysis and Moral Values.* New York, International Universities Press, 1960.
8. Goldstein J, Freud A, Solnit A: *Beyond the Best Interests of the Child.* New York, Free Press, 1973; and *Before the Best Interests of the Child.* Free Press, 1980.
9. Furman E: *A Child's Parent Dies.* New Haven, Yale University Press, 1974.
10. *See Ref* 1.

11. Hook S (ed): *Dimensions of Mind: A Symposium*. New York, New York University Press, 1960.
12. *Matter of Torsney*, 412 N.Y.S. 2d 914, rev'd 420 N.Y.S.2d 192, 394 N.E.2d 262.
13. Moore MS: Legal Conceptions of Mental Illness in Brody B, Englehardt T (eds): *Mental Illness: Law and Public Policy*. Kluwer Academic, 1980.
14. Kuhn T: *The Structure of Scientific Revolutions*. Chicago, University of Chicago Press, 1970, p 2.
15. Hudson WD (ed): *The Is/Ought Question*. New York, St. Martins Press, 1970.
16. Moore MS: Responsibility and the Unconscious. *So Cal Law Rev*, 1980, 53:1563–1675.
17. Walker N: *Crime and Insanity in England*. Edinburgh, Scotland, Edinburgh University Press, 1968, p 82.
18. Ashbrook J: The insanity defense. *Congressional Record*, November 17, 1981, E 5365–6.
19. *See Ref* 4.
20. Redlich F, Bingham J: *The Inside Story: Psychiatry and Everyday Life*. New York, Knopf, 1953.
21. Weber M: Objectivity in Social Science and Social Policy. *The Methodology of the Social Sciences*, translated by Shilis E and Finch H. New York, Free Press, 1949.
22. Rappeport J: Ethics and Forensic Psychiatry in Bloch S and Chodoff P (eds): *Psychiatric Ethics*. New York, Oxford University Press, 1981, p 259.
23. *Id.* at p 264.
24. Dedek J: *Contemporary Medical Ethics*. Sheed and Ward, 1975, p 6.
25. Pollack S: *Forensic Psychiatry in Criminal Law*. University of Southern California Press, 1974.
26. Bazelon: The Role of the Psychiatrist in the Criminal Justice System. *Bull Am Acad Psychiatry Law* 1978, 6:139–146.
27. Estelle v Smith, 451 U.S. 454, 1981.
28. Oath of Affirmation of Governing Principles, Form 161, Oath of Witness, *25 Am. Jur. Pl. and Pr. Forms* (revised), pp 356–357.
29. The Unconscious of a Conservative: A Special Issue on the Mind of Barry Goldwater. *Fact Magazine*, 1964, 1:3–64.
30. *See Ref* 3.

2

Forensic Psychiatry

A Subspecialty

RICHARD ROSNER

The American Academy of Psychiatry and the Law has incorporated into its Ethical Guidelines for the Practice of Forensic Psychiatry the definition of the field that previously had been set forth by the American Board of Forensic Psychiatry:

Forensic psychiatry is a subspecialty of psychiatry in which scientific and clinical expertise is applied to legal issues in legal contexts embracing civil, criminal, correctional or legislative matters; forensic psychiatry should be practiced in accordance with guidelines and ethical principles enunciated by the profession of psychiatry.

This discussion will consider some of the implications of the definition and will explore some of the field's problems and prospects.

The hallmarks of a subspecialty include:

1. The existence of an established and sizable organized body of practitioners of forensic psychiatry.
2. The existence of a body of scientific and clinical data and skills that are unique to the field.
3. The existence of a body of literature that embodies a representative and substantial portion of those unique data and describes or otherwise sets forth those unique skills.
4. The existence of subspecialized fellowship training programs designed

Presidential Address at the Nineteenth Annual Meeting of the American Academy of Psychiatry and the Law in San Francisco, CA, October, 1988. Revised and published by permission.

RICHARD ROSNER • Department of Psychiatry, New York University School of Medicine, New York, New York 10016, and Forensic Psychiatry Clinic of the New York Criminal and Supreme Courts, 100 Centre Street, New York, New York 10013.

to impart the unique data and skills to physicians seeking entry into the field.

5. The existence of an appropriately recognized credentialing organization to certify the quality of the subspecialty training programs.
6. The existence of an appropriately recognized credentialing organization to distinguish between those who claim competence in the field and those who successfully demonstrate that competence.

The largest established and organized body of practitioners in the United States is the American Academy of Psychiatry and the Law, which had its inception in 1969. However, note should be made of the prior existence of the Psychiatry and Behavioral Science Section of the American Academy of Forensic Sciences; that section has been an integral founding constituent of AAFS since its inception in 1948. Thus, forensic psychiatry can document its organized existence for the past 40 years.

The body of scientific and clinical data and skills that are unique to the field are exemplified, in the United States, by the series of annual programs presented under the auspices of AAPL, although it may be more accurate to say that the data and skills are actually embodied in the practitioners of forensic psychiatry and are best exemplified in their practice.

The literature in which the data and skills are set forth is varied. In the United States, it includes the *Bulletin of AAPL,* the *Newsletter of AAPL,* the compilation of landmark cases in mental health and law available through the AAPL Learning Resources Center, and the comprehensive series of books developed by the Tri-State Chapter of AAPL, entitled *Critical Issues in American Psychiatry and the Law* (currently consisting of seven volumes). Outside AAPL, there are the books that have received the Guttmacher Award of the American Psychiatric Association, the American Bar Association's *Mental and Physical Disability Law Reporter,* the American Academy of Forensic Science's *Journal of Forensic Sciences,* and many independent publications such as have been set forth in the core library recommendations of the Accreditation Council on Fellowships in Forensic Psychiatry.

The existence of subspecialty fellowship training programs is attested to by the Association of Directors of Forensic Psychiatry Fellowships. At the present time, there are 20 programs in the United States and four programs in Canada. Through the ADFPF, a descriptive specification of each of the forensic psychiatry fellowships is readily obtainable.

The appropriately recognized credentialing organization to certify the quality of the subspecialty training programs is the Accreditation Council on Fellowships in Forensic Psychiatry, which is sponsored by AAPL and the American Academy of Forensic Sciences, and whose mission has been approved by the American Board of Forensic Psychiatry. The ACFFP's actual implementation of an accreditation process has been one of the principle and successful projects of AAPL during my tenancy as president (1987–1988).

The appropriately recognized credentialing organization to identify those practitioners who have demonstrated their competence in our field is the American Board of Forensic Psychiatry, which is sponsored by the American Academy of Forensic Sciences, the Forensic Sciences Foundation, and AAPL.

Notwithstanding these qualifications for recognition as a subspecialty, the American Board of Psychiatry and Neurology has deferred deciding whether to recognize forensic psychiatry as a defined area in which "special competence" may be demonstrated. The American Psychiatric Association has yet to respond to a request by the American Board of Forensic Psychiatry to recognize our subspecialty. The Accreditation Council on Graduate Medical Education has declined to undertake the accreditation of subspecialty fellowship training programs in forensic psychiatry. The American Board of Medical Specialties has declined to recognize the American Board of Forensic Psychiatry. How is this diffidence on the part of organized psychiatry and medicine to be understood?

The American Board of Medical Specialties has explained that, among other reasons, they have requirements for subspecialty certifying boards with which we in forensic psychiatry are not currently in compliance. For example, candidates for a certifying board recognized by the ABMS must be graduates of an ACGME-accredited subspecialty fellowship. The American Board of Forensic Psychiatry does not presently limit candidates for examinations to psychiatrists who have taken fellowships in forensic psychiatry. The Accreditation Council on Fellowships in Forensic Psychiatry implemented its processes in September, 1988. During October, 1989, the first group of ten forensic psychiatric fellowships were granted accreditation.

The Accreditation Council on Graduate Medical Education declined to undertake the evaluation of subspecialty fellowships in forensic psychiatry because our field does not meet all of their prerequisites. For example, the ACGME only reviews programs in fields whose certifying boards are recognized by the American Board of Medical Specialties.

Thus, the American Board of Medical Specialties requires us first to be possessed of ACGME-accredited fellowship programs, and the Accreditation Council on Graduate Medical Education requires us first to be possessed of an ABMS-recognized certifying board. That there is something intrinsically impossible in these mutually incompatible prerequisites is recognized by all parties, but the policies are not readily modifiable.

There has been no formal clarification of the basis for postponing a decision by the American Board of Psychiatry and Neurology. However, it is bound by the requirements of the American Board of Medical Specialties. Thus, the ABPN would also require those psychiatrists who wish to take an examination in order to demonstrate their "special competence" in forensic psychiatry to be graduates of a subspecialty fellowship program, and would require that such subspecialty programs be accredited.

The American Psychiatric Association has not yet replied to the request from the American Board of Forensic Psychiatry that it recognize forensic psychiatry as a subspecialty; so we do not know how that request is viewed. However, we do know that there is general disagreement within the APA regarding the issue of subspecialization in general.

The only new subspecialty recognized by the APA has been geriatric psychiatry. It is rumored that economic factors were a major concern in the APA's decision. Both internal medicine and family practice, two of the ABMS recognized specialties, had indicated their interest in establishing geriatric subspecialties. There was concern that geriatric internists and geriatric family practitioners might claim that behavioral geriatrics was part of their expertise. Failure to recognize geriatric psychiatry as a subspecialty might have resulted in having psychiatry excluded from a major segment of the therapeutic market. At the present time, there is no other area within organized medicine that is staking out a claim on the area of forensic psychiatry; so there is no fiscal or territorial pressure on the APA to recognize our subspecialty quickly.

A distinction must be made, however, between whether or not forensic psychiatry is a subspecialty, on the one hand, and whether or not organized medicine and psychiatry are ready and willing to recognize forensic psychiatry as a subspecialty, on the other hand. In much the same way as the State of Israel exists regardless of whether the majority of Arab nations recognize it, and the People's Republic of China existed regardless of whether the United States recognized it, the subspecialty of forensic psychiatry exists regardless of whether organized medicine and psychiatry recognize it.

Among the obstacles that we face is the lack of understanding among general psychiatrists, and among the public as a whole, of the adversary system in Anglo-American law, which obliges experts in all fields to be pitted against each other in courtroom testimony. Dr. Paul Fink, a president of the American Psychiatric Association, speaking at the opening ceremonies of the AAPL convention in Philadelphia, cited the spectacle of opposing psychiatric experts as a major public relations problem in forensic psychiatry and called upon AAPL to solve it. Even he, apparently, did not realize that the adversary system was intrinsic to our legal system and beyond the capacity of forensic psychiatry to reform.

As the definition of our subspecialty states, we operate within legal contexts, unlike clinical psychiatry, which operates within therapeutic contexts. This difference was articulated often by the late Dr. Seymour Pollack and was the centerpiece of his presidential message, "Forensic Psychiatry: A Specialty," in 1974 in Volume II, issue 1, of the *Bulletin of AAPL*. Dr. Pollack was particularly clear in stressing that the ends of law are not identical with the ends of therapeutic medicine, in general, and of therapeutic psychiatry, in particular. The requirement of work in a legal context presents the forensic psychiatrist with problems that are not readily understood by clinical practitioners.

At the most elementary level, forensic psychiatrists are asked to substantiate and prove the bases for their opinions. How often does a clinical psychiatrist have to provide, on pain of penalties for perjury, a lucid and cogent explication of the processes by means of which he reached his conclusions? How often does a clinical psychiatrist face the demand that he convince the majority of rational persons listening to his views? To an extent unexperienced in clinical practice, the forensic expert must differentiate between what he sincerely believes, on the one hand, and what he can demonstrate that he knows, on the other hand. The forensic psychiatrist must distinguish between the hard data of our field and the metapsychological theories that purport to explain those data. Further, the forensic psychiatrist is asked to specify the level of confidence that he has in his opinions. In some civil cases decisions are made by a preponderance of the evidence (i.e., a scintilla beyond 50% certainty). In some civil cases decisions are made by clear and convincing evidence (i.e., a greater level of certainty). In all criminal cases decisions are made by proof beyond a reasonable doubt. How often is the clinical psychiatrist required to make such fine delineations as to the certainty of his therapeutic recommendations, let alone called upon to convince impartial hearers that he is correct? No utilization review or medical audit committee is as demanding as a judge or a jury.

The matter of hard data in psychiatry is one that is greatly misunderstood by the general public and by our medical colleagues. It is a commonplace to hear psychiatry accused of being a less substantial field than orthopedic surgery, for example. However, in fact, the hard data of psychiatry are essentially the same as those of every other field of medicine. All that any doctor fundamentally knows is what he sees, hears, touches, smells in the course of his evaluation. (It is difficult to conceive of having to taste anything in the course of a medical or psychiatric examination; maybe the homemade cookies presented by a grateful patient are the exception that proves the rule.) All the behavior we observe, all the words we hear, all the handshakes we feel, all the aromas that waft our way, are the hard data of psychiatry. They are just as real as broken bones and must be given the same serious consideration. We do ourselves a disservice to let accusations of soft data go unchallenged.

In terms of the evaluation of the hard data, orthopedists on the witness stand are seen publicly to disagree just as readily as psychiatric witnesses. To disagree about the interpretation of hard data is common. Every doctor who has attended a clinical pathology conference in the course of medical school training will recall that skilled clinicians in medicine and surgery routinely interpret clinical and laboratory findings in disparate ways. There are multiple valid interpretations of the same findings in many instances.

It is often difficult for the public to fathom the bases of our courtroom disagreements. However, we should be clear in our own minds that there are different levels of professional differences. Some disagreements may be about the hard data themselves (e.g., he slouched in his chair when he spoke to Doctor A., but he sat with erect posture when he spoke to Dr. B.: they disagree about the nature of his posture). Other disagreements may be about lower-level interpretations of the hard data (e.g., Dr. A. thought that he spoke softly, but Dr. B. thought he spoke at a conversational volume: they have a different threshold for using the term "soft"). Some disagreements are about higher-level interpretations of the hard data (e.g., Dr. A thinks the claimant is impaired, but Dr. B. thinks the claimant is malingering). Other disagreements are related to the vagueness of the legal criteria used to determine the psychiatric–legal issue (e.g., Dr. A. thinks that the proximate cause of the emotional trauma was *x*, but Dr. B. disagrees that *x* constituted the proximal cause). All of these different types of professional disagreements can occur; but they do not occur because our data are intrinsically soft. Rather, they are the same types of professional disagreements that are seen when orthopedists or any other physicians testify.

All physicians will disagree with colleagues from time to time. Our disagreements are visible in the courtroom. Our agreements are not visible to the public because there is little incentive for attorneys to present experts who agree.

Some years ago, another president of the American Psychiatric Association, Dr. Alan Stone, addressed the AAPL convention and declared that our field was a "moral minefield." He suggested that there were intrinsic ethical difficulties in our work and implicitly applauded our courage in being undeterred by them. What are these ethical problems that are unique to our work? First, there is the basic fact that the ends of law and the ends of therapeutic medicine are not the same. As a result of working in legal contexts, forensic psychiatrists are asked to put their duty to our society ahead of their duty to the individuals who compose our society. For example, our therapeutic duty is *primum non nocere,* first do no harm. However, when we offer the opinion that a given defendant is competent to stand trial, and our opinion is accepted by the court, the defendant may regard the consequences of our work to be harmful. Similarly, when we offer the opinion that a claimant does not meet the level of impairment required to receive Social Security Disability benefits, and the U.S. government's Social Security Administration accepts our view, the claimant may feel that we have harmed him. However, if we always provided answers to legal questions that served the interests of the persons being evaluated, we would be of no value in legal contexts and the society in which we live would be harmed. Obviously, there are occasions when the interests of the person being evaluated are consonant with the interests of society, and in such cases there is no such ethical tension as in the examples that I have just cited.

The forensic psychiatrist must be prepared, in a way that the clinical psychiatrist often is not, to choose between the well-being of the person he is asked to examine and the well-being of the society as a whole. It is an ethical problem that is not unique to our field. In military psychiatry, the physician is required to place the interests of the nation ahead of the interests of the individual being examined. For example, it may be necessary for the military psychiatrist to declare that an enlisted person is malingering to avoid the dangers of combat. By making such a finding, the military psychiatrist puts the well-being of the person being examined at a lower priority than that of the society as a whole, which must be able to call upon its citizens in its own defense. Similar considerations regarding the duty to society being given priority over the duty to the individuals apply to those situations in which clinical psychiatrists, like all other physicians, are obliged to report gunshot wounds and child abuse. Thus, there is nothing intrinsically alien to medicine or to medical ethics in our field.

Beginning students of moral philosophy are soon made aware of the fact that some ethical tensions are derived from basic conflicting moral theories, i.e., from the fact that there is no fundamental agreement regarding what constitutes moral behavior. Thus, a major portion of the "moral minefield" is due to the nature of philosophy itself, rather than to forensic psychiatry. In gross oversimplification, there are two major schools of moral philosophy in our Western culture. The first, the deontologic school, holds that there are some core rules of moral obligation that are binding on all persons. Perhaps the leading spokesman for this school is the German philosopher Immanuel Kant. The second, the consequentialist or utilitarian school, holds that what makes some behavior right is its desirable outcome. The leading proponents of this school are the Englishmen Jeremy Bentham and John Stuart Mill. To take an extreme example of the disagreement between the two schools, let us examine the issue of whether it is ever right to punish someone who has committed a crime. The deontological school would suggest that a person who has done something good deserves a reward and a person who has done something wrong deserves a punishment. For the deontologic moral philosopher, punishment of a criminal offender is a moral imperative and failure to punish a criminal would itself be a moral wrong. For the utilitarian school, it would be suggested that punishment has a deterrent effect on the perpetrator and on the other potential perpetrators of criminal acts; the consequences of punishing criminals are beneficial to society and those desirable consequences morally justify the punishment.

On the surface, it would seem that deontological and consequentialist moral philosophy complement each other. However, on closer study, it becomes apparent that the two can lead to major disagreements. For the deontological school, it is an imperative to punish a moral wrongdoer regardless of the practical consequences (e.g., no matter what the cost, no matter what the difficulty, even if it required the entire Gross National Product for 100 years to fund the search for one offender). On the other hand, for the utilitarian, it may be more important that some person be designated as the criminal offender and receive publicized punishment, so that other potential criminals will be deterred, even if the person being punished is not the person who actually committed the crime. The deontologists would say that the utilitarians are doubly immoral because they are punishing an innocent person and because they have allowed the truly guilty party to escape punishment. The utilitarians would say that the deontologists are immoral because they are wasting the resources of society on a quixotic project, thereby diminishing the resources that remain to be used to better that society. It would be nice to report that there is some easy way to resolve the fundamental differences between the deontologists and the utilitarians, but no mutually acceptable resolution has been found since the beginning of Western civilization and no one expects a solution to be found in the foreseeable future.

It should be noted that there are disagreements within each of the major schools. Deontologists disagree regarding which rules are morally binding. For example, is it more important always to tell the truth or always to punish criminal offenders? If always telling the truth were to make it impossible always to punish criminal offenders, would that justify sometimes not telling the truth or would that justify sometimes not punishing criminal offenders? Utilitarians disagree regarding which consequences are more important than others. For example, would it be better to spend scarce resources to improve health care for society or to improve police and criminal justice programs; how does one evaluate whether a healthy society is better than a safe society? Thus, apart from the differences between the deontologists and the utilitarians, there is plenty of room for dispute within each of the two philosophical positions.

All moral issues are contaminated by these philosophic disagreements. Thus, it is no surprise that forensic psychiatrists can be caught on the horns of moral dilemmas. What is important is that the forensic psychiatrist should be able to recognize what the nature of the moral problem is. Is it that the requirements of law are different from the requirements of medicine? Is it that the requirements of deontology are different from the requirements of consequentialism? Is it that there is a disagreement about the prioritization of moral obligations? Is it that there is a difference regarding how to evaluate the practical consequences of mutually exclusive moral choices and actions? Sometimes, in the course of careful philosophical analysis it becomes possible to detect imperfect reasoning from agreed-upon premises and to resolve the disagreement. Sometimes, the level of disagreement can be agreed upon, even if the dispute cannot be resolved, thereby narrowing the scope of the dispute.

The thrust of my argument is that forensic psychiatry is not a "moral minefield"; rather, it is that moral discourse is itself a morass of unresolved conflicts. In much the same way that it is not fair to blame the adversary system of Anglo-American law on us, it is unfair to blame lack of moral unanimity on us. It is perhaps incumbent upon the forensic psychiatrist to have some understanding of the roots of moral disputes, if only so as to clarify that the problem rests with philosophy rather than with forensic psychiatry.

The fundamental method of organizing data in forensic psychiatry is not the same as that used in clinical psychiatry. This is because a large part of the data that must be considered in forensic psychiatry is outside the consideration of clinical psychiatry. For example, the legal issues themselves are myriad. In family and domestic relations laws one must consider such issues as juvenile delinquency, child custody, parental fitness, children in need of supervision, abrogation of parental rights, spouse abuse, child neglect, abandonment of children, adoption, and foster care. In criminal law one must be mindful of, among other factors, competence to stand trial, competence to waive representation by counsel, competence to be sentenced, competence to be executed, being guilty but mentally ill, having diminished responsibility, and being not guilty by reason of mental disease or mental defect. Within civil law, the issues include involuntary psychiatric hospitalization, right to refuse treatment, informed consent, competence to participate in do-not-resuscitate decisions, testimentary capacity, competence to become engaged, married, or divorced, contractual capacity, disability compensation, and medical malpractice. None of those psychiatric–legal issues fits into the traditional medical framework of:

Chief Complaint.
History of the Present Illness.
Past Pertinent History.
Physical Findings.
Mental Status.
Laboratory Reports.
Differential Diagnosis.

For every one of the psychiatric–legal issues there are a wide array of legal criteria. Those criteria may be in legislated statutes, in case law determinations by the courts, in administrative codes established by the executive branch of government, or in private contracts (e.g., insurance policies). Just to complicate matters, each of the 50 states and the federal jurisdiction has its own distinct set of laws, cases, codes and valid contracts. While the issues may remain the same, thanks to our federal system of legally independent states, the criteria that are used to decide the issues are a hodge-podge. As before, such legal matters are not readily fitted into the standard data organization framework used in medicine.

Different from clinical medicine's focus on a present condition that is the concern of the patient, is the fact that in forensic medicine the focus may be on the past (e.g., was the person competent to consent to the treatment provided?) or on the future (e.g., will it be safe to transfer this person acquitted by reason of mental disease to a less secure psychiatric facility?). Further, the person who is the focus of the examinations may have no complaint at all; the inquiry comes from a third party whose own health is not under consideration. These contingencies are not part of the routine clinical psychiatric data collection format.

Forensic psychiatry has its own conceptual framework for the organization of the data that are germane to its practice. It is a framework designed to deal with the fact that the method of data organization in forensic psychiatry differs from both that of medicine and from that of law. It is derived from the fact that some special framework is needed to work at the interface between the two fields. In general, forensic psychiatry applies a four-step process:

1. What is the specific psychiatric–legal issue?
2. What are the legal criteria that determine the issue?
3. What are the relevant psychiatric–legal data?
4. What is the reasoning process used to reach a conclusion?

One of the many uses of this outline is that it can reveal the points at which problems exist. In many instances, what is revealed is that the problem lies with the legal system, rather than with forensic psychiatry. In some instances the problem occurs at the first step of the outline: judges and lawyers erroneously ask the wrong questions and then complain about the answers that they receive. For example, the court may ask if a defendant is competent to stand trial; but the real question may be whether the defendant is able to remain acquiescent while his lawyer enters into a negotiated plea bargain on his behalf. In other instances, the problem occurs at the second step of the outline; the criteria set forth in the law are vague and insufficiently specific. For example, who really knows precisely what is meant by "the best interests of the child" when custody issues must be considered? In some instances, the problem occurs at the third step in the outline; judges may insist that we provide answers to questions that are beyond current psychiatric knowledge. A good example of this problem occurred when the United States Supreme Court decided that psychiatrists could legally express an opinion regarding the future dangerousness of persons, notwithstanding the fact that the American Psychiatric Association had filed an *amicus curiae* brief to the effect that such predictions were beyond the scientific competence of psychiatrists. Finally, the problem may be at the fourth step in the outline: the attorney examining the psychiatric expert witness may (on direct examination) not have set forth a series of questions that permit the forensic psychiatrist to demonstrate the rational argument leading from the data to the conclusions or, alternatively, the opposing attorney (on cross-examination) may have prevented the psychiatric expert witness from responding fully and cogently to the questions being posed. After all, once we are on the witness stand, we are largely dependent on lawyers to facilitate and permit the presentation of the logical connections between our data and our opinions.

Much of the difficulty that the medical profession and the general public have in appreciating forensic psychiatry is due to blaming our field for problems that derive from other disciplines. The adversary system comes from Anglo-American law; it is not the creation of forensic psychiatry. The "moral minefield" is derivative from irreconcilable conflicts within the mainstream of Western civilization's moral philosophies. The lack of clear and stable legal criteria for specific legal issues is attributable to social policy decisions made by legislators, judges, and executive administrators.

Given the various problems that cause misunderstanding and misvaluation of forensic psychiatry, what can be done, and what does the future hold for our field? Several cautious predictions are possible. First, the trend towards formal postresidency training in forensic psychiatry is likely to continue. The time will come when any forensic psychiatrist who is not a graduate of an accredited fellowship program will be as dubious a practitioner as a physician who specializes in mental disorders but who has never graduated from a residency in psychiatry. Second, the trend towards recognizing board certification in forensic psychiatry as an important credential for practitioners is likely to continue. Eventually all practitioners will be expected to be certified in forensic psychiatry and the absence of such certification will be grounds to question the qualifications of a witness seeking to provide expert testimony. Third, the importance of educating the general public, the nonforensic general psychiatrists, the specialists in our own field, and the attorneys will continue. AAPL will have an increasingly important role to play as our field continues to mature and its importance is further recognized. Fourth, research in forensic psychiatry will have to increase substantially, so that the scientific data base upon which our opinions rest can become firmer. It has been suggested that many of the questions we are asked in court are not answerable from clinical research data alone (e.g., what percentage of patients with command hallucinations actually obey the commands? Do psychotropic medications work as effectively when administered involuntarily as they do when the patient actively cooperates with the treatment? What factors are related to future dangerous behavior?).

Looking into a crystal ball is always a risky project; sometimes the future is cloudy, sometimes the seer has poor eyesight, sometimes the sphere slips and the shattered shards are undecipherable. These predictions may more likely represent the expectations, perhaps even the hopes, for the field, rather than a guaranteed surety. What we, the current generation of forensic psychiatrists, do in the present is the key to the evolution of forensic psychiatry in the future.

If we recognize that our field has become a subspecialty in psychiatry, and if we act accordingly, then the future of our field is secure. If we are uncertain ourselves, if we falter in our organizational efforts and our commitment to expand the scientific and clinical bases of our work, then the responsibility for delaying general appreciation of our field will rest with us. The future of our subspecialty is in our own hands. It is our task to be worthy of that opportunity.

3

The Role of Traditional Medical Ethics in Forensic Psychiatry

ROBERT WEINSTOCK, GREGORY B. LEONG, AND J. ARTURO SILVA

INTRODUCTION

Traditional medical ethics originated with Hippocrates and a small group of reform-minded physicians in ancient Greece. The concepts of helping and not harming have permeated medical ethics for centuries and have remained a core foundation for the special professional obligations of physicians. The tradition of helping and not harming is most strongly stated in the Latin, *primum nil nocere*, or, first of all, do no harm.

Several years ago, psychiatrist Seymour Pollack formulated a definition of forensic psychiatry which concluded with a statement that the forensic psychiatrist applied psychiatry to legal issues for legal purposes and ends.[1] The forensic psychiatrist was supposed to be ethically neutral in providing consultation to the legal system, and Pollack's definition implied that it was not relevant for the forensic psychiatrist to question the legal purposes or ends in his professional capacity. Such issues were considered appropriate for his "personal morals" or beliefs as a citizen, but not for professional ethics. However, it is far from clear that a definition settles this issue, since definitions can be arbitrary and other definitions are possible. Moreover, surveys of American Academy of Forensic Science (AAFS) psychiatry and behavioral science section members,[2,3] and the tri-state chapter of the American Academy of Psychiatry and the Law (AAPL)[4] have suggested that the majority of forensic psychiatrists,

ROBERT WEINSTOCK, GREGORY B. LEONG, AND J. ARTURO SILVA • Department of Psychiatry and Biobehavioral Sciences, School of Medicine, University of California at Los Angeles, Los Angeles, California 90024, and the Psychiatry Service, West Los Angeles Veterans Administration Medical Center, Los Angeles, California 90073.

at least in the groups studied, do retain traditional medical values as a consideration in their functioning as forensic psychiatrists.

The American Board of Forensic Psychiatry recognized the need for forensic psychiatry to have its own ethics independent of those of attorneys or courts' requirements.[5] The board concluded its definition of forensic psychiatry with a statement that "forensic psychiatry should be practiced in accordance with guidelines and ethical principles enunciated by the profession of psychiatry." The board recognized the need for forensic psychiatry to develop its own ethical guidelines, consistent with medical and psychiatric ethics and not by default to leave the professional ethics of forensic psychiatry to the vagaries of the legal system.

A set of ethical guidelines which do address some fundamental ethical problems has been adopted by AAPL.[6] Although some issues consistent with traditional medical ethical values are addressed in these guidelines, many others found to present ethical problems in surveys of forensic psychiatrists[2-4] are not addressed. The new definition of forensic psychiatry adopted by the board and reiterated in AAPL's ethical guidelines does clarify that the current prevailing view is that the profession itself should determine what is ethically proper for the forensic psychiatrist and not relegate it to the legal system.

Psychiatrist Bernard Diamond[7] recently conceptualized the proper role of the forensic psychiatrist as that of a fiduciary to the legal system. Much as the individual physician and psychiatrist do not provide whatever treatment a particular patient desires, but only what the practitioner agrees would be helpful and consistent with his own values, the forensic psychiatric practitioner should participate only in such a way that he agrees can be useful, promotes better understanding, and functions in a manner consistent with his professional and personal values. In this model, the forensic psychiatrist would not blindly do the legal system's bidding but would do his best to participate only when he could do so honestly in a fiduciary manner, consistent with the profession's values. Such a model could also recognize the autonomy of the legal system much as the current informed-consent model allows for patient autonomy. Negotiation could occur. However, the forensic psychiatrist would not participate in ways he considers harmful or not consistent with his ethics, any more than an individual practitioner would feel obligated to treat an individual patient in such a manner, merely to conform to the patient's wishes. Most psychiatrists, for example, would not wish to treat a corporation executive who wishes to feel less guilty about embezzling money from his company or drug dealer who wishes to experience less conflict in selling drugs to children.

Psychiatrist Alan Stone[8] has described forensic psychiatrists as facing serious ethical dilemmas and conflicts for which medical and psychiatric ethics provide no resolution. He states that a psychiatrist cannot simply adjust to the adversarial system or remain true to one's calling as a physician. Doing whatever possible to help the patient and *primum nil nocere*, constitute the ethical dialectic of the physician's practice. Stone believes that although we know the boundaries of the ethical debate as physicians treating patients, "When we serve the system of justice, we can no longer agree on the boundaries of the debate." He believes this problem exists in all situations in which we go beyond the individual doctor-patient relationship. In his opinion, doctors lose their ethical boundaries when they give other factors such as justice, advancement of science, or political causes greater weight than helping their patients or doing no harm. Moreover, Stone notes that the practical ethical guideline to do everything we can to ease the suffering of our patients is no longer part of the American Medical Association's (AMA's) medical ethics nor is "first of all do no harm." Consequently, there is no current ethical principle by which to declare actions unethical which go contrary to these traditional medical ethical standards.

ORIGINS OF TRADITIONAL MEDICAL ETHICS

A review of the origin of traditional medical ethical values is crucial in an analysis of the ethical problems. According to medical ethics professor Robert Veatch,[9] physicians have been seen as a "profession" in the sense that besides having a body of specialized knowledge they "were committed to a special ethic that bound the members of the profession to special norms, duties and virtues." Physicians have had an ethical tradition that dates back to Hippocrates in ancient Greece and the Hippocratic oath. According to psychiatrist Allen Dyer, "patients and physician alike—with only the vaguest notions of what the oath might actually entail—think of the oath as something morally binding on the physician and requiring obligations to the patient. The oath and the name of Hippocrates still remain in the popular mind as the highest symbol of the physician's dedication to healing and...the oath continues to encourage a fundamental bond of trust among the patient, the physician, and the medical profession" (p 29).[10]

The Hippocratic school of physicians lived and worked on the Greek Island of Cos and emerged about the fifth century B.C. with Hippocrates as its head. The school produced a large body of scientific and ethical writings, but not all writings were authored by Hippocrates. In Rome at the time of physician Galen, 130–200 A.D., there were disputes over authorship.[9] There also are disputes over the date and origin of the oath, but Western physicians trace the foundations of their ethics to Hippocrates and the oath.

Ludwig Edelstein, a scholar on ancient Greece, believed that Hippocrates and the oath were significantly influenced by the Pythagoreans who had a special interest that no harm or injustice be done to people as a result of immoderate or unhealthy eating habits.[11] The oath, according to Edelstein, is almost a pure transcription of Pythagorean ethics (asceticism) with injunctions against abortion, euthanasia (poisons), and surgery as well as strict sexual mores and the keeping of confidences.[12]

The Latin, *primum non nocere*, or, first, do no harm, has become the best-known formulation of traditional Hippocratic medical values. However, many scholars have tried to discover the origin of this formulation without success. Some even consider it to be a revision of the original version.[13] However, related concepts are expressed in the oath and *Epidemics* (Book I, section XI)—a work in the Hippocratic corpus. Their exact meaning differs depending upon the translation from the Greek.

Edelstein's translation of the relevant section of the oath is the most restrictive and reads, "I will apply dietetic measures for the benefit of the sick according to my ability and judgment; I will keep them from harm and injustice."[11] Helping and harming are of equal value and solely dietetic measures for the sick are involved. However, philosopher Paul Carrick and others believe this section refers to other areas of medical practice as well, and not just to dietetics.[11] Another translation of this section is: "I will use treatment to help the sick according to my ability and judgment; I will keep them from harm and injustice." It also has been translated, "I will use treatment to help the sick according to my ability and judgment, but I will never use it to injure or wrong them." This last version gives added strength to the second half of not harming.[13]

The translation by J. Chadwick and W. N. Mann of the Hippocratic oath includes: "I will use my power to help the sick to the best of my ability and judgment; I will abstain from harming or wronging any man by it."[14] A later section of the oath reads, "Whenever I go into a house, I will go to help the sick and never with the intention of doing harm or injury." According to this translation, the oath is not restricted to the physician's treatment of patients but refers to any use of medical powers. Such an interpretation is consistent with seeing medical ethics as pertinent to all aspects of the physician's work.

Chadwick and Mann's translation of the *Epidemics* (Book I, section XI) reads, "Practice two things in your dealings with disease: either help or do not harm the patient."[14] This section has also been translated "as to diseases make a habit of two things—to help—or to do no harm." In one translation it reads, "to help or at least to do no harm."[13] The latter translation with the addition of "at least" comes close to, first, do no harm, with the avoidance of harm as a minimum and necessary characteristic of professional ethical behavior.

Medical ethics professor Albert Jansen agrees that the origin of *primum non nocere* is obscure.[15] However, he states that "do no harm" admonishes physicians that they enter a moral enterprise and exhorts them to "focus their skills on the well-being of patients."

The wider interpretation and translation of the Hippocratic requirement would seem to apply to all uses of medical powers and not merely to the treatment of patients. Such a wider interpretation would include evaluations such as those performed by forensic psychiatrists.

According to Carrick,[11] under no circumstances did the physician's profession "morally permit him to be an accomplice to murder. There are several considerations that render this wider meaning acceptable. First, it is a documented fact that in the Greco-Roman era it was popularly believed that the physician who is skillful at curing, by virtue of this knowledge could also kill. One can find Plato echoing this suspicion in his *Republic*. In book one, Socrates asks Polemarchus: "Who then is the most able when they are ill to benefit friends and harm enemies in respect to disease and health?" to which Polemarchus replies, "The physician."

Anthropologist Margaret Mead considered the Hippocratic oath as marking the first time in history that there was a complete separation between killing and curing. Throughout the primitive world the doctor and the sorcerer were the same person. The person with the power to kill also had the power to cure, including undoing his own killing activities. It marked the first time that the "power to heal was vested in a practitioner who was not also a shaman with the power to harm."[10] Dyer states that the Hippocratic oath was unique among ancient codes in making the healing of patients the single overriding feature. By contrast, an ancient Indian code, the *Charaka Samhita*, obliges the physician to deny services to enemies of his rulers, unattended women, or evildoers. It thereby subsumes the physician's obligations to the interests of the state.[10] In the Hippocratic oath there is to be "equal treatment for males and females, free and slave." The physician must subsume self-interest to what is good for the patient.[10]

The Hippocratic oath thereby required a stricter morality for Hippocratic physicians than was established by Greek law, and was not the norm among medical practitioners at the time. There is no record of any analogous oath or work directed to medical ethics in ancient times. The Babylonians were the first civilization to record laws regulating medical practice in approximately 1727 B.C. under the Code of Hammurabi. This code set forth stiff fines for surgical malpractice but only for those of certain social status.[11] It does not provide a single standard of care for all patients and is not a work about ethics. There is nothing in the code comparable to Hippocratic ethics.

The lack of licensing and regulation of medicine in Greece provided opportunities for charlatanism and abuse and injury of patients. Medicine was merely a craft, and the oath affirms the importance of the physician being committed to and responsible for the welfare of patients who trustingly and naively seek medical help and the technical competence of himself and his peers.[11] The oath expresses a desire and resolve to make oneself and the profession the best they can be: "To be a professional in this sense, is to profess competence and personal integrity not merely at the moment of entry into the ranks of trained healers, but every day of one's working life."[11]

The image of the good physician in the "Hippocratic corpus underwent some transformation in ancient times, from a craftsman's ethic of work done well to the stoic ethic of duty and obligation to mankind and humanity."[12] There is therefore some debate about whether the Hippocratic oath dates back to the time of Hippocrates or whether it is a later development, as late as the second century A.D. Hippocratic writings make no mention of the oath in any other sections.

Medicine was first referred to as a profession in the first century A.D. when Scribonius Largus, a physician at the time of Claudius, so referred to it in his treatise *On Remedies*. He also made the earliest reference to details of the oath. Scribonius, following the middle stoa of Panaetius, with origins also in Ciceros' *De Officiis*, said that each profession has its own ethics, and we "must play the role required by our profession—one which we choose voluntarily." This concept is more demanding than that of the physician as craftsman, and implies a certain nobility of dedication. Perceiving a profession as a special calling is reflected later in Galen's *De Placitis* and in the 18th-century code of Thomas Percival, as well as the original AMA Code of 1848.[12] The later modern view of a profession differed from the earlier stoical one in that it promulgated the image of a special calling with prerogatives of authority and paternalism. Percival saw the physician as "courteous, kind, yet firm, interested yet objective, taking his patient's concerns into account and acting on his behalf. His comportment must be proper; he should inspire confidence." These ideas are similar to some in the Hippocratic corpus. What is new is the concept of medicine as a gentlemanly profession, with the idea of privilege rather than the specific obligations emphasized by Scribonius.

One of the characteristics of a profession which developed is to have its own code of ethics enforced by the profession. Special knowledge was considered necessary to evaluate practitioners and its special ethics was the justification for self-regulation. Increasing professional liability litigation has reduced the justification for these procedures, but does not negate the value of a profession trying to police itself to maintain its standards.

Traditional medical ethics as perceived by physicians and patients alike traces its origins back to the Hippocratic oath and the Hippocratic corpus. These traditions were reintroduced in the 10th century A.D. into Western Europe under the influence of the Christian church. References to the Greek gods were replaced by an infusion not only of Christian religious values, but also the Fifty Admonitions to Physicians of Isaac Israeli and the Code of Ishaq Ibn Ali Al-Ruhawi, both of the ninth century.[12] Hippocratic tradition was rediscovered after obtaining works from Moslem and Jewish sources. In the early Middle Ages the ethics of the Hippocratic oath were first universalized. Its sources were refurbished by the humanism of the great religions and served as a wellspring for much of 19th-century American medical ethics.[12] After the Christianization of Europe, other Greek ethical systems had lost favor, but the Hippocratic ethic was preserved because of its similarity to Christian ethics.[9] The importance of Hippocratic ethics increased in the 10th century, when many Greek writings were recovered from Arabic sources.

Interest in the Anglo-Saxon world in medical ethics did not revive until the 18th century. It had undergone an earlier revival in France and the Continent where medicine had a higher status and the Catholic church had greater influence. In fact, in France confidentiality was seen as absolute, much as in the Hippocratic oath. Thus, the concept of the "professional secret" developed which would not allow testimony in court even with the patient's consent.[16] The value of confidentiality and the professional secret was considered so important for society that no individual patient would be permitted to sacrifice it even voluntarily in a courtroom setting. Only recently have some exceptions developed in France. In contrast, English common law did not contain even a physician-patient privilege.

It was not until the 18th century that interest in medical ethics was revived in the Anglo-Saxon world, when John Gregory published his *Lectures on the Duties and Qualifications of a Physician* based on concepts of Scottish moralists such as David Hume and Frances Hutcheson. In 1789 in Manchester, England, an epidemic struck which overworked the infirmary staff and caused disputes. Thomas Percival was asked to help prevent such disputes, and he wrote his *Medical Ethics*, which presented a scheme for professional conduct which had many features in common with the Hippocratic oath,[9] and became a model for ethical codes in the United States.

In the United States, a dispute among several schools of physicians led orthodox practitioners to found the AMA in 1847. A code of medical ethics that was patterned after Thomas Percival's scheme was developed.

According to Dyer,[10] "traditions at least as old as the cults of Aesculapius and the oath of Hippocrates stress the fiduciary character of medical practice. The fundamental warrant of medical practice is the trust placed in the physician, based on the physician's competence and intention to help or benefit the patient. But being traditional, these ideals are largely unarticulated and inherently ambiguous. In recent years ever more explicit codification has supplemented the received traditions" (p. 47).[10] Dyer's concept seems to imply that more recent ethical codifications supplement traditional medical ethics. However, their absence from any recent codification does not and should not necessarily negate their traditional importance and influence, at least for some of the most basic core characteristics, such as beneficence and non-maleficence.

RELEVANT PHILOSOPHICAL CONCEPTS

Distinctions are sometimes made between professional ethics and morals. However, such distinctions are not generally useful since the terms "ethics" and "morals" have been used interchangeably and in differing contexts. The word "ethics" is derived from the Greek *ethika*, meaning "of or for morals."[11] Philosopher Philippa Foot states that rather than distinguishing between "ethics" and "morals" it is useful to focus on the source of obligations and restrictions of conduct. She distinguishes between professional ethics which stem from special professional obligations and ethical obligations which would apply to any person.[17]

Philosopher Ruth Macklin states that "ethics embraces professional and applied ethics, theoretical concerns in ethics, philosophical and conceptual questions and whatever your group means by 'morals.' Some people construe 'morals' to mean codes of conduct to guide individual or group actions, while 'ethics' is taken to refer to the principle of right action. In the secular philosophical tradition in which I was educated, 'ethical' and 'moral' are virtually synonymous. The difference is only a matter of etymology...It is folly to think that one can rule out an area of conduct as 'inappropriate' simply by defining it one way or another...The fact that your group could probably not reach consensus...does not mean it is therefore a matter of 'morals' rather than ethics."[18]

Psychiatrist Paul Appelbaum has stated, "I have always considered professional ethics to have as their scope consideration of the moral principles that underlie the actions taken by professionals in their professional capacities. The implication of this definition for the issues raised in your letter is that no behavior of psychiatrists as psychiatrists is outside the realm of psychiatric ethics. It may be, of course, that no consensus is possible among psychiatrists as to which principles are relevant to a given professional function (e.g., participation in capital cases), or as to how they should be applied; but that is different from saying that these behaviors are not susceptible to ethical analysis."[19]

Diamond[20] has suggested a division into organizational professional ethics and personal professional ethics:

> Organizational professional ethics are the minimal standards of conduct (ethical, moral, or whatever) below which the practitioner is unacceptable to his peers and, perhaps, assumes legal liability for his conduct. This standard is applicable to all members of the profession, regardless of sex, race, religion, school of thought, training, etc. Examples: sex between therapist and patient, false charges, and deliberately deceiving patients as to need for therapy. Also included here are standards applicable to all members who practice in certain specialized areas. Examples: entering into excessive social or business relationships with patients in psychoanalysis or deep psychotherapy and a forensic psychiatrist who conceals a conflict of interest.
>
> A subcategory of organizational ethics are ideal standards of practice which should be, but are not yet enforceable. That is, standards of ethical practice of the professional leaders, most highly competent practitioners, etc., but which are not enforceable by the professional organization (or the law) because of a lack of consensual agreement that they should represent the general standard of practice. These may be presented as desirable guides for professional practice rather than requirements. Organizational standards of ethical practice sometimes do not distinguish between those which are absolutely required by all, in all circumstances, and those which are guidelines for desirable practice.
>
> The second division of ethics concerns ethical standards accepted by individuals or particular groups of practitioners who for their own personal reasons feel obligated to follow special ethical standards. For example, Catholic psychiatrists may consider it unethical for them to participate in abortion decisions. If one opposes capital punishment one might consider it unethical to evaluate the sanity of a death row prisoner if such evaluation were to be used to certify that he is fit to be executed. The second group may be very strongly held and serve as powerful guides to clinical practice for the persons who subscribe to them, but they cannot be enforced upon all practitioners, even though one might wish to do so, and certainly should not be required of the entire membership of an organization. One must be careful at this point, for frequently strong demands are made for adoption of ethical requirements when, in fact, the ethical concept properly belongs only to a special group of individuals.

In some cases, reason, it would be hoped, can be used to resolve problems in professional ethics. Reason can be most useful when important principles or facts have been overlooked or inconsistencies not appreciated. Difficulties can be most problematic or even impossible to resolve when different values are involved or differing priorities are given to the various values.

Consequentialist or teleological reasoning appeals to consequences such as doing the most good for the most people, e.g., utilitarian philosophy. At the other pole sits deontological reasoning which come from the Greek *deon*, meaning duty, or that which is binding. It appeals not to something extrinsic but to something intrinsic to the situation. For illustration, the pursuit of a worthy utilitarian goal, the patient's health, is constrained by a deontological value, the right to give informed consent.[21] An extreme strict utilitarian position would justify killing an innocent man, if it would be beneficial to society to have someone punished for the crime. It requires deontological values to explain why most people would consider executing an innocent man unethical.

Ethical guidelines are an important start in professional ethics. The latest extensive 1980 revision of the AMA's Principles of Medical Ethics states that the principles "are not laws but standards of conduct which define the essentials of honorable behavior for the physicians" and are "intended as guides to responsible professional behavior, but they are not presented as the sole or only route to medical morality."[22] Philosopher Stephen Toulmin[23] has stated that moral principles, theories, and rules need interpretation to be useful. If guidelines are too highly specific they are not likely to allow the discretion necessary for all sorts of situations. However, if they are so general that they cover every kind of case, they are unlikely to offer clear direction about what to do. Toulmin[23] recommends rules that allow for discretion, since to do otherwise is a denial of uncertainty, because it presupposes that in forming rules and principles, we can think of every kind of situation that could come before us.[24] Psychiatrist Jay Katz[25] has said that people generally have difficulty acknowledging uncertainty and the extent to which it pervades our daily lives. However, such acknowledgment is a prerequisite for careful ethical analysis in complex cases rather than rigid application of an inappropriate rule and an inability to consider other competing values.

When values conflict, and it is impossible to follow one rule or pursue one good without violating another, a moral dilemma is created. Dyer states, "Modern medicine seldom offers us the clear-cut alternatives that could neatly be dissected as *either* good *or* bad, or *either* right *or* wrong. Instead we are offered complex situations in which any course of action compromises certain ethical principles."[10]

Psychiatrist Edward Hundert states that in a moral dilemma, moral values in each side of a case are in conflict because there are a multiplicity of values we hold dear. We can do the right thing by weighing and balancing the scale and acting in the way it tips. The values which are outweighed produce anxiety.[26]

Dyer sees ethics as a process of reflecting on the value judgments we make. He sees analogies to clinical judgment. Much like psychotherapy, he has found that when ethical reflection becomes abstract and remote it is useful to ask "Where is the affect?" as a way of locating ethical conflict.[10]

Hundert has stated that medicine is not value-neutral. It is dedicated to the relief and prevention of suffering. It is therefore not surprising that medicine and law can have conflicting values which can come into conflict since "medicine gives more weight to considerations of welfare than to considerations of justice as compared to the legal profession."[27]

Hundert also believes that what is most needed for medical ethics is to teach physicians a way to think about moral dilemmas. Ethical guidelines are only a start and are insufficient when values and principles are in conflict. Our consciences need to compute how much each value is worth in terms of each of the competing values. These resulting moral principles evolve with our moral experiences in dynamic "reflective equilibrium." He states, "The moral actions we take are determined by the ultimate balance of relative weights assigned to all of the competing values as they arise from the particular facts of a problematic case." Each new dilemma enables us to develop and refine our principles by introducing new patterns of conflicting values. Hundert's model dismisses the simplistic position of those who believe their moral principles are defined in terms of adherence to a consistent action, by emphasizing that consistency applies not at the level of actions but at the level of principles. The patterns of value balancing "characteristics of medicine as a profession gives rise to what is commonly called 'medical ethics'—an ethics that may conflict with that of other institutions within which doctors must make moral decisions."[27]

Philosopher Baruch Brody has developed a model for dealing with moral dilemmas with some similarities to Hundert's model, which he calls the model of conflicting appeals.[28] In his model, various conflicting appeals must be balanced. He states that there are several ways to do this. One model involves a lexical ordering of appeals. Examples are political philosopher John Rawls' system, in which justice (the equal distribution of liberty) should take precedence over a principle justifying some social or economic inequity. Another such system is Veatch's, which states that non-consequentialist principles, such as promise-keeping, autonomy, honesty, avoiding killing, and justice have lexical priority over the consequentialist principle of beneficence. Beneficence, according to philosopher Tom Beauchamp, is defined as "a directive to help others further their important and legitimate interests when we can do so with only minimal risk or inconvenience to ourselves."[29]

However, as stated by Brody, it is difficult to think of any moral appeal which always takes precedence over all others. In order to avoid beneficence always swamping all other appeals, one need only allow that non-consequentialist or deontological principles should sometimes take precedence. In addition, if in a hierarchical approach, a moral appeal always took precedence over any other appeal alone, it is highly unlikely that it also should always take precedence over all other appeals jointly.[28]

Brody also refers to a scale approach to conflict which is very similar to Hundert's approach insofar as each moral appeal is given a differing weight in different circumstances. We then add up all the appeals favoring one action and all the appeals favoring another and come to a conclusion in the given case about which set of appeals takes precedence. The main difficulty Brody has with this approach is that "we have no reason to believe that it is possible to do all the things it requires us to do. Its first task, indicating when a given moral appeal has greater or lesser significance in a particular case is perhaps possible. The second task, constructing a common scale so that we can add the strengths of the various appeals on each side is a different matter" (p. 77).[28]

Brody proposes a modification which he calls the judgment approach. It agrees with the scale approach that we need to develop a theory about when a given moral appeal has greater or lesser significance in a given case and identify all the moral appeals relevant to a given case (which can include both deontological and utilitarian appeals). However, Brody states that moral theory can take us no further, since we have no common measure to use in weighing conflicting appeals. The last process he claims is a process of judgment rather than weighing. Otherwise it is the same as Hundert's approach. It also can include a theory of the significance of a given appeal which ranks the differing "uses of the appeal in terms of likelihood to override other appeals, *all other things being equal*" (p 77).[28] However, judgment is necessary in the last step whose parameters cannot be spelled out consistently by any theory; but the specific circumstances in a specific case must be considered.

This process admittedly is complex and does not produce the simple clear-cut solutions one would like from ethics. Simple problems, of course, can be addressed with simple ethical rules. However, complex problems with values and principles in conflict have no easy solution, which is why they are moral dilemmas.

The judgment approach according to Brody is disturbing because (1) after noting the significance of differing moral appeals the decision maker will often still be unsure what decision to make and would like guidance from moral theory which the judgment approach cannot provide; (2) people's judgments may disagree, although they agree upon the relevant appeals and their significance; and (3) it is open to abuse by those interested in justifying a pre-chosen alternative. However, the reasons Brody gives for accepting it are: (1) by default, because of the problems with other approaches; and (2) it seems to do justice to the reality of moral ambiguity, since good people, after careful examination of the relevant issues, often disagree. A complex model may be what is needed for complex cases.[28]

ISSUES IN FORENSIC PSYCHIATRY

The forensic psychiatrist functions at the interface of the medical and the legal systems which have different and sometimes competing ethical values. Justice David Bazelon, who wanted psychiatrists to "recognize and accede to the higher ethical framework of the adversarial system's search for justice," according to Stone, failed to consider "how the psychiatrists would square the ethical imperative of the healing profession with the adversarial goals of criminal prosecution."[8] As a result of the ethical challenges, Stone[8] stated, "Forensic psychiatry is caught on the horns of an ethical dilemma."

Philosopher Jay Kantor states that the legal system implies that only some persons should not be punished but the implication of the psychological deterministic tradition is that no persons should be punished for their behavior.[30] Psychotherapeutic treatment, according to Kantor, tries to be nonjudgmental and warmly to help a patient overcome feelings of guilt. In contrast, the criminal justice system coldly tries to bring a felon's feelings of guilt to the surface so that he can suffer over them. Kantor gives as the most striking example of the moral inadequacy of trying to separate "objective" medical judgment from their eventual nonobjective use is that of concentration camp physicians in Nazi Germany who gave objective determinations about the fitness of inmates to work in the camp, or by default to be fit only to be exterminated.

Recent works have emphasized the importance of physicians to the Nazi killing.[31,32] Genetic theories about purifying the race, by respected German physicians and scientists who wished to compensate for the recent absence of natural selection in humans resulting from the care given to "genetically inferior" individuals by society, gave intellectual sanction to the killing first of the mentally retarded, then of mental patients, and lastly of Jews and dissidents who were blamed for Germany's loss in World War I. After March 9, 1943 a medical license was required of those making the selections on the railway ramps and supervising the killing in Auschwitz and other extermination camps. Lifton documents the active participation of psychiatrists in the killing of their patients paradoxically described as treatment insofar as it put "life that was not worth living" out of its misery, as well as the doubling process in which a part of a person serves as a whole and which allowed ordinary people who often were not sadistic monsters to do outrageous things.[31] Of course this analogy is not to suggest that current forensic psychiatrists are ever this evil, but only to call attention to what can happen in a system in which fundamental Hippocratic ideals are forgotten and in which physicians separate technical competence from any concern about the outcomes of their endeavors, performed without any consideration of the relevance of traditional medical ethics.

Kantor raises a question about the ethics of a Nazi physician who would have lied about a person's fitness for work or a person's Jewish origin. Such lying would certainly be consistent with doing no harm. Kantor also asks about the ethics of a physician who opposed the death penalty who tried to "save as many condemned as possible from execution, doing anything from giving his evaluees the 'benefit of the doubt' about their competence to outrightly lying about his evaluation."[30] Kantor states that such a physician risks in the microcontext having his judgment no longer trusted by the courts and in the macrocontext "breeding distrust of psychiatry in general." The Nazi physician who would have lied created a more problematic moral dilemma in which most people probably would consider lying ethically appropriate.

Poet Ezra Pound who faced charges of treason illustrates a similar dilemma. In order to save him from harm, a psychiatrist reportedly evaluated Pound as incompetent to stand trial even though the psychiatrist's professional judgment was that Pound was competent. Pound was saved from trial and possible execution because the evaluating psychiatrist, in playing God, believed that Pound was a great poet who deserved special treatment.[30]

Stone similarly raises a question about the ethics of Dr. Leo who testified routinely in order to help Jewish defendants in the Old Bailey in England in approximately 1801. He apparently did so because of the harsh legal system, but became the laughingstock of the court. His frequent participation in court as well as his evasiveness about this fact seem to have been interpreted as automatically undermining his credibility.[8] Stone also has questioned the proper role for psychiatry in his parable of the black army sergeant in which Stone's testimony resulted in the man's conviction and lengthy prison sentence for stealing small items in a system which gave no consideration to racism. Stone believes he was wrong to consider psychiatry "objective" under those circumstances.[33]

PROPOSED RESOLUTION TO ETHICAL PROBLEMS

Although conflicting values of the medical and legal systems can produce ethical dilemmas, ethical solutions probably usually exist. These solutions already are recognized by most forensic psychiatrists in an implicit, if not explicit manner, as shown by their responses to the previously mentioned surveys.[2-4]

In many situations, there is no conflict between values. Helping a defendant in a criminal case may be completely consistent with Hippocratic values. Testifying for the prosecution in a case where the defendant is dangerous and treatment will be offered also may not present significant conflict for most forensic psychiatrists, considering the restrictions posed by current mental health laws. It is true that Hippocratic medical values involved treatment of individual patients, and not efforts to help society. However, it is not a significant extension or departure from the core values of traditional medical ethics to consider the welfare of society as well as of the individual.[34] The 1957 Revision of the AMA's Principles of Medical Ethics included responsibility to society.[9] Later revisions have continued to include this aspect; although, the ethics of becoming societal agents of social control can be complex.[35] Moreover, in resolving financial disputes between parties or child custody suits or preventing someone from succeeding with a false disability claim, or succeeding with a valid disability claim—all do not necessarily involve ethical dilemmas. In only a relative minority of cases does participation on one side or the other significantly conflict with traditional medical ethics. In fact, Appelbaum's[36] standard of truth "to present the truth, insofar as that goal can be approached from both a subjective and an objective point of view," can usually be followed with minimal ethical conflict. Appelbaum[36] recommends that an objective approach to truth requires the psychiatrist to make evident the limitations on his or her conclusions. Subjectively, to present the truth as he or she sees it, the psychiatrist should gather the maximum possible amount of relevant data.

According to Stone,[37] claiming clinical certainty in predictions of dangerousness as routinely done by Texas psychiatrist Grigson in death penalty cases arguably is unethical because it disregards the empirical evidence. Becoming an avid prosecution advocate in death penalty cases, or those in which the recommended punishment appears excessive, can provide ethical problems for many forensic psychiatrists. Nevertheless, honest participation for the defense in these cases could be considered appropriate,[17] and there is no reason for psychiatrists opposed to capital punishment to withdraw from all such cases. It even is possible to support capital punishment in some cases as a citizen yet believe that to advocate it professionally violates traditional Hippocratic ethics.

It sometimes is believed that the only way to appear to be honest in the courtroom is to testify for both sides in different cases and to be prepared to testify for either side if the facts of the case so warrant. Although many people are of this opinion, this recommendation does not obviate the rare "hired gun" who will sell testimony to the highest bidder even if it involves stretching or distorting the truth. The "hired gun" may be prepared to testify for whatever side pays a sufficient fee. Therefore the absence of an ideological motivation or bias does not preclude a financial motivation or bias. The "hired gun" issue was considered the number-one problem by forensic psychiatrists who responded to the first AAFS survey.[2]

As Diamond points out, the crucial distinction between advocacy and a "hired gun" is that the advocate is honest but the "hired gun" is dishonest.[38] The honest advocate still can have an ideological motivation and accept only cases where the facts fit his social philosophy, are consistent with medical ethics, or consistent with what he considers an appropriate fiduciary role to the legal system. The crucial issue is that he is totally honest and turns down cases in which truthful honest testimony does not fit his social agenda or coincide with his personal and professional ethics. He does not twist the facts to help an evaluee or further his social agenda, but tries his best not to participate if he cannot do so in a way that is consistent with his ethics. He is not on one side's payroll or always makes the best case possible for one side regardless of his honest opinion. If his attempt not to participate is unsuccessful because of subpoenas and court rulings and he achieves in an isolated case the opposite result from what was intended, that still does not negate the ethical value of the attempt.[17] Advocacy is therefore not necessarily inconsistent with professional ethics, but dishonesty is, since it destroys respect for the profession in the courtroom as well as in society. There is no reason that ideological motives automatically should lead to dishonesty any more than financial motives.

Respondents to the ethical surveys appear to consider traditional medical Hippocratic values in their functioning as forensic psychiatrists.[2-4] They considered the following to be ethical problems: reporting prison marijuana use despite a promise; writing a seclusion order solely to support prison discipline; or not respecting a competent, not civilly committable prisoner's right to refuse psychiatric treatment. In these situations, traditional Hippocratic ethics seem relevant. Additional situations considered unethical include the following: committing to a position before examining the person, records, or facts; performing a forensic evaluation without attempting to ascertain relevant legal criteria; performing a forensic evaluation without attempting to obtain significant material; or telling only a portion of the truth on the witness stand despite the oath. In this section respondents seem to be opposed to the "hired gun" and to sloppy, incompetent, superficial work.

However, with other forensic issues, traditional medical ethical concerns appear to be even more relevant. Respondents believed there was a duty to protect both the defendant and society regardless of who paid their fee, and not to reveal irrelevant embarrassing material which could be used to press for a settlement.

Regarding death penalty issues there were suggestive trends. A majority did not feel it was an ethical problem to evaluate a defendant's competency to be executed and a slight majority even saw no ethical problem in treating individuals to restore their competency to be executed. Nevertheless, a substantial minority of psychiatrists would consider such treatment as presenting ethical problems or as being contrary to their personal ethical standards as shown by the close vote on this issue. A large majority clearly believed it presented ethical problems not personally to examine a defendant yet give an opinion in a death penalty case despite the United States Supreme Court opinion about its legal acceptability.[39] Respondents apparently recognized that the profession can declare this procedure unethical despite the court declaring it legal. As psychiatrist Howard Zonana states, psychiatric ethics currently require a personal examination for civil commitment.[40] Section 7, Annotation 4 of the APA Annotations[41] states, "the psychiatrist may permit his/her certification to be used in the involuntary treatment of that person." It is, however, ethical to testify in other situations, such as testamentary capacity, without examining the defendant, or to help draw up a psychological profile of a mass murderer without a personal examination. Opinion 7A of the APA Ethics Committee[42] also considers it ethical to testify for the state in a criminal case about the competency of a defendant based on criminal records, without examining the defendant or obtaining approval to render an opinion. However, the death penalty is a problem for which relevant testimony should require special care and caution, considering the extreme importance of the accuracy of such testimony. To quote Zonana, "Is the death penalty less demanding than civil commitment?...The need for reliability might argue for ethical if not legal guidelines regarding the nature and minimal basis for psychiatric testimony."[40]

Respondents to the survey saw an ethical problem in specifically recommending a death penalty verdict or expressing an opinion amounting to a death penalty recommendation. They also agreed with the APA position of not being a participant in a legally authorized execution and saw a need to treat the death penalty differently because of its special seriousness. The earlier survey showed a difference of opinion regarding the ethics of contributing in any way to a death penalty verdict.[2] This difference of opinion suggest that contributing to a death penalty in any way produces ethical problems for approximately half the members of the groups surveyed. Active direct advocacy for the death penalty is problematic ethically for most members; the death penalty is an act of retribution in which the wishes of the law most clearly can come into conflict with traditional Hippocratic ethics.

Consistent with traditional medical values, respondents clearly saw no ethical problems in performing a forensic consultation on a former patient even in a major case, despite the discouragement of this practice in AAPL's current guidelines.[3,4] Psychiatrist Robert Miller discusses this issue further.[43]

The most consistent way to view these findings is that most forensic psychiatrists consider traditional medical ethics as one value that they bring to their consultations to the legal system. Differing practitioners clearly weigh these values differently, but most forensic psychiatrists appear to balance traditional medical values among other values when they consult to the legal system.

The survey results suggest that forensic psychiatrists use methods similar to those recommended by Hundert or to the model of conflicting appeals by Brody, even though these evaluations are more likely to have been made on a preconscious basis by doing what seems or "feels" right. They appear informally to consider traditional medical ethics as one value in this balancing process. Appelbaum[44] has stated that the forensic psychiatrist uses his Hippocratic medical injunction of doing no harm and non-maleficence before and after his evaluation of the forensic issue in question, but not in his evaluating role as a forensic psychiatrist. Perhaps a more appropriate model would consider traditional medical values as one factor even in the evaluation process of the forensic issue insofar as they influence how the evaluation is conducted and how the results are permitted to be used; although, they may be even more relevant in other aspects of the encounter. Even in clinical work, a truthful diagnosis such as antisocial personality may be harmful to a patient.[45]

Although traditional Hippocratic values or biases should not operate in the attempt to reach a truthful honest opinion, they should operate in the decision about whether to participate or in how the opinion will be used—at least to the degree that the forensic psychiatrist has any control over this process. If he determines that some harm would be done to the defendant but good would be done to society, most forensic psychiatrists would probably see no ethical conflict. Other circumstances may differ. For example, if a truthful evaluation would lead to a death penalty verdict, a forensic psychiatrist has the option of trying to withdraw from the case if he believes such participation violates either organizational or his personal professional ethics, even if he might support the death penalty in some cases as a private citizen. Moreover, presentation of mitigating factors in the penalty phase of capital cases can be quite appropriate. Relevant aspects of mental illness may be pertinent in those states which require balancing of aggravating and mitigating factors. Aspects which explain why a person committed the crime may be relevant here even if the legal criteria for an insanity defense are not met. Both the AMA and APA consider it unethical "to be a participant in a legally authorized execution."[41] This section of the Principles of Medical Ethics with Annotations has been narrowly interpreted to refer only to the actual killing. Opinion 1 of the APA Ethics Committee potentially is broader stating that "the overriding meaning of this principle is that the physician-psychiatrist is a healer, not a killer, no matter how well-purposed the killing may be."[42]

Objections sometimes are raised that medical ethics apply only to patients and not forensic evaluees. In addition to the survey results, the *Current Opinions* of the AMA Council on Ethical and Judicial Affairs state: "Ethical standards of professional conduct and responsibility may exceed but are never less than nor contrary to those required by law...In the ethical tradition of Hippocrates and continually offered thereafter, the role of the physician has been a healer...A physician's responsibilities to his patient are not limited to the actual practice of medicine...."[46] In a situation analogous to forensic evaluations, i.e., a pre-employment physical examination by a physician hired by the employer, "no physician-patient relationship exists between the physician and the examinee."

Nonetheless, the information "obtained by the physician as a result of such examinations is confidential and should not be communicated to a third party, without the individual's prior written consent unless it is required by law. If the individual authorizes the release...the physician should release only that information which is reasonably relevant to the employer's decision regarding that individual's ability to perform the work required by the job."[46] Hippocratic ethical tradition is mentioned directly in this section. Also, it is clear that some aspects of medical ethics apply even when evaluees are not patients. Similarly, aspects of medical ethics could apply in a forensic evaluation. The psychiatric profession, of course, can set a higher ethical requirement than the minimum required by law.

There have also been objections that the Hippocratic oath and ethics are outdated. They no longer appear directly in the AMA Principles of Medical Ethics even though they do in the AMA's *Current Opinions*.[46] Abortion today is frequently practiced and even mercy killing is being considered. The Hippocratic oath even prohibited surgery, since Hippocratic physicians were not trained in its practice. Moreover, it has been said that physicians have participated in torture, Nazi death camp selections, and may have even cheered at the Inquisition when souls who were "saved" were burned at the stake. Additionally, recent trends have turned physicians into mere employees with no special ethics. Physician beneficence and paternalism have been replaced by patient autonomy and informed consent with Hippocratic traditions gradually becoming antiquated. Moreover, some believe that medical ethics outside the doctor-patient relationship remain nebulous.

According to ethicist Edmund Pellegrino and coauthor David Thomasma, what is most significant is the ethos and not a formally developed ethic of the physician-patient relationship: "That ethos which is still the dominant influence on how physicians see themselves is that of the benign authoritarian dedicated and competent craftsman who acts in the interest of his patient out of motives as practical as a good reputation and as lofty as a love of mankind" (p 203).[12] They also view some degree of effacement of self-interest as always having been understood as part of a physician's duty, as in the treatment of contagious diseases.[47] Furthermore, they view the fiduciary model as best describing the physician-patient relationship in that the whole person is treated, and that the values of the patient must also be part of the dialogue about medical treatment.[47] Paternalism, although often considered a regressive authoritarian element of Hippocratic ethics, is not necessarily bad. It is not, strictly speaking, always unduly authoritarian, though the Hippocratic physicians may have had little respect for patient autonomy. Paternalism can be considered analogous to the responsibility of a good parent towards a dependent child—namely to promote growth and autonomy when the person is unable to make these judgments.[10] A weak form of paternalism involves making decisions for people only when they are unable to make their own judgments.[29]

Even if much of Hippocratic ethics has become antiquated, the central concepts are not. They still appear to have influenced survey responses of forensic psychiatrists. Those departures from traditional medical ethics, as in

Nazi Germany, are unfortunate and tragic aberrations. They are well combatted by traditional ethics much as in the law where unwritten common law continues to exert influence. While military psychiatrists as "double agents" may inadvertently contribute to the death of their patient by sending him back into battle, as Foot states, there is an important distinction and moral difference between inadvertently killing someone and doing something directly and intentionally to produce the killing.[17] Opposing something wrong is the proper ethical action even if it produces no immediate good result. It may have some good consequence eventually, though, even if no immediate good result is seen.[17]

Although abortion was prohibited by the Hippocratic oath, as was euthanasia, new knowledge has raised questions about the exact point where life begins. Nevertheless, many Catholics as well as others still oppose abortion. Giving a terminal patient the means to kill himself or allowing a terminal patient to refuse life-sustaining treatment is not the same as a physician "giving a fatal draught to anyone" if asked,[14] or deciding himself who warrants euthanasia. Although some aspects of Hippocratic ethics are debatable or have changed, for many centuries, the fundamental aspects have continued to resurface and guide medicine's nobler actions. It still remains a part of the AMA's Opinions.[46]

Unfortunately, knowledge of ethics does not in itself lead to ethical action. Ethical behavior is more complex. An individual physician must also have the will to be ethical. Virtue in physicians has recently received attention in medical ethics as well as what is involved in a physician being virtuous.[48,49] This emphasis marks a resurgence of Aristotelian ethics focusing on excellence in human activity, as in integrity and character.[50] Knowing the ethical thing to do does not help if a physician or anyone else decides to ignore this knowledge.

Moreover, the appropriateness of judging ethical knowledge and behavior by adherence to guidelines or to ethical principles, such as justice, has been criticized by developmental psychologist Carol Gilligan.[51] She states that the morality of caring is at least as important, which takes into account relationships and loyalties and not theoretical justifications based on principles, as emphasized by psychologists Jean Piaget and Lawrence Kohlberg. Gilligan believes that women score lower on many morality tests because women emphasize caring, but that such considerations are not part of the tests. She believes these considerations are not sex-dependent and need more emphasis. As can be seen, the philosophical justifications for professional ethics also can be quite complex.

Much like Diamond,[20] Dyer has written about the two functions of ethics: "Ethics in the upward perspective functions by means of the ego ideal, and ethics in the downward perspective functions by means of the superego. One is beckoned upward by the highest standards of moral perfection, but restricted from falling below certain minimal standards by means of superego strictures, if internalized, and by the possibility of external punishment if necessary" (p 121).[10] Both aspects of professional ethics are helpful and useful. Ethics can serve to guide the motivated practitioner who is striving to find a solution to a complex ethical problem. It also can specify the minimum behavior acceptable to the profession—violation of which could result in ethical sanctions by the profession, and thereby police the actions of practitioners.

Ethical guidelines therefore are the starting point, not the end point, of medical ethics. They often are of no help in complex moral dilemmas with competing ethical values. They are the bare minimum, not the upper limit of ethics in forensic psychiatry, and are far from the last word. Moreover, the presence or absence of a consensus does not, in and of itself, necessarily settle all ethical questions. In fact, it is important to be cautious that the majority are not tyrannical towards a legitimate minority by enforcing its will on the minority if the minority has good reasons for its behavior. Exceptions must be allowed if there are competing and overriding ethical values. An individual forensic psychiatrist also can have his own personal ethical standards which may be more stringent than those required by the profession.

CONCLUSION

A strong case remains for the retention of traditional medical ethical values in the functioning of the forensic psychiatrist. Training in the ethical model of Hundert and the model of conflicting appeals by Brody should be an important part of forensic psychiatric (and general psychiatric) training. Simple guidelines generally are no solution for the complex ethical problems sometimes encountered by the forensic psychiatrist; although they may be helpful in most ordinary cases. Traditional medical values should be one factor in the balancing process—given varying weight by individual practitioners in different circumstances.

If the survey respondents are at all reflective of forensic psychiatrists generally, the results suggest that members informally and on their own already are considering factors such as those discussed in this chapter. Such considerations probably operate when forensic psychiatrists have a moral sense of the ethical thing to do when problems arise. Training in forensic psychiatry should encourage continued consideration of traditional medical ethics as one factor in determining a proper ethical course of action and not dismiss such considerations as "therapeutic bias."[52] Much like values such as public safety, Hippocratic ethics should remain a consideration. However, because of a current lack of consensus, traditional Hippocratic values currently would be given differing emphasis and importance by various practitioners. Some issues such as evaluating death penalty cases without a personal examination achieve a general consensus and warrant inclusion in ethical guidelines.

Rather than being inconsistent, or inappropriately influenced by "therapeutic bias," forensic psychiatrists generally already seem to appreciate the value of retaining traditional core medical values as one consideration in their functioning as forensic psychiatrists. This appreciation should be fostered and encouraged.

REFERENCES

1. Pollack S: *Forensic Psychiatry in Criminal Law*. Los Angeles, University of Southern California, 1974.
2. Weinstock R: Ethical concerns expressed by forensic psychiatrists. *J Forensic Sci* 1986; 31:596–602.
3. Weinstock R: Controversial ethical issues in forensic psychiatry: A survey. *J Forensic Sci* 1988; 33:176–186.
4. Weinstock R: Perceptions of ethical problems by forensic psychiatrists. *Bull Am Acad Psychiatry Law* 1989:17:189–202.
5. Actions of the American Board of Forensic Psychiatry, May 1985.
6. American Academy of Psychiatry and the Law Ethical Guidelines, for the Practice of Forensic Psychiatry. Revised version in Appendix of this volume.
7. Diamond BL: The psychiatrist: Consultant vs activist in legal doctrine. Presented at the 19th Annual Meeting, American Academy of Psychiatry and the Law, San Francisco, October 20, 1988.
8. Stone AA: The ethics of forensic psychiatry: A view from the ivory tower, in Stone AA: *Law, Psychiatry, and Morality*. Washington, D.C., American Psychiatry Press, 1984. Reprinted in Rosner R, Weinstock R (eds): *Critical Issues in American Psychiatry and the Law*, Vol 7, Ethical Practice in Psychiatry and the Law. New York, Plenum, 1990, pp 3–18.
9. Veatch RF: Medical ethics—An introduction, in Veatch RF (ed): *Medical Ethics*. Boston, Jones and Bartlett, 1989.
10. Dyer AR: *Ethics and Psychiatry*. Washington, DC, American Psychiatric Press, 1988.
11. Carrick P: *Medical Ethics in Antiquity*. Dordrecht, Netherlands, D. Reidel, 1985.
12. Pellegrino ED, Thomasma DD: *A Philosophical Basis of Medical Practice*. New York, Oxford University Press, 1981.
13. MacKinnon B: On not harming: Two traditions. *J Med Philos* 1988; 13:313–328.
14. Lloyd GER (ed.): *Hippocratic Writings*. New York, Viking-Penguin, 1978.
15. Jansen AR: Do no harm, in Veatch RF (ed): *Cross-Cultural Perspectives in Medical Ethics*. Boston, Jones and Bartlett, 1989.
16. Shuman DW, Weiner MF: *The Psychotherapist-Patient Privilege: A Critical Examination*. Springfield, IL, Charles C. Thomas, 1987.
17. Foot P: Ethics and the death penalty: Participation by forensic psychiatrists in capital trials, in Rosner R, Weinstock R (eds): *Critical Issues in American Psychiatry and the Law*, Vol 7, Ethical Practice in Psychiatry and the Law. New York, Plenum, 1990, pp 207–218.
18. Macklin R: personal communication, April 19, 1988.
19. Appelbaum PS: personal communication, April 19, 1988.
20. Diamond BL: personal communication, April 25, 1988.
21. Callahan JC: *Ethical Issues in Professional Life*. New York, Oxford University Press, 1988.
22. American Medical Association: *Principles of Medical Ethics*. Chicago, American Medical Association, 1980.
23. Toulmin S: The tyranny of principles. *Hastings Cen Rep* 1981; 11:31–39.
24. Koppelman LM: Moral problems in psychiatry, in Veatch RF (ed): *Medical Ethics*. Boston, Jones and Bartlett, 1989.
25. Katz J: Why doctors don't disclose uncertainty. *Hastings Cen Rep* 1984; 14:25–44.
26. Hundert EM: Competing medical and legal ethical values: Balancing problems of the forensic psychiatrist, in Rosner R, Weinstock R (eds): *Critical Issues in American Psychiatry and the Law*, Vol 7, Ethical Practice in Psychiatry and the Law. New York, Plenum, 1990, pp 53–74.
27. Hundert EM: A model for ethical problem solving in medicine with practical applications. *Am J Psychiatry* 1987; 144:839–846.
28. Brody BA: *Life and Death Decision Making*. New York, Oxford University Press, 1988.
29. Beauchamp TL: *Philosophical Ethics: An Introduction to Moral Philosophy*. New York, McGraw Hill, 1982.

30. Kantor JE: Psychiatry in the service of the criminal punishment system: Some conceptual and ethical issues, in Rosner R, Harmon RB (eds): *Critical Issues in American Psychiatry and the Law*, Vol 6, Correctional Psychiatry. New York, Plenum, 1989.
31. Lifton RJ: *The Nazi Doctors*. New York, Basic Books, 1986.
32. Müller-Hill B: *Murderous Science*, Fraser G (trans). New York, Oxford University Press, 1988.
33. Stone AA: Morality for psychiatry, in Stone AA: *Law, Psychiatry, and Morality*. Washington, DC, American Psychiatric Press, 1984.
34. Mills MJ, Sullivan G, Eth S: Protecting third parties: A decade after *Tarasoff. Am J Psychiatry* 1987; 144:68–74.
35. Leong GB: The expansion of psychiatric participation in social control. *Hosp Community Psychiatry* 1989; 40:240–242.
36. Appelbaum PS: Psychiatric ethics in the courtroom. *Bull Am Acad Psychiatry Law* 1984; 12:225–231.
37. Stone AA: Psychiatry and the Supreme Court, in Stone AA: *Law, Psychiatry, and Morality*. Washington, DC, American Psychiatric Press, 1984.
38. Diamond BL: The honest advocate, in Rosner R, Weinstock R (eds): *Critical Issues in American Psychiatry and the Law*, Vol 7, Ethical Practice in Psychiatry and the Law. New York, Plenum, 1990, pp 75–84.
39. Barefoot v Estelle, 103 S Ct. 3383 (1983).
40. Zonana HV: Critique of a critique. *Bull Am Acad Psychiatry Law* 1984; 12:237–241.
41. American Psychiatric Association: *Principles of Medical Ethics with Annotations Especially Applicable to Psychiatry*. Washington, DC, American Psychiatric Association, 1989.
42. American Psychiatric Association: *Opinions of the Ethics Committee on the Principles of Medical Ethics with Annotations Especially Applicable to Psychiatry*. Washington, DC, American Psychiatric Association, 1985.
43. Miller RD: Ethical issues involved in the dual role of treater and evaluator, in Rosner R, Weinstock R (eds): *Critical Issues in American Psychiatry and the Law*, Vol 7, Ethical Practice in Psychiatry and the Law. New York, Plenum, 1990, pp 129–150.
44. Appelbaum PS: The problem of doing harm. Presented at the 19th Annual Meeting, American Academy of Psychiatry and the Law, San Francisco, October 20, 1988.
45. Weinstock R, Nair M: Antisocial personality—Diagnosis or moral judgement? *J Forensic Sci* 1984; 29:557–565.
46. American Medical Association: Current Opinions of the Council on Ethical and Judicial Affairs (History and sections 5.08, 5.09, 9.08). Chicago, American Medical Association, 1989.
47. Pellegrino ED, Thomasma DD: *For the Patient's Good: The Restoration of Beneficence in Health Care*. New York, Oxford University Press, 1988.
48. Putnam DA: Virtue and the practice of modern medicine. *J Med Philos* 1988; 13:433–444.
49. Veatch RF: The danger of virtue. *J Med Philos* 1988; 13:445–446.
50. Brody H: The physician/patient relationship, in Veatch RF (ed): *Medical Ethics*. Boston, Jones and Bartlett, 1989.
51. Gilligan C: *In a Different Voice*. Cambridge, Harvard University Press, 1982.
52. Pollack S: Psychiatry and the administration of justice in Curran WJ, McGarry AL, Petty CS (eds): *Modern Legal Medicine, Psychiatry, and Forensic Science*. Philadelphia, FA Davis Co. 1980, pp 655–674.

4

Competing Medical and Legal Ethical Values

Balancing Problems of the Forensic Psychiatrist

EDWARD M. HUNDERT

ETHICAL DILEMMAS AND THE BALANCING OF VALUES

> *There are no conclusions in this area which cannot lead to distress. There is no conclusion* worthy *of adopting that* will *not lead to distress. Any position in a complex area such as this which does not produce anxiety is probably too simple to be argued, too unworthy to be held.*
>
> —Willard Gaylin[1]

If there is one feature that is shared by all ethical dilemmas, it is the anxiety we feel even after making what we are sure is the best decision. Unlike other problems, anything worthy of the name "dilemma" almost requires the absence of a really good solution. When we explore the reasons why ethical dilemmas are worthy of their (unfortunate) name, we uncover an important truth about the nature of these difficult problems.

Consider the ethical dilemma of civil commitment in the case of a depressed father of three who is feeling suicidal. There may be important clinical reasons to try to avoid committing him even if his suicidality is severe. Hospitalization will likely be regressive, at least in the short run, and your therapeutic alliance with him will likely suffer, again at least in the short run, if

EDWARD M. HUNDERT • McLean Hospital, 115 Mill Street, Belmont, Massachusetts 02178.

he really is unwilling to sign himself into the hospital and you force him to against his will. Furthermore, the clinical crisis may represent an opportunity to involve his wife and children in his care, bringing them in as supports in a way that could last long after his depression has abated.

But there are also moral reasons to try to avoid committing him. After all, we hold individual liberty to be a preeminent value in this country. Depriving him of such liberty must be considered a negative even when we "have his best interests at heart."[2] Along with his autonomy, we also assign importance to his right to privacy: another value that will be limited if he is committed.

Just as there are moral as well as clinical reasons to avoid committing him, both types of reasons exist on the other side. Clinically, hospitalization may be needed to stabilize his treatment, initiate some new form of treatment, or keep him safe from self-destructive behavior. Morally, there appear to be values equally compelling as those of liberty and privacy. On this side are the values of welfare, both the welfare of the individual and the welfare of others. These others do not just include his family, but also people who cannot even be identified who might be injured if he were, for example, to try to kill himself by driving his car in a dangerous way.

This is not to say that we can separate clinical and moral reasons completely. There is, presumably, at least some moral value that weighs on the side of getting him the treatment he needs just by virtue of its being treatment he needs. Similarly, the clinical value of his participation in his choice of treatments is inextricable from the moral value we attach to his choices just by virtue of their being *his* choices.

If we focus on the moral values that weigh on each side of such a case, we can immediately see why the name "dilemma" is so appropriate. We hold a multiplicity of values dear in contemporary Western society. When the actualities of a case place some of these values on each side of the scale, then we quite literally cannot win. We can do the "right thing" by weighing and balancing the scale and acting according to which way it tips after all the facts and values have been considered. But we will still be left acting against one or another value we hold dear, and so will still be left with some anxiety after doing the "right thing." By virtue of its being a true dilemma, some value or another can never find expression in any action we take. Indeed, our lingering anxiety may well be the only expression we give to the values that were ultimately outweighed in this balancing process. (This is no small point, especially when responding to a critic who would claim, based only on the outcome, "I guess that person's liberty and privacy meant nothing to you." Both in response to such a critic, or to your own self-doubts about the issue, you can discover the value you did attach to his liberty and privacy precisely in your anxiety—in the efforts you took to consider every less restrictive alternative and in the lingering anxiety you still have even when you felt sure no other viable option existed.)

Elsewhere,[3] I have explored some of the features of this model for thinking about ethical dilemmas. It is a model which is relevant to forensic psychiatry in a number of ways. For example, courts appear to agree that this process of weighing and balancing "pros and cons" is precisely what is meant by competent, ethical practice.[4] If you are accused of negligence for failing to commit that patient, who then killed himself and an innocent pedestrian in an apparent suicide using his car, then your best defense (in addition to documentation that you discussed the question with a colleague who agreed that outpatient treatment was still indicated) would be documentation of having gone through this balancing process. Unethical practice could virtually be ruled out by a contemporaneous note which demonstrates how the value of his and others' welfare that might accrue from commitment appeared to be outweighed by the regressive impact of taking away his liberty, privacy, and control of his own care. Competent practice does not require that you predicted his actions correctly, only that you engaged in the process that is here called "ethical decision making" and did not fail to identify any relevant factors weighing on either side.

While this model of ethical problem solving thus has forensic applications for all psychiatrists, it reveals some important aspects of the balancing problems that are faced by forensic psychiatrists in particular. The rest of this chapter will be devoted to exploring these special balancing problems that challenge forensic psychiatrists in their daily practice.

MEDICAL AND LEGAL ETHICAL VALUES: THE GREAT PHILOSOPHICAL DIVIDE

> *The philosophers say life is a moral adventure; I would add that to choose a career in forensic psychiatry is to choose to increase the risks of that moral adventure.*
>
> —Alan Stone[5]

Value balancing is not a new idea, and we may look to philosophers throughout history to learn more about the nature of this process. Philosophers have long known that basic values such as liberty, privacy, and welfare are, to use the philosopher's jargon, "incommensurable." There is no quantitative way to measure these basic values one against the next. Although some philosophers in times past have tried to reduce all values to some common scale (e.g., how much they serve justice or how happy they make us), the modern view recognizes a multiplicity of independently held incommensurable values.[6] Indeed, it may well be, as discussed above, that the anxiety provided by a well-trained mind is ultimately the best (and perhaps only) scale we have to measure how much liberty or privacy is "worth" in terms of how much welfare or safety.

There is, however, a pattern to the particular values that appear to be given more or less weight in certain circumstances. For example, as a purely descriptive statement, it would be fair to say that the medical profession tends to give more weight to welfare and safety considerations (relative to, say, liberty and privacy considerations) as compared with the legal profession, which tends to do the opposite. This pattern is likely preserved through a variety of mechanisms. People may choose a profession because it embodies values they already hold (had I been more concerned with justice than welfare I might have ended up in law school instead of medical school). In the other direction, the professions inculcate the preeminence of certain values in their members (had I gone to law school, I might have been socialized to value liberty more in cases where it conflicts with welfare).

These generalizations about law and medicine are also not new. For centuries, physicians have held up their patient's welfare as the value that drives their profession. In cases where this meant depriving their patient of liberty, of privacy, or even of the truth, these other values were treated as secondary to the patient's health and safety. The law, in contrast, exists to preserve justice, even if a just world might mean a world where some welfare must suffer.

This divergent value structure between law and medicine can be observed most easily when doctors and lawyers talk with one another. When a psychiatrist is feeling the weight of the dilemma of civil commitment most, he or she need only argue the case with the patient's lawyer to see how the professions balance values differently. Typically, a psychiatrist truly ambivalent about that commitment case will begin to argue strenuously for the paternalistic solution as soon as the patient's lawyer takes up the values of liberty, privacy, and self-determination. This is quite similar to the group process of projective identification, where conflicts existing within each party get played out as a conflict between these parties. Indeed, this process often gets enacted in institutional ethics committees on which both lawyers and physicians sit.[3]

The point here is not merely that the two professions take up different values in such cases, but that each always takes up a characteristic set of values. It is this characteristic pattern of value balancing that can in fact be said to give meaning to the terms "medical ethics" and "legal ethics." When someone suggests that "president's ethics" or "congressman's ethics" means anything different from the ethics that apply to all of us, we quickly point out that ethics by definition refers to universalizable rules.[7] Yet, medical and legal ethics mean more than just rules that would apply to any person performing a surgical operation or defending a client in court. They refer to these characteristic patterns of value-balancing that appear in so many ways as medicine strives to preserve welfare and the law strives to uphold justice.

In order to understand the difficulties faced by forensic psychiatrists as they enter the borderland between these value systems, it is important to understand just *how* divergent the two really are. Here the insights of a long philosophical history are invaluable.

Throughout the ages, philosophers have divided ethical theories into two general types: deontological theories and teleological theories. "Deontological" comes from a Greek root meaning "duty"—specifically, the duty to lead a virtuous life. Deontological theories maintain that there are certain virtues (such as honesty, courage, compassion) and certain vices (such as lying, cowardice, selfishness), and an ethical person is one who lives a life embracing the virtues and avoiding the vices. The precise picture of the "virtuous life" depends upon the deontological theory in question. "Teleological," in contrast, comes from a

Greek root meaning "goal" or "end." Teleological theories maintain that there is some goal (such as the greatest happiness for all), and an ethical person is one who acts so as to get closer to this goal. The precise goal depends upon the teleological theory in question, but certainly the most famous is utilitarianism, with its pursuit of the end of maximum welfare for all.

It should immediately become obvious that law and medicine do not merely take up different value systems. As categorized by philosophers for centuries, law and medicine take up value systems on opposite sides of the great philosophical divide, law embodying a deontological ethics based on values such as liberty and justice, and medicine embodying a teleological ethics based on the value of achieving the goal of welfare.

This makes our problem even greater, because different theories conflicting within one "camp" or the other at least have a common language for debate. Although basic incommensurable values are still in conflict, if all the values on both sides of a given dilemma are just deontological (or just teleological) in nature, then the problem is simpler. If privacy, liberty, or honesty must be traded off one against another, we can appeal to our picture of the "virtuous (deontological) life" to decide the matter. Similarly, if welfare, safety, or relief from suffering represent all the relevant values in a given dilemma, we can appeal to our "ultimate (teleological) end" to decide the matter. These types of cases are still truly "dilemmas" in the sense that we will be forced to act against some value we hold dear. But they are considerably more straightforward than those cases that mix deontological and teleological values. Indeed, virtually all of the major ethical issues that appear in the popular press, in professional journals, and in appellate court decisions are issues that force a trade-off between values from each side of this great philosophical divide.

Within this philosophical context, we can better understand the difficulties faced by forensic psychiatrists as they participate simultaneously in processes designed for such divergent moral purposes.

STRANGE BEDFELLOWS: THE PROCESS OF MEDICINE AND THE PROCESS OF LAW

> *...what happens to psychiatrists in the courtroom is actually not a clash of opinion but a clash of lawyers, with psychiatrists in the role of baseball bats. The question is not why psychiatrists disagree, but why they are forced to be baseball bats, and why they accept the role of baseball bats.*
>
> —Gregory Zilboorg[8]

Once we understand how medicine and law are grounded in completely different moral traditions, it becomes easier to see how the two evolved completely different processes to achieve their divergent ends. It is hard to imagine two more contrasting pictures than the traditional views of the physician serving his or her patient at the bedside and the lawyer serving his or her client in the courtroom. For each, there exist completely different sets of rules of proper conduct, tests for relevance of information, views of the individual, concepts of free will, procedures for conducting inquiry, and even concepts of what is real.

This last point cannot be overemphasized. Gutheil and Mills[9] have shown how clinical and judicial investigations not only use different procedures, but also seek different data. The clinical system generally draws upon the scientific method to test hypotheses about truths taken to reside in that which is under investigation. A single empirical observation may necessitate a complete change of theory. Such radical changes as may be generated by these data-driven scientific investigations are antithetical to our theory-driven system of law. The law is by nature conservative; it evolves only through very gradual additions to past law, thus preserving the core of values built into the wisdom handed down through the generations. (Oliver Wendell Holmes[10] thus called our system of law "the government of the living by the dead.")

How these divergent systems result in different concepts of what is real can be seen by comparing the physician or the judge with what might be called the three types of umpires, who offer us a paradigm for differing conceptions of the real. There are, it is said, three types of umpires: subjective, objective, and existential. The subjective umpire says, "There are balls and strikes, and I call 'em the way I see 'em." The objective umpire says, "There are balls and strikes, and I call 'em the way they are." The existential umpire, however, says, "There are no balls and strikes until I call 'em!"

Physicians in general, and psychiatrists in particular, usually view reality somewhere between the views of the subjective and objective umpires. We seek, for example, an objective diagnosis (one that "exists in the patient"), but, especially in treatments such as psychotherapy, we must continually struggle to separate our subjective input from the data we observe. Still, it is always a reality to be sought and found in the clinical material before us.

Judges, in contrast, are existential umpires. By finding the defendant "guilty," the defendant *becomes* guilty, at least in the eyes of the law. As Judge David Bazelon[11] wrote, labeling a person "schizophrenic" does not make him so. In contrast, when a judge or jury labels him "not guilty by reason of insanity" it quite literally does make him so—a feature of legal language J.L. Austin[12] called its "performative" force. Physicians are more likely to say, "All we know for *sure* from the judge pronouncing him guilty is that he is *convicted*. Perhaps we will never know if he was really *guilty*." The law, in contrast, sees guilt as having been determined by the process that led to the judge's performative (existential) pronouncement.

Medical and legal realities also differ dramatically in their approach to probability and uncertainty. It is almost ironic that scientific experiments rely on data proven to very high levels of certainty ("beyond any reasonable doubt" to the $p<0.01$ level) to establish often probabilistic findings. Civil courts, in contrast, use a preponderance of the evidence (just more likely than not at the 51% level) to establish yes-or-no judgments about guilt or innocence. This contrast was noted by Judge Thurman Arnold,[13] who stated in a 1945 decision: "To the psychiatrist mental cases are a series of imperceptible gradations from the mild psychopath to the extreme psychotic, whereas criminal law allows no gradations."

And the procedures mentioned above are indeed suited appropriately to these differing views of reality, controlled experiments being best for "maybe's" and "in-between's" while yes-no judgments are perhaps best produced by that curiosity called the adversarial system.

It is often said that physicians enter a foreign land when they leave their art and science to enter a place where realities are spoken into existence and the "truth" is thought to be discoverable through a procedure that rigidly eliminates a great deal of relevant evidence and that includes techniques such as catching the other side by surprise and obscuring the jury's judgment by appeals to its emotions.[14]

It comes as no surprise that the main reason psychiatrists do not like to go to court is their discomfort with the adversarial system.[15] When they first encounter this system, most physicians are astounded by the techniques used by opposing lawyers, and even more astounded by seeing these two combatants leave the courtroom together for a friendly cup of coffee when the battle has ended. As in the case of their divergent professional value systems, this difference between physicians and lawyers may result both from a self-selection of personality traits in choosing a career and from the socialization of professional education. As Zilboorg[8] noted, "the lawyer is taught emotionally, sociologically, and professionally to be estranged from the people who will become his major concern as a judge or prosecutor or defense counsel.... The physician is taught to become emotionally, sociologically, and professionally one with the people and the medical conditions which are to become his chief concern."

Guttmacher[16] also contrasts these techniques of professionalization, where "medical students are trained at the bedside through close physical contact with the patient and a probing of the most intimate aspects of his personal life." In contrast, he goes on to say: "For the past half century and more, law students have relied chiefly upon the case method for their training, the study of judicial opinions handed down by State and Federal Courts of Appeal. This consists of what Dr. Andrew Watson describes as 'logical and philosophical discussions,' at least thrice removed from the events described.'"

It is difficult to capture the many and varied ways in which these differences between the process of medicine and the process of law reveal themselves. One of the best is Gutheil and Magraw's[17] observation that the legal setting—unlike the clinical setting—is a zero-sum game. In the adversarial setting of the courtroom, there is one winner and one loser, and the sum of the winnings to the winner exactly equals the sum of the losses to the loser. In contrast, the benefits of the collaboration of patient and doctor are additive, even synergistic. The doctor receives payment and the satisfaction of doing his or her job. The patient receives the benefit of the doctor's skill and, when treatment is successful, the continuing satisfactions that pertain to the results of this treatment.

Physicians in court are thus not only unaccustomed to the process of adversarial cross-examination, but find themselves confronted by attorneys who are inclined to view the doctor–patient relationship as a zero-sum game. That is, any benefit to one party tends to be seen as occurring at the expense of the other—a perspective foreign to most physicians.

These contrasts in process and perspective are captured by the differences in emphasis on the beneficial effects versus the adverse effects of medical treatments. Harms, not benefits, are traditionally litigated; courts thus tend to perceive treatments more as "side effect producers" than as beneficial. Physicians, in contrast, emphasize the benefits of treatment, with side effects viewed only as an accompanying necessary evil.

There are, of course, many other important differences between the process of medicine and the process of law. With the contrasting perspectives already discussed as background, let us consider some of these other differences in the context of specific value-balancing problems faced by those psychiatrists who use their medical training to serve the process of law.

BALANCING PROBLEMS OF THE FORENSIC PSYCHIATRIST

> *Here we confront what I believe is still a lingering confusion in the enterprise of forensic psychiatry. The problem is that helping the patient—which is the ethical thesis of the practitioner—becomes the ethical temptation in the legal context. What principle does the forensic psychiatrist have to restrain himself against this temptation? What is his equivalent to the therapist's antithesis of do no harm, particularly when he is cajoled by the lawyers, dazzled by the media spotlight, and paid more than Blue Cross/Blue Shield?*
>
> —Alan Stone[5]

When in 1958 the American Medical Association and the American Bar Association adopted the first "National Interprofessional Code for Physicians and Attorneys,"[18] this document made it clear that physicians must serve the legal process when working in the legal setting. The host of value-balancing problems that arise when physicians are asked to serve the ends of justice rather than health should be apparent from the preceding discussion. Nowhere are these problems more poignant than in the strict requirement, held by most practitioners, that a forensic psychiatrist never become a patient advocate.[19] In serving the ends of justice, they claim that objectivity—not advocacy—is required.

Steeped in the teleological ethic of promoting health and relieving suffering, patient advocacy is, in a sense, the physician's calling. Yet, William Curran[20] warns that the "greatest danger to truth for a forensic scientist is in becoming an advocate. The temptations to advocacy are severe. The strongest of all is the court system itself. Truth is not the objective of most contested cases. The objective is the peaceful settlement of disputes..."

It seems unrealistic to expect psychiatrists to give up their therapeutic philosophy completely when the patient they are examining happens to be a defendant in a civil or criminal matter. Seymour Pollack[21] called this the *therapeutic bias* and considered it to be "the major problem area experienced in the forensic psychiatrist's role/functions." Indeed, although the current professional attitude of forensic psychiatry is to provide testimony for both sides (in part to avoid being pilloried by the prosecution as being defense-biased), it comes as no surprise that many forensic psychiatrists feel more comfortable when acting on behalf of criminal defendants than on behalf of the prosecution.[5,15,21] At the extreme antithesis of the physician's credo to do no harm would be forensic participation in capital cases where a psychiatrist's evidence could lead to the defendant's execution. Most psychiatrists have taken a stand against participation in such cases. Yet, a "therapeutic bias" that makes defense testimony more comfortable and that rules out prosecution testimony in capital cases leaves forensic psychiatrists with a delicate balancing problem in choosing whether to testify in cases where their participation might lead to lengthy prison sentences or other severe punishments. (This is why some practitioners, such as Bernard Diamond, have recommended abandoning the objective forensic role. Dr. Diamond forthrightly tells courts that he only testifies for the criminal defense, because he wishes never to harm anyone.)

The irony of all the stress placed upon maintaining objectivity and avoiding the advocacy role is found in the method by which forensic experts are chosen. Lawyers who retain forensic experts may have some interest in the "objective truth"; but their purpose is essentially to seek support for their client's cause. Typically, they check with many experts and then use only those whose conclusions are favorable to their client's cause. The "objective, independent experts" who appear in court are thus the screened-out results of the *lawyer's* advocacy. This practice is not condemned by the standards of legal ethics, and makes for quite a balancing act on the part of a forensic psychiatrist who would like to make a living. In Curran's[20] words, "The lawyers expect the expert to support the cause of the client. If a forensic science consultant wishes to continue in the field and to be paid to appear in court, it is said that he must 'play the game' according to the court's rules and in compliance with the advocacy system."

As if there were not already enough professional therapeutic bias and systemic bias tending to make forensic psychiatrists less objective experts and more patient advocates, there is also the experience of cross-examination. When forensic psychiatrists are given the distinct feeling from a hostile cross-examiner that they are the ones on trial, it becomes natural to get defensive and advocate even more vigorously than ever.

When forensic psychiatrists overcome this central advocacy problem—through additional subspecialty training, careful choice of cases, and familiarity and comfort with their own weaknesses and limitations—they are still left with a host of other balancing problems. These problems spring from all the contrasts between medicine and the law described above. There are so many ways in which the law's deontological emphasis on process can confound medicine's teleological tendency to want to shortcut these procedures that are seen merely as impediments to a "good outcome."

For example, in strictly limiting the domain of information that may be brought to bear on a case, the legal process may leave a forensic psychiatrist in the position of holding a strong opinion while not allowing an expression of all the reasons for that opinion. In the law, a person's previous "record" will not be allowed into evidence, yet a patient's previous hospitalizations are often the most relevant information a psychiatrist has. Similarly, complaints from a patient's parents that the patient has been calling and threatening to kill them represents hearsay evidence in court. If the parents are unavailable for testimony, the psychiatrist who received those complaints must convey the patient's "dangerousness" (a legal, not a medical, term) without relying on such apparently relevant data.[22] Indeed, this particular problem is so clear that some states now make an exception and allow experts to rely upon hearsay if it is the sort of information usually included in clinical decision making.

This issue raises one of the biggest problems faced by forensic psychiatrists: how to convey their expert opinions in the accurate and neat verbalizations upon which law depends. Although this may at first sound like more of a technical, practical problem than a value-balancing problem, it reflects the latter in many profound ways. Psychiatry, after all, takes a much more complex view of the human organism than does the law.[23] If accurate and neat verbalizations cannot adequately convey these complexities, the law may conclude that psychiatry is meaningless or that the expert has defective knowledge.[16] What counts as a "fact" in a clinical analysis often does not fit neatly into the strict requirements of what is permitted to count as a fact in a legal opinion, especially when that opinion is subject to cross-examination. At the extreme, the diagnostic value of countertransference reactions would hardly stand up in court; yet, in the clinical setting we routinely rely upon our own feelings—fuzzy as they are to articulate—in the assessment of our patient's problems. (It is interesting to wonder whether the advent of biological psychiatry and the DSM approach to diagnosis will serve the courts "better"—but at the expense of those rich complexities that have distinguished psychiatry from other approaches to human behavior and experience.)

Among the human complexities emphasized in psychiatry and virtually ignored in the law is the unconscious. The law necessarily takes a very simple view of free will. If the patient says, "I want out of the hospital," there is little legal room to wonder whether this expresses only one side of a deeper ambivalence. Psychiatrists by training assume that people have at least some mixed feelings about most things, and especially about the things that matter most in life. It may be difficult—or perhaps impossible—to convey these complexities in an inflexible arena designed to wring certainty (guilty or not guilty) from the course of human events. Gutheil and Magraw[17] expand this point to emphasize an even bigger problem with the advocacy issue mentioned above. The therapeutic alliance advocates, in a sense, only for that part of the patient that wants to get better. In "working with the part of the patient that wants to live," the psychiatrist is in some sense *not* an advocate for the part of the patient that wants to commit suicide. How such a complex view of advocacy can find expression in an adversarial framework is anybody's guess.

The law must ignore these complexities and assume a complete free will because the law is there to protect the rights of individuals to autonomy and self-determination. Of course, these rights are legal, not medical, constructs. Where physicians have become involved in the lives of their patients, they have traditionally grounded this involvement in an assumption that they are better trained and more qualified to make decisions affecting their patients' health than the patients who ought to trust them to do what is best. The current informed-consent debate has questioned this assumption, raising the issue of whether all physicians should act more like forensic experts, serving the truth rather than the patient, informing the patient only of objective facts on which the patient should base free choices among the various therapeutic options.

These differing views of the justification for involvement in other individuals' lives creates one of the major balancing problems of the forensic psychiatrist. As increasing numbers of cases deal with the issue of "predicting dangerousness" (the legal view of assessing how violent a patient is), the diverging value systems of psychiatry and law become ever more apparent. As Ciccone and Clements[24] have observed, there is a "considerable difference between prediction of dangerousness for legal purposes (based on notions of accountability and punishment and hence ethically requiring broad safeguards) and prediction of dangerousness for psychiatric purposes (based on therapeutic treatment and patient welfare and ethically requiring different safeguards)." The rationale of benefit to the patient (the traditional medical *parens patriae* principle) requires completely different safeguards than the rationale of social control (the traditional legal application of police powers). A psychiatrist examining a patient for the reason of offering an opinion about that patient's "dangerousness" must apply medical expertise developed for one purpose and use that expertise for another. Such are the balancing problems of the forensic psychiatrist.

At their extreme, these balancing problems constitute examples of what is known as "double agency."[25,26] As in the realm of espionage, a double agent is one who appears to serve two systems that not only have different values, but have values that are in overt conflict one with the other. Commitment cases may sometimes raise a problem of double agency. Is the psychiatrist a patient advocate concerned with the patient's welfare, or is the psychiatrist an agent of social control concerned with the protection of society from dangerous, mentally ill individuals?

In the field of forensic psychiatry, the classic double-agent problem can be seen in the role of prison psychiatrists. Prison psychiatrists are often involved in the voluntary treatment of prisoners who wish to receive such treatments. The traditional medical values would appear to apply in such a therapeutic relationship. But what happens when, in his therapy, a prisoner mentions to his psychiatrist that one of his fellow inmates is planning to escape that evening? This forensic psychiatrist works for the patient, but also for the prison. (In fact, the prison, not the patient, pays the salary.) Here the ethical value-balancing becomes so difficult that the image of a double agent really seems appropriate. Like the army psychiatrist who in wartime is asked by patients to be relieved from duty and is told by the army to get them back to the front as soon as possible, so the forensic psychiatrist in a prison setting must balance two value systems which not only are different, but sometimes are in direct conflict with one another.

Ciccone and Clements[24] also refer to other problems faced not just by prison psychiatrists, but by all forensic psychiatrists. For example, in a specialty generally requiring some amount of empathy and concern for the welfare of the patient, there exist special countertransference problems in dealing with the forensic population, which routinely includes murderers, child molesters, rapists, con artists, arsonists, etc.[27] But such problems are, in effect, clinical rather than ethical balancing problems, and are not the subject of this chapter. Let me therefore conclude this gloomy view of the dilemmas that plague forensic psychiatry by hinting at a little good news as well.

THE COMMON GROUND AND ITS LIMITS: SOME PRACTICAL APPROACHES TO SOME UNSOLVABLE PROBLEMS

> *...there is growing emphasis on the mentalistic aspects of law and an increasing recognition of the humanistic element of justice. I believe that the use of forensic psychiatry for this purpose fulfills deep psychological needs for such justice in our democratic, freedom-loving, individualistically oriented society... Thus I perceive forensic psychiatry as a humanistic tool which the trier uses to reconcile the universal rules of law with justice in the individual case.*
>
> —Seymour Pollack[21]

Given the moral perils of value-balancing inherent in the practice of forensic psychiatry, it comes as no surprise that many thinkers have advocated giving up the enterprise entirely.[5,8,28,29] This position is perhaps best captured by the words of Karl Menninger,[28] who wrote, "We psychiatrists don't belong in the courtroom. We cannot function effectively there. It is not our proper sphere of action. We do not understand the language addressed to us nor convey what we intend to and think we do, using the language we employ. Our performance in the courtroom ritual is a continuation of what is really a fraudulent, discriminatory, undemocratic procedure—that of trying to manipulate psychiatric categories and legal sanctions for the benefit of selected individuals."

In this final section of this chapter, I would like to offer some practical approaches to minimizing the moral peril of forensic psychiatry without actually giving it up entirely. I should note from the start that, as true ethical dilemmas, these balancing problems do not have complete solutions: if they did, they would not be dilemmas as we have defined them. But still, we can try to make a difficult situation better by seeking a framework that strives to minimize those balancing problems that are unavoidable once one enters into the practice of this challenging field.

Before outlining such an attempt at partial reconciliation, it is worth wondering whether this effort is well conceived. Throughout history, ethical codes of conduct have prohibited physicians from practicing outside their area of expertise. Indeed, even the Hippocratic oath contains more promises *not* to do certain things than it does affirmative expressions. As Curran[20] points out, Hippocratic physicians swore never to cut their patients because they were not trained in surgery. This ethical code makes it clear that the physician is not the unthinking instrument of the client. Even if offered a larger-than-usual fee, a Hippocratic physician was never to lower his standards and agree to a request for practices outside his expertise.

We may therefore ask why psychiatrists should even contemplate taking on the additional training required for an expertise in forensic practice. (I shall return to this nontrivial requirement for additional training.) If these special skills are beyond their expertise, why not just add forensic work to the list of forbidden practices?

The short answer to this question is that the law needs psychiatry. The law needs psychiatry for several reasons, not the least of which was expressed in 1810 by Franz Gall,[30] who said that "the measure of culpability and the measure of punishment cannot be determined by a study of the illegal act, but only by a study of the individual committing it." This statement relates both to civil and criminal law, and need not even be limited to the realm of "illegal acts." This chapter has focused on such areas because they create the biggest ethical value-balancing problems. Certain civil issues, such as workmans' compensation, social security and insurance benefits, and certain civil competency questions, sometimes call for psychiatric expertise, and these often pose less problematic roles for forensic psychiatrists. Certainly family law matters of divorce and child custody, while "legal" questions, are often in need of psychiatric expertise, and this seems particularly appropriate.

Yet, even in those civil and especially criminal cases that create the biggest value-balancing problems for forensic psychiatrists, we cannot pretend that the social-control purpose of law (which seems to conflict with the therapeutic role of the physician) is a purpose we physicians are *against*. Certainly criminal social control must be considered not only a necessary legal end, but also a socially desirable one—and most forensic psychiatrists experience little ethical conflict in fact-finding for such purposes.

Perhaps the best practical advice I have seen for minimizing value conflicts in the practice of forensic psychiatry is that of Pollack,[21] who suggested that individual practitioners should avoid participating in those settings and for those ends that make them so uncomfortable as to lose any chance of impartiality in forensic fact-finding. By this advice, the simple exclusion mentioned above of avoiding involvement in cases where testimony might lead to the death penalty is just a bare minimum. It would be a perfectly ethical position for a particular forensic psychiatrist to refuse to be involved in any criminal matters at all. Indeed, it is probably *ethical* to limit criminal case participation to the defense side, so long as this is done with the honesty and openness embodied in Diamond's approach, described above. But this is generally not a practical solution, since it leads to the loss of any ability to at least appear impartial (a characteristic at least as important to the practice of forensic psychiatry as more authentic credentials).

Pollack's advice does not mean that involvement in cases that entail difficult value-balancing problems is therefore to be restricted to unscrupulous practitioners whose "superego lacunae" prevent them from experiencing conflict when they ought to be experiencing conflict. On the contrary, with a presumption of competence and integrity, it is advice that reminds us of the importance of objectivity for ethical forensic work. The advice is not to avoid any uncomfortable situations, but to avoid situations where the level of discomfort will lead to a loss of impartiality. This raises the question of what it means for a forensic psychiatrist to be impartial, and so raises the central question of this chapter.

When the American Board of Forensic Psychiatry set out to create a definition of the field,[31] they determined that forensic psychiatry is the application of psychiatry to legal, rather than medical, purposes. But they also determined that the ethical standards that would apply to this discipline should be the ethical standards of the medical, not the legal, profession. This may seem paradoxical: forensic psychiatrists are to be governed by a teleological ethical system built on the value of welfare, but are to apply their skills to serve the deontological values of the legal system. How can we minimize this inherent value-balancing problem?

Perhaps the most important solution is to understand that ethical forensic psychiatrists should conceive of their role as serving *neither* the individual *nor* the principle of justice. Forensic psychiatrists, like all forensic scientists, assist the courts by serving the *truth*. As was noted above,[20] the truth is not necessarily the goal of the courts; justice is. Yet in helping the courts do their job, forensic psychiatrists must not let their own views of justice influence their assessment of the facts any more than they should let patient advocacy influence this assessment. When a particular view of how justice should be served begins to color a forensic psychiatrist's perceptions of a case, that forensic psychiatrist becomes as biased as when he or she tries to do what is perceived as "best for the patient."

It is no accident that when the American Academy of Forensic Sciences established their Code of Ethics in 1977,[32] the first (and only binding) part required only one thing: truthfulness. Members were required not to misrepresent either themselves (their training, experience, and area of expertise) or any data upon which they based their opinions and conclusions. The second part of this code also contained three guiding principles: to maintain competency through continuing education, to avoid misleading claims in all oral or written work, and to uphold impartiality. The guiding principles were eliminated in the current version.

This view of the role of a forensic scientist makes sense in light of the American Board of Forensic Psychiatry's complex notion that psychiatric expertise can serve the legal system but still fall under medicine's ethical code. On this view, forensic psychiatrists are to serve neither the teleological values of welfare and safety, nor the deontological values of justice and liberty. Simply put, forensic psychiatrists are to dispense *medical knowledge* so that the legal system can dispense justice.

Since this dispensing of justice by the legal system in a given case may require determinations about questions such as *mens rea* (a mentalistic element built into the legal definition of a crime), psychiatrists can assist the courts by offering their expertise about human behavior and motivation—not about justice and liberty. Indeed, Anglo-American law appears to be getting increasingly concerned with the psychological features of human conduct. For example, I mentioned above that competent, ethical psychiatric practice is taken to involve a weighing and balancing of "pro's and con's." This is itself a mentalistic idea. If that malpractice case were brought against you on the ground of negligence, the case presumably would hinge on the *subjective* question of a mental process built into our definition of ethical problem solving!

This increasing concern with the psychological features of human conduct is only one of two aspects of Anglo-American law that Pollack[21] cites as evidence for the law's growing humanism—a value not irrelevant to the purpose of medicine. The other aspect is the law's increasing interest in the individual (again, an interest familiar to the physician). As the law has become more humanistic, it has become less just a body of rules and more a system for individualization in the application of justice. Such individualization began with the insanity defense, which first brought psychiatrists into the courtroom,[33] but has now been extended to include all aspects of civil and criminal proceedings. For a forensic expert wedded to the medical value system, this is good news, because this is where forensic psychiatry can take a leading role.

I say "take a leading role" because psychiatrists can actually reduce the ethical tensions described above when they become agents for positive change. If some of the conflicts arose from the impersonality of a legal system that concentrates on principles and forgets the individual, then forensic psychiatrists can begin to resolve these conflicts by working to change the system. This is true even in the most extreme cases of double agency. As Roth[34] points out, the only solution to the conflict of the prison psychiatrist is for such an individual to begin to function more broadly as a consultant to, and a shaper of, that institutional milieu that generates the conflicts. Of course, no institutional improvement will ever change a prison into a genuine treatment-type institution, nor should it. Still, the prison psychiatrist who aims to make the prison environment more humane and constructive goes a long way toward relieving the problem of double agency. (It is ironic that psychiatrists should become agents of social change just as the courts are becoming a forum for medical progress, as John Malcolm[35] has observed.)

Again, no amount of institutional change will erase all of the ethical tensions inherent in prison psychiatry. But even so, a number of practical approaches may reduce these tensions further. For example, full disclosure to an inmate of limits to confidentiality at the beginning of treatment must be a crucial part of work in this setting. Such clarification of limits to confidentiality is indeed part of any ethical forensic work, since the title "doctor" might mislead a client to believe the usual medical values of confidentiality and advocacy apply. It may be argued that a client will still be misled because of prior assumptions about the proper role of a physician in any setting; but here the expertise of a forensic psychiatrist is doubly important, using psychiatric expertise to assess whether the person has assimilated the disclaimer that has been made.

Although it may sound like a technical or procedural injunction to begin all sessions with a careful disclaimer about the lack of confidentiality, I would maintain that many of the standard techniques and procedures of forensic psychiatry function specifically to reduce the ethical tensions discussed here. Since mixed loyalties may confuse a client, forensic psychiatrists are told to begin all sessions with a clarification of their loyalties and relationships to all relevant parties (again using their psychiatric expertise to stay sensitive to the individual's perception of the evaluator role and particularly to how this differs from a treatment role). Melton *et al.*[26] note that at the extreme, this may require a Miranda-like statement including the specific questions to be addressed, the identities of all parties getting the report, a discussion of the implications of possible findings for the individual, and so forth.

While an explicit statement of the "absence" of the usual medical rules of confidentiality is crucial, confidentiality should not in fact be entirely absent. For example, forensic psychiatrists are taught to respect the privacy of the individual by not addressing issues other than those raised in the referral order, and by not seeking clinical information irrelevant to the referral question. Deep psychological probing is inappropriate when asked to assess competency to stand trial, for instance. This is its own form of confidentiality. Indeed, Melton *et al.*[26] also note that in evaluations involving particularly sensitive subjects (which in the therapeutic setting are assumed to be revealed only because confidentiality exists), forensic psychiatrists need to be especially explicit about their role and write a report qualified by assumed limitations on the amount of information available—or, in some cases, submit no report at all. And confidentiality must still be upheld in not giving reports to parties who should not receive them, and especially in not releasing any information from an evaluation to the media before a trial.

Many of the other rules that govern the practice of forensic psychiatry may also be understood as attempts to reduce the tensions created by the divergence of the medical and legal systems. I have noted the differing views of free will, where the law tends to ignore psychologically deterministic factors so central to psychiatry. We can understand as an attempt to minimize this tension the injunction sometimes made to forensic psychiatrists never to testify to the ultimate legal question, but only to the facts that bear on this question. If the ultimate legal question is, "Was the act voluntary?" then this is for a judge or jury to decide. Forensic expert opinion should be limited to facts that can assist the trier with what is now a legal, not a scientific, question.

Similarly, the divergence noted concerning differing medical and legal views of certainty and probability may be minimized in the requirement that forensic psychiatrists are ethically bound to describe the uncertainty in their conclusions,[26] even if such honesty may unduly diminish the weight courts accord their testimony. Such a requirement entails comfort and familiarity with one's own limitations as well as the limitations of the field. Just as one must be able to anticipate where a level of discomfort might lead to a loss of objectivity by knowing oneself well, it is also important not to overreify psychiatric expertise. Melton *et al.*[26] report a case, for example, in which the court requested a child evaluation in a divorce case to assess the impact of spending one week versus two weeks each year with the mother. Courts may desire this level of certainty from psychiatry, but the ethical forensic psychiatrist respectfully declines such a request, explaining to the court the current state of the art.

Even the most basic practical advice, offered by Gutheil and Appelbaum,[22] that forensic psychiatrists be thorough, well-prepared, and testify to the facts as they believe them, is advice that cannot be separated from the ethics of the profession. There are other ways of looking at "testifying to the facts as you believe them" (i.e., regardless of which side is paying your fee). One is that this is just a mandate to avoid being the proverbial hired gun. Another is that being an ethical forensic psychiatrist takes a great deal of integrity—perhaps more than other physicians who are not exposed to such complex moral perils.

But another way of looking at it is that it is simply another way of saying that forensic psychiatrists have to be objective. The famous retort to a hostile inquiry as to whether "you're getting paid for your testimony, aren't you doctor?" is: "No, I get paid for my time and expertise—my testimony isn't for sale." Testifying to the facts as you believe them is another way of saying that you should *mean it* when you give this famous retort. Only in this way does it even begin to make sense to say that forensic psychiatry serves the truth, rather than welfare or justice. It is no accident that from that first National Interprofessional Code in 1958,[18] codes of ethics have all prohibited the amount of a witness's fee from being contingent on the outcome of the case or on the amount of money damages received by the party calling the witness. Again, such rules of conduct serve to protect the delicate ethical standards on which the profession must stand.

The final point I would like to make about practical approaches for minimizing the tensions inherent in the ethical value-balancing of forensic psychiatric practice revolves around the question of training. I have mentioned that additional training is required if forensic expertise is to be considered a competency of a psychiatrist. Like Hippocratic physicians contemplating surgical procedures, psychiatrists with no forensic training are not prepared to embark on this subspecialized field. This is not only because such psychiatrists do not know what elements must be addressed in various court reports and other such technical aspects of the field. It is also because of the way forensic training itself can service as a practical approach to reducing many of the ethical tensions that have been addressed here.

If some of these tensions result from medicine and law "speaking different languages," then a forensic psychiatrist can minimize such tensions through training in both languages. This does not mean becoming a lawyer. It just means learning to understand and to appreciate the many distinctions that are so important to law and so foreign to most physicians.[22]

This requirement for additional training is about attitudes as much as it is about knowledge. If the natural tendency of physicians to become advocates gives rise to the deepest ethical value-balancing problems of all, then forensic training can minimize these conflicts by inculcating the attitudes more appropriate to an objective evaluator, rather than a supportive advocate. Such training can help enable forensic psychiatrists to abandon the usual therapeutic pragmatism that would see no point in excluding relevant evidence that the legal system deems inadmissible as hearsay. A well-trained forensic psychiatrist has learned not only to understand what hearsay means, but has learned to feel more comfortable assisting a system that demands the exclusion of such evidence.

It is not my purpose to pretend that even all the additional training in the world could eliminate the ethical value-balancing problems of the forensic psychiatrist. These are, as stated, true dilemmas, and my comments here are meant only to suggest ways to minimize the magnitude of these unavoidable conflicts. It is one thing to find a way to understand forensic psychiatry as helping to increase the humanity of the law in individual cases, and so feel that the ends of medicine and law are less divergent than they were before. But it is quite another thing to believe that in a given case, the knowledge of a forensic expert, in helping the courts serve the deontological end of justice, will never lead to a decrease in the teleological end of welfare, because this is simply not true. Ultimately, basic values will always collide in the practice of forensic psychiatry.

For this reason, there is one part of the curriculum of forensic specialty training that must be added to the acquisition of special knowledge and attitudes already mentioned. As Gorman[19] has stated, forensic psychiatrists not only need extra training, but extra training that includes explicit courses in professional ethics designed to address these ultimately unsolvable problems. If there is one practical approach that is the most compelling of all, it is explicit training in the ethical problem-solving process that has been discussed here and that must be part of the daily practice of forensic psychiatry.

What could be a more appropriate way to conclude this chapter?

Acknowledgments

For their helpful comments on successive drafts of this chapter, I would like to thank Drs. Michael Annunziata, Leon Eisenberg, Thomas Gutheil, Alan Stone, Larry Strasburger, and Robert Weinstock. I would also like to express my gratitude to John Malcolm for his useful monograph, *Treatment Choices and Informed Consent*,[35] especially for his interesting final chapter, "Courts as a

Forum for Medical Progress," which stimulated many of the thoughts contained herein. Most of all, I would like to thank my wonderful wife for her never-ending support and encouragement.

REFERENCES

1. Gaylin W: Who speaks for the helpless. *J Am Acad Child Psych* 1979; 18:419–436, p 435.
2. Mill JS: On Liberty (1859). Reprinted in Warnock M (ed): *Utilitarianism and Other Writings by JS Mill*. London, Collins, 1962, pp 126–250.
3. Hundert, EM: A model for ethical problem solving in medicine, with practical applications. *Am J Psychiat* 1987; 144:839–846.
4. *Currie v US*, No. 86-2643 (4th Cir. Dec. 20, 1987).
5. Stone AA: *Law, Psychiatry, and Morality*. Washington, DC, American Psychiatric Press, 1984, pp 73, 68.
6. MacIntyre, A: *After Virtue—A Study in Moral Theory*. London, Duckworth, 1981.
7. Kant, I: *Critique of Practical Reason* (1788). Beck LW (trans). Chicago, University of Chicago Press, 1949.
8. Zilboorg, G: *The Psychology of the Criminal Act and Punishment*. New York, Harcourt, Brace, 1954, pp 112, 41.
9. Gutheil TG, Mills MJ: Legal conceptualizations, legal fictions, and the manipulation of reality. *Bull Am Acad Psych Law* 1982; 10:17–27.
10. Holmes OW: Learning and science; a speech delivered June 25, 1895, in Holmes OW: *Collected Legal Papers*. New York, Harcourt, Brace & Howe, 1920, p 138.
11. Bazelon DL: Psychiatrists and the adversary process. *Scientific American* 1974; 230:18–23.
12. Austin JL: *How to Do Things with Words*. Oxford, Oxford University Press, 1962.
13. *Holloway v US*, 148 F. 2nd 665.
14. Llewellyn K: *Jurisprudence*. Chicago, University of Chicago Press, 1962, p 445.
15. Cooper E: Why psychiatrists shun the court: No room for maybes. *Can Law* 1980; 4:10.
16. Guttmacher MS: *The Role of Psychiatry in Law*. Springfield, IL, Charles C. Thomas, 1968.
17. Gutheil TG, Magraw, R: Ambivalence, alliance, and advocacy: Misunderstood dualities in psychiatry and law. *Bull Am Acad Psych Law* 1984; 12:51–58.
18. National Interprofessional Code for Physicians and Attorneys. *Am Bar Assoc J* 1959; 45:33–34.
19. Gorman WF: Are there impartial expert psychiatric witnesses? *Bull Am Acad Psych Law* 1983; 11:379–382.
20. Curran WJ: Ethical standards, in Curran WJ, McGarry AL, Petty CS (eds): *Modern Legal Medicine, Psychiatry, and Forensic Science*. Philadelphia, F A Davis Co, 1980, pp 36, 29–48.
21. Pollack S: Psychiatry and the administration of justice, in Curran WJ, McGarry AL, Petty CS (eds): *Modern Legal Medicine, Psychiatry, and Forensic Science*. Philadelphia, F A Davis Co, 1980, pp 668, 655–674.
22. Gutheil TG, Appelbaum PS: *Clinical Handbook of Psychiatry and the Law*. New York, McGraw-Hill, 1982, p 341.
23. Capron AM: Harmonies and conflicts in law and biomedical ethics, in Callahan D, Dunstan GR (eds): *Biomedical Ethics: An Anglo-American Dialogue*. New York, New York Academy of Sciences, 1988, pp 37–45.
24. Ciccone JR, Clements C: Forensic psychiatry and applied clinical ethics: theory and practice. *Am J Psychiat* 1984; 141:395–399, p 397.
25. O'Brien-Steinfels M, Levine C (eds): *In the Service of the State: The Psychiatrist as Double Agent*. Hastings-on-Hudson, Hastings Center, 1978.
26. Melton GB, Petrila J, Poythress NG, Slobogin C: *Psychological Evaluations for the Courts*. New York, Guilford, 1987, p 9.

27. Strasburger LH: Treatment of anti-social syndromes: The therapist's feelings, in Reid WH (ed): *Unmasking the Psychopath*. New York, WW Norton, 1986.
28. Menninger K: *The Crime of Punishment*. New York, Viking, 1968.
29. Szasz TS: *Law, Liberty, and Psychiatry: An Inquiry into the Social Uses of Mental Health Practices*. New York, Macmillan, 1963.
30. Quoted in Glueck B: *Studies in Forensic Psychiatry*. Boston, Little, Brown, 1916, p v.
31. American Board of Forensic Psychiatry: Definition of Forensic Psychiatry. Approved at meeting of Board of Directors, May 20, 1985, Dallas, Texas.
32. Newsletter, *Am Acad Forensic Sci* 1977; 3:1–2.
33. Poythress NG: Mental health expert testimony: current problems. *J Psych Law* 1977; 5:201–227, p 201.
34. Roth LH: Correctional psychiatry, in Curran WJ, McGarry AL, Petty CS (eds): *Modern Legal Medicine, Psychiatry, and Forensic Science*. Philadelphia, F A Davis, 1980, pp 704–705.
35. Malcolm JG: *Treatment Choices and Informed Consent*. Springfield, IL, Charles C Thomas, 1988.

II

Models and Guidelines for Ethical Practice

5

The Psychiatric Expert Witness

Honest Advocate or "Hired Gun"?

BERNARD L. DIAMOND

From 1866 to 1872 Isaac Ray and Charles Doe, Justice of the New Hampshire Supreme Court, engaged in correspondence in which they planned the substance and strategy for revision of the traditional McNaughten rule of criminal insanity.[1] This is the first reported example of a psychiatrist working behind the scenes to impact upon a legal decision, and resulted in the historically significant "New Hampshire rule" as set forth in the *Pike*[2] and *Jones*[3] decisions. Dr. Ray and Justice Doe had agreed that there could be no satisfactory legal rule of criminal responsibility of the mentally abnormal offender. Rather, the issue was one of two facts to be decided by the jury: Did the defendant suffer from a mental disease or defect at the time of offense, and was the crime a result or product of the mental abnormality? This was the forerunner and model for the 1954 Durham decision in the District of Columbia.[4]

Despite this remarkable historical precedent, psychiatrists to this day insist that they remain outside of the adversarial system, participating in trials only as detached experts, unbiased, impartial, and uninvolved in the outcome of the trial or appeal. This view has been encouraged by the courts in opinions such as that of Judge David Bazelon in *Washington v United States*[5] where the psychiatric expert is cautioned to have no concern for the ultimate outcome of the case or for the legal meaning of "mental disease or defect." Nevertheless, generations of forensic psychiatrists have actively, but surreptitiously, participated in the adversarial process as a member of the legal team on one side or the other and have been very much concerned with the outcome of the cases in which they testify. I have long maintained that this is inevitable, that the expert cannot possibly remain uninvolved, objective, impartial, and unbiased, and that this is

BERNARD L. DIAMOND • School of Law, University of California at Berkeley, Berkeley, California 94720.

not an improper role for the psychiatrist if his adversarial or advocacy role is made clear to the trier of fact.[6,7]

Finally, in 1985, the United States Supreme Court endorsed the adversarial role for the psychiatric expert in its ruling that an indigent defendant who pleads insanity is entitled to the services of a psychiatrist who will be actively involved in the defense.

> The issue in this case is whether the Constitution requires that an indigent defendant have access to the psychiatric examination and assistance necessary to prepare an effective defense based on his mental condition, when his sanity at the time of the offense is seriously in question...
>
> We therefore hold that when a defendant demonstrates to the trial judge that his sanity at the time of the offense is to be a significant factor at trial, the State must, at a minimum, assure the defendant access to a competent psychiatrist who will conduct an appropriate examination and assist in evaluation, preparation, and presentation of the defense...
>
> The foregoing leads inexorably to the conclusion that, without the assistance of a psychiatrist to conduct a professional examination on issues relevant to the defense, to help determine whether the insanity defense is viable, to present testimony, and to assist in preparing the cross-examination of a State's psychiatric witnesses, the risk of an inaccurate resolution of sanity issues is extremely high. With such assistance, the defendant is fairly able to present at least enough information to the jury, in a meaningful manner, as to permit it to make a sensible determination.[8]

The Court also held that when it is permissible for the State to introduce expert testimony at a sentencing procedure on the issue of dangerousness, the Constitution likewise requires the assistance of a psychiatrist for the defense.

> In such a circumstance, where the consequence of error is so great, the relevance of responsive psychiatric testimony so evident, and the burden on the State so slim, due process requires access to a psychiatric examination on relevant issues, to the testimony of the psychiatrist, and to assistance in preparation at the sentencing phase.[8]

If the Supreme Court now endorses this role of the psychiatrist as advocate, as member of the litigation team, is the Court also endorsing the psychiatric expert as "hired gun"? If not, what is the distinction between the "hired gun" and the adversarial expert witness?

THE "HIRED GUN"

I believe the basic distinction between the psychiatrist as advocate and the "hired gun" is very simple: The advocate psychiatrist is honest; the "hired gun" is dishonest.

The "hired gun" knowingly gives false or misleading testimony. He intentionally violates the oath he, as a witness, takes to "tell the truth, the whole truth, and nothing but the truth." The motive for doing so is usually money; but sometimes there are other reasons such as a desire for publicity, to bolster self-esteem, to please attorneys, police, or insurance companies (thus ensuring continued employment), or to further some personal crusade or belief. Regardless of motive, he violates his oath by giving false information, or false inference from true facts, or by withholding contradictory and conflicting information from the jury.

There is a gray area between the expert who gives evidence that he knows to be false or misleading and the expert who gives false testimony out of stupidity or ignorance. Such experts may deliberately fail to correct their erroneous beliefs by familiarizing themselves with the scientific literature or the consensus of other experts because to do so would eliminate their usefulness to the attorneys that employ them. Often such experts exhibit an extravagant arrogance, claiming that they possess knowledge that is superior to that of the bulk of the scientific community; hence there is no need for them to be familiar with the scientific literature or to testify in accordance with generally accepted scientific principles.

"Dr. Death," the Texas psychiatrist James Grigson, makes such claims. According to a newspaper interview,[9] he has testified in 1400 trials since 1980, including 111 capital cases. In all the capital cases he has testified that the defendant was dangerous and likely to commit criminal acts of violence and be a continuing threat to society. In all but nine of the 111 capital cases, the defendant was sentenced to death. Despite the overwhelming evidence of the uncertainty of such predictions of dangerousness, Dr. Grigson insists that he has the ability to make 100% certain predictions of such future behavior. When confronted by the assertions of the American Civil Liberties Union and the American Psychiatric Association that his predictions had no scientific foundation, his response was to call such charges nonsense. He is quoted as saying "They can say what they want; it hasn't hurt what I do. The people who know me know I'm good, and they keep using me. I don't need the publicity. I don't need more business. I have more business than I can handle."

A psychiatrist frequently used by the prosecution in a Bay Area county testified that the defendant in a criminal trial was sane and responsible. On cross-examination, he revealed that when he went to the jail to examine the defendant, the defendant was sound asleep. He observed the defendant sleeping for about five minutes and did not wake him. He testified that in his experience no psychotic or insane person is able to sleep so soundly; therefore the defendant was not psychotic or insane. This psychiatrist's testimony was usually of about this caliber. A deputy district attorney who often used this expert candidly stated privately that he knew the psychiatrist was an ignoramus and he was sure the jury knew it as well. But by allowing his own expert to be exposed as foolish and ridiculous, this would cause the jury to disregard all psychiatric evidence as foolish and implausible and so discount whatever expert testimony was introduced by the defense, no matter what its quality.

LEGAL DEFINITION OF EXPERT WITNESS

Much of the problem with the "hired gun" would be eliminated if the trial courts were more discriminatory as to who they recognize as an expert. Legislative definitions tend to be vague and tautological. The California Evidence Code states:

> A person is qualified to testify as an expert if he has special knowledge, skill, experience, training, or education sufficient to qualify him as an expert on the subject to which his testimony relates.[10]

Further, the code provides that:

> If a witness testifying as an expert testifies in the form of an opinion, he may not be cross-examined in regard to the content or tenor of any scientific, technical, or professional text, treatise, journal, or similar publication unless:
>
> (1) The witness referred to, considered, or relied upon such publication in arriving at or forming his opinion; or
>
> (2) Such publication has been admitted in evidence.[11]

Such tautological definitions and restrictions are guaranteed to allow idiosyncratic pseudoexperts to take the witness stand and to protect them from exposure of their ignorance of the relevant scientific literature. The conjunctive "or" in the definition of expert allows almost anything to be used to establish the witness credentials and makes it very difficult for the jury to distinguish between the authentic expert, accepted as such by the scientific community, and the maverick expert whose idiosyncratic views are unsupported. Unfortunately, the distinction by the jury is likely to be made on the basis of the witness ability to articulate and persuade, and on how closely the expert confirms the juror's prejudices and commonsense beliefs.

THE HONEST EXPERT WITNESS

I believe the honest expert can, and should, be very much involved in the outcome of the trial in which he participates. He should be very concerned with the uses that the law makes of his testimony and he should resist efforts by the law to interpret psychiatric terms and definitions in ways that do not make scientific sense. Often the outcome of a particular case, especially when appealed, has far-reaching consequences, affecting the destinies of many others in addition to the litigants. In short, the psychiatric expert can, and should be an advocate. "Advocate" is defined in the dictionary as:

1. One that pleads the cause of another...
2. One that defends or maintains a cause or proposal[12]

The psychiatrist's willingness to participate in difficult and financially unrewarding trials may be determined by his personal interest in the broader, social implications of the case. He may hope that his participating as an expert witness will serve as an instrument for enlightenment, education, or social or legal reform. He may hope that his testimony will expose legal procedures that are archaic, unjust, and detrimental to a free society. He may participate as an expert because he wishes to help the underdog, the impoverished, and the have-nots of society. Or he may be an advocate for law and order and conceptualize his role as a protector of society. I see nothing wrong with such motives. They are all admirable reasons for the psychiatrist to involve himself in the intricacies of a legal system which sometimes provides few, if any, personal rewards for such social crusaders. He may seek out cases that offer opportunities to advance his personal social philosophies. Or, having been publicly identified as standing for certain positions, attorneys may seek him out for their cases that involve similar issues.

At the very least, the psychiatrist on the witness stand should be an advocate for the principles of mental health, for the scientific status of psychiatry, and against the misuse of psychiatric evidence. If he is a competent witness, he has invested a large amount of time and energy into his expert opinion and the marshaling of the facts upon which his opinion is based. Necessarily, if he is to be effective, he must strongly advocate his own opinion, presenting it in the most articulate manner and vigorously defending it against the onslaughts of cross-examination. Is such an expert therefore a "hired gun"? I think not if he is competent, scrupulously honest, and does not give false evidence.

LEGAL RESTRICTIONS ON EVIDENCE

A special dilemma arises when the expert's oath as a witness requires him to "tell the whole truth" and, at the same time, the rules of evidence allow, or require, the withholding of certain information from the jury. Such a situation arose in the case of a college student who committed a bizarre murder for highly pathological motives to which he freely confessed. Although sane under the strict "right and wrong" test of insanity, there was ample evidence for a diminished capacity defense. Just prior to the murder, a senseless shooting had been made from a passing car at a woman waiting for a bus. Fortunately for the woman, it was a near miss. After the murder the police suspected that the earlier shooting might have also been done by the defendant. Following extensive interrogation, both in jail and at the scene of the shooting, the police decided that he was not the perpetrator of the shooting.

When examined by the defense psychiatrist, the defendant immediately confessed that he was the one who had done the earlier shooting and that he had lied to the police in denying his involvement. The defense attorney did not wish the psychiatrist to reveal this information to the jury, for fear that if the jury rejected the diminished capacity defense, their concern for the defendant's dangerousness might result in a death sentence. The psychiatrist insisted that the earlier attempt at murder was an essential part of the defendant's pathological behavior, and to omit any mention of it to the jury would be misleading and violate his oath as a witness.

An impasse developed where the attorney refused to allow the psychiatrist to describe the previous murder attempt, and the psychiatrist refused to testify unless he would be permitted to tell the "whole truth." The result was that the defendant pleaded guilty to first degree murder with life imprisonment rather than risk the psychiatric evidence which might have led to the death penalty if the jury were unconvinced of the diminished capacity. The appropriate verdict, because of the psychopathology, would have been manslaughter, or, at most, second degree murder.

An impasse such as this arises whenever information exists that is relevant to the expert opinion of the psychiatrist, but is not relevant to the strictly legal issues of the facts of the crime. The most common example is when previous felony convictions are inadmissible because they are not relevant to the *actus reus*, but are very relevant to the psychopathology introduced as a defense against the *mens rea* of the crime.

There is no doubt that the defense attorney, within the bounds of evidence law, has the right to restrict the evidence that is introduced. But does he also have the right to restrict the testimony of the expert other than by not calling him as a witness? Often attorneys request (and sometimes demand) that the psychiatrist omit significant information from the testimony because of the concern for the negative impact the information may have on the jury. The attorney may not ask the expert certain relevant questions or try to cut short the expert's answers in order to avoid revealing the undesired information. The "hired gun" is more than willing to cooperate with such trial tactics.

Admittedly, there can be differences of opinion about this; but my belief is that if the restrictions on the expert's testimony would result in false, misleading, or incomplete information concerning the basis of the expert's opinion, it would be improper, even unethical, for the psychiatrist to comply with the attorney's demand. The psychiatrist would then have the option to withdraw from the case; the attorney would, of course, have the option of not using him as a witness. It is essential that issues and conflicts of this type be resolved early so that the defendant is not harmed by the necessary last-minute changes in trial strategy.

The courts have attempted to deal with this problem by holding that testimony given by the expert as the basis of his opinion can be used by the jury only to evaluate the opinion of the expert, and not independently for purposes of adjudicating the facts of the case.[13] It is very difficult to estimate the efficacy of such rulings, for jurors may be psychologically incapable of ignoring such facts in their decision making no matter how instructed by the trial judge. However, such rulings may be more useful for appellate courts in determining whether there is sufficient evidence, other than the expert's testimony, to justify the jury decision.

TOTAL DISCLOSURE

It is my personal practice to insist that the defense attorney put the defendant on the witness stand so that the jury can hear from the defendant's own lips the information upon which I based my opinion. I do not want to be just a mouthpiece for the defendant and I do not expect a jury to believe me if I simply relay second-hand statements and information obtained from the defendant. I want the jury to experience the defendant's abnormal thinking and feeling and his account of his behavior and the events of the crime firsthand. Then, I can interpret this information for the jury, explaining its psychopathological significance and its relevance to the legal decision to be made. The defendant has a constitutional right not to testify in his criminal trial; but he does not have a constitutional right to use me as a defense witness against my better judgment as to how I can be honest and effective as an expert.

Related to this issue is my belief that all psychiatric defenses to crime, whether insanity or diminished responsibility (or capacity) should be achieved through total disclosure.[14] Again, the Constitution and various statutory rules of evidence allow many restrictions on the evidence in a criminal trial, including the withholding of many facts from the judge and jury. Such facts are deemed legally irrelevant or improper, even though logically they would seem to be essential for the decision-making process of the jury.

It seems to me, however, that once the strategy of a psychiatric defense has been decided upon, the defendant must waive his rights of concealment and be prepared to reveal everything to the judge and jury. Only through such total disclosure can an effective, believable, and righteous psychiatric defense be achieved. In effect, the defendant says to the jury:

> Although I have the right to remain silent and to conceal my private thoughts, feelings, motives, behavior, and the secrets of my past life from your scrutiny, I choose to waive this right. I waive this right so that you may understand the true nature of my actions and understand that I acted out of irrational, sick reasons rather than the immoral motives alleged by the prosecution. To help you understand this, I will reveal to you my complete life story, my innermost thoughts, emotions, fears, motives, dreams, and hopes, rational as well as irrational, so that you may understand why I did what I did.

I do not think that the psychiatrist can adequately convey this understanding to the trier of fact without the direct assistance of the defendant. Of course, it cannot be expected that a mentally ill defendant will, of his own accord, understand the necessity of this strategy. It is up to the defense attorney, with the assistance of the psychiatrist, to persuade the defendant that this is necessary. If the attorney, or the defendant, is unwilling to use this strategy of full disclosure, then I am unwilling to participate in the trial. I believe this is a proper position for me to take. However, I am not yet quite sure that this should be a generally accepted strategy for all experts under all circumstances. I would like to see more experts commit themselves to this strategic principle and to evaluate the results before deciding on its general acceptability.

RECOMMENDATIONS

There is probably no single measure to be taken against the "hired gun" that would be effective; but a combination of measures by both the legal and psychiatric professional groups might well reduce the problem to minimal proportions. Contrary to the opinion of many of my colleagues, I do not believe that the use of court-appointed experts in any way solves the problem of the "hired gun." Psychiatrists who seek out court appointments often act as if they were employed by the prosecution. Psychiatrists who are defense-oriented may rarely be appointed once their orientation becomes known. Funds for court-ordered psychiatric examinations may be minimal and do not allow for the complete and thorough examinations required by difficult cases. I believe that trial records of the testimony of court-appointed experts, supposedly neutral and impartial, in many jurisdictions, over many years, reveal more blatant incompetence, dishonesty, and bias than adversarial witnesses.

It is often suggested that psychiatric evidence and decisions of competency and responsibility be taken away from the jury and placed before a panel or commission of experts for decision. After such technical and scientific issues have been disposed of, the jury can then decide the issues of guilt or innocence.* There is little doubt that such a procedure is unconstitutional, and persons who make such a recommendation have no understanding of the basic principles of criminal justice law.

More effective remedies against the corruption of the trial process by a "hired gun" would be the following:

First, there must be a clear expression by organized forensic psychiatrists of the boundaries of legitimate psychiatric expertise. Establishment of such boundaries would define organizations, such as the American Academy of Psychiatry and Law, as the relevant scientific community of the so-called *Frye* test.[15] In rejecting expert testimony based upon an early version of the lie detector, the District of Columbia Court of Appeals held that

> ...while courts will go a long way in admitting expert testimony deduced from a well-recognized scientific principle or discovery, the thing from which the deduction is made must be sufficiently established to have gained general acceptance in the particular field in which it belongs.[16]

Thus, the acceptance or lack of acceptance would be defined by consensus of the responsible forensic psychiatrists and, in accordance with the *Frye* test, incompetent and improper testimony could be excluded. Many, but not all, jurisdictions accept the principle of the *Frye* decision. In those that do, difficulty arises because of lack of the expression by competent professional groups as to what is and what is not scientifically valid. If this problem were eliminated, I think more jurisdictions would be willing to require the *Frye* test.

Second, the legislatures and the courts must adopt more rigorous standards for the qualification of experts. A definition, such as that used in California, "A person is qualified to testify as an expert if he has special knowledge, skill, experience, training, or education..."[11] would be much improved if it

*The Louisiana legislature passed a law in 1928 requiring the issue of criminal insanity to be determined by a "lunacy commission" in advance of the criminal trial. The commission determination was to be final and the jury would not decide on the insanity issue. The Supreme Court of Louisiana held that such a procedure was unconstitutional "because it seeks to delegate to a commission judicial powers belonging exclusively to a judicial tribunal and deprives him [the defendant] of his constitutional right to a trial by jury on a question directly pertaining to his guilt or innocence..." *State v Lange*, 123 So. 639, at 639, 168 La. 958 (1929).

substituted "and" for "or." The expert should be qualified by his special knowledge *and* skill *and* experience *and* training *and* education. A deficiency in any one of these qualifications would disqualify him.

Third, the courts should insist that the expert be knowledgeable of the scientific literature on the subject at issue. His testimony should be in accord with the prevailing scientific opinion, as expressed in the literature, or, if not, the burden for accounting for the discrepancy is upon the expert. That burden can never be met just by asserting an unsupported opinion, but must be demonstrated by convincing new scientific evidence relative to the case at trial.

Fourth, the psychiatric expert should be allowed considerable leeway in the form in which he presents his testimony. The usual interrogation by question and answer is not the best way to transmit scientific information.[17] Artificial limitations on the content and scope of his testimony based upon traditional rules of evidence should not be employed. The logic of science, rather than the logic of the law, should be the required standard for the expert's testimony. Total disclosure is mandatory in the logic of science.

Fifth, there cannot be simple reliance on the battle of experts for the exposure of unscientific, irrational, dishonest, or foolish expert testimony. The trial judge must take more responsibility for setting the criteria for expertise and should not hesitate to exclude testimony that does not meet the appropriate standards. At present, the expert is qualified as an expert, the opposing side is given an opportunity to challenge his expert qualifications, and then the expert gives his testimony. Once the expert is qualified, no matter how unscientific, dishonest, or inadequate his subsequent testimony, his evidence is permitted to be considered by the jury. I suggest that, even if the expert is initially qualified, if his subsequent testimony clearly reveals that he is not truly an expert on the issues at trial, the trial judge should take the initiative in disqualifying him and striking his testimony from the record.

Sixth, the law must give up its quest for certainty, its naive belief that certainty can be obtained through science. Scientific knowledge is always approximate, tentative, and subject to revision as knowledge grows. The expert is never justified in expressing his opinion with 100% certainty. There is a level of doubt about every scientific conclusion. In research terminology this is known as the "level of confidence." The meaning of this can, and should, be described and interpreted to the judge and jury. Exaggerated and unsupported expressions of confidence are the hallmarks of the pseudoexpert and must be avoided.

Seventh, the role of the expert in the adversary process should be fully revealed to the trier of fact. I believe it is entirely proper for the expert to serve as a consultant on the litigation team, helping to plan strategy and to unearth relevant facts and information for the attorney. But such activities should not be concealed from the jury and the expert falsely presented as an uninvolved, impartial, objective expert.

Finally, professional organizations must take more responsibility in setting guidelines, defining ethical standards, and, if necessary, exposing and disciplining members of their profession who misuse and abuse the legal principles of expert testimony. In a world in which science and technology are constantly growing, having greater impact on all areas of our life, and becoming increasingly complex and beyond the commonsense understanding of the average person, it is inevitable that expert testimony will be required in legal proceedings to an ever-increasing extent. To avoid the discrediting of both law and psychiatry, the courts and bar associations must take the responsibility for control of the lawyers who willfully encourage irresponsible expertise, and the psychiatric organizations must accept responsibility for the exposure and discipline of their professionals who give unethical and dishonest testimony. The "hired gun" violates his oath as a witness to tell the truth, the whole truth, and nothing but the truth, and therefore cannot be tolerated in our system of justice.

REFERENCES

1. Reik, LE: The Doe-Ray correspondence: A pioneer collaboration in the jurisprudence of mental disease. *Yale Law J* 1953; 63:183–196.
2. *State v Pike*, 49 N.H. 399 (1869).
3. *State v Jones*, 50 N.H. 369 (1871).
4. *Durham v United States*, 214 F.2d 862 (D.C.Cir. 1954).
5. *Washington v United States*, 390 F.2d 444, at 457 (D.C.Cir. 1967).
6. Diamond, BL: The fallacy of the impartial expert. *Arch Crim Psychodynamics* 1959; 3:221–236.
7. Diamond, BL: The psychiatrist as advocate. *J Psychiatry Law* 1973; 1:5–21.
8. *Ake v Oklahoma*, 470 U.S. 68, 105 S.Ct. 1087, 84 L.Ed.2d 53 (1985).
9. *San Francisco Chronicle*, June 19, 1988, p 3. The headline reads " 'Dr. Death' Takes the Stand/Texan specializes in putting criminals on Death Row."
10. California Evidence Code, Section 720(*a*).
11. California Evidence Code, Section 721(*b*).
12. *Webster's Seventh New Collegiate Dictionary*. Springfield, Mass. G & C Merriam, 1972, p 14.
13. *In re Spencer*, 63 Cal.2d 400, 46 Cal Rptr 753, 486 P.2d 33 (1964).
14. Dieden, L, Gasparich, C: Psychiatric evidence and full disclosure in the criminal trial. *Cal Law Rev* 1964; 52:543–561.
15. *Frye v United States*, 293 F. 1013 (D.C. Ct.App. 1923).
16. *Frye v United States*, 293 F. 1013, at 1014 (D.C. Ct.App. 1923).
17. Diamond, BL, Louisell, D: The psychiatrist as an expert witness: some ruminations and speculations. *Mich Law Rev* 1954; 63:1335–1354.

6

The Role of the (Psychiatric) Expert in the Judicial Process

RALPH SLOVENKO

The touchstone for the role of an expert in the judicial process is helpfulness. It is on that basis, for pretrial or trial purposes, that an attorney engages an expert.

An expert may be engaged to serve as a consultant, or as a witness at trial, or both. Before filing a complaint, the lawyer might turn to an expert in order to develop knowledge about a technical area, and to help him frame the complaint and understand relevant issues. The lawyer's knowledge of the subject matter will determine the assistance needed.

Once the complaint is filed, the expert can assist during discovery by identifying documents that should be requested or that routinely exist in a particular enterprise. The expert can also assist in preparing for depositions of lay or expert witnesses, or in identifying licensing agencies and, sometimes, specific persons at agencies who may prove useful.

An expert can be helpful in reviewing and interpreting documents received from adverse parties. The expert, through experience, can determine whether, in fact, the documents are complete. The expert can also assist the lawyer in follow-up discovery, including interrogatories, requests for production of documents, and depositions. The expert may suggest to the lawyer appropriate avenues of inquiry and appropriate cross-examination possibilities.[1]

Experts often play a pivotal role in the development of a case and in its final resolution. Over 95% of tort cases are resolved without a trial. The expert's

This chapter is a development of the author's commentary in the *Journal of Psychiatry and Law*, included by permission. The *Journal of Psychiatry and Law* is published by Federal Legal Publications, Inc., 157 Chambers Street, New York, NY 10007.

RALPH SLOVENKO • Wayne State University School of Law, Detroit, Michigan 48202.

deposition or report is very important in determining whether to go to trial and, correlatively, in determining the amount to offer or accept in settlement. Insurance companies are often strongly persuaded by an expert's report.

At trial, the use of expert testimony poses two interrelated but separate questions. The first is whether the subject matter of the litigation is such that the trier of fact may appropriately receive assistance in the form of specialized knowledge. The second question is whether the witness at hand is qualified to give such assistance.

In resolving the first question, the test under rule 702 of the Federal Rules of Evidence (adopted in 1975) and its state counterparts is whether the testimony of the expert "will assist the trier of fact to understand the evidence or to determine a fact in issue." This "helpfulness" requirement does not limit experts only to subjects beyond the ken of lay jurors (as common law courts often held). It also allows them to aid the jury in understanding even familiar matters, by virtue of experience or training that permits an understanding more thorough or from a different perspective than that provided by ordinary experience.[2]

To be relevant (FRE 401), or helpful (FRE 702), an expert's opinion must be brought out of the realm of speculation and into the realm of reasonable probability; the law deals in "probabilities," not "possibilities." Hence, an opinion based on a "possibility" will not stand up in court, to use a common expression.[3] The Texas Court of Appeals has noted that whether expert testimony expresses probability, as opposed to pure conjecture, is not based upon the semantics of the expert or his use of any particular term or phrase, but rather is determined by the entire substance of the expert's testimony.[4] Usually, however, the testimony of the medical expert must be stated in terms of "reasonable degree of medical probability" or "reasonable degree of medical certainty."[5]

The role of the expert in a particular case is not static. Rather, it evolves. In procuring the expert's agreement to review and comment, the attorney typically treats testimony hypothetically: "If you take the stand...," reviewing the issues and the facts of the case. Once agreeing to serve, the expert is usually expected to act like a fellow traveler, that is, to make the best case he can for the lawyer's client. He is expected to be as persuasive as he can for the client short of fabrication. The system encourages such partisanship. Like it or not, trial is war. Lawyers are generals, fashioning strategies and implementing tactics. Witnesses are mustered into opposing armies. Not only are the immediate parties to a legal action adversaries—plaintiff or state versus defendant—but the witnesses are also labeled as witnesses *for* the plaintiff or *for* the defendant.

To use another metaphor, the adversarial process might be likened to a multilane highway, with several lanes going in one direction and several lanes in the opposite direction. The witness, like the traveler, is expected to go one way or the other. Indeed, any attempt to stand in the middle of the road merely invites disaster from either direction.

In an adversarial system, each side is expected to present its best case on each contested issue. Theoretically, the resulting friction gives the best chance of finding the truth, or at least of airing both sides. Truth emerges, lawyers believe, from the clash of opposing ideas. The system fails when the challengeable goes unchallenged.[6]

At one time the concept of the "impartial expert" found considerable support, as a way to avoid the polemical distortion arising out of the adversarial system. The original version of the ethical guidelines of the American Academy of Psychiatry and Law as well as the American Bar Association's Standards for Criminal Justice, formulated not long ago, also speak to the impartiality of expert witnesses. To most observers of court proceedings, however, they echo hollow. The court's power to appoint an impartial expert, set out in rule 706, is within the discretion of the trial judge but is not frequently used. In fact, rule 706 is the least-used provision of the Federal Rules of Evidence. Dr. Bernard Diamond debunked the idea of an impartial expert in a classic article, "The Fallacy of the Impartial Expert,"[7] and in another article, coauthored with Professor David W. Louisell, "The Psychiatrist as an Expert Witness: Some Ruminations and Speculations."[8] As many would argue, the very concept of the impartial expert is an illusion.

Quite often, lawyers crudely accuse their opponents of "buying" experts, and call them "hired guns." Actually there is nothing unethical about hiring those with favorable opinions, as long as the lawyers do not ask the expert to fabricate or falsify. A "hired gun" is not a "hired liar." In the very nature of things, every event has different versions arising from different perspectives. The famous Japanese film *Rashomon*—a dramatization of the classic enigma of truth—is a metaphor of life, reminding us that there is not one truth but many truths, some valid for one, some for another. In the very nature of perception, events are seen in different ways.

Anterior to the question of what really happened is the question, what is truth? Absolutist notions of truth are in general disfavor. "The strength of Marxist-Leninist teaching lies in the fact that it correctly reflects reality, that it is true," wrote the party journal *Kommunist*. "However many ways of searching for it there may be, there is only one truth concerning its general historical character."[9] That view has little credibility today. In his documentaries—*The Sorrow and the Pity, A Sense of Loss, The Memory of Justice*, and *Hotel Terminus/The Life and Times of Klaus Barbie*—Marcel Ophuls, finding truth to be elusive and relative, casts his net wide so that he catches the next-best thing—the complexity of the human condition, the inherent contradictions of human nature, and its unpredictability.[10]

In some aspects psychiatrists are like biographers or historians. Some training programs in psychiatry call for the writing of reports as though they were biographies. Freud's case histories could have been awarded a prize in literature.[11] Each biographer, though writing about the same individual, will display variation in the story. It is the same with psychiatrists: Variation does not imply falsity. When the same thing occurs in court, however, it is denounced as a "battle of the experts."

Not only are biographers and historians dependent on the sources they use, their special interests will also influence the kind of biography or history written. No one approach, taken by itself, is fully satisfying, nor has any biographer or historian a monopoly on truth.[12]

How then does one delineate fabrication or philosophical conjecture from reality or honest perception? Woody Allen remarked that, after his freshman course in philosophy, he was unable to define reality, but he still knew where to get a good steak. He relied on logic and experience.

With that as prologue, who can say that the opinion of the "impartial expert" called by the court is inherently less biased or more truthful or more objective than that of the witness retained by an adversary? The bias of the impartial expert is simply masked as impartiality, more or less deceiving the fact finder. The traditional adversarial system of examining witnesses for each side by direct and cross-examination is premised more honestly, presuming *ab initio* that witnesses have partiality. The system has evolved for just the purpose of exposing such shortcomings and biases.[13]

At trial, the first step is properly to qualify the witness as an expert. Here, the objective is not only to satisfy fundamental evidentiary and procedural rules, but also to inform the jury about the expert's credentials. The better the credentials, the greater the witness's credibility, and the more weight the jury will presumably give the testimony. At trial, judging from cross-examination, an expert, it seems, should be neither virgin nor prostitute—an expert who has never testified may have difficulty getting qualified, while one who testifies often is discredited as a hired gun.[14]

Various factors, including technological advances and the liberalization of the rules of evidence, have prompted the use of a wider range of experts than ever. In complex or technical cases the expert is often crucial because the evidence is beyond the ken of the jury; but even in a simple slip-and-fall case an expert may be used to establish scientific criteria for walking surfaces or the proper way to maintain premises. Melvin Belli says, "Counsel who choose to proceed without an expert may be flirting with malpractice."[15]

As recently as 30 years ago most tort cases were very simple. Medical malpractice and mass injury, which today constitute 40% of cases, were virtually unknown. New technologies have created "high stakes" litigation where the potential award justifies the expenditure of funds for expert testimony. As a consequence, the use of expert witnesses in recent years has grown rapidly. However, use of experts in court is hardly new. In the 17th century, a treatise listed five classes of experts: locksmiths, cutlers, peruke-makers, washerwomen, and ropemakers.[16] Even earlier, courts called on physicians to help determine whether a defendant was "bewitched."

One may come to court as an "expert" without necessarily being tops in one's field. The term "expert" includes anyone whose knowledge of a subject extends beyond that of the average juror. By legal definition, an "expert" is almost anybody who can reasonably be expected to know more about a given subject than the average person. As rule 702 puts it, anyone with "knowledge, skill, experience, training, or education" which can assist the trier of fact may qualify as an expert. Sometimes the rulings on qualified experts may seem bizarre. Users of narcotics have testified as experts on the identification of a drug.[17] An "expert burglar" has also qualified as an expert witness.[18] A Florida court, however, would not allow a psychologist to testify regarding the proper standard for releasing a psychiatric patient.[19]

Along with the growing complexity of life has come a liberalization of the rules on expert testimony. An expert, unlike an ordinary witness, may now testify not only in the form of an opinion but also, in forming such an opinion, he may rely on inadmissible evidence such as hearsay, if such evidence is customarily or "reasonably relied upon by experts in the particular field."[20] That standard relaxes the foundation for expert opinion, and it has led some attorneys to use experts as a means of "smuggling" otherwise inadmissible proofs into evidence under the guise of foundation for the expert opinion. In criminal cases, the defense expert can, in effect, present the defendant's testimony without the defendant having to take the stand (thereby avoiding cross-examination).

Countering this trend is the doctrine that evidence, though relevant, may be excluded if it is likely to be confusing or misleading. The test, under rule 403, is whether the probative value of the evidence is substantially outweighed by the danger of "confusion of the issues or misleading the jury." This danger is sometimes profound. In the murder trial of Sirhan, four defense psychiatrists and psychologists said Sirhan was a paranoid schizophrenic who was not fully responsible for his actions when he shot Senator Robert Kennedy, while the prosecution experts said he was fully responsible. The experts testifying on both sides admitted that their conflicting statements must have sounded "incredible" to the jury. Even the key defense witness, Dr. Bernard Diamond, conceded that the jury might have trouble believing his testimony that Sirhan killed Kennedy while in a self-induced hypnotic trance.[21]

Helpful? Misleading? A number of critics have charged that psychiatrists (and psychologists) have no useful place in the courtroom. According to these critics, psychiatrists cannot answer forensic questions with reasonable accuracy, and, they say, cannot help the fact finder reach more accurate conclusions than would otherwise be available. In fact, the critics claim, psychiatrists as expert witnesses are not only not helpful but actually more harmful since they tend to mislead by offering testimony with little scientific underpinning.[22]

To evaluate such criticisms, one must first ask why psychiatrists (and psychologists) are called as expert witnesses. Apparently they fill some perceived need, as there is a growing willingness to pay for their services. Is it snake oil? We like to believe that the volume of sales in a marketplace of willing buyers and sellers is a reliable measure of social utility. By this criterion, mental health professionals are of greater use and importance than ever before.

Actually, the attack on psychiatrists as expert witnesses is an attack on the profession itself, nothing more nor less. It is a challenge to psychiatry, but it is entirely reasonable to assume that one who has had special training in understanding people, one who spends his life studying and thinking about people, and treating people for behavioral problems, is in a position to offer relevant and probative testimony about behavior. Is such training and experience irrelevant to issues at trial? Since law deals with behavior, there would be something wrong with a legal process that could not utilize psychiatric or psychological evidence.

In some measure, the law indulges in the ordinary perception that there is a correspondence between character and behavior. The perception of the correspondence is greater when the trait of character represents an enduring attribute of the individual. There are a number of situations where character evidence is directly in issue, for example, in child custody disputes or in negligent entrustment cases. In other situations, character evidence may create an inference that the person acted on the occasion in question consistently with his character.[23]

Traditionally, character testimony has been laden with moral connotations of goodness or badness. The traditional form of "proof" was by compounded hearsay, "reputation in the community." A person was said to be chaste, peaceable, truthful, honest, or the opposite. Such matters are, in essence, opinions, with great potential to appeal to passion or prejudice. Is such to be preferred over careful, studied, psychiatric diagnosis? Is reputation evidence, unschooled opinion, more probative than schooled opinion? One may suggest that the testimony of the psychiatrist and that of the lay witness are both valuable, each in its own way, in different circumstances and at different times. That is recognized in the Federal Rules of Evidence, adopted in 1975: "These [opinions offered to prove character] may range from the opinion of the employer who has found the man honest to the opinion of the psychiatrist based upon examination and testing."[24]

Psychiatric testimony is frequently offered on the issues of causation and extent of injury, elements legally required to establish a right to compensation. On causation, expert opinion may encompass two components. First, opinion may be offered on the actual cause, or "cause-in-fact" of the injury, since cause-in-fact is often treated as a necessary element of the larger issue of proximate or legal cause. Second, opinion may be offered as to whether the actual cause was the "legal" or "proximate cause" of the injury. Expert testimony on cause-in-fact, by itself, presents no great difficulty under rule 702 if the trier of fact may benefit from scientific, technical, or other specialized knowledge and the witness is qualified to provide that knowledge. Expert testimony on proximate (legal) cause, on the other hand, is more problematic. The issue of causation-in-fact—"Did the party's conduct contribute to the plaintiff's injury?"—is often confused with the more complex policy issue of proximate (legal) causation, which is concerned with who should bear responsibility for what happened.[25] It is for the finder of fact to determine proximate cause. As to what is relevant to that determination, Judge Andrews once said, in oft-quoted words, "The problem of proximate cause is not to be solved by any one consideration. It is all a question of expediency."[26]

Even where causation and character are not definitive of substantive rights, our interest as a society in understanding behavior focuses attention on psychiatric testimony. In criminal trials, where so much controversy surrounds psychiatric testimony, we must recall that the trial is very much a morality play. A trial without a psychiatrist is not infrequently bland—without psychiatric testimony, jurors may tend to fall asleep. No wonder then that psychiatric testimony makes headlines. When the public wants some fundamental understanding of what caused the accused to act in the way that he did, trials without psychiatric testimony are neither interesting nor satisfying. Indeed, the press in such cases may supply such "testimony" by obtaining and printing off-the-cuff comments by psychiatrists on any and all facets of the involved behavior.

Our interest in understanding not only *what* but also *why* may explain how at trial the "battle of the experts," as it is called, heightens tension: it prompts the trier of fact to pay attention, stimulates thought, and thereby enhances the deliberations. The evidence can serve as a guideline that the jurors can integrate with their own moral, social, philosophical and religious backgrounds to arrive at an appropriate decision.[27]

Psychiatric testimony, whether or not accepted, broadens the options available to judge and jury. It brings flexibility and an element of humanity into the law. The jury, following their conviction of Jean Harris for the killing of the Scarsdale diet doctor, Dr. Herman Tarnower, wondered why no psychiatric testimony was presented. The jury wanted some excusing evidence, though it may have been conflicting, but got none.[28] Whether in a given case the judge or jury accepts or declines such evidence is for them to decide—but without that testimony, they may have difficulty rationalizing a decision that their sense of community tells them is otherwise fair. The scale is the symbol of justice; but measurement alone would subvert the nature of a trial as a morality play. A trial, of course, has more to do with justice than with show business, but a trial (especially a criminal trial) is a morality play in some measure.[29]

Fundamental to the argument advanced by critics of psychiatric testimony is the idea that psychiatrists have "been continuously plagued by difficulties in achieving reliable classification." They point to the fact that four significantly different diagnostic manuals have been published since 1951, and a fifth is scheduled to appear in the early 1990s.[30] An attorney for the Michigan Protection and Advocacy Service says:[31]

> Psychiatric experts derive their power and prestige, indeed their expert status, on the notion they are medical practitioners, particularly experts in the realm of "mental illness"—should they not be expected to be able to diagnose with some specificity? Anyone can call someone crazy, if craziness is after all a medical domain, then the least one should expect of such an expert is to be acquainted with the taxonomy of their profession. If they cannot identify the malady then it seems questionable whether the same professional can prescribe treatment for it with any accuracy.

Diagnostic categories in psychiatry, however, have less utility than in the rest of medicine. The term currently used in psychiatry to indicate its scope is psycho-socio-biological, but even that does not encompass the true extent of the field's parameters. Dr. John L. Schimel, psychoanalyst, proposes the term: psycho-socio-anthropo-neuro-pharmaco-HMO-cost containment-DSMIII-R-S-T-U-V-W-X-Y-Z-DRG-IRS-bio-medical.[32] Dr. Karl Menninger, the dean of American psychiatry, long railed against psychiatric labelling.[33] In numerous writings and speeches, Dr. Thomas Szasz has criticized the application of the medical model to psychiatry. He tells his audiences that he does not diagnose or treat—he engages in conversation, and he "treats" everyone the same way, he listens and he talks.

One of the more frequent subjects of psychiatric expert opinion is "dangerousness."[34] A determination of "dangerousness" necessarily involves prediction. On this score it is said that psychiatrists, though students of human behavior, are notoriously poor predictors. The critics argue that the difficulty in reaching "correct diagnoses" explains what they see as the high error rate in psychiatric predictions. According to studies, psychiatrists err in the direction of false positives; that is, they are overly inclined to perceive individuals as "dangerous" and to recommend institutionalization. As dangerousness has a low base occurrence, the psychiatrist could make a good impression statistically with negatives. The high incidence of false positives, though often criticized, actually reveals a concern for public safety. On the other hand, when psychiatrists discharge an individual prematurely, they are equally criticized.

Should psychiatrists not testify, who would take their place? Will the witness be the outraged employer, the biased neighbor, the victim? Will there be *any* lay witnesses? A study by the Vera Institute of Justice found that as many as half the witnesses required to come to court for trial simply do not show up. Fear of and dislike for the process are often the stated reasons; but certainly a desire "not to get involved" makes potential witnesses behave like the three monkeys who hear no evil, see no evil, and speak no evil. "With a shooting in a bar," says a police officer, "you'll have 30 people tell you they were in the john at the same time." Thus, in any type of trial, witnesses are increasingly the paid witnesses, the expert witnesses.

Expert testimony is most effective when it augments the testimony of lay witnesses. The expert is useful in summarizing and pulling together the case for the fact finder (judge or jury). More often than not, the fact finder will reject expert testimony that is inconsistent with eyewitness testimony. The claim that experts are usurping the decision-making function of judge or jury is thus unfounded. Trials based solely on expert testimony, without the presentation of eyewitnesses, or "real people," are ridiculed as "dog and pony shows."

In criminal law, the controversy as to mental capacity or responsibility reduces to this: Under what banner will evidence of mental illness be presented, if at all, and what will be the consequences? For instance, under a plea of not guilty (rather than a plea of "NGRI," not guilty by reason of insanity), will an expert be allowed to testify that the defendant did not intend the consequences of his act or did not act volitionally? The courts have held that due process is not offended by a rule that the defendant, unless he pleads NGRI, cannot rebut evidence of intent by presentation of psychiatric testimony.[35] For example, the Tenth Circuit, in *United States v. Esch*,[36] held that in the absence of any legal claim of mental disease or defect, the trial judge is not obliged to but may exclude expert opinion as to the accused's capacity to form the mental state required to commit the offense charged.[37] Moreover, the court said that generalized testimony about the influence of personality traits is excludable as within the common knowledge and experience of lay jurors.[38]

In other words, experts may speak to abnormality but not to normality. The reason generally adduced for this is that the testimony is not helpful, or to put it differently, that the role of the judge and jury must not be usurped by experts unnecessarily testifying on matters within ordinary knowledge. In a case of provocation, the English Court of Appeal said:[39]

> We all know that both men and women who are deeply in love can, and sometimes do, have outbursts of blind rage when discovering unexpected wantonness on the part of their loved ones: the wife taken in adultery is the classical example of the application of the defence of "provocation"; and when death or serious injury results, profound grief usually follows. Jurors do not need psychiatrists to tell them how ordinary folk who are not suffering from any mental illness are likely to react to the stresses and strains of life.

Thus, evidence that an individual is not violent, but is susceptible to provocation in the "ordinary way," has been held inadmissible.[40] An expert witness cannot be an expert on the "ordinary man"—this is the exclusive province of the jury.[41] The jury is said not to need assistance of expert testimony as to, for example, the accused's ability to form the intent to commit the crime (so long as the accused does not fall into the "abnormal" category).[42] The law presumes that, absent evidence of insanity, we are all alike.[43] And, unless one pleads insanity, he is to be judged on the assumption that he has the same capacity as anyone else to determine whether an action is right or wrong, reasonable or unreasonable.

In addition to being "unhelpful," some courts have noted that psychiatric verbiage alone may usurp or supplant the jury's judgment by its capacity to mislead. Description of ordinary occurrences in orphic terms, or diagnostic labels, creates the danger of misleading the jury. The Second Circuit, in *United States v Bright*,[44] upheld the exclusion of testimony about defendant's "passive-dependent personality disorder" unaffected by psychosis or neurosis, reasoning that "couched in simpler language [the psychiatrist] was prepared to testify that appellant was a gullible person."[45] Likewise, instead of "antisocial personality," the expert might say "SOB," but street language, while understandable, would be a breach of decorum. To excuse his wild behavior, heavyweight boxing champion Mike Tyson claimed a diagnosis of manic-depressive. "I was born with this disease," he said. "I can't help it. Maybe that's why I'm successful at what I do."[46] But Dr. A.L. Halpern responded, "Tyson is not, and has never been, a manic-depressive.... The best thing for Tyson would be to get back in the ring."[47] The descriptive term "gorilla" apparently has fallen into disuse, but that might have been a more apt description.[48]

As people do not fit neatly into diagnostic categories, the "battle of experts" is often a "battle of categories." Somewhat tongue in cheek, it could be suggested that, as in the ranking of hotels, experts might use a one to five-star system. Thus, the expert might say, "the defendant is a one-star manic-depressive."

Courts concerned with usurpation of the judge's or jury's function by experts have also held that an expert's opinion on the law of criminal responsibility or insanity itself is considered of no aid to the jury, and could possibly confuse them. An expert witness may not provide a definition of these legal terms for the jury. Thus, a psychiatrist may not testify whether a diagnosis of antisocial or substance-abuse personality is a mental illness within the legal definition of mental illness.[49] However, when it is considered *helpful*, experts are called upon to explain or discuss the law. For example, testimony in the Bess Myerson trial in New York began with the prosecution's presentation of a law professor, who told the jury about divorce procedures in the state. In a session that seemed more like a seminar on matrimonial law than a criminal trial, the prosecutor elicited detailed legal explanations from the professor.[50]

In the same vein, as a rule, expert evidence on the credibility of a witness is not permitted, for the law assumes that it is part of the jury's role, and within its competency, to determine whether a witness' evidence is truthful or not. Thus, in a rape trial, if the prosecutor seeks to introduce psychiatric testimony to the effect that the complainant was limited in her mental capacity and would tend to tell the truth, such testimony will likely be regarded as inadmissible "oath-helping."[51] The law presumes credibility of witnesses, until attacked.[52]

The bar on credibility testimony, however, may be skirted by "consistent with" or "syndrome" evidence. Is the woman falsifying when she claims that she has been abused or raped? Is the child falsifying when she claims abuse? With some exception, courts have allowed an expert to testify that a woman's behavior is "consistent with" that of women who have been abused or raped, or that a child's behavior is "consistent with" behavior of children who have been abused. Indirectly, but in effect, the expert is testifying to the truthfulness of the complainant. While not explicitly directed at witness credibility, testimony that the complainant is or is not suffering rape trauma syndrome, battered woman syndrome, or child sexual abuse syndrome reflects on the credibility of the complainant.[53]

Although polygraph testimony is generally inadmissible, the psychiatric expert may be seen (by some) as an admissible "human lie detector." The "human lie detector" issue came before the intermediate appellate courts in Michigan in a number of cases where the question was, "Is it possible for a child like this to make a false charge?" In *People v Miller*,[54] where the defense sought to have an expert appointed, the request was denied because the purpose was to have the expert offer an opinion on the victim's credibility. In *People v Izzo*,[55] the court held that the trial court committed reversible error by allowing, over defense objection, a psychiatrist to testify that he believed the complainant's story. On the other hand, in another intermediate appellate court decision in Michigan, in *People v Stricklin*,[56] where the defense wished to admit the deposition testimony of a child psychologist that a sexually molested child would be likely to fantasize instances of sexual abuse, the trial judge denied the motion, holding that credibility was for the jury; but the appellate court disagreed. The appellate court held that while an expert cannot be used as a human lie detector, so long as the testimony was based on child development in general and not on the specific child's credibility, the testimony should have been admitted.

In sexual abuse litigation, the theory most frequently advanced by experts is the "sexually abused child syndrome."[57] The expert who recognizes in an alleged victim a certain constellation of symptoms and behaviors will extrapolate to the conclusion that the victim must have been sexually abused. For example, in a Minnesota case, *State v Myers*,[58] the expert described the behavior and symptoms typically exhibited by sexually abused children and the characteristics that the expert had observed in the complainant. The expert then concluded that, based upon the constellation of symptoms and noted behavior, the child had been abused. In *People v Beckley*,[59] the Michigan Court of Appeals held that an expert witness could testify that the actions of a child subsequent to an alleged act of sexual abuse were not inconsistent with those of sexually abused children, so long "as the expert did not give a personal opinion that the child victim was in fact telling the truth." This is, we would say, a roundabout way of attesting to the credibility of the complainant. As for the competency of the testimony, could not the same constellation of symptoms be caused by traumatic events and environmental stressors other than sexual abuse? Even Freud abandoned his early "seduction theory" (roughly, that women became hysterics because they suffered childhood abuse by their fathers) and concluded that they could have developed their hysteria even if they had not been so abused.

An issue arising across the country is whether an expert may testify that observation of a child's use of so-called anatomically correct dolls corroborates an allegation of sexual abuse. The intermediate appellate court in Michigan found this proper, where the witness had been a protective services worker for 10 years, had special training in abuse and neglect, and had extensive experience.[60] The use of anatomically correct dolls has been explicitly authorized by statute in Michigan, but it is subject to challenge.[61]

The majority of states which have considered the admissibility of expert testimony regarding the battered spouse syndrome where a self-defense claim is raised in a homicide trial have ruled such testimony admissible. The courts in these cases, where it is established that the woman has been abused, have allowed expert testimony under the rationale that expert testimony is needed in order to correct the commonsense notion that if the woman had really been beaten badly, over a period of time, she would have left long ago. The expert can explain why the woman would remain.[62] The testimony mimics the talk shows; lawyers call it the "Oprah" effect.[63]

Another "usurpation" or "helpfulness" issue involves the question whether an expert may testify *in general* about the ability of people accurately to observe and recollect. A controversial issue is whether expert testimony assessing eyewitness identification should be admissible evidence. In recent years, a number of defense lawyers in criminal cases have sought to introduce expert testimony with regard to the lack of reliability of eyewitness testimony in general.[64] Most courts have held that the admissibility of such evidence is within the discretion of the trial judge. The crux of these decisions is that such expert testimony comes within the scope of rule 702, and, thus, should not be excluded automatically. At least one federal court has reversed a conviction where the trial court state that such testimony is never admissible. The appellate court held that the judge must exercise his discretion as to the admissibility of such opinions under rule 702.[65] These courts have noted the acceptance of eyewitness identification evidence in the scientific community in recent years, and its possible helpfulness to a jury in explaining counter-intuitive factors that may not develop fully through cross-examination.[66]

Until recently, courts were uniformly skeptical about admitting expert testimony concerning the reliability, in general, of eyewitness identifications. They upheld exclusions of such testimony under a variety of rationales, such as that the evidence has not obtained a suitable level of acceptance in the legal and scientific communities; that the evidence is prejudicial; or that the evidence is within the expertise of the jury. Problems with perception and memory, these courts have said, are easily understood by jurors and can be adequately addressed through cross-examination.

In *United States v Affleck*,[67] the defense counsel argued that the trial judge erroneously prohibited a "memory expert" from testifying. In this case, the expert purportedly would have explained how well or how poorly people are able to remember events over the course of time and why they remember things in the way that they do. The court said: "Under [rule] 702, an expert may be allowed to testify if an untrained layman would not be able to make an intelligent evaluation of the evidence without such expert testimony. Specialized testimony, explaining memory, however, is improper. The average person is able to understand that people forget; thus, a faulty memory is a matter for cross-examination."

In *United States v Moore*,[68] defense counsel sought to counter eyewitness identifications by prosecution witnesses through the expert testimony of Dr. Elizabeth Loftus. Dr. Loftus would have testified about such theories as the "forgetting curve," which shows that memory decreases at a geometric rather than an arithmetic rate; the "assimilation factor," which indicates that witnesses sometimes incorporate inaccurate postevent information into their identifications; the "feedback factor," which demonstrates that witnesses who discuss the case with each other may unconsciously reinforce mistaken identifications; and several other psychological theories relating to eyewitness identification.[69] The trial judge excluded this testimony, stating that he felt the probativeness of eyewitness testimony was not a matter that needed evaluation by experts. The judge went on to say that in any event the admissibility of such testimony was within his discretion. On appeal, the Fifth Circuit said:[70]

> Expert testimony on eyewitness reliability is not simply a recitation of facts available through common knowledge. Indeed, the conclusions of the psychological studies are largely "counter-intuitive," and serve to "explode common myths about an individual's capacity for perception...." For example, it is commonly believed that the accuracy of a witness' recollection increases with the certainty of the witness. In fact, the data reveal no correlation between witness certainty and accuracy. Similarly, it is commonly believed that witnesses remember better when they are under stress. The data indicate that the opposite is true. The studies also show that a group consensus among witnesses as to an alleged criminal's identity is far more likely to be inaccurate than is an individual identification. This is because of the effect of the "feedback factor," which serves to reinforce mistaken identifications. We therefore recognize that the admission of this type of testimony is proper, at least in some cases.
>
> Nevertheless, in the present case we do not find that the district court abused its discretion in refusing to admit this evidence. We have earlier held and we now affirm that the decision whether to admit this testimony is squarely within the discretion of the trial judge and properly so.

A distinction is to be drawn between expert testimony on problems generally of perception and memory and expert testimony that would relate to the specific organic or emotional disorders of a particular witness, whose testimony is alleged to be unreliable on account of these disorders. Ofttimes in a police investigation, statements made by mentally disabled suspects are not so clearly unreliable as to require exclusion. In many cases, despite the fact that the court admits the statement into evidence, questions will remain about the reliability of the statement. The American Bar Association's recently drafted Criminal Justice Mental Health Standards recommend that expert testimony from mental health or mental retardation professionals should be permitted, to allow the fact finder to determine the extent to which the individual's mental disability may have undermined the credibility of the statement.[71] The U.S. Supreme Court, however, has not extended the constitutional rule against involuntary confessions to those statements which are "involuntary" in the sense that they are the product of the suspect's mental disability, but which do not involve coercion on the part of the police.

In *Colorado v Connelly*,[72] the U.S. Supreme Court held that a confession was admissible despite the fact that it was a product of the "command hallucinations" caused by the defendant's mental illness.[73] The majority concluded that to consider such a confession "involuntary" as a constitutional matter, without some form of coercive police conduct, would unduly infringe upon the evidence laws of the state. "[The determination of voluntariness or reliability] is a matter to be governed by the evidentiary laws of the forum," the Court said, "not by the Due Process Clause of the Fourteenth Amendment."[74]

The standards of the ABA recommend, however, the use of expert testimony not on the admissibility but on the reliability or credibility of a mentally disabled defendant's statements. The judge determines admissibility; the jury, credibility. The commentary states: "This allows the trier of fact to determine how much weight to assign to [the] statement."[75] One wonders, then, what degree of "mental competency" will be necessary to produce a credible statement? Putting aside the question of voluntariness, is it a credible statement when one personality of a multiple personality compels another of the personalities to make a confession?[76]

In the case of *Robertson v McCloskey*,[77] the plaintiff filed a defamation suit against the defendant, who allegedly stated that the plaintiff received a preferential transfer out of the battle zone during the Korean War by virtue of being the son of a congressman. Prior to trial, defendant moved to exclude the expert testimony of Dr. Matthew Erdelyi who purported to be an expert in "the psychodynamics of memory and perception." Dr. Erdelyi was to testify that the accuracy of memory dims with time and that in many instances a person can reconstruct or even fabricate the details of a complex event that took place long ago. The suggestion being that the trier of fact should treat the uncorroborated recollection of witnesses about events that occurred in 1950–51 with "considerable caution."

In this case Judge Joyce Hens Green granted defendant's motion to exclude. While acknowledging Dr. Erdelyi's ample qualifications in the field of psychology, Judge Green concluded that his testimony failed to meet the second prong of rule 702, that is, helpfulness to the jury. In the court's view, much of his testimony lay within the ken of the average juror, would be limited to generalities, and would provoke time-consuming rebuttal.[78] Moreover, under the *Frye* test, Judge Green pointed out, plaintiff failed to show that the psychodynamics of memory and perception are sufficiently established to have gained general acceptance in the field.[79] Judge Green wrote, "The cases plaintiff relies on all deal with eyewitness identification, a narrowly defined field that has arisen in order to assure the reliability of criminal convictions; they do not support his assertion that memory and perception experts have been allowed to testify in the federal courts."[80] In sum, Judge Green concluded that the commonsense nature of the testimony, the relevancy problem, the likely confusion and delay engendered by competing experts, and the questionable scientific reliability of the testimony all lead to the conclusion that the testimony would not assist the jury.

In the much-noted decision in 1950 in *United States v Hiss*,[81] the defense on retrial was allowed to present psychiatric testimony that the government witness, Whittaker Chambers, was a "psychopath with a tendency toward making false accusations." Alger Hiss, nonetheless, was convicted.[82] In *Hiss*, the expert testified about a *particular* witness with regard to a *particular* event. In that case, the court, as have other courts, relaxed the standards for admissibility because of its concern for the constitutional rights of a defendant who must rebut charges based on eyewitness identification. The court noted that the outcome of the case depended upon whether the jury believed Chambers, and then cited authority to support the proposition that "the existence of insanity or mental derangement is admissible for the purpose of discrediting a witness."[83]

The courts have divided on that proposition, both before and after *Hiss*, with the majority saying that the testimony is not helpful. The courts allowing the testimony tend to do so because they do not wish to risk reversal of a conviction. Quite often, the courts admit evidence offered by the defense that they would not admit if offered by the prosecution. An example is the admission of the CAT scan by the defense in the Hinckley case.[84] In a Florida case, *Hawkins v State*,[85] the defense psychiatrist would have testified that the complainant did not always tell the truth and had paranoid tendencies. The testimony was excluded at trial, but the state appellate court said that the testimony would have been relevant and admissible for the purpose of discrediting the complainant's credibility, holding it was reversible error not to allow it. Other cases have suggested support for the same proposition.[86]

More often than not, however, courts have rejected psychiatric testimony on witness credibility as an invasion of the province of the jury. By way of illustration, in *United States v Bernard*,[87] the defense offered psychiatric testimony that a key prosecution witness was a sociopath who would lie when it was to his advantage. The evidence was excluded on the ground that it might cause the jurors to abandon their own common sense in determining witness credibility.[88] In *United States v Daileda*,[89] the court held inadmissible psychiatric testimony that a key prosecution witness was a psychopath who was capable of lying, who lacked guilt feelings, and who would lie under the circumstances of the case. Such testimony, said the court, would have invaded the province of the jury.

On the other side of the "helpfulness" coin are those cases that cannot go to trial *without* expert testimony. In almost every case of medical or other professional malpractice, expert testimony for plaintiff is mandatory, not permissive. With few exceptions, the law traditionally has allowed the medical profession to establish its own liability standards. Hence, the plaintiff must prove through expert testimony that the care or skill exercised by a defendant physician was below that exercised by comparable professionals in the community. Even apart from deference to the profession as to standards, courts also have said that expert testimony is necessary in medical malpractice actions because an understanding of the issues of negligence and causation in these cases is ordinarily beyond the knowledge of laymen.[90]

This protective, provider-defined standard of care obliges the plaintiff to produce expert testimony; and in the absence of expert testimony, the defendant physician is entitled to summary disposition. It might be noted that the cost of expert testimony is a significant limitation on the proliferation of malpractice cases. Plaintiffs' attorneys are reluctant to take expensive, risky cases on a contingency fee basis. Were it not necessary to produce expert testimony, these cases would occur with much greater frequency. The more litigation costs, the less litigation there is.

The growing use of the "professional expert," however, has brought a demand for tightening the qualifications of an expert witness, especially in medical malpractice cases.[91] Unquestionably, there are experts who have no business in the courtroom—or, some say, in their own profession. Judge Weinstein put it this way:[92]

> An expert can be found to testify to the truth of almost any factual theory, no matter how frivolous, thus validating the case sufficiently to avoid summary judgment and force the matter to trial. At the trial itself an expert's testimony can be used to obfuscate what would otherwise be a simple case. The most tenuous factual bases are sufficient to produce firm opinions to a high degree of "medical (or other expert) probability" or even of "certainty." Juries and judges can be, and sometimes are, misled by the expert-for-hire.

The Fleming report on tort reform in Michigan, while recognizing the problem, advised against new legislation on the qualification of expert witnesses. It stated: "It is to the clear advantage of the lawyer to use the best and most credible witness [as] inexpert witnesses are not usually difficult to expose." It added, "When one weighs the advantages of mandating the degree of experience required of a witness versus allowing the judge to rule on whether a given witness can qualify as an expert, the virtue of a new requirement is not readily apparent."[93]

However, the Michigan Legislature, pressured by the medical profession, set out criteria, to wit: In cases involving a specialist, the expert must have specialized at the time of the occurrence in the same or a related specialty, and must have devoted, at the time of the occurrence, a substantial portion of his time to practicing or teaching.[94] Previously the expert was not required, as a matter of law, to be of the same specialty as the defendant; thus, a psychiatrist could testify against a psychologist. Michigan and some other states in recent legislation also set out a prescreening provision, which requires that any medical malpractice suit be certified as meritorious by a physician of the same specialty. Inasmuch as the plaintiff must obtain an expert for trial, the effect of the provision is merely to require an earlier retention of the expert.

Attorneys representing plaintiffs in Michigan and elsewhere complain with increasing frequency about the difficulty in obtaining reputable experts. Meanwhile, hospitals pressure physicians on their staff not to consult with plaintiff attorneys on medical malpractice cases. Actually, the professional who testifies occasionally as an expert witness presents more of a problem to the judicial system than the one who testifies frequently. By familiarity, judges and lawyers know the expert who lacks credibility. He can readily be discredited on cross-examination. They know the professionals "who can find a spasm in a statue." It is to be noted that more than 95% of tort cases are settled out of court. The insurance companies as well as the attorneys are familiar with the professional expert and they give little credence to a report prepared by an expert lacking credibility.[95] In contradistinction, the professional who testifies frequently and has credibility is more of an asset to the judicial process than is the professional who testifies infrequently.

Distinct from, and running somewhat counter to, the requirements of "helpfulness" was the traditional rule that an expert was not permitted to give an opinion on the ultimate issue or issues to be decided by a jury. The theory was that such would invade the province of the jury. To use the highway metaphor, the expert could travel near, but not to, the ultimate destination. However, in complex cases involving issues beyond the ken of laymen, a judge or jury may need an expert's opinion on the ultimate issue in order to reach a fair verdict. A review of the jurisprudence indicates an erosion of the ultimate issue doctrine. Opinions on the issues of identity, value, competency or insanity, for instance, all border on ultimate fact issues, yet are generally held admissible. Indeed, more often than not, an expert would not be considered "helpful" if he did not have or would not give an opinion on the ultimate issue. In *Sears, Roebuck & Co. v Haven Hills Farm*,[96] a products liability case, the Alabama Supreme Court not only allowed, but required expert testimony on the ultimate issue of defect.

The Federal Rules of Evidence, as adopted in 1975, and their counterparts in the various states expressly allow expert testimony to embrace an ultimate issue of fact, so long as it is helpful to the trier of fact. Rule 704 abolished the common law "ultimate issue rule." According to the Advisory Committee's notes, the common law rule forbidding that type of testimony "was unduly restrictive, difficult of application, and generally served only to deprive the trier of fact of useful information." Efforts to avoid that prohibition "led to odd verbal circumlocutions which were said not to violate the rule," the committee said. "Thus a witness could express his estimate of the criminal responsibility of an accused in terms of sanity or insanity, but not in terms of ability to tell right from wrong or other more modern standards."[97]

But the abolition of the ultimate issue rule does not mean that all opinions of an expert will be permitted. Since usurpation is still a concern, experts are not allowed to offer opinions embodying legal conclusions. It is for the jury to evaluate the facts in the light of the applicable rules of law. In other words, it is not for the expert to say how the case should be decided. Thus the question, "Did the testator have capacity to make a will?" would be excluded, while the question, "Did the testator have sufficient mental capacity to know the nature and extent of his property and natural objects of his bounty and to formulate a rational scheme of distribution?" would be allowed. The latter opinion would be helpful to the fact finder, the former would be a usurpation of function.

Under rule 704, an expert may voice an opinion only as to the ultimate *factual* issues, not as to the ultimate *legal* issues. The Fifth Circuit said, "Rule 704...does not open the door to all opinions.... [Q]uestions which would merely allow the witness to tell the jury what result to reach are not permitted. Nor is the rule intended to allow a witness to give *legal* conclusions."[98] Louisiana, in a code of evidence adopted in 1988, provides that a witness' opinion is not to be excluded solely because it relates to the ultimate issue in the case, except that, the rule adds with unnecessary but distinct emphasis, "no opinion is allowed as to the guilt or innocence of an accused."[99]

Should psychiatric testimony be excluded merely because it leads to a clash of opinions? Evidence may be excluded, under rule 403, if "its probative value is substantially outweighed by the danger of unfair prejudice, confusion of the issues, or misleading the jury, or by considerations of undue delay, waste of time, or needless presentation of cumulative evidence."[100] Judge Kaufman, writing for the Second Circuit, said that "the unique character of the insanity defense militates against exclusion on the sole ground that the jury would be confused by the clashing opinions of experts." Judge Kaufman went on to state: "In making this legal and moral judgment, the jury should not be shielded from differences of opinion in a profession that can never be entirely devoid of subjective disagreements. Psychiatric testimony should not be excluded solely as a result of an unfounded belief that a jury will not be able to separate the wheat from the chaff."[101] Two years later Judge Pierce of the Second Circuit wrote, "The mere fact that there may be conflicting testimony by experts is not a sufficient basis to exclude such evidence. Indeed, not uncommonly, there is conflict among experts on most any subject."[102]

In *Ake v Oklahoma*,[103] the U.S. Supreme Court said, "Psychiatrists ideally assist lay jurors, who generally have no training in psychiatric matters, to make a sensible and educated determination about the mental condition of the defendant at the time of the offense." The court ruled that the indigent criminal defendant is entitled to a state-provided psychiatrist to examine him and to assist in the preparation of an insanity defense once a threshold showing that such assistance might be helpful is met.

However, in 1984, in the wake of the Hinckley trial and a consequent widespread disenchantment with psychiatric testimony, the federal law on opinion evidence, rule 704, was amended by adding subsection (*b*). The amendment—part of the Comprehensive Crime Control Act of 1984[104]—provides that an expert may testify only as to the defendant's mental disease or defect and the characteristics of such a condition, and may not offer a conclusion as to whether that condition rendered the defendant unable to appreciate the nature and quality of the wrongfulness of his act.[105] Under the amended rule, the latter is an "ultimate issue" to be determined solely by the jury on the basis of the evidence presented.[106] The original rule 704 is now rule 704(a). Rule 704, as amended, reads:

> (*a*) Except as provided in subdivision (*b*), testimony in the form of an opinion or inference otherwise admissible is not objectionable because it embraces an ultimate issue to be decided by the trier of fact.
>
> (*b*) No expert witness testifying with respect to the mental state or condition of a defendant in a criminal case may state an opinion or inference as to whether the defendant did or did not have the mental state or condition constituting an element of the crime charged or of a defense thereto. Such ultimate issues are matters for the trier of fact alone.

Authorities on the law of evidence say that the rationale for subsection (*b*) is that "insanity involves a legal (moral), not a medical, issue, and therefore, no matter how the test for insanity is phrased, a psychiatrist or psychologist is no more qualified than any other person to give an opinion whether a particular defendant's mental condition satisfied the legal test for insanity."[107] The legislative history explains:[108]

> The purpose of this amendment is to eliminate the confusing spectacle of competing expert witnesses testifying to directly contradictory conclusions as to the ultimate legal issue to be found by the trier of fact. Under this proposal, expert psychiatric testimony would be limited to presenting and explaining their diagnoses, such as whether the defendant had a severe mental disease or defect and what the characteristics of such a disease or defect, if any, may have been. The basis for this limitation on expert testimony in insanity cases is ably stated by the American Psychiatric Association:
>
>> [I]t is clear that psychiatrists are experts in medicine, not the law. As such, it is clear that the psychiatrist's first obligation and expertise in the courtroom is to "do psychiatry," i.e., to present medical information and opinion about the defendant's mental state and motivation and to explain in detail the reason for his medical-psychiatric conclusions. When, however, "ultimate issue" questions are formulated by the law and put to the expert witness who must then say "yea" or "nay," then the expert witness is required to make a leap in logic. He no longer addresses himself to medical concepts but instead must infer or intuit what is in fact unspeakable, namely, the probable relationship between medical concepts and legal or moral constructs such as free will. These impermissible leaps in logic made by expert witnesses confuse the jury...Juries thus find themselves listening to conclusory and seemingly contradictory psychiatric testimony that defendants are either "sane" or "insane" or that they do or do not meet the relevant legal test for insanity. This state of affairs does considerable injustice to psychiatry and, we believe, possibly to criminal defendants. In fact, in many criminal insanity trials both prosecution and defense psychiatrists do agree about the nature and even the

> extent of mental disorder exhibited by the defendant at the time of the act.

Long before this change in the law, in the 1967 decision in *Washington v United States*,[109] the District of Columbia Circuit said:[110]

> [T]here is no justification for permitting psychiatrists to testify on the ultimate issue. Psychiatrists should explain how defendant's disease or defect relates to his alleged offense, that is, how the development, adaptation and functioning of defendant's behavioral processes may have influenced his conduct.

How broad is the prohibition of amended rule 704? The legislative history indicates that the amendment was fashioned to preclude "ultimate opinion psychiatric testimony" on the mental state of the defendant in a wide variety of contexts beyond the insanity defense. It was stated: "The rationale for precluding ultimate opinion psychiatric testimony extends beyond the insanity defense to any ultimate mental state of the defendant that is relevant to the legal conclusion sought to be proven."[111] The rule, applicable to both the government and the defendant, prohibits an expert testifying on the ultimate issue with respect to either the existence of a mental element of a crime (a specific intent) or a defense based on a mental condition.[112]

Some recent cases interpret the range of rule 704(*b*) narrowly, while others give it broad scope.[113] In cases where a defense of entrapment is raised, one issue is whether the defendant was predisposed to commit the crime in question. In rebuttal to a defense of entrapment, the prosecutor may show any prior similar criminal conduct of the defendant as well as prior criminal convictions. If the defendant is predisposed to commit the offense, no defense of entrapment exists, even if, for example, in a case involving contraband, a government agent supplies it. Under rule 704(*b*), expert opinion would be precluded upon the question of whether the defendant lacked the predisposition to commit a crime.[114] The restriction is applied in the entrapment context because so much of entrapment is a "mental state or condition" (predisposition or lack of it), and the Senate Note says as much.[115] It seems, however, that rule 704(*b*) should not bar testimony by a psychiatrist about defendant's "susceptibility to influence." Legal scholars say the "susceptibility" is at least one step removed from "predisposition"—a person could be "susceptible" and still not be "predisposed," thus being guilty as charged (rather than not guilty because his criminal act was caused by overly aggressive enforcement efforts.)[116] In *United States v Hill*,[117] the Third Circuit held that the trial judge erred in refusing to allow the defendant to call a clinical psychologist to testify about the defendant's psychological characteristics, subnormal intelligence, and resulting susceptibility to persuasion and psychological pressure regarding his entrapment defense.

The trial of kidnapped heiress Patricia Hearst for alleged bank robbery was a preamendment rule 704 case. There a psychiatrist and a psychologist gave testimony to rebut the defense of duress, stating that Hearst "did not perform the bank robbery because she was in fear of her life," but did it "as a voluntary member of the SLA," and that she "entered that bank voluntarily in order to participate" as "an act of her own free will."[118] Under the amended rule 704(*b*), however, testimony by a psychiatrist or psychologist that a young woman acted "of her own free will" and "voluntarily" would give rise to objection. As these mental qualities are the precise opposite of "duress," testimony directly describing those qualities seems to be what rule 704(*b*) was intended to prevent. According to law commentators, the experts might still testify, however, that defendant seemed "strong" or "determined" or "weak" or "depressed," qualities which bear on the issue while being a step removed from the standard to be applied.[119]

In the prosecution of Captain MacDonald for the alleged murder of his wife and children, a psychiatrist's testimony was offered to support the defense theory that another person committed the crime. The proffered psychiatric testimony that the defendant had a "personality configuration inconsistent with the outrageous and senseless murders of [his] family" was excluded as confusing and misleading under rule 403,[120] but rule 704(*b*) apparently would not bar this kind of evidence. Testimony about a "personality configuration" is character evidence, well removed from intent or lack of it. A psychiatrist would not appear to violate rule 704(*b*) if he testified that the defendant was capable of "loving" or "caring" for people, which presumably would make it less likely that he committed a heinous crime.[121] The court, however, may exclude the expert's testimony as addressing a subject matter within the knowledge and experience of the jury and therefore not meeting the helpfulness criterion of rule 702.[122]

Can expert testimony about mental illness be severed from testimony about the capacity to have and decide among options, such as judging between right and wrong (or ability to conform conduct to the law, where that is the test of criminal responsibility)? Will the fact finder be competent to draw inferences from the mass of psychiatric data? U.S. Attorney Rudolph Giuliani of Manhattan, in a statement in the reform hearings, said, "It would be all gobbledy-gook without the psychiatrist drawing a conclusion as to what he's saying."[123] The Senate Judiciary Committee, however, drawing upon the aforementioned statement of the American Psychiatric Association, traced jury confusion to "leaps in logic" made by experts testifying about ultimate issues.[124]

It remains to be seen whether the courts will extend the rule 704(*b*) prohibition to opinions that "go to the very brink," that is, opinions so closely related to the ultimate issue that they indirectly communicate to the jury the expert's opinion on the ultimate issue.[125] In a rape case, where the insanity defense is raised, would an expert be allowed to testify that at the time of the rape, the accused believed that he was merely dreaming, or did not understand that he was actually having intercourse, or did not understand the nature of the act?[126]

The Senate Subcommittee on Criminal Law explored a hypothetical: A mother on trial for her son's murder claims that she thought she was killing Satan. She asserts the insanity defense, claiming that she was unable to appreciate the nature and quality or wrongfulness of her actions. During the discussion of this hypothetical, Dr. Seymour Halleck stated that the psychiatrist's function is to explore the mother's mental state and to report, if his finding confirmed it, that she truly mistook her victim's identity. Senator Specter then asked, "But if you find that she thought she was killing the devil, would you not necessarily find that she did not know what she was doing or that she did not intend to kill her child? She was intending to kill the devil."[127] Would a court allow the opinion that the mother intended to kill Satan, but exclude the opinion that she did not intend to kill her son? Could the expert testify that the mother believed she was killing Satan, or that she did not understand that she was killing her child, but not that she failed to understand the nature and quality or wrongfulness of her act? That would be a distinction without a difference.[128]

The application of rule 704(*b*) in any given case involves substantial judicial discretion. Quite likely, as the jurisprudence to date indicates, rule 704(*b*) will be interpreted to prohibit only opinions incorporating the statutory language of the insanity defense.[129] In *United States v Edwards*,[130] the Eleventh Circuit observed:

> Every actual fact concerning the defendant's mental condition is still as admissible after the enactment of Rule 704(*b*) as it was before.... [T]he Rule "changes the style of question and answer that can be used to establish both the offense and the defense thereto." ...The prohibition is directed at a narrowly and precisely defined evil.... Rule 704(*b*) forbids only "conclusions as to the ultimate legal issue to be found by the trier of fact."

In *Edwards*, over objection, the government expert testified that people who are not insane can nevertheless become frantic over a financial crisis. The prosecution called the expert to dispute the defense psychiatrist's diagnosis.[131] The government's expert explained why the defendant's behavior—his frantic efforts to pay bills, his manifestations of energy, his lack of sleep, and his feelings of depression—did not necessarily indicate an active manic state. The court concluded, "We think that the doctor played exactly the kind of role which Congress contemplated for the expert witness."[132]

Commentators of the law of evidence have pointed out that rule 704(*b*) is an unnecessary addition to the rules of evidence. Judges can rely on other rules in the law of evidence (rules 403 and 702) to minimize jury confusion and to ensure that expert testimony assists the trier of fact. As with other types of evidence, the judge has the discretion to exclude expert testimony if he finds that its probative value is substantially outweighed by its prejudicial effect, or that its admission would confuse the issues, or create needless delay or waste of judicial resources.[133] The application of rule 704(*b*) to a wide variety of contexts other than the insanity defense is also redundant in view of the traditional law that psychiatric testimony can be offered on *mens rea* only when an insanity plea is entered.

In actual fact, rule 704(*b*) makes expert witnesses less useful to fact finders. It promotes indirect and incomplete testimony, obscures a clear summation of the psychiatric viewpoint, and promotes form of expression over substance. Ultimately, the rule simply ignores the principle that the touchstone in the law of expert evidence is helpfulness.

REFERENCES

1. Curren W, McGarry AL, Shah SA (eds.): *Forensic Psychiatry and Psychology: Perspectives and Standards for Interdisciplinary Practice*. Philadelphia: F.A. Davis, 1986; Brooks, RE: Expert witness, used properly, can expedite fact-finding process. *National Law J*, Sept. 5, 1988, p 20; Miller N: Selecting expert witnesses with litigation savvy. *National Law J*, Oct. 24, 1988, p 44.
2. *In re* Japanese Elect. Prods. Antitrust Litig., 723 F.2d 238 (3d Cir. 1983); *Garbincius v Boston Edison Co.*, 621 F.2d 1171 (1st Cir. 1980).
3. *Spruill v Commonwealth*, 221 Va. 475, 271 S.E.2d 419 (1980).
4. *Ralph v Mr. Paul's Shoes*, 572 S.W.2d 812 (Texas 1978).
5. *Fitzgerald v Manning*, 679 F.2d 341, 350 (4th Cir. 1982); Musslewhite DC: Medical causation testimony in Texas: Possibility versus probability. *Sw Law J* 1969; 23:622. When first asked to express an opinion based upon reasonable medical certainty whether the accident was the competent producing cause of plaintiff's hernia, the expert answered, "It could be. I couldn't say." Pressed further, all he would say was that "it would be about a 90 percent chance that it was caused by [the accident] and 10 percent it wasn't." The court said, "However favorable such odds might seem in some game of chance, a trial is not such a game, and an award of damages cannot be allowed to rest upon speculation and conjecture of that character.... .On this record the jury might or could solve the problem solely by guessing." *Bertram v Wunning*, 385 S.W. 2d 803 (Mo. App. 1965). "Psychological evidence based on possibility is no less speculative and conjectural than like testimony by other experts. Just as we require medical opinions to be based on reasonable medical certainty, so do we require that psychological opinions be based on reasonable psychological certainty." *In re* Interest of D.L.S., 432 N.W.2d 31 (Neb. 1988). *See* Diamond BL: Reasonable medical certainty, diagnostic thresholds, and definitions of mental illness in the legal context. *Bull Am Acad Psychiatry Law* 1985; 13:121; Rappeport J: Reasonable medical certainty, *Id.* at 5.
6. At one time Michigan had a "*res gestae* witness rule" that required the prosecutor to produce in court, and to call to the stand, all witnesses to some event in the continuum of the criminal transaction. The underlying rationale was that, by requiring the prosecution to present the entire transaction, the rule facilitated the search for truth. The litigation costs of the requirement were enormous, as evidenced by the several hundred appellate decisions dealing with issues such as the definition of a *res gestae* witness, the prosecutor's use of due diligence to locate such witnesses, and the prejudice, if any, resulting from the prosecutor's failure to follow the rule's sometimes ambiguous dictates. And, by requiring the prosecutor to call to the stand even adverse witnesses, the rule often contributed to jury confusion. Although the prosecutor could impeach adverse witnesses, the impeachment often did not erase the impression that the prosecutor either had not prepared for trial or simply did not have a case. Grano JD: Implementing the objectives of procedural reform: The proposed Michigan Rules of Criminal Procedure—Part II. *Wayne Law Rev* 1986; 32:1335 at 1396, Gordon RA: Death of the *res gestae* witness rule. *Mich Bar J*, March 1988, p 282.
7. *Arch Crim Psychodynamics* 1959; 3:221.
8. 63 *Mich L Rev* 1965 1335. *See also* Slovenko, R: The opinion rule and Wittgenstein's Tractatus. *U Miami Law Rev* 1959; 14:1 (revised). 24 *ETC.: A Review of General Semantics* 289–303, 1967.
9. Quoted in Wren CS: Italian Reds in visit to Soviet dissident. *New York Times*, Jan. 30, 1977, p 7.
10. Simon J: The Ophuls truth. *National Review*, Dec.30, 1988, p 52.
11. *See* Mahony PJ: *Freud as a Writer*. New Haven, Yale University Press, 1987.
12. "Oh, History," Carl Becker once noted, with puckish piety, "How many truths are committed in thy name!"

13. Goldstein RL: Psychiatrists in the hot seat: Discrediting doctors by impeachment of their credibility. *Bull Amer Acad Psychiatry Law* 1988; 16:225. In one Louisiana case, the expert had just expressed his opinion that the claimant was not suffering from post-traumatic neurosis but was, instead, a malingerer. The attorney asked: "Is that your conclusion that this man is a malingerer?" To which the expert replied, "I wouldn't be testifying if I didn't think so, unless I was on the other side, then it would be a post-traumatic condition." *Ladner v Higgins*, 71 So.2d 242, 244 (La. App. 1954), noted in Slovenko R: The lawyer and the forensic expert: Boundaries of ethical practice. Behav Sci & Law 1987 5:119
14. I owe this observation to Dr. Emanuel Tanay.
15. Belli M: "The expert witness: Modifying roles and rules to meet today's needs. 18 *Trial* 35, 1988.
16. "[There are] five sorts of professional persons, to whom the denomination of experts is applied, and of whose evidence the substance is reported. Locksmiths, to explain the nature of a master-key, known to have been in his possession, and its relation to other keys belonging to the same locks. Cutlers, to say whether there was any relation between a knife found upon the person of the defendant, and another knife which appeared to have been made use of in his committing the murder, but had been found in another place. Peruke-makers, to say whether a few hairs, that had been found in the clenched hand of the deceased, might have been the defendant's, and plucked from his head. Washerwomen, to make a comparison between the shirts and neckcloths of the defendant, and a bloody shirt and neckcloth that appeared to have belonged to the murdered, and to have been stained with blood, in the course and the struggle. Rope-makers, to say whether there was any resemblance between some cords that had been found in the possession of the defendant, and a strange cord which, it was thought, might have been made use of, or provided for the purpose of the murder." *Causes Celebres* 3:309, quoted in Bentham J: *Rationale of Judicial Evidence* 37–38 London, Hunt & Clarke, 1827.
17. *United States v Johnson*, 575 F.2d 1347 (5th Cir. 1978); *People v Boyd*, 65 Mich. App. 11, 236 N.W.2d 744 (1975); Anno., 95 A.L.R.3d 978 (1979).
18. *State v Briner*, 198 Neb. 766, 255 N.W.2d 422 (1977).
19. *Cross v Lakeview Center*, 529 So. 2d 307 (Fla. App. 1988).
20. Rule 703, Federal Rules of Evidence. In Australia, on the other hand, there must be evidence of a "profession or course of study" and of "an organised branch of knowledge in which the witness is an expert," and there must be no reliance on "hearsay knowledge of other incidents." Eggleston R: *Evidence, Proof and Probability*. London, Weidenfeld & Nicolson, ed 2, 1983; Humphrey GF: The law and science. *Med Law* 1988; 7:307.
21. Quoted in Cooney JE: Rising courtroom use of expert witness creates controversy. *Wall Street Journal*, April 20, 1971, p 1.
22. *See*, e.g., Faust D, Ziskin J: The expert witness in psychology and psychiatry. *Science*, July 1, 1988, p 31; discussed in Goleman D: psychologists' expert testimony called unscientific. *The New York Times*, Oct. 11, 1988, p 19. The Faust & Ziskin article in *Science* was the featured lead article. Apparently the only other article on the subject published in *Science*—On being sane in insane places—by David Rosenhan, Jan. 19, 1973, vol 84, p 442—was also a highly critical piece. For a critique of the Rosenhan article, see the discussion by Dr. Robert Wallerstein in the *Bull Menninger Clinic* 1973; 37:526. Dr. Bernard Diamond at the 1988 annual meeting of the American Academy of Psychiatry and Law in a presentation—The image and role of the forensic psychiatrist—questioned whether *Science* was scientific in its selection of articles.
23. Washington Mayor Marion Barry, when under fire for links to a drug suspect, said, "It would be inconsistent with my character, with my integrity, with my veracity, to be involved in such activity or to be around such persons who would knowingly do this." Quoted in Pianin, E, Sherwood, T: Mayor under fire for links to drug suspect. *Detroit News*, Dec. 30, 1988, p 4.

24. Advisory Committee's Note to Federal Rules of Evidence, Rule 405. In *State v Christensen*, 628 P.2d 580 (Ariz. 1981), the appellate court ruled that it was error to exclude psychiatric testimony on behalf of defendant that defendant (charged with killing his wife) had a character trait of impulsive response to stress (a marital argument) since such would help negate the charge of a premeditated plan to kill his wife. In *State v Gonzales*, 681 P.2d 1368 (Ariz. 1984), expert testimony that a rape defendant was retarded was admitted to explain why he failed to seek assistance for the victim while rape was occurring at the hands of alleged cohorts. In *State v Hood*, 346 N.W.2d 481 (Iowa 1984), it was held error to exclude expert testimony of "passive-dependent personality" offered to negate evidence that the accused had the requisite intent to kill her husband. *See* Curran WJ: Expert psychiatric testimony of personality traits. *U Pa Law Rev* 1955; 103:999; Roll S, Foote WE: The inconsistent personality defense, in Muller DJ, Blackman DE, Chapman AJ: *Psychology and Law*. New York, Wiley, 1984, pp 125–132. A number of other courts have been less receptive to such evidence. The usual ruling is that the probative value of the testimony is outweighed by "the danger of unfair prejudice, confusion of the issues, or misleading the jury." Federal Rules of Evidence, Rule 403. In *United States v Webb*, 625 F.2d 709 (5th Cir. 1980), the defendant offered expert testimony of his nonviolent personality to show that it was not likely defendant shot at helicopters over his land. The court said, "Although these days even the most obvious of phenomena [seem to] admit of 'expert' analysis, the opinion rule does not bend so far." See also *United States v MacDonald*, 688 F.2d 224 (4th Cir. 1982), *cert. denied*, 459 U.S. 1103 (1983) ("personality configuration" of defendant allegedly inconsistent with that needed to commit the senseless and violent murder of his family); *United States v Staggs*, 553 F.2d 1073 (7th Cir. 1977) (aggressive tendency toward self rather than others offered on issue of whether defendant had intent to instill fear when he picked up the gun); *United States v West*, 670 F.2d 675 (7th Cir. 1982) (low intelligence offered to show defendant did not know car was a bribe). In criminal cases the accused has the option as to whether to open the door to evidence of "a pertinent trait of character" for the purpose of proving action in conformity therewith on a particular occasion. Federal Rules of Evidence, Rule 404.

    In Woody Allen's play, *Death*, a psychiatrist is asked: "Can you ever really know a person? I mean, know him—not know about him, but know—I mean, actually know him—where you know him—I'm talking about knowing a person—you know what I mean by knowing? Knowing. Really knowing. To know. Know. To know." Allen W: *Without Feathers*. New York, Warner Books, 1976, p 72. In Woody Allen's film *Another Woman*, a college professor discovers she isn't the woman she thought she was.
25. Steinbock DJ, Richman WM, Ray EE: Expert testimony on proximate cause. *Vand Law Rev* 1988; 41:261.
26. *Palsgraf v Long Island R.R. Co.*, 248 N.Y. 339, 162 N.E. 99 (1928). Judge Cooke, in *Derdiarian v Felix Contracting Corp.*, 51 N.Y.2d 308, 314, 414 N.E.2d 666, 670, 434 N.Y.S.2d 166, 169 (N.Y. Ct. App. 1980), stated: "The concept of proximate cause, or more appropriately legal cause, has proven to be an elusive one, incapable of being precisely defined to cover all situations.... This is, in part, because the concept stems from policy considerations that serve to place manageable limits upon the liability that flows from negligent conduct.... Depending upon the nature of the case, a variety of factors may be relevant in assessing legal cause. Given the unique nature of the inquiry in each case, it is for the finder of fact to determine legal cause, once the court has been satisfied that a *prima facie* case has been established. To carry the burden of proving a *prima facie* case, the plaintiff must generally show that the defendant's negligence was a substantial cause of the events which produced the injury."
27. James McElhaney, professor of trial advocacy, writes: "Within the limits of relevance and the constraints of ethics, the lawyer as playwright decides whether and how the trial will be a fascinating experience that will keep the judge and the jury on the edge of their

seats, or a turgid, stultifying affair that will leave everyone in a stupor." McElhaney J: Creating tension. *ABAJ*, June 1, 1988, p 84.

28. Russell R. Leggett, the judge at the trial (now in private practice), expressed the belief that had a jury been given the option of convicting Mrs. Harris of manslaughter, they would have done so and he could have sentenced her to four years rather than the required minimum of 15 for murder. He believes the fault lay not with her lawyer at the trial, Joel Aurnou, but with Mrs. Harris, who refused to allow psychiatric testimony that would have enabled her to seek a manslaughter charge to be introduced. Quoted in Kleiman D: After serving half her term, Jean Harris asks clemency. *The New York Times*, Dec. 8, 1988, p 18.
29. Burton M. Leiser, a professor of philosophy and law, puts it this way: "[I]f the cases have some of the same elements that attract people to melodrama, they also meet important social goals by focusing people's attention on the feelings deep inside themselves that they fear. That is one of the purposes of public trials where people can get a view of the darker side of life. It helps us purge some of the emotions we sometimes have ourselves because we can watch it played out in someone else's life." Quoted in Glaberson W: What compels public interest in Nussbaum? *New York Times*, Dec. 9, 1988, p 17.
30. See Faust D, Ziskin J: *op cit supra*, note 22.
31. Personal communication from Steven Kivari, Nov. 23, 1987.
32. Address at the 21st anniversary meeting of ASAP.
33. Menninger K: *The Vital Balance/The Life Process in Mental Health and Illness*. New York, Viking, 1963.
34. Questions about dangerousness are asked in setting bail, in waiving juveniles charged with serious crimes to adult courts, in sentencing decisions with respect to probation supervision or imprisonment, in decisions concerning civil commitment, in cases involving "sex psychopaths" or "defective delinquents," in sentencing for "habitual offenders," in decisions about the release from confinement of incarcerated offenders, and in the imposition of the death penalty. Dallas psychiatrist James Grigson's inevitable diagnoses in the sentencing phase of death penalty cases of individuals convicted of murder as dangerous sociopaths has earned him the label Dr. Death, but is he wrong or right? Applebome P: Aftermath of "Blue Line": New trial for convict. *The New York Times*, Dec. 8, 1988, p 20.
35. *See, e.g., United States v Gold*, 661 F. Supp. 1127 (D.D.C. 1987); *State v LeCompte*, 371 So.2d 239 (La. 1979). *But see United States v Brawner*, 471 F.2d 969, 1000-1001 (D.C. Cir. 1972) (expressly permitting defendants to introduce expert testimony tending to show absence of any deliberate or premeditated design when insanity defense not asserted).
36. 832 F.2d 531 (10th Cir. 1987).
37. Invoking the defendant's "capacity" to form the mental state required to commit the offense charged is a way to allow psychiatric testimony. Because of "mental abnormality," it is alleged that the accused was unable to form the specific intent—or *mens rea*—required for certain crimes. Only in the rare case, it is observed, will even a legally insane defendant actually lack the requisite *mens rea* purely because of mental defect. In some cases, defendants have attempted to present such theories of defense as the claim that a defendant lacked the *mens rea* to distribute cocaine because of the psychological domination of her mother. *United States v White*, 766 F.2d 22 (1st Cir. 1985). *Mens rea* is generally satisfied by any showing of purposeful activity, regardless of its psychological origins; therefore, it is said, such testimony may mislead the jury about the *mens rea* requirements of a crime. *United States v Pohlot*, 827 F.2d 889 (3d Cir. 1987); Morse S: Undiminished confusion in diminished capacity. *J Crim L Criminology* 1984; 75:1.
38. At a hearing on defendant's offer of proof, it was shown that the psychologist, if allowed to testify, would state that the defendant, a child pornographer, had a "dependent personality," and further that the defendant's values regarding sexuality and nudity were derived from her "rigid" childhood experiences. The defendant in the case was

charged with sexual exploitation of children. There was "no indication of neurosis or mental defect." The court said, "An expert may not substitute her judgment as to the defendant's state of mind by testifying that because of the defendant's personality, she would not have acted in a particular manner.... Absent the suggestion of the presence of a mental disease or defect, a trial court may properly exclude psychiatric opinion about the defendant's capacity to form the mental state required to commit the offense charged.... Even assuming that the psychologist would not have focused solely on defendant's capacity to form the requisite intent, more generalized testimony regarding her personality characteristics was excludable because it addressed a subject matter within the knowledge and experience of the jury and therefore did not meet the helpfulness criterion of [rule] 702.... Defendant testified about her upbringing and her attitudes toward sexuality and nudity. She further testified that she did not believe she was producing sexually explicit pictures and that she had been duped.... The jury was capable of making an intelligent evaluation of that testimony without the assistance of an expert. The trial court was within its discretion in excluding the psychologist's testimony." 832 F.2d at 535.

39. *R v Turner* [1975] 1 Q.B. 34.
40. *Ibid.*
41. *R v Chard* [1972] 56 Cr. App. R. 268; *R v MacKenney* [1981] 72 Cr. App. R. 78, 80.
42. See Bates F: Admissibility—Psychiatric evidence—Towards a coherent policy. 1977 *Canad. Bar Rev.* 178, 186.
43. *Keys v United States*, 346 F.2d 824 (D.C. Cir. 1965); *Bradford v State*, 234 Md. 505, 200 A.2d 150 (1964).
44. 517 F.2d 584 (2d Cir. 1975).
45. *Id.* at 586.
46. Quoted in *Newsweek*, Oct. 3, 1988, p 21.
47. Quoted in Doctor: Tyson not manic-depressive, *Detroit Free Press*, Oct. 5, 1988, p 2-D.
48. There is indication that some psychiatrists are avoiding jargon. The other evening at a gathering a woman said, "I'm manic. I go in the basement and scream." Her husband, a psychiatrist, said, "You're not manic. You're crazy."
49. "Legal definitions are beyond the expertise of doctors.... [A]n expert's opinion as to the law of criminal responsibility or insanity is of no aid to the jury, and could possibly confuse them." *People v Anderson*, 421 N.W.2d 200 (Mich. App. 1988).
50. Lubasch AH: A law professor is first witness to take the stand in Myerson trial. *The New York Times*, Oct. 6, 1988, p 16; Note: Expert legal testimony, *Harv Law Rev* 1984; 97:797.
51. Oath-helping is an ancient practice. In olden times, as developed in Roman Law and preserved in medieval law, the oath actually decided the issue, rendering judicial discretion unnecessary. It operated as absolute proof, binding upon the judge. The oath was not incidental to testimonial evidence, but rather, the reverse was the case: witnesses supported the oath. Indeed, testimony did not originally constitute an independent means of proof, but was merely a means of fortifying the litigants' oath. At best, the witnesses swore with the party as compurgators and did not individually testify to the truth of facts within their knowledge (a compurgator is one who under oath vouches for the blameless character or conduct of an accused person attempting thereby to vindicate him). At times, testimonial evidence was treated as equivalent to the oath. Thus, Mohammed said: "Thy two witnesses are his oath." *See* Freckelton IR: *The Trial of the Expert.* Melbourne, Oxford University Press, 1987, p 44; Silving H: The oath. *Yale Law J* 1959; 68:1329; *R v Kyselka* [1962] 37 C.R. 391 (Ont. C.A.); *R v Burkart & Sawatsky* [1965] 3 C.C.C. 210, 45 C.R. 383. "It is well settled that an expert witness may not render an opinion as to a complainant's veracity in criminal sexual conduct cases." *People v Miller*, 418 N.W.2d 668 (Mich. App. 1987).
52. See Rules 601-610, Federal Rules of Evidence.
53. *State v Jensen*, 415 N.W.2d 519 (Wis. App. 1987) (testimony that complainant's "acting

out" behavior was consistent with that exhibited by sexually abused children); *State v Haseltine*, 352 N.W.2d 673 (Wis. App. 1984) (admission of psychiatrist's opinion that defendant's daughter was an incest victim, which was an opinion that she was telling the truth in her allegations of sexual contact by defendant, constituted error that was prejudicial in view of fact that daughter's account of sexual assault was not corroborated by independent evidence); see McCord D: Syndromes, profiles and other mental exotica: A new approach to the admissibility of nontraditional psychological evidence in criminal cases. *Ore Law Rev* 1987; 66:19, Slovenko R: Syndrome evidence in establishing a stressor. *J Psychiatry Law* 1984; 12:443, Comment: The syndrome: Problems concerning the admissibility of expert testimony on psychological profiles. *U Fla Law Rev* 1985; 37:1035.

54. 165 Mich. App. 32 (1987).
55. 282 N.W.2d 10 (Mich. App. 1979).
56. 162 Mich. App. 623 (1987).
57. Murray DE: Expert testimony in sexual abuse litigation. *For the Defense*, July 1988, p 14. Dr. Richard Gardner says false allegations occur in the context of a "parental alienation syndrome." In this disorder, he writes, we see not only programming of the child by one parent to denigrate the other parent, but self-created contributions by the child in support of the preferred parent's campaign of denigration against the nonpreferred parent. While most authorities find the overwhelming proportion of child allegations to be true, Gardner states that the vast majority is fabrication. Gardner RA: *The Parental Alienation Syndrome and the Differentiation Between Fabricated and Genuine Child Sex Abuse.* Cresskill, NJ, Creative Therapeutics, 1987, p 274.
58. 359 N.W.2d 604 (Minn. 1984).
59. 161 Mich. App. 120 (1987).
60. *People v Garrison*, 166 Mich. App. 557 (1988).
61. Mich Comp. Laws Ann. §600.2163a(3). Does a child's play correlate with the child's prior experiences? Some research has indicated that the use of the dolls itself generates sexual-like play with them, and in at least one controlled study, most children played with the dolls in many ways. See Gabriel RM: Anatomically correct dolls in the diagnosis of sexual abuse of children. *J. Melanie Klein Soc.* 1985; 3:400. Dolls often misused in dealing with suspected sex abuse victims. *Psychiatric News*, Jan. 20, 1989, p 4. For this reason, use of dolls as evidence might be challenged as inherently unreliable, the statute on admissibility notwithstanding. *See Frye v United States*, 54 U.S. App. D.C. 46, 293 F. 1013 (1923).
62. The courts in a number of cases have held the testimony admissible. *See, e.g., State v Kelly*, 478 A.2d 364 (N.J. 1984); *Terry v State*, 467 So.2d 761 (Fla. App. 1985); *People v Torres*, 488 N.Y.S.2d 358 (1985); *State v Gallegos*, 104 N.M. 247, 719 P.2d 1268 (1986). In *Ibn-Tamas v United States*, 407 F.2d 626 (D.C. Circ. 1979), the court found that, while the subject matter was beyond the realm of understanding of the jury and that the expert was qualified, the defendant failed to establish that the battered woman syndrome was generally accepted by the scientific community.
63. *See* Mather V: The skeleton in the closet: The battered woman syndrome, self-defense and expert testimony. *Mercer Law Rev* 1988; 39:545; Comment, Battered-woman-syndrome testimony and the jury: The question of admissibility. *NYLS Rev* 1987; 32:79.
64. Murphy JP: An evaluation of the arguments against the use of expert testimony on eyewitness identification. *U Bridgeport Law Rev* 1987; 5:21. Defense lawyers a decade ago began trying to call on psychologists to help them challenge eyewitness' testimony. But judges generally disallowed the testimony, letting jurors determine for themselves whether eyewitness testimony was accurate. In 1983, however, the Arizona Supreme Court overturned a conviction on the ground that the judge refused to let a psychologist testify in a murder case about the psychological research. A year later, the California Supreme Court made a similar decision, and appellate courts subsequently held that the

juries were entitled to hear about research on eyewitnesses' reliability. More than 100 psychologists have since testified in various cases as experts on eyewitness memory. Bishop JE: Memory on trial/Witnesses of crimes are being challenged as frequently fallible. *Wall Street Journal*, March 2, 1988, p 1.

65. *United States v Downing*, 753 F.2d 1224 (3d Cir. 1985).
66. *United States v Blade*, 811 F.2d 461 (8th Cir. 1987).
67. 776 F.2d 1451 (10th Cir. 1985).
68. 786 F.2d 1308 (5th Cir. 1986).
69. See Wells GL, Loftus E (eds.): *Eyewitness Identification/Psychological Perspectives*. New York, Cambridge University Press, 1984; Loftus EF, Schneider NC: "Behold with strange surprise": Judicial reactions to expert testimony concerning eyewitness reliability. *UMKC Law Rev* 1987; 56:1.
70. 786 F.2d at 1312.
71. American Bar Association, *Criminal Justice Mental Health Standards*, Chap 7.
72. 107 S. Ct. 515 (1986).
73. In this case the defendant had approached a police officer on the street in Denver and said he wanted to confess a homicide. The policeman told him of his rights to remain silent and have a lawyer present. The man said he understood, and proceeded to confess to the killing of a 14-year-old girl and to lead police to the scene and to other evidence. Later the defendant told a psychiatrist that God's voice had told him to confess. Citing his history of mental illness and the psychiatrist's opinion that he was insane, the Colorado courts barred the use of the confession and subsequent statements. They said these statements had been involuntary and that the defendant's waiver of his rights had been ineffective. The prosecutor appealed to the U.S. Supreme Court.
74. *Id.* at 502. In *Wold v State*, 430 N.W.2d 171 (Minn. 1988), the defendant appealed from an order denying his motion for postconviction relief following his conviction for first-degree murder. He contended that the trial court erred in admitting statements he made to police following his arrest because his intoxication, combined with his limited intelligence, precluded him from knowing, intelligently, and voluntarily waiving his Fifth Amendment rights. The Minnesota Supreme Court affirmed the conviction.
75. Commentary to Standard 7-5.8.
76. This is an actual case (reported by Dr. Hubert Miller to author, Nov. 10, 1988). See Melton GB, Petrila J, Poythress NG, Slobogin C: *Psychological Evaluations for the Courts*. New York: Guilford Press, 1987, p 7; Grano J: Voluntariness, free will, and the law of confessions. *Va Law Rev* 1979; 65:858, 886.
77. 680 F. Supp. 408 (D.D.C. 1988).
78. *Id.* at 411.
79. The test which has gained general acceptance throughout the United States for establishing the reliability of scientific methods was first articulated in the leading case of *Frye v United States*, 54 U.S. App. D.C. 46, 47, 293 F. 1013, 1014 (1923). Under the *Frye* standard, before scientific opinion will be received as evidence at trial, the basis of that opinion must be shown to be generally accepted as reliable within the expert's particular scientific field. Thus, if the validity of a new scientific technique is in controversy in the relevant scientific community, or if it is generally regarded as an experimental technique, expert testimony based upon its validity cannot be admitted into evidence. *Reed v State*, 283 Md. 374, 391 A.2d 364 (1978).
80. 680 F. Supp. at 412.
81. 88 F. Supp. 559 (S.D. N.Y.), *aff'd*, 185 F.2d 822 (2d Cir. 1950), *cert. denied*, 340 U.S. 948 (1951).
82. Discussed in Slovenko R: *Psychiatry and Law*. Boston, Little, Brown, 1973, pp 40–60.
83. 88 F. Supp. at 599.
84. *United States v Hinckley*, 525 F. Supp. 1342 (D.D.C.), *aff'd*, 672 F.2d 115 (D.C. Cir. 1982).
85. 326 So. 229 (Fla. App. 1976).

86. *See, e.g., United States v Partin*, 493 F.2d 750 (5th Cir. 1974), *cert. denied*, 434 U.S. 903 (1977); *Sinclair v Turner*, 447 F.2d 1158 (10th Cir. 1971), *cert. denied*, 405 U.S. 1048 (1972); *United States v Allergetti*, 340 F.2d 254 (7th Cir. 1964), *cert. denied*, 390 U.S. 908 (1968); *Goldstein v State*, 447 So.2d 903 (Fla. Dist. Ct. App. 1984); *Bonner v State*, 59 Ga. App. 737, 1 S.E.2d 768 (1939); *Walley v State*, 240 Miss. 136, 126 So.2d 534 (1961); *Bouldin v State*, 87 Tex. Crim. 419, 222 S.W. 555 (1920). "Testimony on the truthfulness or untruthfulness of a witness can be distinguished from evidence of drug or alcohol use that may affect a witness' ability to perceive or to recall her perceptions." *Seelye v State*, 429 N.W.2d 669 (Minn. App. 1988).
87. 490 F.2d 907 (9th Cir. 1974), *cert. denied*, 416 U.S. 959 (1975).
88. The court said: "Credibility...is for the jury—the jury is the lie detector in the courtroom. Judges frequently instruct juries about factors that the jury may or should consider in weighing the veracity of a witness. In this respect it can be said that judges assume that they have certain expertise in the matter, and that juries have less of that expertise than judges. It is now suggested that psychiatrists and psychologists have more of this expertise than either judges or juries, and that their opinions can be of value to both judges and juries in determining the veracity of witnesses. Perhaps. The effect of receiving such testimony, however, may be twofold: First, it may cause juries to surrender their own common sense in weighing testimony; second, it may produce a trial within a trial on what is a collateral but still an important matter. For these reasons we, like other courts that have considered the matter, are unwilling to say that when such testimony is offered, the judge must admit it. The admissibility of the proffered testimony was for the judge, and in deciding whether to admit expert testimony, 'the trial judge has broad discretion...and his action is to be sustained unless manifestly erroneous.'.... We think that the testimony of the type offered in this case should be received only in unusual cases, such as *United States v Hiss*. And by referring to that case we are not saying that it would have been error to exclude the testimony there offered and received." 490 F.2d at 912–913.
89. 229 F. Supp. 148 (M.D. Pa. 1964).
90. See, *e.g., Thomas v McPherson Community Health Center*, 155 Mich. App. 700, 400 N.W.2d 629 (1986).
91. See Richards B: Doctors seek crackdown on colleagues paid for testimony in malpractice suits. *Wall Street Journal*, Nov. 7, 1988, p B-1.
92. Weinstein J: Improving expert testimony. *U Richmond Law Rev* 1986; 20:473, 482.
93. Slovenko R: Tort reform legislation, *Med Law* 1988; 7:103.
94. MCLA §600.2169(1)(*a*)(*b*).
95. Here is a quote from a brief: "As everyone who has ever practiced law knows is that if you don't have a meritorious case, go to the inventive Dr.—, so that he can make something out of nothing."
96. 395 So.2d 991 (Ala. 1981).
97. Advisory Committee's Note to Federal Rules of Evidence, Rule 704.
98. *Owen v Kerr-McGee Corp.*, 698 F.2d 236, 240 (5th Cir. 1983).
99. Art. 704, La. Code of Evidence.
100. Federal Rules of Evidence, Rule 403.
101. *United States v Torneiro*, 735 F.2d 725, 734 (2d Cir. 1984).
102. *United States v McBride*, 786 F.2d 45, 51 (2d Cir. 1986).
103. 105 S. Ct. 1087 (1985).
104. 18 U.S.C. §17.
105. Columnist Andy Rooney, after pointing out that the five psychiatrists hired by the prosecution all testified that Hinckley was sane and the five psychiatrists for the defense all testified Hinckley was insane, said: "The average person...can reach one of two conclusions about psychiatrists: Either psychiatrists can be bought, or psychiatry is such an inexact science that it is worthless. I don't want any psychiatrists mad at me, so I'll

leave it to them to say which of these two categories they fall into." Syndicated column, June 14, 1982, quoted in Resnick PJ: Perceptions of Psychiatric Testimony: A Historical Perspective on the Hysterical Invective. *Bull Am Acad Psychiatry Law* 1986; 14:203.

106. Federal Rules of Evidence, Rule 704, as amended by 18 U.S.C. §20. See *United States v Hillsberg*, 812 F.2d 328 7th Cir. 1987).
107. Giannelli P, Imwinkelried E: *Scientific Evidence*. Charlottesville: Michie, 1986, §9-3(B), p 286.
108. S. Rep. No. 225, 98th Cong., 1st Sess. 230 (1983).
109. *Washington v United States*, 390 F.2d 444 (D.C. Cir. 1967).
110. 390 F.2d at 456.
111. 1984 U.S. Code Cong. & Admin. News 3182.
112. *United States v Frisbee*, 623 F. Supp. 1217 (D.C. Cal. 1985).
113. In *United States v Brodie*, 858 F.2d 492 (9th Cir. 1988), involving a charge of willful failure to file federal income tax returns, an accountant's testimony that would have stated an opinion as to the taxpayer's willfulness, a mental state which is an element of the crime charged, was excluded under rule 704(*b*). The testimony was also held inadmissible as bolstering the credibility of the defendant.
114. *United States v Prickett*, 604 F.Supp. 407 (S.D. Ohio 1985).
115. Congress intended the provision to extend "beyond the insanity defense to any ultimate mental state of the defendant that is relevant to the legal conclusion sought to be proven...*e.g.*, premeditation in a homicide case, or lack of predisposition in entrapment." S. Rep No. 225, 98th Cong., 1st Sess. 231 (1983); *US Code Cong & Admin News* 1984, p 3413. Various appellate courts have stated that rule 704(*b*) is not limited in application to cases where the defendant raises an insanity defense. The clear language of the rule, according to the courts, applies to testimony relating to the mental element of any crime or defense. See *United States v Alvarez*, 837 F.2d 1024 (11th Cir. 1988) (inference that defendants were aware of contraband aboard a vessel); *United States v Dotson*, 817 F.2d 1127 (5th Cir. 1987) (inference that defendant intentionally evaded his income taxes).
116. Mueller CB, Kirkpatrick LC: *Evidence Under the Rules*. Boston, Little, Brown, 1988, p 728.
117. 655 F.2d 512 (3d Cir. 1981).
118. *United States v Hearst*, 563 F.2d 1331, 1350–1351 (9th Cir. 1977) (testimony properly received under preamendment rule 704).
119. Mueller CB, Kirkpatrick LC: *supra* note 116, p 729.
120. *United States v MacDonald*, 688 F.2d 224, 227–228 (4th Cir. 1982) (under rule 403, no error to exclude as confusing and misleading), *cert. denied*, 459 U.S. 1103 (1983). Author Joe McGinniss, in a best-selling book, devotes 663 pages to building a case that the physician did it. McGinniss J: *Fatal Vision*. New York, Putnam, 1983. Dr. Robert Sadoff, who examined Dr. MacDonald in 1970, 1975, and 1979, says he would say again what he said before: "Dr. MacDonald's personality is not consistent with the type of personality likely to commit this crime. I think that it is very unlikely that he could have done this. I base this statement today, not only upon my previous examination of him, but upon his total actions and behaviors over the 13 years since the murder." A prosecution psychologist, Hirsch Lazaar Silverman disagrees: "This man is a pathological narcissist. His personality is such that under certain pressures he would revert to violence." Quoted in Breo, DL: *Extraordinary Care*. Chicago, Chicago Review Press, 1986, pp 140–141.
121. Mueller CB, Kirkpatrick LC: *supra* note 116, p 729.
122. *United States v Esch*, 832 F.2d 531 (10th Cir. 1987); discussed *supra* note 36.
123. National Mental Health Association: *Myths & Realities*. Hearing Transcript of the National Commission on the Insanity Defense, 1983, p 30.
124. S. Rep. No. 225, 98th Cong., 1st Sess. 231 (1983), quoting APA statement on the insanity defense, reprinted in *Am J Psychiatry* 1983; 140:681.

125. Carlson RL, Imwinkelried EJ, Kionka EJ: *Materials for the Study of Evidence*. Charlottesville, Michie, 1988 (suppl), p 45.
126. Comment, Resurrection of the Ultimate Issue Rule: Federal Rule of Evidence 704(*b*) and the Insanity Defense, *Cornell Law Rev* 1987; 72:620, at 639.
127. S. Rep. No. 225, 98th Cong., 1st Sess. 271 (1983).
128. Carlson RL, Imwinkelried EJ, Kionka EJ: *supra* note 99, p 45; Comment, Resurrection of the Ultimate Issue Rule: Federal Rule of Evidence 704(*b*) and the Insanity Defense. *Cornell Law Rev* 1987; 72:620, 638.
129. *United States v Davis*, 835 F.2d 274 (11th Cir. 1988) [expert testimony that a person suffering from multiple personalities, in and of itself, does not indicate that a person is unable to understand what he is doing, not prohibited by rule 704(*b*)]; *United States v Hillsberg*, 812 F.2d 328 (7th Cir. 1987) (psychiatrist not permitted to give opinion as to whether, at the time of the shooting, the accused had the capacity to conform his actions to the requirements of the law); *United States v Alexander*, 805 F.2d 1458 (11th Cir. 1986) [rule 704(*b*) held not to violate the equal protection clause of the Constitution]; *United States v Buchbinder*, 796 F.2d 910 (7th Cir. 1986) (expert could not testify as to whether the defendant had the requisite mental state to defraud, but could testify as to the extent of defendant's depression over son's death).
130. 819 F.2d 265 (11th Cir. 1987).
131. At trial, the defendant did not contest his role in the bank robbery, but argued that he was insane at the time that he committed the offense. His ex-wife and an old friend testified that they believed him to be incapable of criminal activity. The crux of the defense case, however, was the testimony of the defense psychiatrist who noted that the defendant had endured a difficult past and was "off the wall." The doctor testified that he had a "very, very strong suspicion" that the defendant suffered from "manic-depressive" illness at the time of the offense. The government countered with the rebuttal testimony of another psychiatrist and concluded from the defendant's description of events that he was not in "an active manic state" at the time of the robbery because his actions were reasonably well controlled and goal directed.
132. 819 F.2d 262 at 265.
133. Weinstein J: Improving Expert Testimony. *U Richmond Law Rev* 1986; 20:473; Comment, Resurrection of the Ultimate Issue Rule: Federal Rule of Evidence 704(*b*) and the Insanity Defense, *Cornell Law Rev* 1987; 72:620.

7

The Impartial Expert

Myth or Reality?

HENRY C. WEINSTEIN

The question posed by the title of this chapter is of more than mere academic interest at the present moment in the history of forensic psychiatry in the United States. As this book was in the process of being published, the American Academy of Psychiatry and the Law after vigorous debate eliminated the word "impartiality" from its ethical guidelines,[1] replacing it with the word "honesty" (see Appendix).

I would be less than candid if I did not state, at the onset, that I favor the use of the word "impartial." Indeed, I am a strong proponent of this position, and this chapter is an opportunity for me to justify my viewpoint and to present some of the reasoning supporting it.

This chapter is based upon a talk I gave at the Fourteenth Annual Conference of the Tri-State Chapter of the American Academy of Psychiatry and Law, January 14, 1989. The title of the conference was "Impartiality and Advocacy in Mental Health and the Law." The first part of the conference was titled "The Psychiatrist and the Judicial Process: Scientific Expert or 'Hired Gun'?" and the title of my talk during this first part was "The Impartial Expert: Myth or Reality?" Thus, even before we began, the participants were presented with a formidable series of complex words and concepts: "impartiality," "advocacy," "scientific," "hired gun"—even "myth" and "reality."

I began my talk to my colleagues by relating an incident that had occurred not long before the conference. I had received a telephone call from a lawyer who told me that he represented a particular university—an Ivy League university. He said that he had gotten my name from a friend of mine—a mentor, as a matter of fact, who is rather a celebrity in psychiatry. So, these two things, the

HENRY C. WEINSTEIN • Forensic Psychiatry Service, New York University Medical Center/Bellevue Hospital Center, 550 First Avenue, New York, New York 10016.

fact that this renowned university was calling me and that my mentor had suggested my name to them, started me off on what, I guess, was something of a "high."

He explained why he was calling: there was a will dispute involving a legacy to the university. The legacy, he noted, was substantial. (So, I felt, I think, even more important.) The deceased, the testator, had been hospitalized a number of times with a diagnosis of paranoid schizophrenia. The will was being contested on this basis. He was calling me to ask whether I would be willing to be retained as the expert for the university and consult with its Office of Counsel.

I tentatively agreed and he began to tell me some of the background details. The deceased had been a single person and had left his entire estate to the university. As part of the litigation contesting the validity of the will, the testator's original treating psychiatrist (in the hospital) had submitted a statement to the effect that his former patient, because he "carried" the diagnosis of paranoid schizophrenia, could never have been competent to sign a will.

As I was listening, I began to assess the situation and recalled thinking that this opinion violates some of the most elementary principles of the practice of forensic psychiatry. Namely, that competency is both context-related and often variable over time and, further, relates to the particular moment in question: in this case when the will was signed. I mentioned this to my new employer, who was clearly pleased to hear me say this. I asked about the other psychiatrist's forensic qualifications. (Was I subtly putting him down?) And, as I asked for further details, it might be inferred that I felt that the university, insofar as I could tell at that point, had a good case and could probably get the money. Before long, I noticed I was speaking in terms of "we."

What was happening to me? I believe that I was undergoing a powerful process of "identifying" with my new employer and his view of the case.

In their chapter on "The Psychiatrist as Expert Witness," Curran and McGarry, addressing their concerns about undue familiarity between one particular lawyer in a case and the psychiatrist who is the expert, and the problems that can be caused by such a situation, state that

> to maintain impartiality, both attorneys should be treated with the same professional courtesy and distance, avoiding undue familiarity.[2]

Appelbaum[3] also has pointed out that "expert testimony...is inevitably affected by the delicate courtship that goes on between experts and the attorneys with whom they work." Why a "delicate courtship'? What does he mean by this? Appelbaum then continues, perhaps in the way of an explanation, that

> experienced attorneys begin every encounter with a new expert, whether by letter, by telephone, or in person, with an effort to present the case from the point of view most favorable to their client. This initial contact has a tendency to imprint in the expert's mind a particular approach to the case.

The "experienced attorney" has thus begun a complex courting ritual. What should the reaction of the expert be?

> Of course, experienced forensic clinicians are aware of this technique and train themselves to a certain degree of skepticism when dealing with new cases.

So, Appelbaum suggests that the expert take a "skeptical" attitude. Why? Because the presentation of his case by the attorney constitutes "a perspective that must be overcome if the expert is to reach a conclusion adverse to the attorney with whom he works." And, according to Appelbaum this is a "subtle process of identification."

In his book, *The Powers of Psychiatry*,[4] Jonas Robitscher, in the chapter in which he describes the development of the use of expert witnesses in the courts, points to the problems that arise because different experts, like different psychiatrists in general, have different beliefs and attitudes. Referring specifically to the "battle of experts" in an insanity defense case, he notes that:

> Because one psychiatric expert might have a very different attitude from another on the all-important questions of free will and the ability to control action, psychiatrists could be found to testify persuasively for either the prosecution or the defense. In famous criminal cases we have been more aware of the psychiatrist for the defense, spinning out a theory by which the jury could, if it wished, find the defendant not guilty by reason of insanity, but in all but the most obvious cases, there is equal scope for the prosecution's psychiatrist to make a case for conviction.

Parenthetically, it is worth considering another aspect of the expert's state of mind. Presumably ethical, presumably insightful, the psychiatric expert must cope with an extensive array of inner influences that would tend to prejudice his attitude and move him away from impartiality. For example, it has been my experience that most thoughtful and erudite discussions of such influences rarely take into account the expert's need to snare a well-heeled client. How close does this not-so-subtle need bring the expert to being biased, even a "hired gun"? In any event, these influences which affect the beliefs and attitudes and therefore the approach of the expert to his work, is the principle subject of this chapter insofar as they relate to the expert's impartiality.

I am addressing one aspect of the psychiatrist-expert's inner mental state, specifically the expert-psychiatrist's attitude toward the merits of the legal issue at hand. Some words that have been used to characterize this attitude are: "hired gun," "biased," "adversarial," as well as "neutral," "impartial," and "objective." Most prominently, and most controversially, the word "impartial" is used extensively in the Ethical Guidelines for the Practice of Forensic Psychiatry of the American Academy of Psychiatry and the Law.

An entire section, Section IV, of these Guidelines are devoted to this subject. The title is "Impartiality and Objectivity." It states:

> The forensic psychiatrist functions as an expert within the legal process. Although he may be retained by one party to a dispute in a civil matter or the prosecution or defense in a criminal matter, he adheres to the principles of impartiality and objectivity. His clinical evaluation and the application of the data obtained to the legal criteria are performed in the spirit of such impartiality and objectivity. His opinion reflects this impartiality and objectivity.

The Commentary to this section takes up a number of specific situations where the issues of impartiality and objectivity might be at risk of being compromised. These include a "treating psychiatrist" agreeing to be an expert witness in a case involving his patient; the importance of interviewing all parties in a custody case; remuneration to an expert witness that involves a contingency fee; opinions rendered without personal examination of a party; and the importance of distinguishing between opinions based on facts and opinions based on inferences and impressions. The Commentary sets forth the underlying principles as follows:

> The adversarial nature of our Anglo-American legal process presents special hazards for the practicing forensic psychiatrist. Being retained by one side in a civil or criminal matter exposes the forensic psychiatrist to the potential for unintended bias and the danger of distortion of his opinion. It is the responsibility of the forensic psychiatrist to minimize such hazards by carrying out his responsibilities in an impartial and objective manner.

The careful way this commentary is written is intended to alert the practicing forensic psychiatrist to "the potential for unintended bias." The implication is, of course, that no honest forensic psychiatrist would approach his work in a consciously or intentionally biased manner. Be that as it may, this section of the Guidelines, and the use of the term "impartial" aroused some controversy. At the time of their adoption by the membership of the Academy[5] a small but vocal group of colleagues expressed concern that the inclusion of the word "impartial" could be used to attack the opinions of forensic psychiatrists on the basis, as I understand it, that it is impossible to be perfectly and absolutely impartial. Others called attention to the fact that one of our most respected colleagues, Dr. Bernard Diamond, seems to have taken a different view in his seminal article entitled, "The Fallacy of the Impartial Expert."[6]

In my role as the Chairman of the Ethics Committee of AAPL, I was one of the principal drafters of these guidelines, and, understandably, I disagreed. After some discussion, a vote was taken and the guidelines were passed. It was agreed, however, that the use of the term impartiality in the guidelines would be reconsidered by the academy. Recently, it has been suggested that the term impartiality be dropped from the guidelines.[7]

The history of the guidelines is illuminating in this regard. From its very inception, the members of the academy have been concerned about ethics and ethical issues.[8] In a draft of suggested guidelines in the late 1970s Jonas Rappeport[9] had included the following statement:

> Reports should reflect sound clinical judgment and not be adversarial in nature.

There is no mention of the term impartiality, but rather the admonition not to be "adversarial." Using Rappeport's draft, the AAPL Committee on Ethics proceeded to craft a more detailed set of guidelines. A decision was made, early in this process, to use the development and adoption of these guidelines as an educational experience for the members of the academy. So the committee proceeded slowly and deliberately, involving, to the extent possible, the entire membership of the academy. Thus, Rappeport's draft was sent, in the form of a request for comments, to all the members of AAPL. There were many responses, and over the years of deliberations there were more than 20 drafts that the committee considered.

I shall use the material from some of these drafts to begin our study of the use of the term "impartial." As the responses to the first circulated draft were evaluated, a new set of headings were developed. The ensuing rewritten guidelines began with a preamble and ended with a discussion of procedures for handling complaints of unethical conduct. Between were the major headings and topics: confidentiality, consent, impartiality, and qualifications. The section on impartiality was created to include Rappeport's principles that the expert's opinion is based on the data and is not adversarial. However, as regards impartiality, the term appeared, during this laborious process, as an idea that the forensic psychiatrist is obliged to try to be impartial. It is gently put:

> ...the forensic psychiatrist strives toward impartiality."[10]

Thus, we were struggling with the problem, as adumbrated by Rappeport's guidelines, of the forensic psychiatrist functioning in the adversarial process and the effect of the adversarial process upon the practitioner. To cope with this powerful process the committee changed the phrase "strives towards" to the phrase "adheres to the principles of."

> Although he may be retained by one party to a dispute in a civil matter or the prosecution or defense in a criminal matter, he adheres to the principles of impartiality and objectivity.

The purpose was clearly to present this idea in the strongest way possible. Now, as hopefully I have made clear, everybody who has thought about this subject is usually well aware of the famous article by Bernard Diamond mentioned above, titled "The Fallacy of the Impartial Expert."

Diamond begins this article by noting that

> It is quite generally assumed that the battle of the experts, that always disconcerting and often sensational disagreement of psychiatrists on testifying on issues of legal insanity and criminal responsibility, could be eliminated through the device of the neutral or impartial expert.

Note that Diamond seems to use these words "neutral" and "impartial" synonymously. The context is the use of a court-appointed expert rather than experts retained by the two sides in a dispute or, more specifically, for Diamond, a criminal case.

> Such a neutral expert witness is supposedly outside the traditional adversary system of the courts. Not in the employment of either the defense or the prosecution, but acting in the name of the court, such a witness presumably can remain detached and objective.

Diamond adds two more words, "detached," and "objective," and he is clearly discussing the expert retained by the court rather than either party to the dispute. This must be kept in mind as we proceed with our analysis. Diamond's concern is that the use of this "device" is probably never effective in eliminating the personal biases of the expert, and is therefore invariably misleading in that it may give a false impression of freedom from such bias.

For our purposes, Diamond's central point is this: There are forces at work in the legal process that make true, total impartiality impossible. Even the expert who makes a deliberate effort to be impartial, must, as a result of coming to an opinion that will inevitably favor one side or the other, yield to a "close operational identification with one side of the conflict" and therefore "does become an advocate."

> Because his testimony does in fact support one side of the legal battle, he, if he is at all human, must necessarily identify himself with his own opinion, and subjectively desire that "his side" win.

Diamond then points to another aspect of the legal process that creates such an identification—cross-examination. As a result of the usually inevitable fact that the expert's opinion favors one side in a dispute, it is the duty of the other side to cross-examine and, indeed, to "attack" the expert and his opinion.

"It is absurd," Diamond states, "to pretend that the psychiatric expert remains neutral under such a legal procedure. For the sake of his own ego integrity he must identify himself with his own opinions and become the advocate for those opinions. But in proportion as those opinions favor one side or the other, the witness loses his hypothetical impartiality."

But, it is important to appreciate that Diamond is speaking of the "impartial expert" in the sense of the expert who is retained by the court, not one side or the other, the expert who is "supposedly outside the traditional adversary system." He has demonstrated that this is, in certain respects, an illusion, that the adversarial system itself has a subtle, or perhaps not-so-subtle effect, and creates a (perhaps unrecognized) bias.

And yet, on the other hand, Diamond clearly concedes "that both legal and medical codes of ethics demand the impartiality of the expert witness," but, he stresses (and this I believe is the crux of my disagreement with Diamond):

> The desirability of such an ideal must not blind us to the reality that the ideal is seldom, if ever, achieved.

Diamond is concerned that the *label* of impartial is misleading and that "impartiality" is, as he puts it, an "ideal."

He caricatures the expert who, seeking perfect impartiality, confounds the ideal with the real, and attempts to take a posture of an "aloof detached facsimile of impartiality that masks his secret hope for victory of his own opinion."

> Such a detached witness may be totally unconscious of the innumerable subtle distortions and biases in his testimony that spring from this wish to triumph.

Thus, as I understand it, Diamond is critical not of an ideal of impartiality, but rather of an uncritical acceptance of the term as a description of the true inner mental state of the expert witness. He thus uses the opportunity to comment upon the use, in the legal process, of the court-appointed "impartial" expert, as potentially and dangerously misleading.

How do the new AAPL Guidelines deal with these two aspects of "impartiality?" As to the first, the use of the court-appointed expert, the guidelines clearly do not favor one system over the other. They clearly contemplate the use of experts retained by either side. But they do warn about partiality and bias.

It was clear to the Committee on Ethics, from a number of sources, that our members were concerned about the problem of the "hired gun," the expert who would proffer any opinion in order to further the cause of the litigant who was paying. The committee decided to bring this difficult subject into the guidelines in what we hoped would be a delicate manner. We stated:

> The impression that a psychiatrist in a forensic situation might distort his opinion in the service of the party that retained him (the so-called hired gun) is especially detrimental to the profession and must be vigorously avoided.

As the guidelines went through numerous changes, refinements, and modifications, this sentence was retained. However, just before they were finally presented to the membership—when they were in their tightest, most condensed state (as much like the Ten Commandments as we thought they could be) it was agreed that in this context the inclusion of the phrase "hired gun" was "unseemly." So, it was cut.

When we use this pejorative term, hired gun, we are reflecting upon the expert's state of mind: specifically, that expert's state of mind, or intent, as regards his expert opinion. And, to make matters even more complicated, we sometimes do so notwithstanding the individual's subjective assessment of his own state of mind. In other words, for example, a particular colleague may want to regard himself as impartial or fair or unbiased, but nonetheless is seen by others as favoring one type of a client or another (such as the defense or the prosecution in criminal matters). Is this being a hired gun? I don't think so. The implication of being a hired gun is that one would consciously and intentionally distort or change one's true opinion for the sake of, or in the service of, the party that pays. It certainly can get very complicated as we attempt to assess someone's intent; but I believe this is what we are really addressing. Why? One reason is, as Diamond noted, that as participants in this judicial process we are committed to the truth. The hired gun, by definition, disregards this priority. He is anything but "impartial." In his strong partiality he introduces a serious distortion into the process and thereby creates the potential for unfairness in a process that seeks, most of all, fairness—as an aspect of justice. The "hired gun" is thus more than "unseemly." He is a menace to the judicial process and is therefore universally condemned as unprofessional, immoral, and unethical. I would argue that for reasons of professionalism, morality, and ethics, the psychiatric expert must be impartial. If this medicine is too strong, I would accept the modification that the psychiatric expert must *strive* for impartiality. Does this sound familiar?

Before going any further with this argument I would like to pause briefly and examine the word impartial. Impartiality, as an adjective, is grouped synonymously with words such as fair, just, equitable, unprejudiced, unbiased, straightforward, dispassionate.[11] These adjectives broadly mean "showing no evidence of favoritism, self-interest, or the indulgence of one's likes and dislikes."

"Fair," which has the widest range, can imply any of the foregoing senses. "Just" stresses being in accordance with a code of what is legally and ethically right and proper. "Equitable" also implies justice, but less from the standpoint of a rigid code of rules than from a sense of what is in the best interests of all concerned in a given issue. It therefore may imply justice tempered by reason or compromise. "Unprejudiced" means without preconceived opinions or judgments, especially those adverse to a person or a thing, and not soundly based. "Unbiased" implies straightness of judgment or behavior, in the absence of self-interest, prejudice, or emotionalism. "Straightforward" suggests what is frank and honest rather than devious. "Dispassionate" means free from coloring by strong personal feelings or emotions.

These words give us a groundwork of meaning as we examine a number of words that appear or appeared prominently in the AAPL Guidelines. "Objectivity" implies a detachment that permits a person to observe and judge without undue reference to his own experience and without indulgence of his sympathies. That objectivity is required of the psychiatric expert is, I believe, generally accepted.

What of "impartiality"? Impartiality emphasizes the absence of favoritism in deciding an issue. The word partial, on the other hand, means favoring one person or side over another. I have mentioned that I presented many of these thoughts in a talk to my colleagues of the Tri-State Chapter of AAPL at a conference titled "Impartiality and Advocacy in Mental Health and the Law." Clearly, impartiality was meant to contrast to advocacy, so let us consider the word "advocate." To advocate means to support one side in a dispute, and this is quintessentially the job of the attorney. I raise this point here because the word advocate also had an interesting history in the development of the AAPL Guidelines. Diamond had pointed out that it was inevitable that the expert "identify himself with his own opinion and become the advocate of those opinions."

This point was taken up by another group at the same time that the earliest drafts of the AAPL Guidelines were being drafted. The American Bar Association in the early 1980s had gathered a large interdisciplinary group to develop criminal justice mental health standards. A number of members of AAPL, including myself, were also members of this ABA group and became aware of various precepts of the legal profession on these issues.

Thus, for example, it was clearly and emphatically stated by the ABA group that the role of the expert witness was that of "an independent and impartial expert."[12] Thus, on the issue of impartiality, the ABA standards are clear. The Commentary to one section on expert testimony states that

> As with other expert witnesses, a mental health or mental retardation professional testifying at trial serves as an impartial witness called to inform and assist the trier of fact. Therefore, the professional in formulating his or her expert opinion should conduct an evaluation that is impartial and objective and that results in clinical findings that are derived impartially and objectively.[13]

In regard to the issue of advocacy, however, the ABA standards note that

> Once the expert's opinion is formulated, however, the mental health or mental retardation professional should serve as a proponent for the opinion reached.

This is in essence what Diamond had pointed out. Is this a contradiction? The ABA standards go on to state that

> Although the expert is in essence an advocate or proponent for the opinion formulated in the evaluation, it is proper to characterize the expert as "an impartial witness" so long as the expert's evaluation was performed impartially and objectively.

The commentators to the Bar Association standards note that this position "represents a middle ground between those who would view the professional as an adversary witness and those who would view the professional as wholly impartial and disinterested." They then cite Diamond for the former position and Halleck for the latter, nonadversarial role, quoting Halleck:

> When he takes the witness stand the psychiatrist becomes a person committed to the process of truth seeking no matter how the truth may conflict with his own ideologies.... The psychiatrist's abandonment of the adversarial role when taking the witness stand should put him in a very comfortable position. Once the thought of "winning the case" is temporarily dissociated from his consciousness, the psychiatrist has no duty other than of telling what he knows as clearly as possible.

To distinguish the psychiatric expert witness' advocacy of his opinion from his initial impartial approach to the evaluation of the facts and the formulation of that opinion, an early draft of the AAPL Guidelines provided that

> once having arrived at his opinion, he may become an advocate for that opinion, but his opinion and any of his testimony based on that opinion should not be distorted by the adversarial nature of the proceedings.

In the consideration of subsequent drafts of the guidelines, this sentence was first shortened and then moved to the commentary, and then omitted altogether. The discussions of the Ethics Committee related to the ambiguity and confusions created by this statement since it seemed to confuse the role of the expert with that of the attorney.

In this regard it is instructive to note that in the 1985 Supreme Court Case of *Ake v Oklahoma*[14] the role of the expert psychiatrist became an issue. So much so that in his dissent, Justice Rehnquist felt called upon to state that "a psychiatrist is not an attorney whose job is to advocate."

The AAPL Guidelines link impartiality and objectivity. And, although the term objectivity does not seem to have aroused much concern, I would like to examine it from one perspective. The word objectivity is used to mean "free of emotion, surmise, or personal prejudice." But it also has the inference of "scientific."

Recall that the subtitle of the session at which I spoke on these matters was "The Psychiatric and the Judicial Process: Scientific Expert or 'Hired Gun.' " Writing in the journal *Science*, Faust and Ziskin,[15] in an important article titled "The Expert Witness in Psychology and Psychiatry," undertake a broad-ranging attack questioning the value of psychological and psychiatric expert testimony. Of this I shall cite only two points. The first, which they make after a significant marshaling of scientific evidence, is that

> Expert evidence is readily subject to abuse due to its highly subjective nature and vulnerability to biases.

At another point they state that the difference in opinions between experts may be the result of different backgrounds, prejudices, and biases.

> This diversity in theory and practice breeds the divergence in opinion that makes the battle of experts a regular courtroom occurrence.

So, again and again, we are shown that forensic psychiatric experts are different from each other. They have their different backgrounds, different beliefs, and here, different theories and practices. How could they be impartial? I remind you that the title of this chapter is "The Impartial Expert: Myth or Reality?" and I hope to present an answer to this question, but I would first like to pause to reflect on still one more word, consideration of which I believe may help us better to understand the problems we face as forensic psychiatrists and may further point in a direction of resolution of the question posed by this chapter.

The word is "neutrality." Recall that it was Diamond who used the term "neutral" as synonymous with "impartial," when the expert is appointed by the court rather than retained by a particular side to the conflict. He regards it as "absurd" to think that the expert remains neutral in the context of the adversarial system.

It happens that this particular word—neutrality—has additional resonances for the psychiatrist. It is a word quite familiar to those trained in dynamic psychiatry and psychoanalysis.

Freud, writing on the need for the analyst to control his impulses, said:

> Our control over ourselves is not complete.... In my opinion, therefore, we ought not to give up the neutrality towards the patient, which we have acquired through keeping the counter-transference in check.[16]

Thus Freud regarded countertransference as an impediment to psychoanalytic work. At first he dealt with the manifestations of unconscious countertransferences in the analyst, and later added that acting upon countertransference could involve conscious thought, and gave the example of giving in to tender feelings toward a patient.[17]

But it is well accepted that analysts are "influenced every step of the way by motivation arising from personal individual psychologies."[18] To deal with this, and "to restore analytic neutrality," the analyst analyzes the countertransference. As Loewald has put it,

> analytic neutrality is not exempt from transference-countertransference dynamics. It is one of their valid and fragile outcomes.... The analyst's understanding of transference-countertransference is used to determine the content, form, and timing of interpretations.... The issue with regard to the analyst's countertransference is how it plays its essential part in the analytic process, and under what conditions it interferes.[19]

Countertransference is inevitable. It is inevitable because each of us has our own ideologies, belief, opinions, likes, and dislikes. What is required is self-scrutiny and self-analysis to restore analytic neutrality on the one hand, or impartiality on the other.

By striving for analytic neutrality, the analyst reaffirms that analysis, as Freud has said, is "founded on truthfulness." The analyst is alert to the countertransference. He does not deny it, he does not act upon it. Shapiro, in his paper "On Neutrality," refers to this principle as a "guide to action and proper technique."[20]

The analogy that I am proposing is that as necessary as neutrality is to psychoanalysis, so too is impartiality to forensic psychiatry. The analyst is not "neutral" in relation to his opinion about the patient's inner conflicts. It is his approach that is "neutral" in the sense of unbiased, unprejudiced.

So too, as forensic psychiatrists, when we "strive" for impartiality, we are alert to our biases and prejudices. We do not deny them, and we do not act upon them. We watch ourselves: a form of self-analysis. Our work, as we clearly state in our guidelines, is performed "in the spirit of such impartiality." We compare our imperfect selves to the ideals set forth in our guidelines. One of those ideals is impartiality.

Diamond, in the article cited extensively, concluded with a list of utopian conditions which might make him reconsider the opinions he had expressed. One of these relates to a time when

> psychiatrists, through their own enlightenment and self-understanding, can be relied upon to detach themselves from their own prejudices and refrain from homogenizing their moral judgments with their medical opinions.

I believe that Diamond is referring to impartiality in the sense that I am defining it. It is an ideal. Recall that Diamond referred to this ideal as "desirable." So perhaps we have, by inference, Diamond's agreement to include the ideal of impartiality in our guidelines, which I believe is the place to set forth our ideals.

We all "strive" to achieve our ideals. So, I would further suggest that rather than eliminate the word impartiality, we should perhaps once again include the phrase that the forensic psychiatrist "strives toward impartiality."

I turn now to answer the question posed by the title of this chapter. Is the impartial psychiatric expert a myth or a reality?

What is a myth? The word comes from the Latin for "tale." There are two definitions of the word myth. One is that a myth is a story, a traditional story dealing with supernatural beings or heroes, a fiction or half-truth or a notion based on tradition or convenience more than on fact.

The other definition is that a myth is a recurring theme that appeals to the consciousness of a people by embodying its cultural ideals. It was based on this latter definition that Joseph Campbell named his book *Myths to Live By*.[21] In that book he states

> It has always been on myths that the moral orders of society have been founded.

So my answer to the question posed by this chapter: the impartial expert: myth or reality? is that the impartial expert is both a myth and a reality. Impartiality is a myth—an ideal—in that it is a goal that we strive to achieve. But it is also a reality because it is a real goal, truly a "myth to live by." It is a goal that we strive to achieve on the road to truth as we seek to contribute to fairness in the legal process.

These issues, like the other issues that are dealt with in our AAPL Guidelines are, fundamentally, issues of morality, of the moral order. Our guidelines present our beliefs, our ideals. They command our loyalty, our faith. They provide for cohesion, for vitality, and for the exercise of our creative powers.

REFERENCES

1. Ethical Guidelines for the Practice of Forensic Psychiatry, *Newsletter of the American Academy of Psychiatry and the Law*, April 1987, pp 16–17.
2. Curran WJ, McGarry AL: The psychiatrist as expert witness, in Curran WJ, McGarry AL, Shah SA: *Forensic Psychiatry and Psychology*. Philadelphia, Davis, 1987.
3. Appelbaum PS: In the wake of *Ake*: The ethics of expert testimony in an advocate's world. *Bull Am Acad Psychiatr Law* 1987; 15:15–25.
4. Robitscher, J: *The Powers of Psychiatry*, Boston, Houghton Mifflin, 1980.
5. May 10, 1987.
6. Diamond BL: The fallacy of the impartial expert. *Arch Crim Psychodynamics* 1959; 3:221–236.
7. Weinstock R: Report of the Ethics Committee, American Academy of Psychiatry and the Law, to the Executive Committee, April 14, 1989.
8. Personal communication: A. Halpern, M.D.
9. For a discussion of this material and some historical information see, Weinstein, HC: How should forensic psychiatry police itself? Guidelines and grievances: The AAPL Committee on Ethics. *Bull Amer Acad Psychiatr Law* 1984; 12:289–302.
10. The American Academy of Psychiatry and the Law, *Ethical Guidelines for the Practice of Forensic Psychiatry*, Second Draft, July 1985. (It is important to note that there were many "internal" drafts that the Committee was working with over the years. The Second Draft was the second presented to the membership in the form of a request for comments.) Compare Appelbaum, cited in Ref. 3, "the process of striving for objectivity and impartiality."
11. *The American Heritage Dictionary of the English Language*, Boston, Houghton Mifflin, 1981.
12. American Bar Association: Standards for Criminal Justice, 3-3.3(*a*), 4-4.4(*a*) and commentary.
13. American Bar Association: Criminal Justice Mental Health Standards, 7-3.14 (1984).
14. *Ake v Oklahoma*, 105 S.Ct.1087 (1985).
15. Faust D, Ziskin J: The expert witness in psychology and psychiatry. *Science* 1988; 241:31–35.
16. Freud S: Observations on transference love. (1913) *Standard Edition*, Vol 12, London, Hogarth, 1958.
17. Tyson R, Renick O: Panel, Countertransference theory and practice. *J Amer Psychoanal* (1986); 34:699–708.
18. Owen Renik in panel cited in Ref. 17.
19. Hans Loewald in panel cited in Ref. 17.
20. Shapiro T: On neutrality. *J Amer Psychoanal* 1984; 32:269–282.
21. Campbell J: *Myths to Live By*. New York, Viking, 1972.

8

Ethical Issues Involved in the Dual Role of Treater and Evaluator

ROBERT D. MILLER

Of all the medical specialties, psychiatry has the longest history of accepting the dual role of providing individual treatment to patients and providing expert opinions and management of persons perceived to be dangerous to society. For much of its history, the majority of psychiatrists in the United States were employed in prisons and public mental hospitals, where their major roles were perceived (at least by their employers) as serving the interests of the state in resolving criminal cases and protecting the public.[1,2] With the growth of academic psychiatry and the differentiation of private, individual psychotherapy from public psychiatry in the 1940s, an increasing number of psychiatrists have left the public sector for a more traditionally medical, autonomous private practice.[3,4]

As private and academic practitioners began to predominate within psychiatry, the ethical codes developed by their professional organization emphasized an individual psychotherapy approach to areas such as confidentiality.[5] Critics began to point out the ethical dilemmas involved in the public sector when psychiatrists practiced in a "society-oriented" as opposed to a "client-centered" mode.[6-9]

As the trend toward individual practice extended to the subspecialty of forensic psychiatry,[10] the modal forensic interaction also came to be conceptualized as a private evaluation done at the request of an attorney or judge.

ROBERT D. MILLER • Forensic Center, Mendota Mental Health Institute, 301 Troy Drive, Madison, Wisconsin 53704; Department of Psychiatry and Law School, University of Wisconsin–Madison, Madison, Wisconsin 53706; and Department of Psychiatry, Medical College of Wisconsin, Milwaukee, Wisconsin 53226.

Since the great majority of such evaluations are undertaken voluntarily by private practitioners, the recent forensic Ethical Guidelines developed by the American Academy of Psychiatry and the Law[11] reflect that discontinuous relationship.[11] The Commentary to Guideline IV (Confidentiality) states:

> A treating psychiatrist should generally avoid agreeing to be an expert witness or to perform an evaluation of his patient for legal purposes except in minor matters. The demands of a forensic evaluation may require that other people be interviewed and testimony can adversely affect the therapeutic relationship.

While such a blanket position may be appropriate for the majority of private evaluations, it does not adequately take into account the continuing exigencies of legitimate public practice, particularly in forensic hospitals which have the dual responsibility to evaluate and to treat patients; it creates a double standard of practice by ignoring clinical reality in a variety of public practice situations; and it does not deal with a number of particular issues which have arisen recently, such as duties to report a variety of patient behaviors considered to pose threats to society. This chapter will use the still embryonic professional ethical guidelines which are relevant to forensic practice to analyze the question of the potential for dual agency inherent in combining the treatment and evaluation roles from a number of aspects, and attempt to differentiate those situations in which treating psychiatrists should avoid providing expert testimony about their patients from those in which such activities are appropriate and even preferred. I will divide the issues into a series of dichotomies for greater simplicity of analysis, realizing that there is considerable overlap among the various categories.

PRIVATE VERSUS PUBLIC PRACTICE

The majority of forensic psychiatrists practice in private or academic settings,[3,10,12] and thus professional ethical guidelines have reflected their practices and ideologies. There is a significant difference in the degree of autonomy characteristic of private versus public practice. Private practitioners, whether in individual, group, or academic practice settings, are essentially free to choose the type of services they provide, and the types of patients or agencies to whom they provide those services. They are therefore usually able to "avoid agreeing to be an expert witness" if they choose to do so. In the case of evaluations requested concerning persons whom they are not already treating, private psychiatrists are of course free to decline, and the great majority of them do. Those who specialize in forensic practice may choose to accept such referrals, but they are free not to, and can thus ensure that they do not mix their roles as treaters and evaluators if they choose not to do so.

There are exceptions, of course, even for private practitioners. Patients who come for clinical psychotherapy may subsequently end up in court in a variety of situations, such as child custody conflicts or after alleging psychic trauma. In such situations, private psychotherapists may find themselves subpoenaed to testify as to their client's or former client's mental state at some past time. While some judges have held that the confidentiality of the psychotherapeutic relationship protects the clinician who declines to testify without his patient's consent,[13] most have ruled that the court's need for relevant evidence overrides confidentiality, and have compelled testimony under threat of contempt.[14,15] Presumably, psychiatrists who testify under court order would not be considered to have violated any official ethical principles, as all professional ethical codes provide exceptions for legally mandated duties. However, many therapists would still object strongly to such court orders, based on what Diamond[16] calls "personal ethics," a matter of individual conscience, as opposed to "professional ethics," that which an organized profession has determined to impose on all its members.

Clinicians in the public sector generally do not have the freedom of choice available to private practitioners, although their personal moral preferences may be the same. Clinicians employed at state forensic facilities in particular are usually required as part of their jobs to provide both treatment and evaluation for the same patients, and staffing rarely permits the luxury of separating the roles by having different staff perform them. Despite significantly greater variety in severity of criminal charges in which defendants' mental states are called into question than had previously been the case,[17] the majority of patients in forensic facilities are still charged with serious crimes, not "minor matters," and public employees thus are placed in a potentially greater bind by ethical prohibitions designed essentially for private practitioners who have choices to exercise. In addition, while the consequences of evaluation itself may be less severe in the case of "minor matters," the impact on the therapeutic relationship might be equally deleterious.

Economic factors also frequently differentiate the two practice settings. Because of the contingency fee system common in civil practice, there are stronger financial incentives for evaluators in civil cases to produce opinions useful to their referral sources than exist in criminal evaluations, the great majority of which are performed by salaried public practitioners.[18]

While it might be argued (and has been in the analogous case of the quality of care provided by state civil mental hospitals prior to the reforms of the 1970s[19]) that ethical clinicians should simply refuse to practice in such situations, such simplistic solutions avoid rather than address the issues. If the "ethical" practitioners abandoned the public system, they might feel better as individuals, but the system would go on, and without the benefit of internal critics who are in the best position to effect what changes are possible.

While such arguments may appear to be merely utilitarian, or what Modlin[20] calls situational or marketplace ethics, they assume that the ethical prohibitions against the dual role are appropriate; as I shall argue subsequently, I believe that this is also a simplistic answer to the problem which ignores both reality and the potential benefits available when the same clinicians provide both evaluation and treatment.

CIVIL VERSUS CRIMINAL PRACTICE

The nature of the dual role of treater and evaluator also may differ, depending upon whether it exists within a criminal or civil framework. In many ways, the potential problems are fewer with criminal evaluations. First, the rights of criminal defendants are much more carefully spelled out in statutes and court decisions, and procedures for protecting those rights are correspondingly more explicit, than is the case with civil procedures.[21] Virtually all psychiatric evaluations of criminal defendants are prospective in the sense that the court orders a particular clinician or facility to perform an examination of the defendant's mental state as it relates to competency to perform a specified set of actions (such as to understand Miranda rights, to plea-bargain, or to proceed to trial), or as it relates to the defendant's mental state at the time of the alleged crime. The scope of the evaluation is thus somewhat limited, and thus easier both to perform and to explain to the subject. The distinction between treatment and evaluation is thus easier for both the clinician and the defendant to understand, and the potential for blurring the roles is thus reduced. In addition, the adversarial nature of the legal process is also more easily understood by criminal defendants than by civil litigants, and defendants are less likely to become confused about the role of the evaluator.

Civil evaluations typically involve more complex issues, such as psychic trauma or child custody, in which the issues to be considered more closely resemble those typical in more standard psychiatric evaluations, and thus pose a greater likelihood that the evaluatee will believe that the evaluator is operating in a traditional physician's role with a patient, despite any warnings given by the evaluator.

Thus, the parameters of the relationship with a criminal defendant are usually specified prior to the initial contact, permitting the clinician to inform the evaluatee at the outset of the nature of the evaluation (see Section 10, below). Although a clinician who has been treating a patient in conventional private psychotherapy occasionally becomes involved unexpectedly in a criminal case,[22,23] such involvement is quite unusual, and is much more frequent in civil cases.

There is some inevitable conceptual overlap with the previous dichotomy between private and public practice, since virtually all civil evaluations are performed privately,[12] while the majority of evaluations performed by forensic psychiatrists in the public system are criminal, either inpatient or outpatient. But the clearer adversarial framework and the more explicit procedural rules established by courts and legislatures for criminal evaluations make it easier to separate the roles of evaluator and treater in such situations.

On the other hand, the court-mandated treatment of forensic patients (both to restore competency to stand trial and after a finding of insanity) is almost invariably carried out in the public sector, often in forensic hospitals,[18,24] and thus frequently requires a combination of treatment and evaluation to be provided by the same clinicians.

TYPE OF TREATMENT INVOLVED

Psychotherapy

The major problem cited by critics of combining the roles of treater and evaluator is misrepresentation or betrayal of the confidentiality of the therapeutic relationship, with damage potentially accruing to the patient through the impact of the forensic opinion itself, as well as more generally damage to the ability of clinicians to provide effective treatment due to the destruction of the trust which is essential for psychotherapy.[7-9,25]

While these are certainly significant concerns, their impact is somewhat contextual, depending upon the nature of the therapy in question. There is no doubt that traditional long-term psychotherapy, both insight-oriented and supportive, requires considerable trust between patient and therapist. In such situations, it is clear that the role confusion and potential conflicts of interest involved in the dual role of treater and evaluator present serious difficulties.

Such conflicts are more frequent in the context of the treatment of forensic patients, chiefly because the possibilities of the therapist being called upon to provide expert testimony are more numerous. Some of these situations will be discussed in more detail below; but they typically involve predictions of future dangerousness based on information gained during therapy. While it is clear from the standpoint of society and its judicial representatives that treating therapists have the most comprehensive knowledge of their patients, and are therefore presumably in the best position to make accurate predictions, it is equally clear from the standpoint of the patient's treatment (which may be essential for the ultimate reduction of the dangerousness about which society is legitimately concerned) that patients cannot be expected to be appropriately self-disclosive if they have cause to fear that their revelations will be used against them by their therapists.[26]

In nonforensic treatment, while there is less risk of having to testify against one's patient, there is also less likelihood that the patient will have been informed of the possibility of such testimony at the beginning of therapy. In addition, the problem of overidentification with a patient who has been in treatment for some time might cause a therapist to err on the side of supporting a patient's wishes against professional judgment.[27] Another possible consequence of overinvolvement arises when patients are involved in civil litigation which could result in their receiving compensation which therapists consider both justified and necessary for them to regain control over their lives. Although a recent study indicates that there is little objective evidence to support the assertion that such situations significantly influence the course or outcome of therapy,[28] the danger exists in individual cases nevertheless.

Pharmacological Therapy

Although it has been argued that there is no evidence to support the assertion that psychotropic medication is effective when administered involuntarily,[29] most psychiatrists who have experience treating committed patients would probably agree that it is quite effective when used for appropriate clinical indications, whether the patient consents or not. It may be, therefore, that the conflicts introduced by the dual role may be less problematic with patients who require psychotropic medication, particularly antipsychotic medication, as an essential part of their treatment.[26] Since the majority of forensic patients in treatment under court orders suffer from major psychoses,[30,31] the problems inherent in the dual role may again be less with such patients, since their trust and cooperation is not as essential for the efficacy of psychopharmacological treatment.

It must be pointed out, however, that although medications can be administered without a patient's cooperation in inpatient facilities and in some outpatient settings, the establishment of trust in therapists is often essential over the long term to ensure that patients continue taking their medication once court jurisdiction is removed. The type of therapeutic alliance which may be jeopardized by the therapist acting as evaluator as well as treater may not even be possible with many acutely psychotic patients; but once the medication has exerted its maximum effects, if therapy is to extend beyond pharmacology, its efficacy will depend upon patients' confidence and trust in their therapists.

Therefore, even within the class of medication treatment of forensic patients, it will make a difference whether or not the therapy is to be long-term, with the goal of restoration of the capacity to return to relatively independent community living (such as in the treatment of insanity acquittees or sex offenders) or whether the treatment goals are more limited, as in the case of restoration of competency to stand trial. In the latter case, the assumption by the clinician of both roles may be less destructive, as no therapeutic relationship has been established, and the patient is unlikely to return to the same clinician for subsequent treatment. The problem of generalization from experience with one therapist to subsequent treatment remains, however.

THE ORDER OF ASSUMPTION OF THE ROLES

The impact of combining treatment with evaluation frequently depends upon the order in which the roles are assumed. Most problematic is the situation in which an ongoing relationship has been established solely on a treatment basis and the therapist is unexpectedly required to provide an expert opinion concerning the patient. As mentioned previously, one such category of evaluations includes situation in which the patient's mental state becomes an issue in litigation, such as child custody or psychic trauma. Another category which has become prominent in the literature (if not in the courtroom) more recently is that of the protection of society from dangers posed by patients. This latter category will be addressed in more detail below.

When therapy is sought for purely clinical reasons, and the therapist's initial evaluation has not turned up any reason to suspect a subsequent need for expert testimony (such as previous dangerous behavior, a troubled marriage, or a recently accident allegedly resulting in emotional problems), there is little likelihood that the patient will have been warned at the beginning of therapy that the therapist might be called to testify about him or her, and the greatest potential danger to the therapeutic alliance exists.

In the forensic context, the order is often reversed, with evaluation for competency to stand trial or criminal responsibility preceding treatment. Since evaluations are (or *should* be) always preceded by explicit warnings of the purpose and potential outcomes of the evaluation, and given before a therapeutic alliance has formed, and often to patients whose severe mental disorders preclude the formation of such an alliance at that time, the damage in practice is often less.[26]

Wisconsin has recognized this distinction in its civil commitment statutes; the evaluation done within 3 days of admission and presented at the probable cause hearings are performed by hospital staff, while the subsequent evaluations for the final commitment hearings held within 14 days of admission are performed by evaluators independent of the hospital.[32]

There are problems, however, even when the evaluation role precedes treatment. Some patients will develop such a strong negative transference to the evaluating clinician that it will be impossible subsequently to establish an effective working relationship, even if the initial treatment (particularly with medications) is effective.

Another type of problem may arise if a clinician who initially evaluates a person privately for legal purposes subsequently assumes the role of treater. If the outcome of the legal procedure was unsatisfactory to the prospective patient, he or she may blame the evaluator, consciously or unconsciously, and be unable to develop an appropriate alliance during treatment. Even if the therapy itself proceeds effectively, the appearance of conflict of interests or "ambulance-chasing" can pose significant ethical problems for the clinical professions, even if the patients in question do not object.[33]

TREATERS AS DECISION MAKERS

An even more difficult ethical and therapeutic dilemma arises when clinicians are called upon not just to offer opinions to courts or other judicial decision makers, but to preside over hearings and actually make the decisions in question. Such roles exist almost exclusively in forensic contexts, and are less common than formerly, when courts officially deferred to clinical judgment much more often than is the case today. Nevertheless, they continue to exist in many jurisdictions in a variety of forms.

Obviously, the potential for damage to a therapeutic relationship is significantly increased when therapists serve as the final decision makers, rather than as advisers. Legislatures and regulatory bodies have recognized this problem, and have generally prohibited clinicians serving as decision makers from being directly involved in the patient's treatment.

Involuntary Civil Commitment

Examples of such roles include those jurisdictions in which clinicians have the statutory authority (and increasingly, the responsibility) to hospitalize patients involuntarily under civil commitment without a judicial hearing, such as California.[34] In such situations, the admitting clinicians are also often called upon to provide testimony at the initial judicial hearing, held within a few days of admission. Not only do such procedures create an even more adversarial relationship between therapists and patients then mere testimony, but the potential exists for greater destruction of therapeutic potency if the court overrules the clinician's original decision to hospitalize.

Sexual Psychopath Laws

A number of states created statutory schemes in the 1950s and 1960s to permit diversion of certain types of recidivist criminals into the mental health system. Called sexual psychopath or defective delinquent laws, they accepted current clinical thinking that treatment would both rehabilitate the criminals and provide greater protection for the public.[35] Since such schemes were conceived as therapeutic rather than as punitive, the decision-making power was often delegated to clinicians, an abdication which has been criticized by Halleck.[36] While the majority of such programs, and the statutes that established them, have been abolished, some remain.

In one such system, the Wisconsin Sex Crimes Law (which was repealed in terms of new commitments, but not in terms of continuing authority over those convicted prior to 1980) provides two release procedures. One is a modified parole board with an independent psychiatrist, a law professor, and a member of the state parole board. The other involves staff from the treating facility serving as hearing officers, and making their recommendations to the Secretary of the state Department of Health and Social Services.[37] While the regulations prohibit treating clinicians from serving as hearing officers, because patients are transferred between units in the Forensic Center, it is often difficult to find a hearing officer who has not had some treatment or administrative responsibility over the patient at some time. One patient went so far as to file a lawsuit over this very issue.[38]

When the hearing officer is not permitted to make autonomous decisions, but rather is instructed for policy reasons not even to recommend release, as has happened under the Wisconsin system,[36] the ethical problems go beyond the potential damage to individual therapeutic relationships, and place hearing officers in the position of appearing to apply clinical judgment when in reality they are totally agents of social control. The American Psychiatric Association Ethics Committee has issued an opinion that it is unethical for psychiatrists to participate in such hearings under such circumstances.[39]

Pacht and Halleck,[27] referring directly to the Wisconsin sex crimes procedures, also point out that the pressures on therapists to recommend release (and thus to adopt the usual therapist's role of supporting patients) is strong and makes it difficult to make an objective decision, particularly when the burden of proof lies on the patient to prove that he is no longer dangerous.

Right to Refuse Treatment

Although they have seldom been explicitly pointed out in the clinical literature, potential conflicts also exist when clinicians attempt to treat committed patients against their wills. Most states now recognize a qualified right for competent patients to refuse treatments such as psychosurgery, aversive conditioning, electroconvulsive therapy, and psychotropic medication.[40] All provide, however, mechanisms for challenging such refusals through determination of incompetency to make treatment decisions. While some states provide for full judicial hearings, most permit the decisions to be made by clinicians, either ones independent of the facility,[41] or even clinicians from the same facility as long as they are not directly involved with a patient's treatment.[42]

Although most clinicians who have written on the subject clearly prefer clinical to judicial decision making with respect to overriding patients' rights to refuse medication,[43] it has not previously been conceptualized as another example of the dual role of treater and evaluator. In all systems of determination of patients' competency to refuse treatment, treating clinicians serves as initial evaluators, and their recommendations are presented to the decision makers quite analogously to expert opinions in other types of legal decision making. In fact, that role is clearest in those jurisdictions with judicial determinations, since in most of those jurisdictions, in addition to the role as initial evaluator, treating psychiatrists are also appointed in effect as guardians for their patients who are found incompetent to make treatment decisions.

EXPLICIT DUTIES TO WARN OR TO PROTECT

The General Duty to Protect Third Parties

As if there were not enough problems with situations in which therapists are required to respond to requests for information and expert opinions about their patients, recent legal developments have established that therapists may also have duties to take action without waiting for requests. Because of the recently discovered "special relationship" between therapists and patients,[44] society now looks upon therapists as protectors of the public from the behavior of patients in treatment, and, most recently, from other therapists. Although courts for many years have found therapists liable for acts committed by hospitalized patients,[45] the *Tarasoff* decision[44] and its progeny in other states have extended that responsibility to outpatient clinicians as well.[46-49]

The duty to release confidential information without patient consent to prevent danger to the public has been a part of the ethical codes of the American Psychiatric Association,[5] the American Psychological Association,[50] and the National Federation of Societies for Clinical Social Work[51] for some time, without any significant outcry in the professional literature. But once the courts and legislatures began to define the duty themselves and to hold therapists financially liable for its breach, therapists forget their own ethical codes and complain that externally mandated breaches of confidentiality are unethical and will surely lead to the extinction of psychotherapy as we know it.[46] Once again a double standard is applied; when private and academic practitioners find themselves held to the same standard which has applied to public and hospital-based practitioners for years, the cries of ethical dilemmas are suddenly heard in the land.

The Duty to Report Child Abuse

Another duty, which psychotherapists share with a number of other professionals, is that of reporting suspected child abuse. While this duty raised ethical questions when it was first created in every state in the 1960s, it has become generally accepted as necessary and effective in preventing further abuse. In the situation contemplated by the originators of such statutes, there is technically no duality, since the report is made concerning the child who is abused. Critics pointed out, however, that while the child might technically be the identified patient, the legally responsible persons were the parents, who were most likely to be the subject of the reports. It was argued that reporting suspected child abuse violated the rights of the parents, and also that the threat of reporting might prevent parents from bringing their injured children in for treatment, whether they had been abused or not.[52]

While those arguments have died out in the last decade as reporting has become accepted, there is a subset of cases which continue to raise troubling ethical problems. While most child abuse comes to light through examination of the injured children, it may also come to the attention of therapists who are treating the abusers themselves. It is thus similar to the more general duty to warn, with the significant difference that most statutes require reporting past abuse even when there is no danger of future abuse (such as when the children have already been removed from the parents, or in the case of child sexual molesters who have been removed from their victims by the courts and are in treatment in inpatient forensic facilities[53]).

In the case of the treatment of sex offenders, it is certainly possible to warn them at the outset of treatment that reports will have to be made of any child abuse they have caused for which they have not already been prosecuted, and most forensic facilities do so by policy.[53] But there remains the significant dilemma of encouraging patients to be appropriately self-disclosive in therapy while warning them at the same time that "anything they say may be held against them."

The Duty to Report Sexual Abuse by Previous Therapists

A growing number of states have created a newer duty, modeled after the established child abuse reporting statutes, under which psychotherapists are encouraged or required to report sexual abuse by previous therapists which is reported to them by their current patients.[54] The rationales of the two sets of statutes are similar, in that both attempt to prevent future abuse by removing the abuser from a situation in which further abuse can occur, although the second main purpose of child abuse reporting laws, to ensure treatment for the victims, is unnecessary in the case of sexually abused patients who are already in therapy.

The few statutes that have been enacted to date differ from each other in one important area: some, like the Minnesota statute,[55] can be interpreted to *require* therapists to report sexual abuse revealed during therapy, even without their patients' consent, or over their objections. Such statutes track child abuse reporting statutes, which are also mandatory rather than permissive, and obviously value prevention of future abuse over the rights of an already abused patient. The obvious dilemma created by such statutes is that they may require therapists to force a patient who has already been abused once to submit to the consequences of an investigation she or he may not be psychologically prepared to handle, and thus further complicate the course of therapy, particularly since she has not been abused by another therapist.[54]

By contrast, statutes such as that recently passed in Wisconsin,[56] are permissive in that they require therapists to obtain informed consent from their patients before making reports, even reports that omit the name of the alleged victim. While such procedures will perhaps be less effective in identifying abusers, they have the advantage of eliminating the ethical dilemmas posed by their mandatory counterparts.

Prosecution of Mental Patients

When persons with mental disorders that do not significantly impair their responsibility for their behaviors commit illegal acts while under the control of clinicians (as while involuntarily hospitalized), those clinicians may feel compelled to behave more like police than therapists.[57,58] Although therapists are not required by any statutes or regulations to report past criminal acts by their patients, there are times when it appears, for any of a number of reasons, that initiation of criminal prosecution is the most appropriate course of action for a therapist to take.

In some cases, prosecution is appropriate because the "patient" has chosen to assume that role in preference to accepting appropriate and justified responsibility for his actions, and to permit him to hide behind the shield of a simulated mental disorder would be to grant him virtual carte blanche to commit crimes without consequences. By initiating criminal charges, the therapist not only refuses to condone the actions of a calculating criminal, but also opposes the type of blatant misuse of process which jeopardizes the chances of genuinely mentally disordered persons to avail themselves of the legitimate protections of the criminal law.

In other cases, the patient's mental disorder is genuine, but the therapist feels that it is necessary for treatment to progress that the patient accept responsibility for those of his actions over which he does in fact have control, including criminal ones. Bringing criminal charges (which in such cases are rarely carried through) may be clinically necessary in order to force the patient to accept that responsibility.

In the first type of situation, therapists may appear to be clearly violating their duties to their patients by initiating criminal charges; but I would argue[58] that when such "patients" attempt to take advantage of the patient role for nontherapeutic purposes, they have relinquished any rights they may have had to benefit from the professional duties of therapists, and cannot expect the protections of therapeutic support and confidentiality available to those genuinely in need of such protections.

And in the latter case, prosecution (or the threat of prosecution) becomes an integral part of treatment itself, is done solely for the patient's benefit (as is clearly demonstrated by the reluctance of police and prosecutors to follow through on the criminal complaints), and thus is not a true example of dual agency, although patients may initially perceive it as such.

ADVANTAGES OF COMBINING TREATING AND EVALUATING

While the presence of legal duties to perform both roles, such as the *Tarasoff* duty, the duty to report abuse of children or patients, and the combined duties to evaluate and treat which exist in most state forensic facilities, might exempt clinicians from any legal professional consequences of combining the roles, that does not mean that the personal ethical dilemmas are also eliminated. There are, however, some situations in which I would argue that the same clinician serving both as treater and evaluator not only violates no ethical guidelines, personal *or* professional, but is actually more appropriate both for the patient and for society.[60]

Halleck[36] argues that the double-agent role may be beneficial in situations in which the state and the patients' overt interests coincide, and even when a patient initially disagrees with the results (such as is frequently the case in involuntary civil commitment). But he also points out that some patients may feel betrayed by the results of such interactions, and this distrust may generalize to future therapeutic relationships.

Unusual Clinical Conditions

One such situation is that in which the clinical condition is unusual, requiring special expertise to diagnose and to treat, particularly in the forensic context. Such conditions as posttraumatic stress disorder,[61] multiple personality disorder,[62] pathological gambling,[63] pathological intoxication,[64] and pedophilia[65] have perhaps been overrepresented in forensic populations since their acceptance in DSM-III,[66] and other proposed diagnoses, such as paraphiliac rapist, would also be likely to be utilized frequently in court if included in a future Manual.

There are several reasons why these diagnoses are increasingly found (or at least claimed) in forensic populations. By their very nature, persons with these disorders are more likely than those with most other disorders to commit criminal or tortious acts, and therefore many defense attorneys have become sufficiently knowledgeable about them to raise the issues when their clients appear to fit in one of the categories. Since experts on these conditions have generally argued that they are underdiagnosed in part because they are not suspected by general psychiatrists, attorneys represent another group with motive to suggest the presence of such conditions.

Because of the higher incidence of diagnosis (even if not actual occurrence) of these disorders in forensic populations, the clinicians assigned to evaluate and treat persons suffering from them have the opportunity to develop a level of expertise which is not readily available to the general psychiatrist.

Prediction of Future Behavior

A related justification for combining the roles of evaluator and treater is that the combination should be expected to improve clinicians' abilities to provide the courts with certain types of legally relevant predictive opinions. In what has become the most common situation, private evaluators make predictions about a variety of issues, including restoration of competency to stand trial, future dangerousness, and response to treatment, often without sufficient personal experience with the treatment of forensic patients to form the basis for accurate opinions.[10]

Continuity of Care

Another potential advantage of the combined role is that it can provide continuity of treatment for forensic patients, and help to integrate the legal and clinical facets of their experience. Strasburger[67] argues that it can be devastating for mentally disordered persons to hear the opinions derived from forensic evaluations for the first time in court, without the opportunity for the evaluators to explain them and to discuss them with the patients. I would certainly agree, and have pointed out[68,69] that the best solution to the dilemma is for evaluators to share their opinions and the reasons for their conclusions with those they have evaluated at the time of the evaluation. Strasburger[70] has pointed out that such discussions may not be possible in the case of private evaluations, particularly those performed at the request of opposing counsel, in which legal strategic reasons may prevent evaluators from disclosing their opinions to patients lest the information become available to opposing counsel. This reality provides another example of the advantages that can accrue when evaluations are performed in the context of an ongoing clinical as well as legal relationship, which is usually possible with inpatient evaluation and treatment, but often logistically or procedurally difficult with outpatient evaluations.

Also, in contrast to the more usual view that adversarial legal proceedings can disrupt a therapeutic alliance,[71] Ensminger and Liguori[72] have pointed out that the alliance may actually be strengthened by such proceedings (assuming that the court accepts the treating clinician's recommendations) when the patient realizes that an objective, independent decision maker reinforces the clinical position.

The Right to Refuse Treatment

The various legal and clinical issues surrounding the right to refuse treatment provide another example of the advantages of combining evaluation and treatment. Jurisdictions that have accepted the right have established various procedures for the determination of a patient's competency, several of which require evaluation and decisionmaking by independent clinicians.[43] But in all cases, it is clinically as well as legally important that those responsible for the patient's treatment plan provide the basic information concerning the need for the proposed treatment and the patient's capacity to understand the need for that treatment.[73] It would be difficult for independent evaluators in necessarily limited evaluations to determine patients' competency to make treatment decisions, and inappropriate for them to attempt to convince patients to accept such treatment, a necessary step in most procedures for determining patients' competency to refuse treatment.

SEPARATION OF TREATMENT FROM EVALUATION

Despite the potential advantages of combining the roles discussed in the previous section, it is clear that in many situations there advantages in separating them. Some states have attempted to address the problem (although generally in response to perceived conflicts of interest, not out of concern for preservation of therapeutic alliances) by statutorily separating the roles, as Wisconsin has done in the case of civil commitment,[32] pretrial evaluations for criminal responsibility,[74] and evaluations for release from commitments following insanity acquittals.[74] Even if treaters are required to provide clinical information to decision makers, it may be possible to minimize the negative effects of such testimony by refraining from asking ultimate questions (such as whether the patient is ready for release).[27]

Such separation may also be established procedurally within a treatment facility. If it can be predicted from initial contacts that a forensic evaluation and resulting testimony will permanently disrupt a therapeutic alliance, it may be possible to assign an evaluating therapist different from the one who will ultimately provide treatment. Additionally, it may be possible to separate the administration of psychotropic medications and/or disciplinary functions, (typically the most contentious parts of treatment) from psychotherapeutic approaches by assigning different therapists to those roles. Such a separation may be particularly important if the patient suffers from a disorder which requires specific expertise both to evaluate and to treat (such as multiple personality disorder or certain types of sexual disorders).

Unfortunately, even such attempts to separate the roles may not be completely successful in achieving the desired results in terms of preservation of therapeutic alliances. Even if treating clinicians do not testify directly in legal proceedings, independent evaluators usually consult previous and current clinical records as part of their evaluations, so the supposed separation of treatment and evaluation, even where it is explicitly established, is seldom complete in practice. Patients will learn at their hearings that some of the information upon which the evaluator's opinion is based was derived from clinical records from his treaters, and the same problems will exist. And while avoidance of answering ultimate questions has been recommended on a variety of theoretical grounds,[27] even its most ardent supporters admit that in practice it is frequently impossible to present comprehensive clinical information without essentially answering ultimate questions in the process, even if only indirectly.[75] If such legal fictions do not deceive judges and juries, it is not surprising that they also fail to convince patients that their treating clinicians are not directly (and adversely) involved in the decision-making process.

Even if attempts at separation are made through using different clinicians for evaluation and treatment, patients, particularly if they have paranoid disorders, may still generalize from one clinician to all. It may therefore not be possible to separate the roles completely in practice; but such efforts as have been presented here are still effective in many cases, and should be attempted whenever ongoing therapeutic relationships have been established.

WARNINGS TO PATIENTS AT THE BEGINNING OF A RELATIONSHIP

Warnings at the Outset of a Forensic Evaluation

It might seem that explicitly informing patients at the outset of a formal evaluation for legal purposes might help to separate the roles of evaluator and treater. It is well established that clinicians evaluating criminal defendants have a legal[21] as well as an ethical[5,11] duty to inform those they evaluate of the purpose of the evaluation and the disposition of any report generated in advance of the evaluation.

Unfortunately, the distinction is often lost on patients in practice, for several reasons. First, as Halleck[36] points out, in order to inform the patient as to the purpose of the evaluation, the evaluator must understand it, and frequently does not, either because the referring source has not made the request sufficiently clear ("Evaluate Mr. X's mental state," or "Perform a psychiatric evaluation"), or because the evaluator is unfamiliar with the legal definitions of the conditions to be evaluated, and confuses the criteria for one evaluation with those for another.[76] In such situations, evaluators may end up testifying on issues different from those they explained to the patients they evaluated, as happened most notoriously in *Estelle v Smith*.[21]

Secondly, even if the request is exact, the evaluator understands it completely, and explains it carefully and accurately to the patient, it is clear from empirical studies of Miranda warnings in the criminal justice system[77,78] and similar warnings to patients facing civil commitment,[79] that few persons, either criminal defendants or mental patients, fully understand what they are being told. There is even some evidence[79,80] that complete disclosure of the purposes of evaluation may even have the unintended and paradoxical effect of inducing the misapprehension in patients that they are in fact involved in a confidential treatment relationship rather than a legal evaluative one. Thus, while such warnings are absolutely required, both legally and on the basis of professional ethics, they may in practice be ineffective. Evaluators must therefore continue to monitor the evaluation process carefully, and to give additional warnings if they perceive patients to be disclosing information which appears to be counter to their expressed interests.

Third, evaluators can no longer necessarily assume that even private evaluations done at the request of the patient's attorney will be protected by the attorney-client privilege, particularly in criminal cases. Although the U.S. Supreme Court has held that criminal defendants with apparent mental disorders are entitled not only to expert evaluations of their competency to stand trial and criminal responsibility, but also expert consultation in the preparation of the defense case,[81] it has so far avoided ruling on the larger issue of discoverability by the prosecution of expert opinions provided to the defense. Because of the nationwide trend toward a retrenchment from individual rights and greater consideration for protection of the public, prosecutors are increasingly pressing for access to the results of evaluations done for the defense but not presented by the defense at trial (which would almost guarantee that the opinions generated would be supportive of the prosecution's case).[82] As they have been successful in some of their efforts, evaluators must be careful in the guarantees that they give patients being evaluated, and aware of the applicable statutory and case law in the jurisdiction in which the evaluation is being done.

Warnings during the Course of Clinical Practice

All these problems exist even in the relatively simple situation in which a clinician knows in advance of contact with a patient that at least one purpose of that contact will be to provide a legal opinion to a third party. Unless clinicians are prepared to read a lengthy and complicated list of hypotheticals to every new patient they see (which would most probably serve either to confuse or frighten most of them away), it is unlikely that patients coming in voluntarily for clinical treatment can effectively be warned about all the circumstances under which the clinician might be called upon to provide expert opinions about them to courts or other third parties. Perhaps the best that clinicians can do under the present circumstances is to be alert for signs that such opinions might be sought (such as threats of violence, difficulty disciplining a child, or serious marital strife), and to warn patients immediately upon recognizing such signs that expert opinions might well be called for in such situations.

THE SPECIAL CASE OF COMPETENCY FOR EXECUTION

Although ethical principles do not usually depend on the circumstances of particular cases, or on the consequences of rendering particular opinions, it cannot be denied that the finality of the death penalty places clinical participation in the decisions surrounding it on a different level of ethical discourse. While it is clear that actual direct participation in the execution itself is out of bounds for all physicians, there is no professional consensus on related issues, such as whether mental health professionals should participate as expert witnesses in any or all phases of a capital prosecution. At one pole, Resnick[83] argues that there is no ethical distinction between treating a condemned inmate who has been found incompetent for execution and evaluating that defendant's competency to stand trial. The National Medical Association also adopts a consistent position which finds no ethical problems in evaluating and treating condemned but incompetent inmates, reasoning that clinicians have an ethical responsibility to provide treatment to all persons in need of it, regardless of the subsequent nonclinical consequences.[84] Others[85] would support evaluation of competency for execution but not treatment to restore such competency; while still others[86] would provide evaluations of competency to stand trial and criminal responsibility, and even provide opinions in capital sentencing hearings in capital cases, but not become involved in the issue of competency for execution itself.

Unlike other types of treatment under involuntary circumstances, such as civil commitment, treatment to restore competency to stand trial, or treatment of persons committed after findings of not guilty by reason of insanity or under sexual psychopath laws, a significant number of clinicians would refuse to provide treatment to restore competency for execution under any circumstances. Even those who would provide the treatment generally refuse also to provide subsequent legal evaluation of their patients' competency to the courts.[87]

Clinicians at Florida State Hospital, which has had the greatest experience with the dilemma, have developed an uneasy division of labor, under which hospital clinicians provide the treatment, but are not called upon to provide opinions or testimony on the issue of competency, which is provided by independent clinicians (who, however, have access to the hospital's treatment records, thus again preventing in practice the complete separation of treatment and evaluation).[88,89]

The only legal approach which deals satisfactorily with the clinical dilemma is that found in Maryland[90] and Great Britain,[91] both of which require automatic and permanent commutation of a death penalty to life imprisonment without the possibility of parole upon a finding of incompetency for execution. Such a provision relieves clinicians of the special problems inherent in treatment which, if successful, would have the effect of removing the last barrier to execution; but it of course at the same time makes the prospect of malingering even greater than would be the case if temporary incompetency would result only in temporary delay in execution.

CONCLUSIONS

As long as the mental health professionals are perceived to have unique information of value to legal decision makers, and unique skills in dealing with the mentally disordered which are of use to society in general, some degree of double agency is inevitable. Even in the simplest situation, involving an explicit request for a specified forensic evaluation, with no treatment relationship required, it is frequently impossible to avoid some aspects of the dual role, even if only in the mind of the evaluatee.

It is not useful to pretend that such conflicts do not exist, or that we could somehow avoid them altogether if only we practiced "ethically." While it is true that many of the more overt dilemmas can be avoided by eschewing practice in public, especially forensic, systems, I would argue that such a course would merely turn us into a profession of ostriches, righteously burying our heads in the sands of "pure" clinical practice while ignoring the real, practical problems that will continue to exist around us. If those who have well-developed ethical senses choose to leave the fray, it can only mean that it will be left to practitioners who are less sensitive to the problems, and would be therefore a type of abandonment of patients for whom we can provide the best (if imperfect)protections from misuse by an adversarial system often more interested in protecting the dignity of its own practices than providing justice to our patients.

It is essential that we acknowledge the reality of dual agency at all levels of current clinical as well as forensic practice, and continue to discuss them within our professions as well as to advocate for such changes as would have significant impact in reducing or eliminating unnecessary conflicts. Those practices that appear to be unacceptable to the great majority of practitioners, such as failing to warn persons being formally evaluated for the courts of the purpose of the evaluation, or perhaps serving as both treater and evaluator of condemned inmates found incompetent for execution, should be incorporated into what Diamond[16] calls "professional ethics," where they might ultimately form a sufficiently powerful consensus to permit changes to be made in statutes or court decisions. More controversial issues, which Diamond would classify as falling under "personal ethics" need to be continuously debated, if for no other reason than to educate clinicians who have not recognized them to be problems.

It is essential that ethical principles be developed with the strong input of those who practice on the front lines as well as those who recline in ivory towers and view the fray from afar. We should not attempt premature closure on difficult questions by codifying abstract theory into rigid principles that do not fit the everyday reality of clinical and forensic practice in *all* types of settings.[92]

It is also essential that such discussions permeate our training programs, which have perhaps heretofore had too much of a tendency to be satisfied with providing pat answers, rather than raising the difficult and ultimately unanswerable questions which reflect the reality of our practices.

REFERENCES

1. Halleck SJ: American psychiatry and the criminal: An historical review. *Am J Psychiatry* 1965; 121:Supplement i.
2. Smith CE: Psychiatry in corrections. *Am J Psychiatry* 1964;120:1045–1049.

3. Dietz PE: Forensic and non-forensic psychiatrists: An empirical comparison. *Bull Am Acad Psychiatry Law* 1978; 6:13–22.
4. Knesper DJ: How psychiatrists allocate their professional time: Implications for educational and manpower planning. *Hosp Comm Psychiatry* 1981;32:620–624.
5. American Psychiatric Association: American Medical Association Principles of Medical Ethics With Annotations Especially Applicable for Psychiatry. Washington DC, American Psychiatric Association, 1978.
6. Szasz TS: *Law, Liberty and Psychiatry*. New York, Macmillan, 1963.
7. Hollender MH: Privileged communication and confidentiality. *Dis Nerv System* 1965; 26:169–175.
8. Hastings Center: In the service of the state: the psychiatrist as double agent. *Hastings Cen Rep*, special suppl, April 1978.
9. Monahan J (ed): *Who is the client? The ethics of psychological intervention in the criminal justice system*. Washington DC, American Psychological Association, 1980.
10. Kaplan LV, Miller RD: The courtroom psychiatrist: Expertise at the cost of wisdom? *Int J Law Psychiatry* 1986; 9:451–468.
11. American Academy of Psychiatry and the Law, Ethics Committee: Ethical Guidelines for the Practice of Forensic Psychiatry. *Newsletter Am Acad Psychiatry Law* 1987; 12(1); 16–17.
12. Miller RD: The harassment of forensic psychiatrists outside court. *Bull Am Acad Psychiatry Law* 1985; 13:337–343.
13. *In re Roth*, 394 A.2d 419 (Pa. Sup. Ct. 1978).
14. *In re Lifschutz*, 2 Cal.3d 415, 85 Cal.Rptr. 829, 467 Pac.2d 557 (1970).
15. *Caesar V Mountanos*, 542 F.2d 1064 (9th Cir. 1976).
16. Diamond B: in Rosner R, Weinstock R (eds.) *Critical Issues in American Psychiatry and Law*, vol 7. New York, Plenum Medical Books, 1990, p. 38.
17. Rachlin S, Stokman CLJ: Incompetent misdemeanants—Pseudocivil commitment. *Bull Am Acad Psychiatry Law* 1986; 14:23–30.
18. Miller RD, Germain EJ: Inpatient evaluation of competency to stand trial. *Health Law in Canada* 1989; *9*(3):74–78, 92.
19. Solomon H: Presidential address to the American Psychiatric Association. *Am J Psychiatry* 1958; 115:1–9.
20. Modlin HC: The ivory tower v. the marketplace. *Bull Am Acad Psychiatry Law* 1984; 12:233–236.
21. *Estelle v Smith*, 451 U.S. 454, 101 S.Ct. 1866 (1981).
22. Hudgins RW: Murder by a manic-depressive. *Int J Neuropsychiatry* 1965; 1:381–383.
23. Ratner RA: Mania, crime, and the insanity defense: A case report. *Bull Am Acad Psychiatry Law* 1981; 9:23–32.
24. Wisconsin Statutes Chapters 971.14(5) and 971.17.
25. Gutheil TG: Prosecuting patients (ltr). *Hosp Comm Psychiatry* 1985; 36:1320–1321.
26. Miller RD: The treating psychiatrist as forensic evaluator in release decisions. *J Forensic Sci* 1987; 32:481–488.
27. Halleck SJ, Pacht AR: The current status of the Wisconsin Sex Crimes Law. *Wis Bar Bull* 1960:17–26.
28. Modlin HC: Compensation neurosis. *Bull Am Acad Psychiatry Law* 1986; 14:263–271.
29. Cole R: Patients' rights vs. doctors' rights: Which should take precedence? Paper presented at conference, *Refusing Treatment in Mental Health Institutions: Values in Conflict*. Boston, November 10, 1980.
30. Pasewark RA, Pantle ML, Steadman HJ: Characteristics and disposition of persons found not guilty by reason of insanity in New York State, 1971–1976. *Am J Psychiatry* 1979; 136:655–660.
31. Heller MS, Traylor WH, Ehrlich SM, Lester D: Intelligence, psychosis and competency to stand trial. *Bull Am Acad Psychiatry Law* 1981; 9:267–274.
32. Wisconsin Statutes Chapter 51.

33. Sadoff RL, Tanay E: Should the forensic evaluator be the treater? Panel presented at the 15th Annual Meeting of the American Academy of Psychiatry and the Law, Nassau, Bahamas, October 27, 1984.
34. California Welfare and Institutions Code ## 5000-5404, 1967, effective 1969 (Lanterman-Petris-Short Act).
35. Weiner BA: Sexual psychopath laws. In Brakel SJ, Parry J, Weiner BA (eds): *The Mentally Disabled and the Law*, ed 3, Chicago, American Bar Foundation, 1985.
36. Halleck SJ: The ethical dilemmas of forensic psychiatry: A utilitarian approach. *Bull Am Acad Psychiatry Law* 1984; 12:279–288.
37. Miller RD: The Terry hearings to determine the release of offenders committed under Wisconsin's Sex Crime Law. *Wis Bar Bull* 1988; 61(1): 17–19.
38. *State v Post*, Case No. I-7439 (Milwaukee Cty. Cir. Ct., September 1984).
39. American Psychiatric Association Ethics Committee: Opinion, expressed in a letter to the author from William L. Webb, Jr., M.D., Chair, APA Ethics Committee, April 18, 1986.
40. Miller RD: *Involuntary Civil Commitment of the Mentally Ill in the Post-Reform Era*. Springfield, IL, Charles C. Thomas, 1987, pp 129–170.
41. Bloom JD, Faulkner LR, Holm VM, Rawlinson RA: An empirical view of patients exercising their right to refuse treatment. *Int J Law Psychiatry* 1984; 7:315–328.
42. Zito JM, Lentz SL, Routt WW, Olson GW: The treatment review panel: A solution to treatment refusal? *Bull Am Acad Psychiatry Law* 1984; 12:349–358.
43. Appelbaum PS: The right to refuse treatment with antipsychotic medications: retrospect and prospect. *Am J Psychiatry* 1988; 145:413–419.
44. *Tarasoff v Regents of the University of California*, 118 Cal. Rptr. 129, 529 P.2d 553 (1974); 17 Cal.3d 425, 551 P.2d 334 (1976).
45. Miller RD, Doren DM, Van Rybroek GJ, Maier GJ: Emerging problems for staff associated with the release of potentially dangerous forensic patients. *Bull Am Acad Psychiatry Law* 1988; 16:309–320.
46. Stone AA: The *Tarasoff* case and some of its progeny: Suing psychotherapists to safeguard society, in *Law, Psychiatry and Morality*. Washington DC, American Psychiatric Press, 1984.
47. Appelbaum PS, Meisel A: Therapists' obligations to report their patients' criminal acts. *Bull Am Acad Psychiatry Law* 1986; 14:221–230.
48. Felthous AR: Liability of treaters for injuries to others: Erosion of three immunities. *Bull Am Acad Psychiatry Law* 1987; 15:115–125.
49. Weinstock R: Confidentiality and the new duty to protect: The therapist's dilemma. *Hosp Comm Psychiatry* 1988; 39:607–609.
50. American Psychological Association: Ethical principles of psychologists. *Am Psychol* 1981; 36:633–638.
51. National Federation of Societies for Clinical Social Work: Responsibilities of clinical social workers. Cited in Loewenberg F, Dolgoff R: *Ethical Decisions for Social Work Practice*. Itasca, IL, F.E. Peacock Publishers, 1985.
52. Newberger EH: The helping hand strikes again: Unintended consequences of child abuse reporting. *J Clin Child Psychol* 1983; 12:307–311.
53. Miller RD, Weinstock R: Conflict of interest between therapist-patient confidentiality and the duty to report sexual abuse of children. *Behav Sci Law* 1987; 5:161–174.
54. Gartrell N, Herman J, Olarte S, Feldstein M, Localio R: Sexual abuse of patients by therapists: Strategies for offender management and rehabilitation. *Hosp Comm Psychiatry* 1988; 39:1070–1074.
55. Minn. Stat. Ann. Secs. 148A.01-148A.06, Supp. 1987.
56. 1987 Wisconsin Act 380, published May 2, 1988, amending Wisconsin Statutes Chapter 940.22.
57. Hoge SK, Gutheil TG: The prosecution of psychiatric patients for assaults on staff: a preliminary empirical study. *Hosp Comm Psychiatry* 1987; 38:44–49.

58. Miller RD, Maier GJ: Factors affecting the decision to prosecute mental patients. *Hosp Comm Psychiatry* 1987; 38:50–55.
59. Appelbaum PS, Meisel A: Therapists' obligations to report their patients' criminal acts. *Bull Am Acad Psychiatry Law* 1986; 14:221–230.
60. Miller RD: The treating psychiatrist as forensic evaluator. *J For Sciences* 1984; 29:825–830.
61. Apostle DT: The unconsciousness defense as applied to post traumatic stress disorder in a Vietnam veteran. *Bull Am Acad Psychiatry Law* 1980; 8:426–430.
62. Kluft RP: The simulation and dissimulation of multiple personality disorder. *Am J Clin Hyp* 1987; 30:104–108.
63. McGarry AL: Pathological gambling: A new insanity defense. *Bull Am Acad Psychiatry Law* 1983; 11:301–308.
64. Perr IN: Pathological intoxication and alcohol idiosyncratic intoxication—Part I: Diagnostic and clinical aspects. *J Foren Sci* 1986; 31:806–811.
65. Resnick PR: Necrophilia, murder and insanity. Presented at the 18th Annual Meeting of the American Academy of Psychiatry and the Law, Ottawa, Canada, October 16, 1987.
66. American Psychiatric Association: *Diagnostic and Statistical Manual of Mental Disorders*, ed 3, revised. Washington DC, American Psychiatric Press, 1987.
67. Strasburger LH: Crudely, without any finesse: The defendant hears his psychiatric evaluation. *Bull Am Acad Psychiatry Law* 1987; 15:229–233.
68. Miller RD: Forensic testimony (Letter). *Newsletter Am Acad Psychiatry Law* 1988; 13(1):24.
69. Miller RD: Should forensic evaluators be informed of evaluators' opinions prior to trial? *Bull Am Acad Psychiatry Law*, 1989; 17:53–59.
70. Strasburger LH: Response (Letter). *Newsletter Am Acad Psychiatry Law* 1988; 13(1):24.
71. Amaya M, Burlingame W: Judicial review of psychiatric admissions: The clinical impact on child and adolescent patients. *J Am Acad Child Psychiatry* 1981; 20:761–776.
72. Ensminger JJ, Liguori TD: The therapeutic significance of the civil commitment hearing: An unexplored potential. *J Psychiatry Law* 1978; 6:5–44.
73. Miller RD, Bernstein MR, Van Rybroek GJ, Maier GJ: The impact of the right to refuse treatment in a forensic patient population: Six-month review. *Bull Am Acad Psychiatry Law* 1989; 17:107–119.
74. Wisconsin Statutes Chapter 971.17.
75. Melton GB, Petrilla J, Poythress NG, Slobogin C: *Psychological Evaluation for the Courts: A Handbook for Mental Health Professionals and Lawyers*. New York Guilford Press, 1987.
76. Bukatman BA, Foy JL, DeGrazia E: What is competency to stand trial? *Am J Psychiatry* 1971; 127:1225–1229.
77. Bursten B: Voluntariness of waiver of Fifth Amendment rights. *Bull Am Acad Psychiatry Law* 1979; 7:352–362.
78. Grisso T, Manoogian S: Juveniles' comprehension of Miranda warnings. In Lipsitt PD, Sales BD (eds): *New Directions in Psycholegal Research*. New York, Van Nostrand Reinhold, 1980.
79. Miller RD, Maier GJ, Kaye M: The right to remain silent during psychiatric evaluation in civil and criminal cases—A national survey and an analysis. *Int J Law Psychiatry* 1986; 9:77–94.
80. Gutheil TG, Appelbaum PS: *Clinical Handbook of Psychiatry and the Law*. New York, McGraw-Hill, 1982.
81. *Ake v Oklahoma*, 470 U.S. 68, 105 S.Ct. 1087, 84 L.Ed.2d 53 (1985).
82. Friedenthal JH: Discovery and use of an adverse party's expert information. *Stanford Law Rev* 1962; 14:455–488.
83. Resnick P, Discussion at the Spring Scientific Meeting of the Midwest Chapter of the American Academy of Psychiatry and the Law, Cincinnati, April 4, 1987.
84. National Medical Association Section on Psychiatry and Behavioral Sciences: Position statement on the role of the psychiatrist in evaluating and treating "death row inmates," Washington DC, undated.

85. Rappaport J, Roth LH: Resolved: It is unethical for psychiatrists to diagnose or treat condemned persons in order to determine their competency to be executed. Debate presented at the Annual Scientific Meeting of the American Psychiatric Association, Chicago, May 13, 1987.
86. Appelbaum PS, Sargent DA: Resolved: It is unethical for psychiatrists to diagnose or treat condemned persons in order to determine their competency to be executed. Debate presented at the Annual Scientific Meeting of the American Psychiatric Association, Chicago, May 13, 1987.
87. Miller RD: Evaluation of and treatment to competency to be executed: A national survey and an analysis. *J Psychiatry Law* 1988; 16:67–90.
88. McClaren H: A model mental health system for death row—Evaluation of competency for execution following *Ford v Wainwright*. Presented at the 18th Annual Meeting of the American Academy of Psychiatry and the Law, Ottawa, Oct 18, 1987.
89. Radelet ML, Barnard GW: Treating those found incompetent for execution: Ethical chaos with only one solution. *Bull Am Acad Psychiatry Law* 1988; *16*:297–307.
90. Annotated Code of the General Public Laws of Maryland, 1987 Cumulative Supplement, Article 27, Par. 75A(9)(d)(3).
91. Duff R: *Trials and Punishments*, 1986, p 15.
92. Hundert EM: A model for ethical problem solving in medicine, with practical applications. *Am J Psychiatry* 1987; 144:839–846.

9

Ethical Considerations of Giving *Miranda*-Type Warnings in Psychiatric Evaluations in Criminal Cases

GREGORY B. LEONG, J. ARTURO SILVA, AND ROBERT WEINSTOCK

INTRODUCTION

Just over two decades ago, the Supreme Court in its landmark *Miranda* decision afforded specific rights to criminal defendants.[1] Based primarily upon the Fifth Amendment, the *Miranda* warning includes informing the criminal defendant of the right to remain silent and that any of his or her statements have potential adverse legal consequences. Although the initial context of the *Miranda* ruling involved law enforcement personnel within the criminal justice system, the operational effects of *Miranda* have since permeated forensic and general psychiatric practice.

Psychiatry has adopted the usage of related "*Miranda*-type" warnings as part of professional psychiatric and forensic psychiatric ethical guidelines.[2-4] *Miranda*-type warnings closely resemble the informed consent process.[5] Informed consent contains the following three concepts: (1) voluntariness of the consent, (2) materiality of information provided to the patient about treatment, including relevant information about the diagnosis and risks and benefits of proposed treatment(s), and (3) competency to consent—the capacity to make a

---

GREGORY B. LEONG, J. ARTURO SILVA, AND ROBERT WEINSTOCK • Department of Psychiatry and Biobehavioral Sciences, School of Medicine, University of California at Los Angeles, Los Angeles, California 90024, and the Psychiatry Service, West Los Angeles Veterans Administration Medical Center, Los Angeles, California 90073.

rational judgment based upon the medical information present.[6,7] Using the informed-consent model, *Miranda*-type warnings contain elements of voluntariness, materiality of information provided to the examinee about the nature and purpose of evaluation, including possible limits of confidentiality and to whom such confidentiality may be breached, and competency to be evaluated. In some forensic situations, however, psychiatric evaluation may be statutorily mandated so that the voluntariness and competency aspects associated with the informed consent paradigm are not operational.[5] In addition, *Miranda*-type warnings serve to minimize ethical dilemmas posed by the double-agent role frequently encountered in both forensic and ordinary clinical settings.[8]

Ethical considerations associated with *Miranda*-type warnings in general psychiatric practice in clinical situations involving involuntary hospitalization, the duty to warn and/or protect (*Tarasoff*-type duty), and child abuse reporting have been previously discussed.[9] These clinical situations occur in the civil system, although child-abuse reporting can lead to involvement in the criminal justice system. Only in the context of civil commitment in a limited number of jurisdictions have *Miranda*-type warnings that include a right to remain silent been legally required.[10,11] *Miranda*-type warnings are not legally required in the context of a *Tarasoff*-type duty or child abuse reporting, but may be ethically appropriate.[9] Compared with the general clinical setting, legal rules and consequences play a greater role in the forensic setting and consequently affect psychiatric ethics to a greater extent. In the forensic setting, *Miranda*-type warnings play an integral part in the psychiatric evaluation as a result of the legal and essentially nontherapeutic context of evaluation.

This chapter focuses upon ethical considerations associated with usage of *Miranda*-type warnings in the practice of psychiatry in forensic settings in the criminal justice system. We exclude discussion of civil forensic cases. Monetary recompense is usually the stated goal in these civil matters and thus a separate set of ethics becomes involved when economic incentives are at stake. Although *Miranda*-type warnings have ethical relevance in civil cases, it is less likely that patients or examinees will need to be as thoroughly informed, as they generally have an adequate grasp of the matter. Moreover, these individuals (plaintiffs) are often prepared by their attorneys for both "friendly" and "adversarial" psychiatric evaluations.

CONTEXT OF *MIRANDA*-TYPE WARNINGS IN FORENSIC EVALUATIONS

In the criminal justice system, those individuals who undergo psychiatric evaluations have already been given the *Miranda* warning when apprehended. Moreover, some defendants do not candidly speak with anyone without the presence of their attorney. This makes psychiatric evaluations, including those requested by defense counsel, difficult to carry out.

In spite of the context of psychiatric assessment within the criminal justice system, the defendant may still misconstrue the consultative and essentially nontherapeutic role of the forensic evaluator. Forensic evaluators are generally psychiatrists or clinical psychologists, who carry the title of "doctor," thereby implying a helpful individual. They can also be skilled at making people feel at ease and come across as trustworthy.

Issuing a *Miranda*-type warning may not be an alien concept to forensic psychiatry, however, several factors may affect its clinicolegal impact. Ethical analysis thus depends upon discussing these factors that can affect the outcome of legal proceedings. With regard to *Miranda*-type warnings, psychiatric ethics only indicate that they be given. Indeed, a mentally ill defendant may not have sufficient awareness of the nature and purpose of the evaluation, especially its potential deleterious consequences. Some individuals may be so mentally disordered that they would lack the capacity to understand the meaning of a *Miranda*-type warning. Even if it is decided that some minimal level of awareness on the part of the defendant is ethically required before undertaking evaluation, the level of awareness that would be ethically feasible cannot be easily determined either clinically or legally. A review of empirical studies has found limitations to the goal of providing actual informed consent.[6,7] By analogy, it can be reasonably expected that similar limitations would hold for understanding *Miranda*-type warnings.

The level of a defendant's awareness of a *Miranda*-type warning raises several dilemmas. Do psychiatric ethics require that a minimum level of awareness of the *Miranda*-type warning vary with the severity of potential adverse legal consequences? For example, should potential capital punishment require a different level of awareness of *Miranda*-type warnings than a potential maximum penalty of a six-month incarceration? Should a psychiatrist proceed with an evaluation if the defendant is incapable of understanding its purpose in a capital case? When the purpose of the criminal justice system becomes retribution, does that increase the ethical requirement for clear and comprehensible *Miranda*-type warnings? Answers to these questions are difficult, as what may be deemed ethical from a psychiatric viewpoint is not always clear. Psychiatric ethics may necessitate concern even in situations where the law has no concern.

Police personnel use standard wording when issuing *Miranda* warnings. Similarly, should forensic psychiatrists also adopt standard wording when giving *Miranda*-type warnings? Changing the wording of a *Miranda*-type warning could imply to the defendant a message that could affect the expressed content of the interview and thereby change a psychiatric opinion and subsequent legal outcome. However, standard wording may preclude an effort to make certain the defendant has understood it. Extra effort may be ethically required in important cases. Standard wording could result in merely the appearance of a warning being given. Even in the medical setting, few patients truly understand standard consent forms.[12] The manner in which a *Miranda*-type warning is issued by the forensic examiner may also influence the ensuing interview. Operationally, in addition to the wording, the forensic psychiatrist's affect and demeanor when giving a *Miranda*-type warning may influence the interview and hence the legal outcome.

Miranda-type warnings ordinarily are given only once. After some time, "slippage," or decrease of the effect of a *Miranda*-type warning may occur.[4] Skillful and adept interviewers may help place the defendant at ease and, although performing an accurate clinical evaluation, negate the legal impact of the *Miranda*-type warning. Therefore, should forensic psychiatrists repeat the *Miranda*-type warning, and on what basis should it be repeated? Should the potential legal penalty dictate whether *Miranda*-type warnings are to be repeated, or only if slippage occurs? How much slippage needs to occur before a *Miranda*-type warning is reissued? What effort should be required to look for possible slippage when the defendant begins to give legally incriminating statements? And what are the effects of repeated and possibly unnecessary *Miranda*-type warnings on the forensic evaluation?

The legal context of forensic evaluation may affect the ethical considerations involved in issuing *Miranda*-type warnings. Since the nature and purpose of a specific type of forensic evaluation may have relevance to the ethical inquiry, different psychiatric-legal situations are discussed separately below.

Competency to Stand Trial Evaluations

In competency to stand trial (CST) evaluations, the issue of understanding a *Miranda*-type warning or obtaining informed consent for the evaluations is essentially moot. For a CST evaluation, a doubt is raised as to whether the defendant has "sufficient present ability to consult with his attorney with a reasonable degree of rational understanding...and...a rational as well as factual understanding of the proceedings taken against him."[13] Hence, it is likely that a defendant incompetent to stand trial would be similarly incapable of displaying sufficient awareness or understanding of the meaning of a *Miranda*-type warning. Clearly, if the defendant were required to be sufficiently aware of a *Miranda*-type warning before a CST evaluation, it could paralyze the legal process in these cases. In CST evaluations, it would seem that giving a single *Miranda*-type warning, whether or not the defendant is sufficiently aware of it, would generally satisfy ethical concerns.

A problematic issue in CST evaluations is the revelation of data that may have adverse legal consequences for the defendant. A unanimous Supreme Court ruling in *Estelle v Smith*[14] seems to protect the defendant against the use of any deleterious data from a pre-trial CST evaluation as evidence during the trial. In *Estelle v Smith*, an effort to utilize information given by the defendant in a CST evaluation during the penalty phase of the defendant's trial to determine whether the defendant met the legal standard for capital punishment was overturned in part because an appropriate *Miranda*-type warning regarding potential uses of the pretrial CST evaluation was not given. Nevertheless, exposure of information during a CST evaluation may indirectly lead to adverse consequences for a defendant.[15] It is well known that juries do not ignore evidence in many cases even if the judge orders them to do so. Thus, if the psychiatrist reports such information, it could be used to advantage by the prosecution against the defendant.

Reconstructive Evaluations

Often forensic psychiatrists are requested to assess by reconstruction the defendant's mental state at the time of the commission of an alleged offense. These reconstructive evaluations involve issues such as legal insanity, *mens rea*, diminished capacity, specific intent, and legal unconsciousness.

Frequently, defendants who undergo reconstructive evaluations are simultaneously assessed for competency to stand trial. A defendant who is not competent to stand trial may prevent a clinically reliable reconstructive evaluation. If a defendant is not competent to stand trial, the data obtained from a psychiatric evaluation may not reflect the historical mental state at the time of the alleged offense, as the present mental state is impaired and, by inference, data obtained from the evaluation could be unreliable. Alternatively, it is possible that a mentally disordered defendant may better be able to reveal the extent and details of his or her illness, including the thinking at the time of the alleged offense, only while he or she is still sufficiently disorganized to be incompetent to stand trial. Recovery from mental illness can frequently lead to denial and an inability to recall thoughts and behaviors at the time of the alleged crime. Ethical problems can occur when the mentally disordered and incompetent-to-stand-trial defendant is also incapable of understanding a *Miranda*-type warning about potential uses of psychiatric evaluation. For instance, if the defendant is unable to understand the *Miranda*-type warning about an insanity defense evaluation but is found not to meet the criteria for an insanity defense on the basis of forensic assessment, especially utilizing the restrictive M'Naghten criteria presently followed in about half the states,[16] some of the information revealed by the defendant in the pretrial CST and reconstructive assessment may later have harmful consequences to the defendant.

Assessment of a historical mental state has potential legal consequences for the defendant. If a legally relevant mental state existed at the time of the instant offense, a defendant's criminal responsibility may be absolved or reduced. A defendant generally would be satisfied with a reduction in criminal responsibility in order that he or she face less severe legal consequences. However, in the case of a determination of legal insanity, it may not necessarily be a desirable legal outcome. Arguably, the more severe the punishment is for a crime, the more likely a finding of legal insanity would be of legal benefit to a defendant. For example, a penalty of life imprisonment without the possibility of parole or the death penalty may be easily seen as less legally and clinically desirable than lengthy or lifetime commitment to a psychiatric facility. On the other hand, the possibility of long-term commitment in a psychiatric facility as opposed to a relatively short penal sentence may be seen as less legally desirable, although not necessarily less clinically desirable. Thus, it is difficult to gauge what is actually preferable for an individual defendant. Besides this simple analysis, the forensic psychiatrist may be unaware as to the legal strategy the defendant's attorney is pursuing, the attorney's belief as to what constitutes a favorable outcome for the client, and the mentally ill defendant's idiosyncratic beliefs and preferences for the trial outcome. Without knowing the particular defendant's legal options, the task of the forensic psychiatrist becomes more difficult from an ethical perspective concerning how much and what should be revealed to the defendant by *Miranda*-type warnings about the potential consequences of the forensic evaluation.

The problem of dissimulation or simulation of sanity[17] may be operating during or prior to the start of the forensic interview. A *Miranda*-type warning could serve to place defendants who consciously or unconsciously fear being considered "crazy" on alert to feign an absence of symptoms. Repetition of the *Miranda*-type warning throughout the interview could continually reinforce such a defendant's need to conceal mental illness in order to simulate sanity. Most often, however, defendants with a need to simulate sanity will do so regardless of the purpose of the examination and regardless of warnings. Therefore, it is unlikely that a *Miranda*-type warning will encourage withholding of helpful information in this case. Alternatively, a full and thorough explanation by the psychiatrist or the attorney of the need to discuss symptoms could facilitate more openness from the defendant. However, it would be important not to end up encouraging antisocial individuals to feign insanity by overly extensive explanation of the benefits of displaying psychosis.

Perhaps a more difficult ethical task occurs when assessing mental state at the time of the crime in potential capital cases. If a not guilty by reason of insanity (NGRI) plea is raised, a finding of an insufficient basis for legal insanity has potential severe legal harm for a defendant. The exposed data from NGRI evaluations may not be protected from prosecutorial use. When the legal stakes are this high, the ethics surrounding the *Miranda*-type warnings appear to take on additional importance. The number and method of *Miranda*-type warnings given may very well affect the legal outcome for these defendants.

Evaluations of Dangerousness in Noncapital Cases

Forensic psychiatrists often participate in assessing the level of dangerousness of defendants committed to psychiatric hospitals after trial court determination of NGRI or mentally disordered sex offender (MDSO) status. Evaluations for dangerousness of NGRI acquittees and MDSO committees generally take place near the end of their commitment and serve as a partial basis for extension of commitment beyond the term of the original "sentence." Though MDSO statutes have been repealed in many jurisdictions, those committed under old MDSO statutes continue to require psychiatric evaluation for possible extension of their commitment. The number of NGRI acquittees that face extension of their commitment is likely to remain unchanged for the foreseeable future. Thus, forensic psychiatrists will continue to participate in evaluations of dangerousness in NGRI acquittees and MDSO committees. Given the legal rules of NGRI and MDSO extensions, it is possible to have perpetual extensions of the original commitment and thus have lifetime commitment by statutorily defined criteria which may be less stringent than that for civil commitment under other circumstances. Hence, the legal risk to an NGRI or MDSO individual may indeed be great, though not at the level of capital cases where the specter of death looms. Given the possible legal harm to these individuals, a *Miranda*-type warning would seem to have particular relevance in commitment extension cases.

From a legal viewpoint, the Supreme Court in *Allen v Illinois*[18] has asserted that *Miranda* warnings are not required prior to undertaking a MDSO extension evaluation. In *Allen v Illinois*, the Supreme Court cited the civil (noncriminal) nature of the MDSO extension evaluation. In the case of NGRI acquittees, they may represent a special class of individuals that defy the usual civil-criminal dichotomy.[19] In spite of a legal ruling such as *Allen v Illinois*, forensic psychiatric ethics require giving *Miranda*-type warnings before undertaking MDSO and similarly, NGRI dangerousness commitment extension examinations.

The commitment extension of NGRI and MDSO individuals who have "served" their commitment or "sentence," poses ethical questions. After generally long periods of commitment and presumably psychiatric treatment during this time, such individuals may remain essentially clinically unchanged and therefore continue to represent a danger. Further commitment may not effect a clinical change to the extent that the statutorily defined level of dangerousness is then not met. Potential long-term and even lifetime commitment would seem ethically to require careful use of *Miranda*-type warnings. This may be especially true when the NGRI or MDSO individual's commitment time has surpassed the maximum time of confinement a non-mentally ill offender would have served in a penal institution for the identical crime. However, should the person clearly be dangerous, a forensic psychiatrist might not wish to explain the nature and purpose of the examination in such a way as to encourage the person to conceal evidence of dangerousness.

NGRI and MDSO extension cases frequently present with some clinical improvement and it may be exceedingly difficult to assess an individual's degree of danger to others, since the person will have been confined for so long that there may be no way reliably to assess how the patient will do in a setting outside the structured and supervised institutional milieu.[20] The context of evaluation is different from the context of prediction. If these individuals do not cooperate with forensic evaluation, the psychiatric facility treating the individual and simultaneously petitioning for commitment extension would have an unopposed clinical opinion supporting extension. Alternatively, cooperation with an extension evaluation may have legally beneficial effects for the individual, as a favorable psychiatric report could depend in part on the degree of cooperativeness during the clinical interview. Often it may realistically be impossible to determine dangerousness in such circumstances and the opinion may be more reflective of unstated evaluator biases. Is a forensic evaluator ethically required to inform a defendant of his biases if these biases are clear? Is the evaluator ethically required to inform a defendant when the outcome of such evaluations is predetermined to be negative and the procedure a sham, as some have claimed is true in MDSO release hearings in Wisconsin?[21] *Miranda*-type warnings may have some legal impact on the ultimate clinical opinion, and hence legal outcome in these situations.

Presentence Capital Case Evaluations

The most attention and controversy concerning *Miranda*-type warnings has probably been focused on death penalty cases. In contrast to other legal sanctions, death may be viewed as an irreversible process. Parenthetically, in the abstract sense, all legal sanctions may be considered at least partially irreversible. Nonetheless, the notion of the finality of death gives forensic psychiatric evaluation in potential capital cases significant meaning. One commentator fervently argues that performing assessments that are applied to capital sentencing proceedings is inherently unethical.[22]

In *Estelle v Smith*, the Supreme Court defined the legal contours regarding *Miranda* warnings for presentence psychiatric evaluation in capital cases.[15] In *Estelle v Smith*, a psychiatrist who evaluated the defendant for competency to stand trial testified at the sentencing phase of the trial and gave his opinion about the defendant's future dangerousness based upon data from his CST evaluation. The psychiatrist's testimony served as a partial basis for the imposition of the death penalty. The Supreme Court vacated the death penalty for two reasons. The first reason was that the psychiatrist had failed to provide a *Miranda*-type warning, in violation of the Fifth Amendment, prior to his CST evaluation if he was going to use the data for anything other than a CST assessment. The second reason was the defendant's right to counsel, or Sixth Amendment right, was violated with respect to the CST evaluation on which the death penalty was in part based. However, even though *Estelle v Smith* was a nine-to-zero decision, not all the justices agreed that a Fifth Amendment violation had occurred, since the statements used by the psychiatrist were not used to prove guilt, but rather for determination of the severity of punishment. The Sixth Amendment issue appeared to have unanimous support. Parenthetically, *Estelle v Smith* is not felt to address directly the results of pretrial evaluation on issues other than dangerousness; nor does it outline constitutional protections, if any, when the defendant initiates evaluation or introduces his own expert witness.[15]

In capital cases, like noncapital cases, repetitions of the *Miranda*-type warning, because of apparent slippage by the defendant, may give the defendant an impression or message, either conscious or unconscious, of the need to withhold data. The implicit message a *Miranda*-type warning is likely to communicate to the defendant is that he or she is guilty and the less said the better. This would seem to run counter to the legal presumption of "innocent until proven guilty." Such an inhibitory effect by repeated *Miranda*-type warnings may occasionally be legally detrimental to the defendant. Not all defendants are "wise" enough to determine what data may be detrimental to their cases. For those defendants with major mental disorders, a partial defect in logical cognitive processing may further impair the free flow of data needed to formulate an opinion with reasonable medical probability, especially for reconstructive evaluations. Thus, the use of *Miranda*-type warnings could have unpredictable effects upon capital-case forensic evaluations, as neither a beneficial nor a detrimental effect can be predetermined for specific data that may be withheld. However, traditional medical ethics might require an attempt to limit revelation of incriminating data that could lead to a death penalty sentence, especially if such information were in part revealed because the evaluator was perceived as intrinsically helpful. It would seem ethically improper if the evaluator utilized in any way the traditional helpful role of physicians to assume a role analogous to an undercover police detective.

The manner in which the *Miranda*-type warning is explained to the capital case defendant deserves attention. When informing the potential examinee of the nature and purpose of the evaluation, disclosure of its potential relation to the death penalty could easily influence the subsequent evaluation, especially when competency to stand trial and/or insanity evaluations are not yet completed. As discussed above, data necessary for psychiatric opinions that may be legally beneficial to the defendant occasionally may be withheld because the *Miranda*-type warning can convey the implication that all data may be legally harmful to the examinee. Most often, however, clearly explained and repeated *Miranda*-type warnings likely would be beneficial to the defendant in capital cases.

Many capital-case evaluations fall under the cloak of the attorney-client privilege or so-called "confidential" evaluations. In states where confidential evaluations are permitted, an extensive *Miranda*-type warning would seem to be less necessary, as the attorney needs all available data and the opinions flowing from he data adequately to undertake optimal defense of the case. However, it is still ethically necessary to inform a defendant of the nature and purpose of the examination and with whom the examination may be shared.[4] Failure to inform the defendant of the fact that it may largely be the attorney's decision whether to make the psychiatric evaluation public, or "nonconfidential," could lead to the defendant being defensive and concealing potentially helpful information. It would seem that nonconfidential evaluations, to which both prosecution and defense have access, would necessitate a stricter adherence to a clearly understood *Miranda*-type warning. It is conceivable that differences in *Miranda*-type warnings given by forensic psychiatrists for confidential and nonconfidential evaluations may affect the psychiatric opinion. Nonconfidentially appointed psychiatrists may also be placed at a clinical "disadvantage" when trying to gather data for opinion making as the defendant's attorney may instruct the defendant to withhold certain details from these psychiatrists, as opposed to the confidentially appointed forensic psychiatrist whose data gathering remains a product of the attorney-client privilege.

Postsentence Capital Case Evaluations

Even after the final judicial decision is rendered in capital cases and no intervening executive orders have come forth to avert a legally authorized execution, a death row inmate who suffers from a mental disorder to the degree that he or she qualifies for incompetency to be executed may be able to prevent execution. The Supreme Court has recently affirmed the incompetency to be executed concept.[23]

The recent literature contains several ethical analyses about psychiatric participation in the competency to be executed process.[24-28] Many commentators recommend staying away from participating in this controversial process because of its close association with death. Even so, psychiatric participation may be deemed ethically appropriate when an opinion supporting incompetency to be executed is offered. Diamond[29,30] contends it is possible to perform an honest evaluation, become an honest advocate, and participate in criminal cases only if a totally honest opinion would be helpful to the defendant, and the opinion is confidential to the defense attorney. Such a procedure may be especially appropriate in death penalty cases. Rappeport and Roth[31] argue that the psychiatrist's role is consultative to the legal system and no violation of psychiatric ethics occurs so long as the psychiatrist is not a participant in the actual execution.[31] A survey of forensic psychiatrists (and a few forensic psychologists) showed variance of opinion regarding the ethics of professional participation in competency-to-be-executed evaluations.[32] Moreover, there is no scientific or philosophical evidence to support fully either position. Nonetheless, for a position that would allow for an opinion in support of competency, *Miranda*-type warnings appear to be especially relevant. Participation in a restoration-of-competency evaluation after a prior finding of incompetency presents a similar ethical dilemma.

Ethical questions might be raised if the psychiatrist becomes too avid an advocate for the death penalty in his or her professional capacity. For those forensic psychiatrists who equate restoration of competency to doing harm, the pull to exaggerate incompetency or to ignore malingering in such cases presents a serious ethical conundrum. Although this might be consistent with the traditional medical role of preserving life, a lack of total honesty tends to undermine any reliance on psychiatric testimony and presents the problems associated with that of a "hired gun." Nevertheless, the additional factor of proximity to death makes the use of the *Miranda*-type warning potentially powerful in deciding what data the death row inmate transmits to the examining psychiatrist.

CONCLUSION

As physicians, psychiatrists attempt to adhere to the principles of medical ethics, including the traditional Hippocratic principle of *primum non nocere*, or "first do no harm." In forensic psychiatry, especially in the milieu of the criminal justice system, information gathered in psychiatric assessments and used in the formulation of psychiatric-legal opinions may have harmful consequences for evaluated individuals. Since confidentiality frequently cannot be maintained for psychiatric evaluation in the criminal system, *Miranda*-type warnings serve to define the limits of confidentiality to the examined individual prior to psychiatric evaluation.

Miranda-type warnings are specifically legally required prior to undertaking psychiatric evaluation in potential capital cases. Further, *Miranda*-type warnings are necessary in all situations from the psychiatric ethical perspective. Although giving *Miranda*-type warnings is seemingly straightforward, the forensic situations discussed strongly suggest that ethical problems still remain how the *Miranda*-type warning is given, or the number of times the *Miranda*-type warning should be repeated. Given the multiplicity of legal and psychiatric parameters of a particular case, clear-cut answers to operationalize *Miranda*-type warnings are lacking. Either overconcern or underconcern with *Miranda*-type warnings may impact the clinical interview and the subsequent psychiatric opinion and legal outcome. Latent values of the individual evaluator often determine the extent of such warnings and differences in the type and extent of a warning, dependent on the nature of a specific evaluation.

Appelbaum[33] contends that psychiatrists should protect as much as possible information disclosed by the patient, and that warning a patient of the potential for disclosure of an evaluation's contents undermines the ethical basis of confidentiality, since patient information ordinarily should be kept confidential. However, he only discusses forensic settings in which a doctor-patient relationship exists. In the forensic settings described in this chapter, the traditional doctor-patient relationship is not present. A consultant-client relationship more aptly describes the professional relationship in the forensic situations described herein. However, even in these forensic situations, medical ethics still applies. How much weight to give various aspects can be a matter of controversy. We agree that psychiatric ethics require breaches of confidentiality to be kept to a minimum, even in the context of psychiatric evaluation in the criminal justice setting. *Miranda*-type warnings can serve to reduce the ethical problem associated with any breach of confidentiality. Nevertheless, they raise other perplexing issues. The complexity of the situational legal factors in criminal cases make ethical analysis especially difficult when considering the extent and nature of *Miranda*-type warnings.

REFERENCES

1. *Miranda v Arizona*, 384 U.S 436 (1966).
2. American Psychiatric Association: *Principles of Medical Ethics with Annotations Especially Applicable to Psychiatry*. Washington, D.C., American Psychiatric Association, 1985.
3. American Psychiatric Association: Official actions: Guidelines on confidentiality. *Am J Psychiatry* 1987; 144:1522–1526.
4. American Academy of Psychiatry and the Law: *Ethical Guidelines*. Baltimore, American Academy of Psychiatry and the Law, 1987.
5. Sadoff RL: Ethical issues in forensic psychiatry. *Psychiatr Ann* 1988; 18:320–323.
6. Tancredi L: Competency for informed consent: Conceptual limits of empirical data. *Int J Law Psychiatry* 1982; 5:51–63.
7. Lidz C, Meisel A, Zerubavel E, *et al*: *Informed Consent: A Study of Decision Making in Psychiatry*. New York, Guilford Press, 1984.
8. Simon RI: The psychiatrist as a fiduciary: Avoiding the double agent role. *Psychiatr Ann* 1987; 17:622–626.
9. Leong GB, Silva JA, Weinstock R: Ethical considerations of clinical use of *Miranda*-like warnings. *Psychiatr Q* 1988; 59:293–305.
10. Miller RD, Maier GJ, Kaye M: *Miranda* comes to the hospital: The right to remain silent in civil commitment. *Am J Psychiatry* 1985; 142:1074–1077.

11. Miller RD, Maier GJ, Kaye M: The right to remain silent during psychiatric examination in civil and criminal cases—National survey and an analysis. *Int J Law Psychiatry* 1986; 9:77–94.
12. Casseleth B, Zupkis R, Sutton-Smith K, *et al*: Informed consent—Why are its goals imperfectly realized? *N Engl J Med* 1980; 302:896–900.
13. *Dusky v United States*, 362 U.S. 402 (1960).
14. *Estelle v Smith*, 451 U.S. 454 (1981).
15. Slobogin C: *Estelle v Smith*: The constitutional contours of the forensic evaluation. *Emory Law J* 1982; 31:72–138.
16. Callahan L, Mayer C, Steadman HJ: Insanity defense reform in the United States-post-Hinckley. *Ment Phys Disability Law Rptr* 1987; 11:54–59.
17. Diamond BL: The simulation of sanity. *J Soc Therapy* 1956; 2:158–165.
18. *Allen v Illinois*, 106 S. Ct. 2988 (1986).
19. Parry J: The civil-criminal dichotomy in insanity commitment and release proceedings: Hinckley and other matters. *Ment Phys Disability Law Reprt* 1987; 11:218–223.
20. Monahan J: Prediction, research, and the emergency commitment of mentally ill persons: A reconsideration. *Am J Psychiatry* 1978; 135:198–201.
21. Miller RD: personal communication.
22. Ewing CP: "Dr. Death" and the case for an ethical ban on psychiatric and psychological predictions of dangerousness in capital sentencing proceedings. *Am J Law Med* 1983; 8:407–428.
23. *Ford v Wainwright*, 106 S. Ct. 2595 (1986).
24. Appelbaum PS: Competence to be executed: Another conundrum for mental health professionals. *Hosp Comm Psychiatry* 1986; 37:682–684.
25. Salguero RG: Medical ethics and competency to be executed. *Yale Law J* 1986; 96:167–186.
26. Radelet M, Barnard G: Ethics and the psychiatric determination of competency to be executed. *Bull Am Acad Psychiatry Law* 1986; 14:37–53.
27. Ewing CP: Diagnosing and treating "insanity" on death row: Legal and ethical perspective.s *Behav Sci Law* 1987; 5:175–185.
28. Mossman D: Assessing and restoring competency to be executed: Should psychiatrists participate? *Behav Sci Law* 1987; 5:397–409.
29. Diamond BL: The psychiatrist: Consultant vs. activist in legal doctrine. Presented at the 19th Annual Meeting of the American Academy of Psychiatry and the Law, San Francisco, October 20, 1988.
30. Diamond BL: The honest advocate, in Rosner R, Weinstock R (eds): *Ethical Practice in Psychiatry and the Law.* New York, Plenum, 1990.
31. Usdin GL, Appelbaum PS, Sargent D, *et al*: Resolved: it is unethical for psychiatrists to diagnose or treat condemned persons in order to determine their competency to be executed. Presented at the 140th Annual Meeting of the American Psychiatric Association, Chicago, May 13, 1987.
32. Weinstock R: Controversial ethical issues in forensic psychiatry: A survey. *J Forensic Sci* 1988; 33:176–186.
33. Appelbaum PS: Confidentiality in the forensic evaluation. *Int J Law Psychiatry* 1984; 7:285–300.

10

Ethical Issues in Forensic Psychiatry

ROBERT L. SADOFF

Forensic psychiatry has been established as a subspecialty of psychiatry in the past two decades. The initiation of the American Academy of Psychiatry and the Law as the outstanding organization of forensic psychiatrists in the country, the founding of the American Board of Forensic Psychiatry in the late 1970s, and finally, the development of specialized training programs and fellowships in forensic psychiatry, all attest to the growth and presence of the subspecialty. In many ways, forensic psychiatrists serve as the spokespersons for psychiatry, as they attain exposure, both in court and in the media, commenting on principles of psychiatry and mental health. The changes in mental health legislation and the increase in psychiatric malpractice claims have also served to enhance the subspecialty of forensic psychiatry.

Forensic psychiatry may be defined as that subspecialty of psychiatry in which individuals are examined and evaluated within a legal context, either civil or criminal. In criminal cases, the forensic psychiatrist may examine the defendant at any stage of the criminal proceedings, beginning with the investigative phase, through the accusatory phase, the pretrial phase, the trial stage, and, finally, the posttrial proceedings. Determination of competency or criminal responsibility and recommendation for disposition are issues addressed by the forensic psychiatrist in a criminal setting.

In civil-legal cases, the forensic psychiatrist may offer an opinion with respect to civil competency, or in domestic relations disputes in which child custody or visitation is the major issue, in assessment of damages in personal

Originally published in *Psychiatric Annals.* Revised and reprinted by permission.

ROBERT L. SADOFF • Department of Psychiatry and Center for Studies of Social-Legal Psychiatry, University of Pennsylvania School of Medicine, Jenkintown, Pennsylvania 19046.

injury and malpractice cases. In psychiatric malpractice cases, he may offer an opinion with respect to liability, as well as damages. In administrative legal matters regarding commitment and patients' rights, the forensic psychiatrist is often at the forefront, providing evaluations, examinations, and forensic consultations.

How is the forensic psychiatrist regulated in his practice? Certainly, he is regulated by the same ethical and legal guidelines that affect physicians and psychiatrists in general. However, because of the special nature of his work, the American Academy of Psychiatry and the Law deemed it necessary to provide ethical guidelines for the practice of forensic psychiatry. These guidelines were recently adopted by AAPL, and focus primarily on four areas: confidentiality, consent, impartiality and objectivity, and qualifications.[1] "Impartiality and objectivity" recently were revised to read, "honesty and striving for objectivity" (see Appendix).

CONFIDENTIALITY

With respect to confidentiality, the forensic psychiatrist is guided, as are all psychiatrists, by the statement of ethics for physicians that has been applied to psychiatrists, as follows: "A physician may not reveal the confidences entrusted to him in the course of medical attendance, or the deficiencies he may observe in the character of patients, unless he is required to do so by law or unless it becomes necessary in order to protect the welfare of the individual or of the community."

The forensic psychiatrist may encounter situations in which confidentiality may become difficult. The examining forensic psychiatrist must indicate to the person examined that he is not a treating doctor and that he may not be able to keep confidential any material that is divulged to him. He must indicate that there is no secrecy and the examinee must be careful about his communications because, especially in criminal cases, they may be used against him in court.

The forensic psychiatrist must also be aware that the legal proceedings are adversarial in nature, and when his records are subpoenaed by an attorney, he must take precautions and be certain that the subpoena is valid and the attorney is authorized to have the information contained in the records. Sometimes the opposing attorney will demand a hearing before the judge prior to the psychiatrist releasing his records. Once the judge orders records released, the psychiatrist should provide the information in response to the court order. Court orders are commands; subpoenas are demands.

When conducting evaluations in correctional settings, the psychiatrist must alert the individual examined that there is a limit to confidentiality, and that he may need to report information that could be construed as leading to violent behavior, escape, or self-destructive behavior. The responsibility for the individual examined in a correctional setting still belongs to the warden or the head of the institution, and not to the psychiatrist.

In some cases, individuals will tell a psychiatrist that they have killed other people in the past. What is the duty of the psychiatrist in such cases? In other cases, defendants will indicate that they are planning to harm witnesses against them. Must the psychiatrist speak out and reveal these communications? In the second instance, the psychiatrist is obliged, as in any other branch of medicine, to prevent violent behavior, and will need, under the Tarasoff doctrine, to communicate these threats if they are believed likely to occur. In the first instance, the psychiatrist should explore with the patient his communication about killing others in the past. Sometimes, individuals brag or have fantasies about what has occurred in their lives, and may not be truthful. A helpful suggestion is to have the patient communicate these events to the authorities as part of his therapy. There is no duty to report a past crime.

When treating an individual on probation, parole, or in a conditional-release situation in criminal cases, the forensic psychiatrist must clarify with the patient at the outset the limitations on confidentiality. He must report attendance, and may be obliged to report communications that will be damaging to the patient or to others. The psychiatrist will be able to keep most communications confidential in such settings; but there are limitations that must be clarified at the beginning, both with the patient and with the authorities responsible for the patient under treatment. Failure to clarify at the outset could lead to very difficult ethical problems later about confidentiality. Especially with the antisocial personality or the borderline personality disorder, the psychiatrist must be clear about not being seduced into hearing information that may not be shared. For example, the sociopathic individual or borderline may tell the psychiatrist, "This information I do not want you to tell anyone, but it will be helpful in my treatment." Under such conditions, the psychiatrist should stop the patient and announce that there are limitations on confidentiality, and he may not be able to comply with the patient's wishes.

Because the legal situation is adversarial, the forensic psychiatrist who is approached by an attorney for one side may not accept assignment by the other side in the same case. Once he has been consulted, he is likely to be kept from working for the other side because he has been privy to confidential information that would negatively affect the side that approached him initially. However, it should be pointed out that, on occasion, lawyers will list forensic psychiatrists as their experts without ever contacting them, thereby preventing them from being called by the other side. This is not fair practice and should be reported by the psychiatrist when it occurs.

INFORMED CONSENT

Perhaps the most important concept in the treatment of patients is that of informed consent. In psychiatry generally, the patient's informed consent is necessary before treatment can occur. The psychiatrist must give the patient sufficient information on which the patient can then base an intelligent and informed consent to treatment of a particular nature. The psychiatrist should tell the patient what to expect from the treatment, including side effects and positive effects. He should also tell the patient what alternative forms of treatment are available and the effects and side effects. Finally, the psychiatrist should tell the patient the effects of no treatment at all. In this way, the patient may choose what type of treatment he wishes to accept. Too often, the psychiatrist tells the patient only about the treatment he is to give, and not the alternative forms that are available, and may be helpful to the patient.

The psychiatrist should write in the record essentially what he told the patient, and that the patient appeared to understand and accept the treatment offered. It is not wise to write every side effect that is anticipated, since one can never get them all, and it would take excessive time away from treatment to list all side effects. However, with the use of psychotropic medication it is important to list tardive dyskinesia as a side effect, and to discuss this effect with the patient. It is also important to follow the patient during the course of treatment, not only personally, but also with records that may be reviewed later in the event of an untoward reaction.

In forensic psychiatry, informed consent is especially important. The psychiatrist approaching an individual for an examination should give him what are sometimes loosely called "psychiatric Miranda warnings." This warning is especially important in criminal cases, when the psychiatrist is examining the defendant for the prosecution or for the court. In those cases, the psychiatrist must alert the defendant that he is a psychiatrist, and that he has been appointed by the court or retained by the prosecution to conduct the examination. The defendant should also be told that whatever he says will be written down and put into a report that will be sent to the prosecutor and/or the court, and will be used in the prosecution of his case. The defendant should also be given the option that he does not need to divulge incriminating information, and does not even need to respond to the questions posed by the psychiatrist, especially if the responses will be incriminating. In some jurisdictions, this matter is handled effectively by legislation, but in others, the defendant is mandated to speak to the prosecution-appointed psychiatrist if he intends to plead insanity.

It is not enough in informed-consent issues merely to give the information to the patient. The psychiatrist should be aware that the patient understands the information as given, and can incorporate that information into a decision-making process, so that his consent is truly voluntary, intelligent, and informed. This means the psychiatrist must explain, in a manner that the patient can understand, the effects and side effects of treatment, or the consequences of talking with the psychiatrist. It should also be pointed out that treatment is different from examination, and for the patient in a criminal setting to agree to treatment, he should be told exactly the parameters of the treatment and the limits on confidentiality, as noted above.

Finally, in criminal matters, the forensic psychiatrist should not examine a defendant for the prosecution before he has obtained effective counsel. It is deemed unethical for the psychiatrist to conduct such an examination before the defendant has been properly prepared by his attorney for the consequences of such a forensic examination.

HONESTY AND STRIVING FOR OBJECTIVITY

Perhaps the next two sections are more particular for the forensic psychiatrist than for psychiatry in general. The issue of honesty and striving for objectivity certainly arises in the treatment of individuals by the general psychiatrist. However, in adversarial cases within the law, the forensic psychiatrist may be obtained by one side or the other. Despite this fact, the psychiatrist must maintain as much honesty and objectivity as possible when conducting the initial examination. He must not be swayed by the fact that the defense attorney is paying him for the examination. Similarly, his psychiatric judgment and opinion must not be influenced by the fact that he is being paid by the plaintiff in a civil case. One way of avoiding such influence is to have the payment made in advance. Some psychiatrists may fear that if their opinion does not help the attorney who is retaining them, he will not be inclined to pay them. If the psychiatrist is paid in advance, he has no concern about being paid and may retain his objectivity. If the lawyer does not like the psychiatrist's opinion, at least he knows it is an honest opinion, and will have to work with that. Some lawyers, of course, will continue to search for an opinion that will help their side.

Maintaining objectivity and honesty, however, does not mean that the psychiatrist rushes to the other side if his opinion is helpful to them. He must maintain the confidentiality of the side that retains him. In criminal cases, the psychiatrist working for the defense may not be called by the prosecution if his opinion is not helpful to the defense and he is not called to testify. In civil cases, however, the discovery rule indicates that anyone having seen the plaintiff, either for the plaintiff's attorney or for the defendant's attorney, may be called to testify by the side that feels that testimony will be helpful.

Honesty and striving for objectivity do not preclude the psychiatrist from maintaining his opinion even under good cross-examination. Thus, the ethical forensic psychiatrist may be an advocate for his opinion, but should not become an adversary for it. In other words, the psychiatrist should present his data and his findings as objectively as possible and maintain his stance, even under cross-examination. However, if cross-examination weakens his opinion, he should be honest enough to admit that, and not maintain his viewpoint even in the face of logical opposition.

Retainer fees for testimony are also important in maintaining objectivity. The psychiatrist may fear that if his testimony is weakened in court, he may not be paid by the side calling him to court. Thus, it is important to have been paid in advance, so that cross-examination that does logically and effectively weaken the testimony will be acknowledged honestly by the expert, who will not cling desperately to his original opinion for fear he will alienate his attorney and not be paid.

We have heard, too often, about the "battle of the experts" that tends to weaken the public image of psychiatry. The image can be strengthened and enhanced when the psychiatrist provides effective testimony and appears logical and credible under cross-examination. He does not maintain his stance simply because he is a psychiatrist and that is his opinion, but maintains it because the objective data tend to support his conclusion and his opinion.

The forensic psychiatrist providing a report to the court should also maintain the type of honesty and objectivity necessary in medicine. The report should be balanced, credible, and complete. The psychiatrist should be able to support his conclusions with reasonable data, obtained through examination, and to communicate these conclusions effectively, even to a lay jury.

In cases of domestic-relations disputes, it is important for the objective and honest forensic psychiatrist to examine all parties. When that is prohibited by law, the psychiatrist should announce initially that his examination was restricted to the people whom he did examine. It is clear that the psychiatrist can give a better evaluation of an individual following a personal examination; however, the person may not be available, legally or practically, for such examination. For example, in cases of will contests, the testator is often deceased. In these cases, again, the psychiatrist must acknowledge the source of his evaluation and opinions.

Striving for ethical objectivity can be enhanced when the treating psychiatrist does not act as a forensic expert. It is unwise for the treating psychiatrist to attempt to testify in court, even though lawyers and judges may believe that his testimony is the most effective because he knows the patient best. In many cases this is true; but the legal arena is a difficult one for the treating psychiatrist. There is an inherent bias on the part of the treating psychiatrist to help his patient. Therefore, he could not effectively testify against his patient and expect to resume treatment after the court setting. In another sense, the treatment situation is altered as soon as the psychiatrist enters the courtroom to take on a different role with his patient than as therapist. Finally, there is the concern about economic conflict of interest when the treating psychiatrist testifies, especially in a personal injury matter, recommending further intensive and long-term treatment with him.

As in all forms of medicine and psychiatry, contingency fees are prohibited; that is, if the psychiatrist testifies effectively, he will then obtain more money. This puts the profession of psychiatry in an untenable position. Another reason for obtaining retainer fees is to avoid the accusation of contingency fees. For the very reason that attorneys do accept contingency fees, and may lose the case, the psychiatrist should be paid by the plaintiff's attorney in advance.

QUALIFICATIONS

Finally, the issue of qualifications is important in forensic psychiatry. The jury is impressed by the qualifications of the expert, and the weight of testimony often goes to the experiences and the credentials of the expert witness. When forensic psychiatrists misrepresent their training or their experience, the effect on the proceeding is apparent. It is unethical and fraudulent for a psychiatrist to misrepresent himself in court.

On a final note, the American Academy of Psychiatry and the Law has decided to turn over all complaints of an ethical nature to the American Psychiatric Association, because the procedures are extensive, and APA has the mechanism for handling disciplinary actions in ethical breaches.

REFERENCE

1. Ethical Guidelines for the Practice of Psychiatry as adopted by The American Academy of Psychiatry and the Law, October 1987, revised October 1989.

11

Adjudication of AAPL Ethical Complaints

A Proposal

ABRAHAM L. HALPERN

An issue that was very controversial within AAPL for a long time was the question of adoption of a definition of forensic psychiatry. Prior to 1985 a frequently quoted definition ran as follows: "Forensic psychiatry is the application of psychiatry to legal issues for legal ends."[1] Some members felt that such a definition left our profession open to misuse and to the temptation on the part of forensic psychiatrists to practice in accord with legal, not psychiatric, ethical canons. After a great deal of debate and consultation with a number of senior AAPL members, the following definition was submitted to the American Board of Forensic Psychiatry and subsequently adopted on May 20, 1985: "Forensic psychiatry is a subspecialty of psychiatry in which scientific and clinical expertise is applied to legal issues in legal contexts embracing civil, criminal, correctional or legislative matters; forensic psychiatry should be practiced in accordance with guidelines and ethical principles enunciated by the profession of psychiatry." Linking the ethical prong to the functional prong in one definition was disturbing to some; but the authors of the definition felt fully vindicated when it was included in AAPL's *Ethical Guidelines for the Practice of Forensic Psychiatry*,[2] adopted by the membership at the Semiannual Meeting in Chicago on May 10, 1987.[3]

AAPL's Ethical Guidelines are intended to supplement *The Principles of Medical Ethics with Annotations Especially Applicable to Psychiatry*, promulgated by the American Psychiatric Association. An example of how important it is that

ABRAHAM L. HALPERN • Department of Psychiatry, New York Medical College, Valhalla, New York 10595, and Department of Psychiatry, United Hospital Medical Center, Port Chester, New York 10573.

these documents be read together can be seen in Section 5 of AAPL's Guidelines concerning "Qualifications" ("As regards expert opinions, reports and testimony, the expert's qualifications should be presented accurately and precisely"), and Section 2 of the Principles of Medical Ethics ("A physician shall...strive to expose those physicians...who engage in fraud or deception").

Here is an actual case in point: Dr. X, a member of AAPL, provided attorneys who engaged him with a curriculum vitae that included the following false claims: certification in psychiatry by the American Board of Psychiatry and Neurology; appointment as Associate Professor of Columbia University School of Medicine; publication of an article in the June 1965 issue of the *American Journal of Psychiatry*; and Editor of the *American Journal of Forensic Psychiatry*. Should this case come before the Ethics Committee of the APA, it may well be considered relatively trivial, and dismissed on the promise of the accused physician that he will correct his curriculum vitae. This case was in fact handled recently by the New York State Health Department's Office of Professional Medical Conduct. That body concluded that there was insufficient evidence to support charges of professional misconduct for formal disciplinary proceedings and the case was closed.[4] This decision was rendered even after it was brought to the attention of the officials that the psychiatrist was reported to have pled guilty to a federal fraud charge[5] and a state bribery charge.[6] Members of AAPL might feel that such a disposition is inappropriate, if not frivolous.

AAPL's "Ethical Guidelines for the Practice of Forensic Psychiatry" contains canons that do not appear in the APA's code of ethics. For example, under the Guidelines, AAPL would consider it unethical were a forensic evaluation performed on *any person* charged with criminal acts prior to his access to, or the availability of, legal counsel. The APA Annotations, however, preclude the psychiatric evaluation only in the case of *adult* defendants.

Since membership in the APA is a requirement for all AAPL members, one might think that the problem of enforcement would readily disappear with the adoption of AAPL's ethical guidelines by the American Psychiatry Association. However, experience has shown that it can take years to effect changes in codes of ethics. Furthermore, it is a well-recognized and much deplored fact that ethical complaints are processed with glacial speed under present procedures.

With all of this in mind, it is proposed that AAPL adopt procedures for handling ethical complaints against Academy members along the lines recommended by the American College of Physicians Ethics Committee.[7] The ACP's procedures, which include a review, hearing, and sanctions, constitute a process that is fair and effective. Should such procedures be adopted, a complaint of unethical forensic psychiatric practice by an Academy member would be submitted, along with supporting documentation, to the President and Medical Director of the Academy. They, along with the relevant Chapter President or, if there is no relevant chapter president, the president-elect of the Academy, would evaluate the material, including a response from the affected member to the president's notification to the member that an ethical complaint has been filed against him. If these officers were to decide that further study were necessary, a hearing would be called within 30 days.

The hearing committee would consist of at least three senior members of the Academy, appointed by the relevant chapter president or the president-elect of the Academy if there were no relevant chapter president. As such proceedings would be intra-Academy, not judicial, neither the Academy nor the member being questioned would be represented by an attorney. (If, however, the Academy were to decide to have an attorney participate on its behalf, the member under review would be allowed one as well.) Failure of the affected member to provide the information requested within 14 days, or failure of the member to appear before the hearing committee when requested to do so, without good cause shown, would in itself be considered a violation of AAPL's ethical code and would result in an appropriate sanction.

Within 30 days of the hearing, the hearing committee would make a recommendation on the case which would be sent along with written findings to the president of AAPL, the medical director, and the member under review.

There would be four possible sanctions: 1) a letter of reprimand; 2) a period of probationary membership; 3) suspension of membership; and 4) permanent revocation of membership.

The member would be advised that reporting laws of the jurisdiction in which the hearing was to be held might require the Academy to report action taken regarding membership status or to report evidence of unethical or unprofessional physician conduct.

The hearing committee's recommendations and findings would then go to the ethics committee for review. The ethics committee's recommendation would subsequently be forwarded to the executive council (or board of directors, if AAPL were to establish such an entity) for review and implementation, and to the affected member.

It is further proposed that action by AAPL on a complaint of unethical forensic psychiatric practice should not be obstructed, terminated, or rendered moot, by the resignation of an accused member after the complaint has been registered and before the case has gone through the process described above.

An alternative to the four formal sanctions mentioned is considered by the author to be essential to the effective handling of violations of AAPL's ethical guidelines. The option herein proposed is that of *caution*, constituting an *informal* notice to a violator by AAPL's governing body on the recommendation of the ethics committee. A caution would not be reportable to a state agency or to another organization to which the AAPL member belongs (such as the American Psychiatric Association) as a formal disciplinary action against the physician. Nor would it be reportable as an "adverse action" to the central nationwide data bank formed by the Health and Human Services Administration "to collect and disseminate disciplinary and malpractice information on physicians and dentists."[8]

One reason for recommending this step of informal caution is that experience has shown that relatively minor violations are rarely reported to ethics committees and, when reported, are not processed by ethics committees which heretofore have been frequently hampered by cumbersome procedural rules and have been hard-pressed to handle on a timely basis serious, let alone minor, charges of unethical conduct. It is common knowledge that a serious violation has never been processed from start to finish by any psychiatric association in a reasonable period of time, other than by the resignation or death of the accused psychiatrist.

A more important reason lies in the fact that in many instances physicians, including psychiatrists, against whom serious charges of ethical violations are brought, have previously been involved in generally minor ethical practices over a prolonged period of time. It is my belief that a mechanism that permits an ethics committee to hear a complaint informally and issue a caution which is not designated as a disciplinary action and is not subject to reporting could have a most salutary effect in correcting the conduct of the physician in question.

Thus, it is my contention that dealing with minor ethical violations can have a preventive effect and reduce the likelihood of future misconduct.

Formal ethics committee actions are not only required to be reported to state licensing authorities in many jurisdictions but, to an ever-increasing extent, must be reported by the physician on an application for a state medical license, application for membership on a hospital medical staff, application for a position in a health maintenance organization or other employment, and, extremely troubling indeed, applications for professional liability insurance.

Is it small wonder that ethics committees are most reluctant to consider minor violation complaints or that accused physicians resist with every legal device available (even engaging specialist attorneys at astronomical fees) any effort on the part of an ethics committee to reach a *formal* finding against them?

SUMMARY

A method for processing complaints of unethical forensic psychiatric practice is described. Formal and informal measures are outlined. The steps recommended would provide AAPL members accused of violations of the Academy's ethical guidelines all the process that is due without causing procedural paralysis by an overabundance of due process.

REFERENCES

1. Pollack S: Forensic psychiatry—A specialty. *Bull Amer Acad Psychiatry Law* 1974; 2:1, p 2.
2. Ethical Guidelines for the Practice of Forensic Psychiatry. *Newsletter Amer Acad Psychiatry Law* 1987; 12:1, pp 16–17.
3. Ethical Guidelines. *Newsletter Amer Acad Psychiatry Law* 1987; 12:2, p 12.
4. Letter, Leanne Raga, Health Program Administrator, Office of Professional Medical Conduct, New York State Department of Health, to AL Halpern, Jul 1, 1987.
5. Meislin RJ: Testimony portraying darker side of Manes. *The New York Times*, Oct 13, 1986, p B1.
6. Kates B, McCoy K: Friedman lawyer hits a "smear." *New York Post*, Oct 15, 1986, p 3.
7. Policy is established for ethical complaints. *Am Coll of Physicians Observer*, Jan 1986, p 4.
8. National repository formed for "adverse" data on doctors. *The Palm Beach Post*, Dec 31, 1988, p 5A.

12

Ethical Problems Regarding Sex between Therapist and Patient

SPENCER ETH

The sexual exploitation of patients by their therapists has been a perennial thorn in the side of psychiatry. Surveys of therapists have revealed that 5–10% have engaged in sexual activity with patients, while about 40% of psychiatrists admit knowing at least one such colleague. Forensic psychiatrists are also subject to sexual misconduct, although the national organization, the American Academy of Psychiatry and the Law, has traditionally relied on the far larger American Psychiatric Association (APA) to adjudicate such charges against its members. An examination of the workings of a large APA District Branch Ethics Committee suggests that psychiatrists can successfully investigate, discipline, and deter unethical behavior by colleagues. Although due-process considerations impose certain limitations on ascertaining the veracity of some allegations of sexual abuse, the ethics committee remains a viable means to safeguard the standards of our profession.

DIMENSIONS OF THE PROBLEM

Accounts of what today would be considered the sexual exploitation of patients by their psychotherapists can be found throughout this century. In a letter to his disciple Ferenczi, Freud cautioned: "You have not made a secret of the fact that you kiss your patients and let them kiss you. Now I am assuredly not one of those who from prudishness or from consideration of bourgeois

SPENCER ETH • Veterans Administration Medical Center, Los Angeles, California 90073; Department of Psychiatry and Biobehavioral Sciences, University of California at Los Angeles, Los Angeles, California 90024; and Department of Psychiatry, University of Southern California School of Medicine, Los Angeles, California 90033.

convention would condemn little erotic gratifications of this kind. But that does not alter the fact that with us a kiss signifies a certain erotic intimacy. We have hitherto in our technique held to the conclusion that patients are to be refused erotic gratifications."[1] Elsewhere, Freud explained his rationale for sexual abstinence during treatment as a case where "ethical motives unite with the technical ones to restrain him (the analyst) from giving the patient his love."[2] Forty years later Leon Saul still found it necessary to present four fundamental reasons why psychoanalysts must not succumb to the temptation to gratify an erotic transference by indulging in sexual relations with their patients.[3] Greenson, too, is emphatic in reminding therapists that "There can be no compromise. One cannot permit even the most innocent and partial of erotic gratifications... Perhaps at no other time is the analytic attitude of compassionate, restrained humanness and firmness so absolutely necessary."[4]

Sexual indiscretion continued, albeit no longer defensible as treatment. In fact, there is overwhelming evidence that erotic contact is quite harmful to patients.[5] As noted, surveys of therapists have consistently revealed that 5–10% have at some point in their professional careers engaged in this behavior.[6,7] A recent study of psychiatrists involved a questionnaire mailed to one-fifth of all American psychiatrists under the age of 65.[8] A total of 1,442 (26%) responded by June 1985, of whom 80% were male; 6.4% acknowledged having had sexual conduct (defined as contact intended to arouse or satisfy sexual desire in patient, therapist, or both) with their own patients. Two-thirds of these offenders had been involved with just one patient, the remainder with two or more. Significantly, about 70% stated that sexual relations commenced after termination, usually within the first six months. Of these psychiatrists, 41% sought consultation in response to their sexual involvement with patients, and 1.6% indicated that they themselves had been victims of sexual exploitation in their own treatment experience. A 1981 survey of the Washington Psychiatric Society produced strikingly similar results.[9] More than half of the members responded, with 6.6% (7.9% of the male and 2.2% of the female) conceding that they had had sexual contact with patients.

The prevalence of sexual abuse by therapists will come as no surprise to psychiatrists—in fact, 39% of those surveyed replied that they personally knew psychiatric colleagues who had been sexually involved with patients.[10] Yet, the overwhelming majority of all psychiatrists (98%) believe that therapist-patient sexual contact is always inappropriate and usually harmful to the patient.[11] This position is clearly articulated in the Principles of Medical Ethics with Annotations Especially Applicable to Psychiatry: "Sexual activity with a patient is unethical."[12] Further, Simon opines in his forensic psychiatry text that sex with a patient is malpractice per se.[13] A review of 25 civil cases of sexual exploitation found that 23 were won by the patient against the defendant psychiatrist.[14] Of the APA insurance program claims, 27% were for improper treatment, usually in the form of sexual misconduct. These claims accounted for 10% of all losses (P. Slawson quoted in *Psychiatric News*, November 4, 1983).

Given that about 6% of psychiatrists engage in unethical behavior that frequently becomes known to colleagues, how well is our profession responding to this pattern of misconduct? Ten years ago Zitrin and Klein described the experience of their American Psychiatric Association District Branch Ethics Committee in handling complaints.[15] During a four-year period, 44 allegations of improper conduct by members were considered, of which only five involved violations of the prohibition against sexual relations with patients. The Ethics Committee voted for a finding of unethical conduct in only two of the 44 cases; in many other instances the charges were felt to be justified, though lacking sufficient proof. This seemingly meager outcome appears representative of the national trend. During 34 years (1950 through 1983) the APA found less than 100 members guilty of unethical conduct.[16] In this context Alan Stone, a former president of APA, has ample reason to decry our profession's competence in disciplining and deterring sexual activity between therapist and patient: "There is almost a total lack of capacity to act."[17]

FINDING THE TRUTH

Contrary to this gloomy diagnosis, our local District Branch Ethics Committee is alive, well, and active. A careful review of our procedures will demonstrate a focused response to the problem of sexual misconduct. The Ethics Committee is authorized to receive written, signed complaints in order to recommend action, including admonishment, reprimand, suspension, or expulsion from the district branch of the American Psychiatric Association. Upon receipt of a complaint against a member, the ethics committee secretary writes to the patient to request a consent for release of information from the treating psychiatrist. This is necessary to enable the psychiatrist to respond openly to the allegations of unethical behavior.

We have chosen to exclude anonymous accusations or complaints filed by an unnamed patient or patient's therapist against a former psychiatrist. Bouhoutsos argues forcefully against this procedural requirement, since it could deter a sexually exploited patient from lodging a complaint.[18] For instance, some patients harbor guilt or shame about their role in the affair and may be unwilling publicly to confess having been used, having been seductive, or even having been in psychiatric treatment. Other patients may be reluctant to trust the psychiatric profession or to become involved in a bureaucratic process. A few patients, however victimized they may have been, hesitate to provoke trouble for the offending psychiatrist.

A way to relieve the patient of the burden of initiating a complaint is by transferring the responsibility to the exploited patient's new therapist. In the APA survey, 56% favored mandatory reporting.[10] A statute obligating therapists to do just that was enacted in Minnesota in 1985.[19] It requires the reporting of any physician who engages in sexual contact or seductive or demeaning behavior with a patient, while providing immunity for the reporter. The sole exception is for information obtained from an offending physician during his treatment, if the doctor has already limited his practice. However, a mandatory reporting law has the effect of forcing the psychiatrist to violate confidentiality regardless of the patient's wishes, as in the child-abuse model, which was designed to protect endangered dependent children. Knowing that certain secrets cannot be kept may in itself deter sexually abused patients from seeking needed treatment. There are other difficulties with complaints from current psychiatrists about former psychiatrists. The treating psychiatrist has, in fact, only hearsay knowledge of the incident.[20] Direct evidence from the patient is necessary for resolution of the serious allegation of sexual abuse. Hence, it is preferable for the current therapist to assist the patient in filing a formal complaint and then to offer emotional support to the patient during its adjudication.

CASE EXAMPLE

> Dr. Jones wrote to our ethics committee to complain that Dr. Smith, a member in good standing of our district branch, had sexually molested her patient 18 years before when he had been in practice in the Midwest. The unnamed patient had been an adolescent at the time and only recently in her treatment disclosed the details of the abuse. The ethics committee decided that there shall be no statute of limitations on alleged ethics violations, although special consideration would be extended in cases where medical records have not been preserved or where the standards of ethics have changed.[21] Therefore, because Dr. Smith is a member of our district branch we would take action if, and only if, the patient herself authorized Dr. Smith to release information about her treatment with him. The patient refused to reveal her identity by giving consent, and the case was closed without the psychiatrist being notified of the anonymous complaint.

After receipt of a signed complaint and consent, the ethics committee informs the patient of the procedures to be followed and the potential sanctions against members found guilty of an ethics violation. The ethics committee provides assistance, if needed, to the patient in presenting evidence to support the allegations. The accused psychiatrist is given copies of all complainant materials, including the consent form, the Principles of Medical Ethics with Annotations Especially Applicable to Psychiatry, and the Opinions Pamphlet of the APA Ethics Committee.[12,22] The psychiatrist is invited to reply to the allegations. The patient's complaint and the psychiatrist's response are then carefully reviewed by two members of the ethics committee, who independently report their findings at a meeting of the full ethics committee. The committee considers whether the misconduct alleged by the patient constitutes a specific violation of the Principles of Medical Ethics (Sections 1–7).[12] If so, the Committee then decides whether there is probable cause to proceed with an investigation and hearing.

This is a crucial juncture, and commentators have voiced concern that ethics committees might shy away from conducting hearings, either because of anxiety or bias. Moore notes that "Members have unrealistic fears of legal retribution (and) what promises to be an unpleasant experience."[16] However, the current APA malpractice policy affords appreciable protection from liability for ethics committee members acting in good faith. Our Committee has been able to recruit the active participation of 20 psychiatrists, who generally experience service on the committee as a privilege and not a burden.

Before scheduling a hearing, the ethics committee asks the complainant patient whether other actions have been taken against the respondent psychiatrist. The committee will defer a hearing until any criminal (rape), civil (malpractice), or licensing-board proceedings have been concluded. Judicial and administrative actions may increase in frequency as a result of the passage of new laws in several states.[19] The procedures for evidence collection (i.e., subpoena powers) and the potentially serious penalties in the other judicial arenas justify our delaying consideration. The committee is also alert to the potential use of ethics hearings as a devious means to expose legal strategies that may be employed in future litigation. After the other matters have been resolved, we routinely request records from the court and/or the licensing board and will include this material in our subsequent deliberations. Unfortunately, some out-of-court settlements bind the patient to withdraw all ethics complaints.

The ethics committee hearing panels are composed of at least three members, one of whom is designated as the Chair. The district branch legal counsel reviews the materials in preparation for the hearing and is prepared to assist in conducting the hearing under the direction of the Chair. Legal counsel assumes responsibility for assuring that the respondent psychiatrist's right to due process is protected. In addition, the respondent psychiatrist is permitted representation by an attorney who has access to all materials and is given the opportunity to examine witnesses. Due-process considerations have prompted the committee to disregard a respondent psychiatrist's personal characteristics (i.e., marital status, sexual orientation, etc.) and the existence of prior ethics complaints.

The hearing panel, in the presence of the respondent psychiatrist and his attorney, interviews the complainant patient, who may be accompanied by an attorney, therapist, or support person. The complainant patient is encouraged to present all available evidence corroborating the accusations. The respondent psychiatrist, through his attorney or the panel, may question the complainant regarding the merits of the allegations. The ethics committee is cognizant of the presumption of innocence of the respondent psychiatrist and of its duty to protect the complainant patient from psychological harm during the hearing. The committee therefore excuses the complainant patient from the hearing prior to testimony of the respondent psychiatrist and his witnesses.

In the hearing the respondent psychiatrist typically relies on certain defenses, such as that the alleged misconduct did not occur. Rather, the accusation is interpreted as a product of the patient's erotic fantasies, psychosis, or as a retaliation for perceived disappointment or rejection in the transference. The psychiatrist will often want the panel to infer that no sexual abuse occurred by virtue of the fact that the patient continued in therapy or delayed reporting the incident. Less commonly, the psychiatrist will admit having engaged in a personal relationship with the complainant, but insist that the treatment had terminated before the affair began. In this instance, the psychiatrist may contend that former patients are adults and have the right to associate with whomever they wish. The American Psychiatric Association's new annotation states "Sexual involvement with one's former patients generally exploits emotions deriving from treatment and therefore almost always is unethical."[12] We consider this issue on a case-by-case basis according to "the extent to which this was exploitation of the therapeutic relationship."[22] Some committee members would go further by supporting explicit guidelines prohibiting sexual relations with former patients regardless of the time elapsed.[23]

Often, allegations of sexual misconduct reduce to the patient's accusation countered by the psychiatrist's insistence that the incident never happened and the patient should not be trusted. Rarely is there physical evidence (i.e., photographs) or eyewitnesses (i.e., sexual contact during group therapy). We will ask the patient if the psychiatrist had any distinguishing marks (i.e., an appendectomy scar), but hardly ever obtain such corroboration. The hearing panel must then decide whom to believe. Although on occasion other ethical misconduct allows the committee to discipline the respondent in any case. Our district branch ethics committee has adopted a standard of clear and convincing evidence for establishing proof of guilt.[24] This standard is intermediate between the preponderance of the evidence standard of tort law and the beyond-a-reasonable-doubt standard of criminal law. The United States Court of Appeals for the Federal Circuit has promulgated a similar "substantial evidence" standard for adjudication of sexual harassment accusations in the workplace.[25] This court also recognizes that conflicting testimony must be expected.

After the hearing panel has deliberated with its counsel and applied a clear and convincing standard of proof, a vote is taken of panel members on each charge. A two-thirds vote is required to confirm a finding that the respondent psychiatrist violated the Principles of Medical Ethics. A report of the hearing panel is drafted by counsel and presented by the hearing panel Chair to the full ethics committee, which by majority vote considers approval of the report. The ethics committee Chair will convey the report to the district branch council for final action. The council receives the report, with the respondent psychiatrist's name omitted. The psychiatrist's identity is not relevant to the facts of the case and should remain confidential. The trial of approval ends with reviews by the APA Ethics Committee. If the final decision is that no ethics violation occurred, the complainant patient and the respondent psychiatrist are immediately notified to that effect. The ethics committee carefully phrases its letter to the complainant to the effect that the evidence was insufficient to support the allegations, rather than imply that the committee thought the complainant was lying or crazy.

If the decision is adverse to the respondent, the ethics committee notifies the psychiatrist, but not the complainant, and advises the respondent of the right to appeal to the APA Ethics Appeals Board. If that option is taken, the ethics appeals board will hold its own deliberation and may affirm the original action or reduce or reverse the decision. Only then is the patient told of the outcome. Whenever the sanction is expulsion, the APA Board of Trustees must ratify that action by a two-thirds vote. The name of a member expelled for an ethics violation will be reported in *Psychiatric News* with specification of the violation found.

Having confirmed an act of sexual misconduct, the ethics committee must then confront the issue of physician impairment. Perhaps the offending psychiatrist's behavior was a consequence of mental illness calling for treatment and not punishment. The psychodynamics of sexually abusing therapists have been explored in some depth in the literature.[26,27,28]

The committee encourages psychiatric treatment and emotional support, and has included a specific recommendation for therapy in its reports. However, the severity of psychopathology and need for treatment rarely overrules the companion penalty for ethical misconduct. We have seen seemingly contrite psychiatrists suffering from depression appeal very mild sanctions. In addition, the committee may impose supervision. As Zelen recommends: "When a troubled therapist has been identified, not only should the profession offer him or her "therapy," but it also must monitor his or her work, discreetly but effectively."[29] Finally, by California law, a professional society disciplinary action that leads to restriction of membership privileges of more than 30 days in any calendar year must be reported to the State Licensing Board (Business and Professions Code Section 805).

CONCLUSION

It has been written that the psychiatrist engaging in sexual relations with his patient runs "no risk of unfavorable action for the local ethics or grievance committees (are) composed of men more like himself than otherwise."[30] Our ethics committee, 30% of whom are women, takes exception to this characterization. We volunteer hundreds of hours of our time and are budgeted over $10,000 of district branch funds each year in vigorously investigating and adjudicating allegations of sexual misconduct by our colleagues. Our procedures have been legally challenged and have been upheld by the Federal Court of Appeals. Recently published data seem to indicate an actual decrease in the percentage of therapists reporting sexual intimacies with their patients.[31] The conspicuous attention focused on this problem by ethics committees promises to fulfill the claim that "the purpose of all this activity is to protect the integrity of our profession."[16]

REFERENCES

1. Jones E: *Life and Work of Sigmund Freud*, vol 3. New York, Basic Books, 1957, p 163–165.
2. Freud S: Observations on transference-love (1915). *Standard Edition*, vol 12. London, Hogarth press, p 169.
3. Saul LJ: Erotic transference. *Psychoanal Q* 1962; 31:54–61.
4. Greenson RR: *The Technique and Practice of Psychoanalysis*, vol 1. New York, International Universities Press, 1967, p 226.

5. Pope KS, Bouhoutsos JC: *Sexual Intimacy Between Therapists and Patients*. New York, Praeger, 1986.
6. Kardener S, Fuller M, Mensh I: A survey of physicians' attitudes and practices regarding erotic and nonerotic contact with patients. *Am J Psychiatry* 1976; 133:1324–1325.
7. Holroyd JC, Brodsky AM: Psychologists' attitudes and practices regarding erotic and nonerotic physical contact with patients. *Am Psychologist* 1977; 32:843–849.
8. Gartrell N, Herman J, Olarte S, *et al*: Psychiatrist-patient sexual contact: results of a national survey, I: Prevalence. *Am J Psychiatry* 1986; 143:1126–1131.
9. Derosis H, Hamilton JA, Morrison E, *et al*: More on psychiatrist-patient sexual contact. *Am J Psychiatry* 1987; 144:688–689.
10. Gartrell N, Herman J, Olarte S, *et al*: Reporting practices of psychiatrists who knew of sexual misconduct by colleagues. *Am J Orthopsychiatry* 1987; 57:287–295.
11. Herman JL, Gartrell N, Olarte S, *et al*: Psychiatrist-patient sexual contact: Results of a national survey, II: Psychiatrists' attitudes. *Am J Psychiatry* 1987; 144:164–169.
12. American Psychiatric Association: *The Principles of Medical Ethics with Annotations Especially Applicable to Psychiatry*, 1989 Ed. Washington, DC, APA, 1989.
13. Simon RI: *Clinical Psychiatry and the Law*. Washington, DC, American Psychiatric Press, 1987.
14. Smith JT: Therapist-patient sex: Exploitation of the therapeutic process. *Psychiatr Ann* 1988; 18:59–63.
15. Zitrin A, Klein T: Can psychiatry police itself effectively? The experience of one district branch. *Am J Psychiatry* 1976; 133:653–656.
16. Moore RA: Ethics in the practice of psychiatry: Update on the results of enforcement of the code. *Am J Psychiatry* 1985; 142:1043–1046.
17. Stone AA: Legal implications of sexual activity between psychiatrist and patient. *Am J Psychiatry* 1976; 133:1138–1141.
18. Bouhoutsos JC: Therapist-client sexual involvement: A challenge for mental health professionals and educators. *Am J Orthopsychiatry* 1985; 55:177–182.
19. Gartrell N, Herman JL, Olarte S, Feldstein M, Localio R: Management and rehabilitation of sexually exploitive therapists. *Hosp Comm Psychiatry* 1988; 39:1070–1074.
20. Stone AA: Sexual misconduct by psychiatrists: The ethical and clinical dilemma of confidentiality. *Am J Psychiatry* 1983; 140:195–197.
21. Cummings NA, Sobel SB: Malpractice insurance: Update on sex claims. *Psychotherapy* 1985; 22:186–188.
22. American Psychiatric Association: *Opinions of the Ethics Committee on the Principles of Medical Ethics* (1985 Ed). Washington, DC, APA, 1985.
23. Sell JA, Gottlieb MC, Schoenfeld L: Ethical considerations of social/romantic relationships with present and former clients. *Prof Psychology* 1986; 17:504–508.
24. Borenstein DB: Standards of proof for ethics committees of professional organizations. *Hosp Comm Psychiatry* 1987; 38:711–712.
25. *Anthony Mazza v U.S. Postal Inspection Service*, 86-1598, August 4, 1987.
26. Kardener SH: Sex and physician-patient relationships. *Am J Psychiatry* 1974; 131:1134–1136.
27. Marmor J: Some psychodynamic aspects of the seduction of patients in psychotherapy. *Am J Psychoanal* 1976; 36:319–323.
28. Claman JM: Mirror hunger in the psychodynamics of sexually abusing therapists. *Am J Psychoanal* 1987; 47:35–40.
29. Zelen SL: Sexualization of therapeutic relationships: The dual vulnerability of patient and therapist. *Psychotherapy* 1985; 22:178–185.
30. Davidson V: Psychiatry's problems with no name: Therapist-patient sex. *Am J Psychoanal* 1977; 37:43–50.
31. Pope KS, Tabachnick BG, Keith-Spiegel P: Ethics of practice: The beliefs and behaviors of psychologists as therapists. *Am Psychologist* 1987; 42:993–1006.

III

Applications

13

Prediction of Dangerousness in Different Contexts

BARUCH A. BRODY

INTRODUCTION TO THE PROBLEM

Psychiatrists are called upon by the legal system to provide many services. This is particularly true, of course, of forensic psychiatrists. As Bloom and Rogers[1] have pointed out, psychiatric input often seems mandated by statutes, even though this does not necessarily mean that any particular psychiatrist is required to participate in the proceeding in question. This use of psychiatry has resulted in many criticisms and questions. This chapter will focus on one set of criticisms related to the willingness and capacity of psychiatrists to predict dangerousness.

Psychiatrists are called upon in a variety of contexts to make predictions about the likelihood of a patient's acting in ways that endanger others. Among the contexts that might be mentioned are the following: (1) Most civil commitment statutes allow for involuntary commitments when the patient, as a result of his or her mental illness, is dangerous to self or others. Psychiatrists are called upon by the courts to certify the presence of a mental illness and to ascertain whether the patient is dangerous to self or to others. (2) Many sentencing statutes provide for psychiatrists to examine patients to see whether, as a result of personality disorders, they have a propensity towards dangerous criminal activity. Such offenders receive greater punishments. In the extreme case, such offenders would be executed rather than receive a jail sentence. Psychiatrists are then called upon by the courts to ascertain the probability of a patient's committing further dangerous acts. (3) Court decisions, following *Tarasoff*, have placed a duty upon psychiatrists to protect potential victims of

---

BARUCH A. BRODY • Center for Ethics, Medicine, and Public Issues, Baylor College of Medicine, Houston, Texas 77030.

patients' violent acts. Psychiatrists who discharge patients, or who don't admit patients, who later go on to commit violent acts, face the threat of liability for these dangerous acts. In Appelbaum's[2] apt phrase, they are led to participate in the "new preventive detention" by keeping as patients those who are dangerous, even if there is little that can be done for the patients therapeutically.

The capacity of psychiatrists reliably to predict dangerousness has, of course, been challenged for many years. As early as 1974, a task force of the American Psychiatric Association[3] concluded that:

> ...the state of the art regarding predictions of violence is very unsatisfactory. The ability of psychiatrists or any other professionals to reliably predict future violence is unproved. (p 30)

A very similar conclusion was reached by Stone[4] in his extremely influential review of the prediction of dangerousness, a review that emphasized both the poor success rate of predictions and the bad false-positive problem in predicting any phenomenon with a low base rate.

Where does all of this leave the practicing psychiatrist? A number of possible approaches could be adopted. At one extreme is the position that since psychiatrists do such a poor job at predicting dangerous behavior, they should stop making such predictions. The way to do that is to not participate in any legal proceedings where psychiatrists are called upon to make such predictions. At the other extreme is the position that since society has decided to employ such predictions in making a variety of decisions, and since psychiatrists are best capable of making such predictions, psychiatrists, as responsible professionals and citizens, should participate in legal proceedings where they are called upon to make such predictions. Many less extreme positions are, of course, possible.

I am particularly interested in exploring the question of adopting a consistent policy on this issue. Should an individual psychiatrist or a group of psychiatrists deal with this issue in the same way in all contexts in which predictions of dangerousness are involved, or are there reasons for adopting a different approach in different contexts? Is it, in particular, appropriate to adopt a far more cooperative attitude towards predicting dangerousness when one is testifying concerning involuntary commitment than when one is testifying in a sentencing hearing? That is the issue on which this chapter will focus.

It is helpful in this connection to examine some reports of the American Psychiatric Association on the prediction of dangerousness. In a 1984 task force report,[5] the APA adopted a recommendation calling for only a modest level of involvement in predictions of dangerousness. To quote the Task Force's report:

> We have previously noted the limitations of predicting violence. Considerable evidence has been accumulated by now to demonstrate that long-term predictions by psychiatrists of future violence is an extremely inaccurate process. The most that can be said about any individual is that a history of past violence increases the probability that future violence will occur...In addition, the psychiatrist may wish to comment on factors in the individual's environment that are likely to increase (e.g., alcohol, rejection by a girlfriend), or decrease (e.g., taking psychotropic medication) the probability of future violence. (p 208)

By way of contrast, the APA's own Guidelines for Legislation on the Psychiatric Hospitalization of Adults[6] calls upon psychiatrists to examine patients and make recommendations about involuntary confinement based in part on whether the person is likely to cause harm to others. Commenting on that provision, Stromberg and Stone, main figures in drafting those guidelines, have the following to say:

> Studies have shown that psychiatric predictions of future danger, like other clinical, sociological, and actuarial predictions, are not very reliable. Because we lack better guidance, however, society has called upon psychiatrists and psychologists to make such predictions. To ensure some minimum degree of reliability, the Model Law requires that predictions of such dangerous conduct be based on recent behavior of the person. (p 90)

Is this type of difference justified? If not, can its appeal be explained? Three strategies can be identified. The first emphasizes the difference in the reliability of predictions of dangerousness in different settings and contexts. The second emphasizes differences in the therapeutic connection of predictions of dangerousness in different settings and contexts. The third emphasizes differences in fundamental attitudes toward different systems involved in different settings and contexts. I shall argue that the first two strategies, which would *justify* the difference, fail. I shall also argue that only the third strategy offers an account that at least *explains* these differences, but that it in turn has implications of considerable significance.

DIFFERENCE IN DEGREES OF RELIABILITY

The first strategy takes its point of departure from a well-known and often-cited article by Monahan[7] on second-generation studies of the prediction of violent behavior. One of Monahan's crucial points was that predictions of dangerousness might be far more reliable in the short-term context of a violent patient presenting in a community setting than in the long-term context of a convicted criminal facing sentencing and being evaluated for potential dangerousness after he or she is discharged years later from prison. Such a differentiation in reliability would justify psychiatrists testifying in civil commitment hearings while still hesitating about testifying in sentencing hearings.

The studies referred to by Monahan are by Rofman and his colleagues[8] and by Yesavage and his colleagues[9]. A later study by McNiel and Binder[10] could be cited as well. Let us review the findings of these three studies to see whether they will support the conclusions suggested by our first strategy.

Rofman and his colleagues compared actual incidents of violence by hospitalized patients who were involuntarily committed as dangerous to others with actual incidents of violence committed by patients who were not admitted on that basis. They found a significant difference between the numbers of incidents during the first 20 days, but no difference at all afterwards. During the entire hospitalization, 41% of the dangerous patients committed a violent act, while only 8% of the others did. Rofman and colleagues summarized their conclusions as follows:

> This preliminary retrospective study indicates that the clinical determination of dangerousness by physicians who send people to a typical psychiatric Veterans Administration medical center for emergency psychiatric commitment predicts the patients at risk of in-hospital assaultive behavior to a statistically significant degree...This finding supports the hypothesis that predictions of dangerous behavior have validity when the time of prediction and the time of validation are relatively close together. (p 1063)

Yesavage and his colleagues examined 84 involuntarily committed patients, 46 of whom were admitted as dangerous to others and 38 of whom were not. They found a greater trend towards violence in the first seven days after commitment among those who were committed as dangerous to others than among those who were not, although this trend did not reach the level of statistical significance. It is worth noting that in terms of physical assaults, only 26% of those committed as dangerous and 16% of those not committed as dangerous actually committed a physical assault. Their own conclusion is that:

> So it may be that with a large number of subjects, some of our results which just missed significance would become significant. On the other hand, the lack of significance with the present number suggests that whatever differences exist in the ward behavior and psychiatric status of patients who were and who were not considered dangerous to others are not of large magnitude. Its final implication is that although the dichotomy between these two groups of patients has serious implications for incarceration, it appears to be paralleled by small differences in behavior on the ward after an admission. (p 1148)

The most recent study is that of McNiel and Binder. They examined 101 patients who were admitted involuntarily, 47 as dangerous to others and 54 on other grounds. Looking at both physical and verbal assaults and the need for seclusion and restraint, they found a significant difference in assault-related events between the dangerous patients (34 of 47, or 72%) and the nondangerous patients (16 of 54, or 30%). Even when confined just to physical assaults, a difference existed between the dangerous patients (13 of 47, or 28%) and the nondangerous patients (4 of 54, or 7%). This difference was found entirely in the first 72 hours after admission and led the authors to draw the following implications:

> Our findings have implications for the continuing controversy regarding the appropriateness of dangerousness as a criterion for emergency civil commitment...The results of the present study suggest that emergency commitment based on dangerousness does seem to protect society, in that a large percentage of patients judged to be dangerous did become violent in the hospital. Furthermore, our findings suggest that the rate of false-positive predictions of dangerousness is not as high in the emergency commitment setting as it may be in other settings. (p 199)

We have seen then that two studies seem to support the ability to predict dangerousness in the short-term emergency setting. The one study which does not support this ability is not that challenging because there was definitely a greater trend towards dangerous behavior by those predicted to be dangerous. Can we therefore conclude that psychiatrists should adopt a different stance towards predictions of dangerousness in the context of involuntary confinement than towards predictions of dangerousness in sentencing hearings just because the former is far more reliable than the latter?

I think not. There are three related issues that need to be considered. The first had to do with the definition of dangerous assault-related behavior in these studies. The second has to do with the false-positive rate found even in these most favorable studies. The third has to do with the period of dangerousness examined in these studies as compared to the period of dangerousness looked at in cases of civil commitment. Let me elaborate upon each of these points.

When we are predicting dangerousness, what are we predicting? A straightforward answer would be any physical assault. If that is the definition, then the results of these studies are less impressive than they might appear initially. In the McNiel and Binder study, for example, only 13 of the 47 patients (28%) judged to be dangerous actually committed a physical assault. While significantly larger than the percentage of patients not judged to be dangerous who committed a physical assault (4 of 54, or 7%), this percentage means that the overwhelming majority of patients judged to be dangerous did not commit a physical assault. McNiel and Binder treat many of them as engaged in an "assault-related event" because they threatened others and/or engaged in abusive verbal behavior and/or were secluded and restrained. But is this really justified? A lot will depend upon how threatening was the verbal behavior, and we just don't know. Similar issues arise for the Yesavage study and for the Rofman study. Yesavage reports that 65% of the dangerous patients committed an assault-related event, as opposed to 47% of the nondangerous group, but in terms of physical assaults, the difference comes to 26% for the dangerous group versus 16% for the nondangerous group. Rofman's data does not allow for the same numerical analysis, but we can say that of the 52 incidents involving the 24 dangerous patients, only 22 involved either a completed battery or an attempt that would have been completed were it not for immediate staff physical intervention. In short, then, my first problem with these studies is that they may be overemphasizing the quality of the predictions of dangerousness by excessively broadening the definition of assault-related events.

We turn to the second issue of the false-positive rate. What percentage of the patients judged to be dangerous actually committed violent assault-related events during the period in question? It depends, of course, upon the definition of violence, but Table I illustrates the data clearly. The false-positive rates are obviously very high if we only consider physical assaults and become more acceptable only on the questionable broader definition.

There is, of course, a very difficult general question about what constitutes an acceptable false-positive rate in civil commitment hearings. That question is equivalent to the question of what standard of evidence of dangerousness is required in order to commit someone. Stone and Stromberg, in their commentary on the APA Guidelines,[6] correctly point out (p 115) that most courts want clear and convincing evidence of dangerousness, of the order of 75% certainty, as opposed to a mere preponderance of evidence of dangerousness (>50%

Table I. Studies of Validity of Predicting Dangerousness

	Percent who committed physical assaults	Percent who committed some assault-related behavior
Rofman study	N/A	41%
Yesavage study	26%	65%
McNiel & Binder study	28%	72%

This means that we can state the false-positive rate as follows:

	Percent incorrectly predicted to commit physical assaults	Percent incorrectly predicted to commit some form of assaultive behavior
Rofman study	N/A	59%
Yesavage study	74%	35%
McNiel & Binder study	72%	28%

certainty) or proof beyond a reasonable doubt (95% certainty). If this is true, then a false-positive rate of about 25% is the most that is acceptable, and that is almost reached only in the McNiel and Binder study, and then only using the broadest definition of assaultive behavior. So even in these best studies, there may be an unacceptably high false-positive rate even in the short-term prediction of dangerousness.

McNiel and Binder[10] have the following to say about this difficult set of issues:

> Although many complex issues are involved in developing policy regarding civil commitment...our data warrant consideration when comparisons are made between the relative costs (e.g., loss of liberty) and benefits (e.g., protection of the community from harm) of emergency civil commitment based on dangerousness. (p 199)

They are certainly right in saying that, since it is only their data that show the false-positive rate as sufficiently low to meet the currently accepted social comparison embodied in the clear and convincing evidence rule. In order to make their case persuasive, however, they will have to justify their broad definition of the type of assault-related behavior that counts, for on a narrower definition, their false-positive rate is still unacceptably high.

I turn finally to the issue of the length of time involved in the prediction of dangerousness. It is useful to remember, before we turn to this issue, that psychiatric testimony of dangerousness may be involved in several stages of involuntary civil commitment. In my state (Texas), for example, the statutes[11] call for psychiatrists to be involved in the prediction of dangerousness before a person is admitted for emergency detention (24 hours), before a person is confined under an order for protective custody while awaiting a court hearing for court-ordered mental health services (14–30 days), before a person is confined under an order for temporary mental health services (90 days), and before an already confined person is further confined under an order for extended mental health services (12 months). Such a scheme, with various modifications, is not atypical. The question I want to raise is whether the second generation of research on dangerousness justifies claims of the reliability of predictions of dangerousness over this extended period.

The answer to this question is not encouraging. Rofman[8] found no difference between those predicted to be dangerous and those not after 20 days, and he found few violent acts from either group after that time. Yesavage[9] only studied the first seven days after hospitalization. McNiel and Binder[10] only studied the first three days after hospitalization. In short, then, the only study that went beyond the first week of hospitalization found that, at later stages, dangerous patients were no more likely to commit assaultive acts than nondangerous patients, and that neither group was very likely to commit assaultive acts. If these new studies are to be used as the basis for justifying a psychiatric involvement in short-term predictions of dangerousness during involuntary civil commitment hearings, they can at most justify a psychiatric involvement at the earliest stages.

Our first strategy for justifying psychiatric involvement in civil commitment hearings while resisting psychiatric involvement in sentencing hearings was based upon the idea that the short-term predictions of dangerousness involved in the former are far more reliable than the long-term predictions of dangerousness involved in the latter. This strategy is far from successful at this point. To begin with, given the current research, it at most justifies psychiatric involvement at the earliest stages of involuntary civil commitment. Secondly, and more importantly, the false-positive rate, even in the best studies, may well be unacceptably high unless we define the dangerousness we are trying to predict in much too broad a fashion.

DIFFERENCES IN THERAPEUTIC IMPLICATIONS

The second strategy takes its point of departure from reflections on the recent history of involuntary civil commitment statutes. Its crucial point is that, as a result of that history, psychiatric predictions of dangerousness in civil commitment proceedings are the only technique available for psychiatrists to ensure that those who need treatment get that treatment. That is why they are justified; psychiatric predictions of dangerousness in sentencing hearings, however, are not justified because they lack that therapeutic value. Let me elaborate upon this explanation and justification of the difference between the settings.

The history of the recent changes in civil commitment laws is well-known and can therefore be summarized briefly. The classical criterion for involuntary civil commitment was simply the patient's need for treatment. This came under challenge in the 1960s by reformers who were rightfully concerned about the vagueness and arbitrariness of that standard, about the warehousing of unwanted individuals who received no treatment, and about the resulting loss of civil liberties. In 1969, California became the first state to redefine the criterion for involuntary confinement so that major emphasis is placed on dangerousness to self or others. California has been followed in this regard by nearly every other jurisdiction; but what the new standards mean both in theory and practice varies greatly from one jurisdiction to another.[12] This change did not take place without some opposition,[13] but that opposition really did not crystallize until the seminal publication of Stone,[4] which argued for a return to a more therapeutic approach with clearer criteria for confinement (severe mental disorder leading to major distress for the patient, effective treatment available, patient refuses it but is incompetent to refuse, and the treatment would be accepted by a reasonable person). This approach would delete any reference to the issue of dangerousness to others. Danger to self would, of course, be part of the distress criterion. This approach was not adopted in full by the APA in its Guideline for Legislation,[6] but it was very influential on those guidelines. Like the Stone criteria, the APA Guidelines require that the person be suffering from a severe mental disorder, that effective treatment be available, and that the patient refuses (or at least does not, because he or she cannot, consent to) the treatment while being incompetent to decide about undergoing treatment. It deletes the Stone requirements of distress and of reasonableness and substitutes the requirement that the person is likely to cause harm to self or to suffer substantial deterioration (which is the distress criterion) *or* that the person criterion is likely to cause harm to others. It is crucial to note that the harm to others is really out of place here. Without it, the APA Guidelines, like the Stone criteria, would be using involuntary civil commitment as a way of forcing incompetent sick individuals to receive the care from which they would benefit and which they desperately need. This therapeutic paternalistic model would be acceptable to most commentators, for it is a form of weak paternalism which has been eloquently defended by such authors as Feinberg[14] and Beauchamp and Childress.[15] With it, the APA Guidelines are really a hybrid of an essentially therapeutic model with dangerousness to others thrown in as a concession to what continues to remain the predominant legal approach in most states, the nontherapeutic approach adopted in the 1970s.

With this background in mind, we can now present the second strategy's argument which runs as follows: It would be better if states were to adopt the therapeutic standards advocated in Stone's original proposal (adding, if necessary, the APA's concession on dangerousness to others). In fact, they mostly have not. But psychiatrists who testify about dangerousness to self and others actually succeed in producing the desired outcome since, as studies show, the results of operating under the dangerousness scheme and the revised therapeutic scheme are very similar. Predictions of dangerousness are, therefore, justified in civil commitment proceedings because of the appropriate therapeutic result reached, even if they are not justified by their reliability. An analogous argument is unavailable in criminal sentencing hearings, and that fact, combined with their unreliability, results in the conclusion that psychiatrists can have at most a limited role in presentencing predictions of dangerousness.

This strategy is supported by at least one major study conducted by Monahan and his colleagues.[16] They looked at patients who had been involuntarily committed under the California dangerousness standard, and they asked psychiatrists to evaluate whether or not these patients would have been committable under the therapeutic model. At least when they examined patients who were involuntarily committed for more than a minimal emergency period, they found that 84% were committable under the therapeutic criteria advocated by Stone. The authors of the study drew the following conclusion from it:

> Likewise, procedures for civil commitment as theoretically divergent as the Stone-Roth model and the California dangerousness standard may tend to converge in practice to commit the same patients...Despite enormous shifts in virtually all states from treatment-oriented to danger-oriented commitment statutes, approximately the same number of people continue to be civilly committed, year after year, law after law. It may be that abjuring dangerousness and returning to a medical model of commitment would not substantially alter this pattern of stability. (p 1271)

It is not far to move from this observation to the suggestion of the strategy we are considering, viz., that psychiatrists can continue to make predictions of dangerousness in civil commitment proceedings because the patients being committed under that standard are ones that ought to be committed anyway.

I have a number of problems with this justification for predictions of dangerousness. One has to do with the accuracy of the claim that the two standards coincide. The other has to do with whether the sameness of outcome, to the extent that it exists, is as relevant as this second strategy suggests.

The very large overlap found in the Monahan study presented above only holds for a small group of patients they studied, the ones not released after an emergency three-day confinement. When one looks at Monahan's data on emergency 72-hour commitments, the situation appears very different. Monahan found that the majority of patients who were committed under the California dangerousness statute were not committable under the therapeutic model advocated by Stone, primarily because they did not have a severe mental disorder (which Monahan identified with being psychotic). This result is very compatible with a recent study of emergency commitments by Hoge and colleagues[17] in Massachusetts. Of the 80 patients who refused treatment and were committable under the Massachusetts dangerousness statute, only 46 (57%) were committable under the Stone therapeutic approach. They found that most of the patients did have a severe mental disorder (since, quite correctly, they did not identify this just with being psychotic); but they found that a majority were competent to refuse treatment and were therefore not committable under the Stone therapeutic approach. So the first thing to note is that psychiatrists temporarily committing patients under the dangerousness standard are committing a large percentage of patients whose commitment probably cannot be justified under the therapeutic approach, and that undercuts this second strategy.

Hoge's study is quite properly very sensitive to this question of competency, and raises important challenges to how Monahan and his colleagues treated that issue in their study. The moral strength of the Stone therapeutic approach is that it restricts involuntary commitment to incompetent patients, thereby employing only the weak paternalism which nearly all commentators accept. Many patients committed as dangerous do not meet this crucial criterion of incompetency, and that means that we cannot justify involuntarily committing them using questionable predictions of dangerousness on the grounds that they are committable anyway on the morally justifiable paternalistic standards embodied in the Stone therapeutic approach.

Even if the two standards did overlap to a greater degree, however, I would still be unhappy with the justification offered by the second strategy. It has an air of duplicity about it. It says, after all, that one may legitimately recommend commitments on grounds of dangerousness, knowing that those predictions may be unreliable, because the patients being committed should be committed anyway on other grounds. Our moral sensitivities involve a concern not only with whether the outcome is appropriate (should this patient have been committed?) but also with whether the process leading to that outcome was appropriate (was the process a fair process?). Even if the two standards did overlap sufficiently, so our concern about the outcome was satisfied, a process that involved an inappropriate standard being used by people who did not believe in it anyway seems inappropriate.

ONE FINAL EXPLANATION AND ITS IMPLICATIONS

We have so far examined two strategies which purport both to explain and justify the difference in psychiatric attitudes towards predictions of dangerousness in different contexts and we have found them wanting. In this final section, we will propose a strategy to explain, but not necessarily to justify, the difference, and we will discuss some implications of adopting that strategy.

The point of departure for this explanation is the simple observation that the world of psychiatry and the world of the criminal law appear initially to represent fundamentally different ways of thinking about human beings and their actions. Following upon this observation, this final strategy suggests that psychiatrists are more comfortable about playing a role (e.g., predicting dangerousness) in areas of the law (e.g., involuntary civil commitment) that seem to embody their presuppositions about human behavior than in playing the same role in areas of the law (e.g., sentencing criminals) that seem to embody different presuppositions about human behavior. Let me elaborate.

Michael Moore has recently articulated[18] the apparent discrepancy between the psychiatric conception of human behavior and the criminal justice conception of human behavior as follows:

> A prominent example is provided by the century-old debate between psychiatrists and lawyers about determinism and responsibility. Psychiatry is often painted (by both lawyers and psychiatrists) as a scientific, deterministic worldview that leaves no room for free will and responsibility, whereas law is often painted (again, by both groups) as a system of thought that takes free will as its unquestionable first postulate. Given these supposedly contradictory starting points the disciplines are often thought to be incommensurable. (p 1)

Moore thinks that this discrepancy is more apparent than real, and the main goal of his book is to explain why the discrepancy is only apparent; but none of that takes away from the fact that many continue to see these two conceptions of human behavior as conflicting and irreconcilable. The apparent discrepancy becomes most troubling when psychiatrists confront the sentencing process. Psychiatrists asked to predict the dangerousness of convicted offenders understand that such predictions are to be used for assessing responsibility and degrees of punishment; and they may feel that the dangerousness is more indicative of a personality disorder or another mental illness that calls for understanding and treatment rather than condemnation and punishment. This is why they are reluctant to participate by predicting dangerousness, and why they emphasize the uncertainty of such predictions. No such conflict is present when psychiatrists are asked to predict dangerousness in civil commitment hearings, and that is why they are more comfortable about making such predictions and why they downplay the uncertainty of such predictions.

None of this in any way justifies the discrepancy we have been trying to understand; but it certainly offers an explanation of the discrepancy. I would like to suggest it as a plausible explanation. I would also like to call attention to certain implications arising from accepting this explanation and rejecting the earlier justifications.

I would note at least the following: (1) The psychiatric community would probably do best to advocate further revisions of involuntary commitment statutes to reflect more adequately the realities of the inability to predict dangerousness. The original Stone proposal made a great deal of sense, both because its moral justification for commitment was so strong and because it eschewed predictive judgments of dangerousness. It should be supported. (2) The psychiatric community needs to make it clear that is has no demonstrated expertise in predicting dangerousness in the long run, and no real role in the sentencing process. Allowing psychiatrists to testify, but suggesting that they confine themselves to the obvious (e.g., a past record of violence is somewhat predictive of future violence) is a way of avoiding saying what needs to be said. (3) There is a real need to confront the challenge raised by Moore to determine whether the criminal justice system and the mental health system can present a coherent and unified picture of human beings and their behavior.

REFERENCES

1. Bloom JD, Rogers JL: The legal basis of forensic psychiatry. *Am J Psychiatry* 1987; 144:847–53.
2. Appelbaum P: The new preventive detention. *Am J Psychiatry* 1988; 145:779–785.
3. American Psychiatric Association: *Clinical Aspects of the Violent Individual.* Washington DC: American Psychiatric Association, 1974.
4. Stone A: *Mental Health and Law.* Washington DC: U.S. Dept of Health, Education, and Welfare, 1975.
5. Task Force on the Role of Psychiatry in the Sentencing Process: Psychiatry in the sentencing process, in *Issues in Forensic Psychiatry.* Washington DC: American Psychiatric Press, 1984.

6. American Psychiatric Association: Guidelines for legislation on the psychiatric hospitalization of adults, in *Issues in Forensic Psychiatry*. Washington DC: American Psychiatric Press, 1984.
7. Monahan J: The prediction of violent behavior: Toward a second generation of theory and policy. *Am J Psychiatry* 1984; 141:10–15.
8. Rofman E, Askinazi C, Fant E: The prediction of dangerous behavior in emergency civil commitment. *Am J Psychiatry* 1980; 137:1061–64.
9. Yesavage J et al: Short-term civil commitment and the violent patient. *Am J Psychiatry* 1982; 139:1145–49.
10. McNiel D, Binder RL: Predictive validity of judgments of dangerousness in emergency civil commitment. *Am J Psychiatry*, 1987; 144:197–200.
11. *Vernon's Annotated Revised Civil Statutes of the State of Texas*, 1988 Ed: Articles 5547-27, 5547-36, 5547-50, 5547-51.
12. Mestrovic S, Cook JA: The dangerousness standard: What is it and how is it used. *Int J of Law and Psychiatry* 1986; 8:443–69.
13. Treffert D: Dying with their rights on. *Am J Psychiatry* 1973; 130:1041.
14. Feinberg J: Legal paternalism: *Canad J Philosophy* 1971; 1:105–24.
15. Beauchamp T, Childress J: *Principles of Biomedical Ethics*, Ed 2. New York: Oxford University Press, 1983.
16. Monahan J, Ruggiero M, Friedlander HD: Stone-Roth model of civil commitment and the California dangerousness standard. *Arch Gen Psychiatry* 1982; 39:1267–1271.
17. Hoge S et al: Limitations on psychiatrists' discretionary civil commitment authority by the Stone and dangerousness criteria. *Arch Gen Psychiatry*, 1988; 45:764–9.
18. Moore M: *Law and Psychiatry*. Cambridge: Cambridge University Press, 1984.

14

Treating Patients Who Threaten Violence

Ethical Concerns

SPENCER ETH AND MARK J. MILLS

The problem of violence in contemporary American society is both complex and compelling.[1] Interpersonal violence can occur in many forms, with death due to intentional injury being the most serious, though not the most common violent crime. In 1980 the United States homicide rate reached 10.6/100,000—the highest rate recorded this century. The lifetime risk for being a victim of homicide is 1/240 for whites and 1/47 for blacks. Further, the prevalence of nonfatal assault is about 100 times greater.[2]

Given its frequency, it is not surprising that psychiatrists and other mental health professionals directly encounter issues of violence in a variety of ways: from treating aggressive patients and assisting crime victims, to testifying as expert witnesses and working in prisons. In each of these activities the psychiatrist is confronted with a challenging array of ethical dilemmas.[3] Rather than attempt to survey the entire field, we will instead focus on one specific clinical situation that raises many of the common ethical questions facing the practicing psychiatrist—how to manage best the patient who threatens violence.

SPENCER ETH • Veterans Administration Medical Center, Los Angeles, California 90073; Department of Psychiatry and Biobehavioral Sciences, University of California at Los Angeles, Los Angeles, California 90024; and Department of Psychiatry, University of Southern California School of Medicine, Los Angeles, California 90033. **MARK J. MILLS** • Department of Psychiatry and Biobehavioral Sciences and Program in Psychiatry and Law, University of California at Los Angeles, Los Angeles, California 90024.

CASE EXAMPLE

Consider the following hypothetical case example:

Jim Smith is a 25-year-old machinist who presented to Dr. Jones, a psychiatrist, complaining of feeling like he was losing control of his mind. Jim, who had no previous history of psychiatric treatment, lived alone and readily admitted to being uncomfortable around people. He reported that over the preceding few months he had had occasional thoughts that other workers were talking about him behind his back. He has lately become very concerned that his supervisor is "out to get me." Jim reported feeling so upset at work each day that he needed three or four beers at home each night to calm down. He denied other substance use and was in good physical health. Jim stated at one point in the interview that unless things "let up" he might have to "hurt someone in self-defense." He refused to elaborate about his plans.

Jim was raised as an only child. He recalls feeling "out of it" during school; his grades were mediocre, he had no friends, few acquaintances, and never dated. Although he has been involved in several "brawls," he has no history of arrests. One year ago his parents were killed in a single-vehicle automobile accident. He has felt "numb" about their death ever since. On mental status examination Mr. Smith presented as a shy, quiet, neatly dressed young man in some distress. His speech was clear and coherent, and he was oriented in all spheres. Memory functions tested grossly intact. The patient became guarded when asked about psychotic symptoms, and at times throughout the interview he seemed to be responding to internal stimuli. His associations were somewhat loose, and his affect was constricted. The patient failed to endorse symptoms of depression, mania, or suicidality.

Dr. Jones reached a tentative clinical impression of schizophreniform disorder, which he shared with his patient. Dr. Jones then recommended voluntary psychiatric hospitalization to commence intensive treatment, but Mr. Smith declined by saying, "That ain't for me." After further discussion, Mr. Smith reluctantly agreed to consider a trial of medication on an outpatient basis. Mr. Smith was given a prescription for a neuroleptic, and a return appointment was scheduled for the following week.

INFORMED CONSENT PARADIGM

Mr. Smith seeks an outpatient consultation with Dr. Jones, who examines Mr. Smith, recognizes the vague threat of violence, diagnoses a psychiatric illness, and recommends treatment. This routine medical transaction reflects the prevailing informed consent model of the doctor-patient relationship.[4] "Informed consent is the basis of all psychiatric intervention and without it no psychiatric intervention can be morally justified."[5] The ethical foundation for the importance of consent is the natural right of man to freedom and liberty.

This concept of self-determination is conveyed by the term autonomy and is generally seen as a necessary attribute for the full status of personhood. The priority value associated with exercising personal choice over one's destiny is independent of the consequences of the decision. Autonomy can have meaning only if one is free to make the wrong choice, however, unfortunate though the outcome may prove to be. In a medical context, the doctrine of informed consent holds that "physicians should be placed under an affirmative duty to acquaint patients with the important risks and plausible alternatives to a proposed procedure."[6] Failure to provide the opportunity for informed consent can be considered an assault on the patient's autonomy.

Many professionals reading the preceding analysis will object to the diminished role ascribed to the physician. In ancient Greece physicians were required to intervene whenever the disease was responsive to treatment, irrespective of the patient's wishes. To refrain from caring for the sick under any circumstances constituted a breach of medical ethics. This philosophy was codified as the Hippocratic oath and has remained a testament to the glorious tradition of medical paternalism. The core of medical paternalism is helping another person without personal gain, and its ethical justification is altruistic beneficence. Although delivering needed medical care is a praiseworthy act, the good it serves may be nullified when the deed is performed against the patient's will. "Individuality and autonomy have long been central values in Anglo-American society and law. Decision making by competent professionals does not provide an adequate substitute for patient choice."[7]

The priority given to informed consent presupposes an autonomous moral agent, which in turn is dependent on mental competence. "Competent persons possess both the right and the ability to give informed consent; incompetent persons have neither the requisite ability nor the right."[8] Competence is a legal concept referring to the mental capacity or ability to perform a specific act, such as consenting to treatment. Under common law all adults are presumed to be competent to consent until a court adjudicates otherwise. A patient does not automatically become incompetent as a result of psychosis, dementia, or any other psychiatric disorder. Competency determination is an especially vexing problem because the law does not recognize the clinical reality of marginal competence for those patients whose cognitive functioning is unclear, fluctuating, or equivocal. Furthermore, each court will rule according to statute and precedent within their own particular jurisdiction.

Psychiatrists must have a sense of which patients might be incompetent to consent to treatment and should receive judicial scrutiny. Culver and colleagues have promoted a standard of competency for psychiatric patients that appears both legally and ethically sound. They hold that a patient is competent to decide about a proposed psychiatric treatment if the following criteria are fulfilled: (1) "The patient knows that the physician believes the patient is ill and in need of treatment," (2) that "this particular treatment may help the patient's illness," and (3) "the patient knows he or she may be called upon to make a decision regarding this treatment."[9] Applying these notions to our case example, it is reasonable to conclude that Mr. Smith is competent because he has not been declared incompetent by a court and because his psychiatric illness does not impair his cognitive abilities to the extent that he cannot appreciate the nature of the treatment situation, whatever the effect the illness may have on his judgment and insight.

Dr. Jones evaluated his patient Mr. Smith and found him to be suffering from a psychotic illness, schizophreniform disorder, whose natural history may be associated with a progression of symptoms. Mr. Smith is dysphoric and requests help. In addition, Dr. Jones recognizes the presence of vague aggressive fantasies associated with paranoid ideation. Dr. Jones suggests psychiatric hospitalization as the treatment of choice, but his patient refuses. Because this clinical interaction is operating within the constraints of the informed consent model, Dr. Jones should then offer other treatment strategies, including an outpatient trial of neuroleptic medication. Although this less desirable alternative may compromise patient care, it is a form of treatment acceptable to Mr. Smith. "Medical decision making involves the interwoven, overlapping, and often competing claims of personal autonomy and professional competence. The challenge of regulating medical decision making is to allocate the proper weight to each of these values. The task is both difficult and important, for the conflict may be between professional defined correct choices in matters ultimately involving life and death, and no less a value than self-determination."[7] Psychiatrists must face the limits of their therapeutic effectiveness. Not only are our treatments imperfect, but "there is no reason to do all that we can do because agencies of therapy are on hand or because we believe our judgment about the circumstances is superior to the patient's."[10]

CIVIL COMMITMENT PARADIGM

Mr. Smith leaves Dr. Jones' office with a prescription and a return appointment. Let us assume the following ensues thereafter: A very tense Jim Smith arrives 20 minutes late for his next session with Dr. Jones. He glances around the room before telling his psychiatrist that everything has gotten worse. He tried the medicine, but it made him feel "weird," and he "flushed it down the john." Work has become unbearable. Jim is convinced that his supervisor is calling him "faggot" on the shop floor. He reluctantly admitted that he has heard a man's voice commanding him to kill his tormentor. The day before the session Jim purchased a handgun and ammunition, which he carries in the trunk of his car. He ominously predicted that at any minute he might "explode" and "get even with the bastard." He then announced that "shrinks" are worthless and that he "won't be coming back." At that point Dr. Jones asked Jim to wait for a few moments, permitting Dr. Jones to leave the office to call the police in order to initiate involuntary psychiatric hospitalization.

The deteriorating clinical situation has demanded a shift from an informed consent to a civil commitment model of psychiatric treatment. The consequent abrogation of a competent patient's right to autonomous choice generates considerable ethical controversy. Comments in the psychiatric literature have ranged from a belief that compulsory treatment is morally impermissible to a conviction that every citizen should have the right to be committed to the care of a psychiatric service.[11] Despite the general acceptance of civil commitment by psychiatrists, the profession must be prepared to defend any course of action that sacrifices a patient's freedom. "Involuntary confinement is the most serious deprivation of individual liberty that a society may impose (regardless of the name under which it parades)."[12] In fact, between 1974 and 1979 at least 34 states substantially modified their civil commitment statutes away from criteria based on psychiatrically defined need for treatment to some explicit finding of dangerousness and tighter procedural controls.[13] Let us examine the legal and ethical rationale for this fairly dramatic evolution in the rules governing civil commitment and the practical difficulties these changes have spawned.

Civil commitment of the mentally ill is substantively justified on the basis of two historic powers of the state. Parens patriae is the state's authority to care for, protect, or treat persons who are unable to provide these services for themselves. The *parens patriae* doctrine offers a mechanism for the state to compel mentally incompetent persons to receive treatment. However, *parens patriae* alone is insufficient to override a competent person's autonomous refusal to accept the care. The inherent right of the state to protect the safety and welfare of its citizens is referred to as the police power. This power is usually exercised through the criminal law, though it may also apply to enforce medical interventions, such as quarantine. The police power of the state may be called upon to detain mentally ill persons in need of treatment, but only when they are also dangerous. Just as the *parens patriae* doctrine cannot justify the confinement of the nondangerous mentally ill, the police power of the state cannot be used to incarcerate the dangerous but not mentally ill. To do so would constitute preventive detention. Probably more than half of all violent felons will commit crimes after release from prison, "yet the courts have no legal basis of ordering their continued confinement on mere apprehension of future unlawful acts, and must await until another crime against society is committed or they are found insane in proper mental health proceedings before confinement may again be ordered."[14] It seems a peculiar consequence that the joining of the *parens patriae* and police powers of the state has as a result that: "Of all the identifiably dangerous groups in society, only the mentally ill are singled out for preventive detention, and they are probably the least dangerous."[15] Presumably the benefits to the patient and society of the treatment of the potentially violent mentally ill outweigh the costs of civil commitment, though this equation is scorned by the mental health bar.[16]

In most states a determination by the physician of a mental illness and an associated danger to self or others is necessary and sufficient for civil commitment. Procedural safeguards are generally in force offering the patient an early opportunity for a judicial hearing with legal representation. The psychiatrist, as an agent of the state, has the burden of demonstrating mental illness, dangerousness, and that treatment in a less restrictive setting is inappropriate. The standard of proof for these elements is clear and convincing evidence, intermediate between the civil standard of preponderance of the evidence, and the criminal standard of evidence beyond a reasonable doubt.

The moral justification for civil commitment has resulted in an extraordinary emphasis being placed on the concept of dangerousness. The finding of dangerousness in a psychiatric patient allows the psychiatrist to compel hospitalization over the patient's objections. Despite its practical importance, "psychiatrists cannot agree upon the criteria for dangerousness, nor can they predict it accurately, nor can they guarantee that persons who are not dangerous will not be labeled as such and confined."[17] What is the foundation for this rather sweeping indictment of the psychiatric determination of dangerousness? To begin with, dangerousness has never been consistently or adequately operationally defined. It is largely unclear what domain of behaviors is to be deemed dangerous. Compounding the difficulty of definition, "no instrument has yet been developed that can predict violent and dangerous behavior in a reasonably accurate and satisfactory manner."[18]

Although psychiatrists are called upon to characterize a patient dichotomously as either dangerous or not, dangerousness is more properly viewed as a continuum of risk determined by many factors. An assessment of dangerousness would include the patient-specific risk factors, such as a history of violence, the presence of paranoia and psychosis, the use of disinhibiting substances, availability of weapons, etc. Other interpersonal and situational variables would also need to be considered, including the existence of an identifiable victim. To add further complexity, it has been suggested that rater bias operates as well. The patient's race, social class, physical appearance, the time of day, and background of the interviewer have all been cited as suspect factors influencing the psychiatric decision to commit "dangerous" patients.[19] Finally, because violence, even among a high-risk group of patients, is an infrequent event, there is a statistical tendency to overpredict, especially since a false negative error might lead to tragedy. Is it any wonder that "there is simply no empirical evidence that psychiatrists or any other clinicians can clinically identify who will be dangerous beyond the accuracy anyone could attain simply by the probability of chance"[20]? Since the vast majority of errors in predicting future violence results in the unnecessary deprivation of liberty of the mentally ill, the Canadian Psychiatric Association has recommended restricting civil commitment to a smaller, more narrowly defined group of "dangerous" patients: "It would seem that only in cases of patients who repeat the same pattern of dangerous behavior which responds favourably to psychiatric treatment but recurs when the patient discontinued such treatment may there be justification in treating a patient against his will on a preventive basis."[21]

Violence remains a major public health concern regardless of how unsophisticated and imprecise our predictive abilities may be. Moreover, there is an undeniable clustering of violence within a subpopulation of the mentally ill. For instance, a substantially higher prevalence of schizophrenia was found among men convicted of homicide than would be expected in the general population.[22] In addition, the increased arrest rate among the postdischarge mentally ill is a function of a higher rate of prehospital criminality and the fact that even ex-patients without a criminal record are arrested five times more often for violent crimes than the local population.[23]

It is particularly important to note that the literature criticizing the clinical prediction of violence was based primarily on research involving institutionalized patients or prisoners who were subsequently released. This study group contrasts markedly with the typical outpatient evaluation conducted in the psychiatrist's office or emergency room. An investigation of Veterans Administration patients, held on an emergency basis, showed that in the first 45 days of psychiatric hospitalization the involuntary patients had a 41% probability of assault, compared with an 8% rate for the voluntary admissions.[24] Thus, although little is known about how accurately violent behavior can be predicted in many circumstances, it may nonetheless be possible to predict it accurately enough to be useful for the purpose of civil commitment to reduce threat of imminent danger.[25] By so doing, the patient will receive treatment, society will be protected, and ultimately the patient may come to believe that it was indeed fortunate that he or she was hospitalized against their will.[26] Policymakers have recognized this wisdom, as reflected in the "recent shift toward increased reliance on judgments of psychiatrists when clinical needs and legal rights conflict with the underlying assumption that psychiatrists can be trusted to make decisions that are both clinically sound and uphold their patients' rights."[13]

DUTY-TO-PROTECT PARADIGM

Dr. Jones' decision to commit Mr. Smith appears to be legally and ethically appropriate, given the clinical picture. Let us posit that while Dr. Jones was phoning the police, Mr. Smith bolts from the office and cannot be found. Dr. Jones then contacts Mr. Smith's supervisor, alerting him that he may be in peril.

Confidentiality of doctor-patient communication has enjoyed a long and enduring tradition in medicine. It is specifically recognized in the Hippocratic oath ("What I may see or hear in the course of the treatment or even outside of the treatment in regard to the life of men, which on no account one must spread abroad, I will keep to myself holding such things shameful to be spoken about") and in the current Principles of Medical Ethics of the American Medical Association ("A physician shall safeguard patient confidences within the constraints of the law").[27] Two types of explanations have been proposed to explain the importance of confidentiality. The first suggests that divulging secrets is an insult to human dignity and an a priori wrong. The other argument holds that violations of confidentiality deter new patients from entering treatment and current patients from revealing charged material. Hence, the benefits of a policy of strict confidentiality transcend the good that would come from routine disclosure.

In 1976 the California Supreme Court handed down its second, definitive, and by now famous *Tarasoff* decision. This case arose after a University of California student killed his estranged girlfriend, Tatiana Tarasoff. The student had been in treatment at the University Mental Health Service, where he had discussed his stormy relationship. Following her death the victim's parents sued the University for negligence. In its ruling the court created a psychotherapist duty to protect: "When a therapist determines or pursuant to the standards of his profession should determine, that his patient presents a serious danger of violence to another, he incurs an obligation to use reasonable care to protect the intended victim against such danger."[28] There followed an immediate outcry from the psychiatric community warning of the dire consequences that would follow any psychotherapist obligation to violate confidentiality.[29] Fortunately, these fears have largely proved unfounded. In fact, over the ensuing decade, a series of similar decisions have expanded the duty-to-protect doctrine far beyond the borders of California.[30] Let us examine the ethical, legal, and clinical rationale for adopting this duty.

The objection to the imposition of a duty to protect is the implication that protection would require warning the intended victim, which would then necessitate a violation of psychiatrist-patient confidentiality. But confidentiality is not and has never been sacrosanct. Physicians have long recognized that their ethical responsibility to the law and to the public compelled notifying the authorities of patients diagnosed as having certain contagious diseases. More recently every state has enacted laws mandating physicians to report cases of suspected child abuse. Similar legislation is being promulgated for elder abuse. Acceptance of the obligation to report abuse reflects an acknowledgment by physicians that confidentiality is not absolute. No doctor can in good conscience be bound to silence in the face of violence perpetrated against an innocent victim; psychiatrists are no exception. "It is, indeed, difficult to formulate a moral argument against the position that therapists should act to protect those whom they believe to be endangered, as should all human beings."[31]

It can be shown to be ethical and legal to breach confidentiality in order to protect third parties from becoming victims of violence; but is it also therapeutic for the patient? At the very least, the *Tarasoff* doctrine "is not as unmitigated a disaster for the enterprise of psychotherapy as it once seemed."[29] One empirical study of clinical practice concludes that "the *Tarasoff* decision is not inimical to good clinical practice and may actually be beneficial to it."[32] Suggested mechanisms cited in the literature for a therapeutic effect have included shifting "the treatment of interpersonal violence from an intrapsychiatric model to a model more interactionist in perspective,"[33] and forging an alliance with the patient's ambivalence.[34]

Approaching the *Tarasoff* doctrine as a three-stage process may promote rather than disturb clinical care.[31] First, the psychiatrist gathers data for the assessment of the patient threatening violence. Our prototypical Dr. Jones evaluated Mr. Smith, diagnosed a serious psychiatric disorder, and negotiated an outpatient treatment plan. When the initial treatment failed and the threat of violence escalated, Dr. Jones took the reasonable clinical step of arranging for involuntary hospitalization. This plan provides intensive psychiatric treatment for the patient and insures safety for the potential victim. Finally, after a breakdown in the implementation of civil commitment, Dr. Jones anticipating imminent violence, notifies the intended victim as a further measure to lessen the danger of physical harm. Although our hypothetical case example ends with the discharge of a duty to protect through delivering a warning, Dr. Jones' clinical involvement would continue through the hospital and aftercare phases of treatment. It is likely that issues of aggression would remain a prominent focus of therapeutic attention.

CONCLUSION

In this chapter we have explored three areas of ethical concern in the treatment of potentially violent psychiatric patients. The importance of the therapeutic alliance with patients is unquestioned, as is its ethical counterpart, voluntary informed consent. When a patient appears on the verge of losing control of aggressive impulses and no longer wishes to participate in psychiatric treatment, civil commitment may become necessary. In those instances where there is danger, law and ethics permit the psychiatrist to confine the patient for involuntary treatment. This act, performed when less restrictive alternatives are not feasible, temporarily curtails the patient's liberty in order to treat the mental illness that may be compromising autonomy, and to neutralize the threat of violence. We contend that clinical practice, the law, and medical ethics all complement each other to benefit the patient and society, while simultaneously preserving the integrity of the role of physician.

There are those unusual situations when all appropriate clinical interventions have failed to reduce the likelihood of patient violence directed against an identifiable third party. The psychiatrist's clinical, legal, and ethical duty to protect life may then force a breach of doctor-patient confidentiality in the form of a warning to the intended victim. The psychiatric treatment of violence-prone patients is admittedly difficult, but good clinical care is nearly always congruent with the standards of law and ethics. We believe that our legal rules and ethical codes offer support to the psychiatrist, and should not be perceived as a deterrent to treating patients who threaten violence.

REFERENCES

1. Glazer D: Violence in society, in Lystad M (ed): *Violence in the Home: Interdisciplinary Perspectives*. New York, Brunner/Mazel, 1986.
2. Rosenberg ML, Mercy JA: Homicide: Epidemiologic analysis at the national level. *Bull NY Acad Med* 1986; 62: 376–399.
3. Lion JR: Ethical issues and violent behavior. *Am J Soc Psychiatry* 1984; 4(3):9–11.
4. Eth S, Robb JW: Informed consent: The problem, in Kentsmith DK, Salladay SA, Miya PA (eds): *Ethics in Mental Health Practice*. Orlando FL, Grune & Stratton, 1986.
5. Redlich F, Mollica RF: Overview ethical issues in contemporary psychiatry. *Am J Psychiatry* 1976; 133:125–136.
6. Katz J: *The Silent World of Doctor and Patient*. New York, Free Press, 1984, p 59.
7. Shultz MM: From informed consent to patient choice: A new protected interest. *Yale Law J* 1985; 95:219–299.

8. Roth LH: Competency to consent for or refuse treatment, in Grinspoon L (ed): *Psychiatry 1982: Annual Review*. Washington, DC, American Psychiatric Press, 1982.
9. Culver CM, Ferrell RB, Green RM: ECT and the special problems of informed consent. *Am J Psychiatry* 1980; 137:586–591.
10. Reiser SJ: Refusing treatment for mental illness: Historical and ethical dimensions. *Am J Psychiatry* 1980; 137:329–331.
11. Clare AW: Ethical issues in psychiatry. *Practitioner* 1979; 223:89–96.
12. Livermore JM, Malinquist CP, Meehl PE: On the justifications for civil commitment. *Univ Penn Law Rev* 1968; 117:75–96.
13. Schwarcz HI, Appelbaum PS, Kaplan RD: Clinical judgments in the decision to commit: Psychiatric discretion and the law: *Arch Gen Psychiatry* 1984; 41:811–815.
14. *In re Williams*, 157 F supp 871 (1958).
15. New York Civil Liberties Union: Objections in involuntary admission to mental hospitals. *Psychoanal Rev* 1971; 58:385–394.
16. Lansdorf RG: The involuntary commitment of adults: An examination of recent legal trends. *Psychiatr Clin N AM* 1983; 6:651–660.
17. Mestrovic SG, Cook JA: The dangerousness standards: What is it and how is it used? *Int J Law Psychiatry* 1986; 8:443–469.
18. Shah SA: Dangerousness and civil commitment of the mentally ill: Some public policy considerations. *Am J Psychiatry* 1975; 132: 501–505.
19. Appelbaum PS, Hamm RM: Decision to seek commitment. *Arch Gen Psychiatry* 1982; 39:447–451.
20. Steadman HJ: The right not to be a false positive: Problems in the application of the dangerous standard. *Psychiatr Q* 1980; 52:84–99.
21. Cahn CH: The ethics of involuntary treatment: The position of the Canadian Psychiatric Association. *Canad J Psychiatry* 1982; 27:67–74.
22. Taylor PJ, Gown J: Violence and psychosis I—Risk of violence among psychotic men. *Br Med J* 1984; 288:1945–1949.
23. Soswsky L: Explaining the increased arrest rate among mental patients. *Am J Psychiatry* 1980; 137:1602–1605.
24. Rofman ES, Askinzi C, Fant E: The prediction of dangerous behavior in emergency civil commitment. *Am J Psychiatry* 1980; 137:1061–1064.
25. Monahan J: The prediction of violent behavior: Toward a second generation of theory and policy. *Am J Psychiatry* 1984; 141:10–15.
26. Kane JM, Quitkin F, Rifkin A, Wagner J, Rosenberg G, Bernstein M: Attitudinal changes of involuntarily committed patients following treatment. *Arch Gen Psychiatry* 1983; 40:374–377.
27. Bloch S, Chodoff P (eds): *Psychiatr Ethics*. New York, Oxford University Press, 1984.
28. *Tarasoff v Regents of the University of California*; reargued 17 Cal 3d, 551 p 2d 334, 131 Cal Reptr 33 (1976).
29. Stone AA: *Law, Psychiatry and Morality*. Washington, DC, American Psychiatric Press, 1984.
30. Mills MJ, Sullivan G, Eth S: Protecting third parties: A decade after Tarasoff. *Am J Psychiatry* 1987; 144:68–74.
31. Appelbaum PS: Tarasoff and the clinician: Problems in fulfilling the duty to protect. *Am J Psychiatry* 1985; 142:425–429.
32. Beck JC: When the patient threatens violence: An empirical study of clinical practice after Tarasoff. *Bull Am Acad Psychiatry Law* 1982; 10:189–201.
33. Wexler D: Patients, therapists and third parties: The victimological virtues of Tarasoff. *Int J Law Psychiatry* 1979; 2:1–28.
34. Wulsin LR, Bursztajn H, Gytheil TG: Unexpected clinical features of the Tarasoff decision: The therapeutic alliance and the "duty to warn." *Am J Psychiatry* 1983; 140:601–603.

15

Ethics and the Death Penalty

Participation by Forensic Psychiatrists in Capital Trials

PHILIPPA FOOT

Psychiatrists, who may or may not specialize in legal work, are called on to participate in capital punishment cases at several points in the legal process. For instance, their opinions may be requested in the determination of fitness to stand trial, and on mental state at the time of the crime, particularly in connection with the insanity defense. After a declaration of guilt they may be involved in the sentencing process, where questions as to mitigating circumstances will often be about mental stress and psychological history. They are also asked to predict future dangerousness and the possibility of rehabilitation. Finally, psychiatrists may (though much less frequently) be asked to pronounce on "fitness to be executed."

Psychiatrists, particularly those who work in public institutions, may also find themselves treating defendants accused of capital offenses, when the hope is that through treatment the accused will become fit to stand trial. Very occasionally, they may be asked to treat prisoners on death row who have been pronounced unfit to be executed, who may thereby be restored to a sufficient degree of sanity to be taken to the execution chamber.

Even apart from this last, surely bizarre, possibility, forensic psychiatrists have become increasingly worried about the morality of participating in capital trials; and this is true of some of those who support capital punishment as well as those who oppose it. The work that they are asked to do has increased considerably since the Supreme Court decisions on *Furman v Georgia*[1] and *Gregg v Georgia*[2] have forced those states wishing to keep or institute capital punishment to make arrangements for sentencing hearings, when aggravating

PHILIPPA FOOT • Department of Philosophy, University of California at Los Angeles, Los Angeles, California 90024.

and mitigating circumstances will be considered, as well as the possibility of future rehabilitation.

In this paper I shall try to sort out some of the moral issues involved in work of this kind. But first a word about the different types of moral questions that can arise when the obligations of members of a particular profession are under review. I would divide them as follows.

Firstly, there are the special obligations that belong to members of a profession, acting professionally, where these obligations are independent of any question of the moral status of the institution, practice, or procedure within which the obligations arise. Obligations of this type are usually referred to as matters of professional ethics, though they could just as well have been called matters of professional morality. This kind of obligation can come from a number of distinguishable sources. The obligations may have to do with the standards of work in the profession stemming from the importance of some task that is especially its own. It may, however, come rather from the opportunities and temptations of persons placed in the position in which their profession places them, for instance, in being able to exploit vulnerable people. Or again, it may come from the special role and purposes that belong to this profession.

The second, theoretically distinct, class of questions has to do with the special case in which moral doubts are raised about a certain practice or institution. In such cases there are particular obligations falling upon those whose profession makes them liable to be asked to participate in this practice. It seems that they must be especially sensitive to doubts about the practice, because they will have to decide whether their consciences will allow them to participate. If the practice is a morally unjustifiable practice then there is a *prima facie* case for nonparticipation, though, as we shall see, the moral question may in a particular instance be more complex than this.

We can illustrate the difference between the two types of moral questions by referring to the stand taken by the AMA about the participation of doctors in the process of execution. The *Current Opinions of the Judicial Council of the AMA 1984* states "A physician, as a member of a profession dedicated to preserving life when there is hope of doing so, should not be a participant in a legally authorized execution" though it is added that a physician may make a determination or certification of death.[3] While it is increasingly difficult for medical or paramedical personnel to observe this rule in view of the use of lethal injection as a method of execution, we see here the first puzzling doubt about the moral duty of physicians in respect of capital punishment. If even paramedical professionals refused to prepare and administer lethal doses, the only possible effect of this would be to swing the pendulum back to more barbarous ways of killing. The professionals would have kept their own hands clean, but would have increased rather than decreased the sum of human suffering. At the moment, however, I am not concerned with these dilemmas, but only with the ground of the objection to participation. We notice that the AMA was not raising doubts about the morality of capital punishment, but giving an opinion about the role that doctors should play in it, whatever its moral status. It was being suggested that because theirs is a healing and life-preserving role, *they* should not take part in a procedure that has a conflicting aim. The moral objection was of the first of the two types distinguished a few paragraphs back.

PROFESSIONAL ETHICS

Let us now discuss psychiatrists' moral obligations of the first type, those that would most naturally be said to fall under the heading of professional ethics. These in their turn fall naturally into two groups: those that do and those that do not depend on the special aims of the profession. The obligation to which the Judicial Council of the AMA was referring in the document just quoted did, of course, have to do with the *aims* of the medical profession; and we may start with this kind of objection to the participation by psychiatrists in capital penalty trials.

It is evident that the aims of psychiatry are of the same general type as of those of the nonpsychiatric medical profession. Psychiatrists, like other doctors, consider themselves bound by something like the Hippocratic oath. How then are they justified in examining or treating individuals where their testimony or treatment is part of a process designed to bring about the death of some of these persons, and where this testimony or treatment may contribute substantially to that outcome? It is true that by participating they are not aiming at the death of a particular person, as are doctors administering a lethal dose. Nevertheless, death is the conditional aim of any murder trial in which the prosecution is seeking the death penalty. The purpose is that if the defendant is found guilty, and if the mitigating circumstances do not outweigh the aggravating circumstances, he should be put to death. The psychiatrist knows that if he gives an honest opinion, as the standards of his profession require him to do, he may, in effect, be bringing about the death of a person whom he has examined and perhaps even treated.

How, then, can the participation of psychiatrists in capital cases be defended, even on the assumption that execution is a morally unobjectionable penalty for certain murders? The chief defense against this kind of charge of violating professional ethics, brought against forensic psychiatrists who make themselves available for murder trials in jurisdictions operating with the death penalty, depends on various distinctions of *role* within the profession. It is pointed out that not all the professional work of a psychiatrist has healing as its aim. For, just as physicians sign death certificates, make assessments for insurance companies, and so on, so psychiatrists have many professional duties conducted not on behalf of the persons they examine but, rather, on behalf of others who have a legitimate interest in the state of their mental health. So, for example, psychiatrists give opinions on the necessity of confining some people not so much for these people's own good as for the protection of those whom they might otherwise harm.

Can this precedent be argued in favor of the psychiatrist's participation in capital legal processes? It seems to me that this can be argued, but that its force must not be exaggerated. What is being said is, in effect, that the profession of psychiatry can be seen as having two parts, almost as if there existed two professions using a number of the same skills, sharing much of their training, and often carried on by a single person. As belonging to one subdivision of the profession, the psychiatrist stands in a professional relation to a patient, and is bound to see his implicit contract to be that of healer and life preserver to this patient. This does not mean that in case of great necessity he may not consider it his duty to warn other individuals, or even authorities, of a threat of danger from the patient, as in a *Tarasoff*[4] type of case when he is justified in breaking the implicit contract. It does, however, mean that, with such exceptions, he is bound to the patient in matters such as the divulging of confidential material without his consent. Where courts so rule, he may have to divulge it; but he should oppose this and mitigate its effects when he can. His patient, whether accused person, defendant, or convicted murderer, is someone *in his care*.

The role of assessor, as much bound to the general interest as to the person he examines, is different, and it will often be possible, and almost always desirable, to keep the roles distinct, so that the same person will not stand in the two different relationships to the same defendant. I am aware, of course, that the attempt to separate out the role of psychiatric healer from that of psychiatric assessor meets practical difficulties, particularly in the case of psychiatrists working in forensic medical facilities. Nevertheless, it may be possible even there, and should be urged. It is sometimes argued that there is disutility in this separation of the two roles, because it is important that someone who is assessing defendants in the legal system should have experience of treating the kind of person whom he is to examine; but this objection seems weak, given that what is being suggested is not a separation of persons who habitually take one role rather than another, but only a separation of role in respect of a single defendant.

There is, therefore, some defense for the participation of psychiatrists in death penalty proceedings coming from the theoretical and often practical separation of the roles of healer and assessor, Nevertheless, it seems to me that it is right to be uneasy about the conflict between the aims of the medical profession and of the courts in a death penalty jurisdiction, and to be wary of the arguments of those who seem to believe that a new role can be created by a difference of purpose, as if the legitimacy of setting aside the principle of nonmaleficence were not exactly what is in question. It is not, after all, possible to see doctors as having other roles *of equal importance* to that of healer. In spite of the other things that they are called on to do, psychiatrists and other doctors must surely be seen *primarily* as healers, with *primum non nocere* as their guiding light. It is true that the doctor does not have a duty even to a patient to ward off any evil that may threaten him; he does not even have a duty to ward off a threat of death from any and every source, as if a doctor had a special duty to go into the water to save someone from drowning. Our question, however, is about the use of medical skills to participate in a process that is set up to result, in certain circumstances, in the subject's death.

I am not, therefore, entirely convinced by the argument put forward by Paul Appelbaum[5] to the effect that the separation of roles solves the problem of the conflict between the aims of the psychiatrist as healer and the psychiatrist in his role as assessor for the courts. He suggests that the forensic psychiatrist (or "forensicist") has a quite different aim from the treating psychiatrist, and should therefore be trying to realize different moral goods, such as the working of justice or the good of society. Forensic psychiatry is the application of psychiatry to legal issues for legal, not therapeutic ends, and here therefore "the argument that the principle of non-maleficence will be violated if harm results to the evaluee is irrelevant."

Appelbaum's suggestion is to be respected, because it is so open about the separation that he endorses. It is infinitely superior to the somewhat disreputable attempts of some to make out that the psychiatrist who serves the courts in capital cases is, despite appearances, actually adhering to the principles of nonmaleficence. That dubious kind of defense has been made in two different ways. In the first place, it has been suggested that the doctor should see himself as ministering not to the individual patient but rather in the role of healer to society as whole. This is dangerously close to the "biomedical vision" of the Nazis that recommended the "excision" of "diseased" individuals in the interest of the whole societal "organism," and we need not say very much about it. That it was crucial to the way in which the Nazis persuaded otherwise reputable doctors to play a leading role in their exterminations and experiments has been well documented by Robert Jay Lifton,[6] and it is strange that it should make even the briefest appearances in contemporary discussions of the ethics of forensic psychiatry, as Charles Ewing reports that it does.[7] The other attempt to reconcile the role of physician as healer with that of agent of the criminal courts is just as extraordinary and as unacceptable. Its adherents use neo-Hegelian arguments to try to show that in getting a guilty person punished, the forensic psychiatrist is actually serving him by carrying out the real will expressed in his implicit acceptance of the punishment attached to his crime.[8]

Appelbaum's arguments are of a quite different order of merit from these ridiculous theorizings. Nevertheless, his thesis has curious implications that may make us pause before accepting it. It would, though he does not mention it, remove all objection to even the most direct participation by doctors in the process of execution. The courts could ask them to kill the condemned because in such a role they would be "forencisists," not healers, legitimately serving the ends of the courts and having no duty of nonmaleficence.

I have been emphasizing the aim of doctors as healing, and protecting against the threat of death. Against this the precedent of army doctors may be argued. Do they not certify recruits as fit for active service, and do they not treat wounded soldiers so that they may go back into battle? That case is, however, different. Army doctors do not aim at the death of the recruits and soldiers whom they examine and treat, *nor are they working for people who do have this as even a conditional end.* It is usual in moral philosophy to distinguish aiming at a result (either as an ultimate end or a means to this end) from doing that which will forseeably but regrettably bring it about. This is an important, though sometimes controverted, doctrine, and clearly has application here.

Uneasiness about the compatibility of the ends of a psychiatrist as doctor and of the capital penalty processes in which he is asked to participate should therefore remain. Nevertheless, it would surely be wrong for psychiatrists to refuse to participate in any capacity at any stage of capital proceedings. It is true that if he does participate he may unintentionally be instrumental in bringing about the death of the subject whom he examines or treats, and that even refusing to work for the prosecution is not a perfect safeguard against this, given that if he discovers prejudicial evidence and is not called as a defense witness he may be subpoenaed by the other side. Nevertheless, certain kinds of participation may be seen as likely to be favorable rather than neutral or inimical to the defendant's interests. Defendants often need psychiatrists, for instance when a defense of not guilty by reason of insanity is being put forward. And psychiatric testimony can be especially important in the sentencing stage of capital trial in the many jurisdictions in which there is a statuary basis for mounting a mental illness defense in the capital penalty trial. Although Lawrence White has argued, citing George Dix and studies made by students at Stanford Law School, that this defense often fails to impress juries, he also points out that

> A recent U.S. Supreme Court decision has provided a constitutional basis for mounting a mental illness defense. In *Ake v Oklahoma,* the court held that an indigent capital defendant is entitled to access at public expense to a psychiatrist for purposes of evaluation and possible testimony.[9]

It seems, therefore, that if psychiatrists refused to participate in any way in capital trials this would not serve defendants, so that the argument for this refusal which is based on an incompatibility between the healing aims of the profession and the threatening nature of a capital process are not in the end compelling. Asking himself *where* he should participate, a psychiatrist might decently be guided by his loyalty to the principle *primum non nocere,* and the idea of treating a defendant on death row in order that he should be made fit to be executed is surely repugnant; but probably he should not take the aims of his profession as a reason for refusing to participate altogether.

Still leaving aside the question of whether there are special reasons for nonparticipation stemming from the dubious morality of capital punishment itself, there are, however, considerations of professional ethics other than that of the "psychiatrist as healer" that tell against participation in capital penalty trials. It can be said, for instance, that it is impossible to maintain the usual principles of confidentiality, and that however many warnings are given about possible self-incrimination, a defendant talking to a psychiatrist usually finds it almost impossible not to regard the psychiatrist as his doctor.

There is also the problem of maintaining professional integrity in face of the tendency of juries, and even judges, to overestimate the reach of psychiatric expertise. This problem is particularly serious where psychiatrists are asked to make predictions about the future dangerousness of defendants, as they frequently are in the sentencing phase of capital trials, because a great body of evidence shows that these predictions are totally unreliable, except perhaps when they concern the immediate future.[10,11,7] It is therefore surprising that the report of the Task Force on the Role of Psychiatry in the Sentencing Process, which is in general strongly critical of claims to predict violence, should leave a place for an individual psychiatrist "who believes that he or she has sufficient data to make some type of probability prediction."[12] There does not seem to be the slightest chance that juries or judges will recognize that psychiatrists who predict future dangerousness are not speaking with any kind of professional competence, even if these psychiatrists (unlike the notorious and much discussed Dr. Grigson[7]), refrain from making confident predictions.

Nor is it easy to accept the view of those who believe that it is for the courts to determine the utility of psychiatric participation, and that it would be arrogance for a psychiatrist to refuse the court's request. Charles P. Ewing was right to point out that professionals also have obligations that derive from the ethical standards of their professions.

> Are psychiatrists and psychologists who testify that a capital defendant is dangerous—and thus deserving of the death penalty—practicing their profession in an ethical fashion? The answer to this question lies not in judicial reasoning or law, but rather in the ethical standards of the psychiatric and psychological professions.[7]

The Supreme Court of California was upholding an important principle ruling in *People v Murtishaw* (1981)[13] that there had been error in a lower court's admission of testimony forecasting that a defendant would commit violent and possibly homicidal acts in prison, since there was no reason to believe the witnesses' prediction was immune from the general unreliability that attends predictions of future violence generally. But so long as a number of jurisdictions make such predictions the crucial determinant, or at least a determining factor, in death penalty sentencing, psychiatrists surely have the duty to take their own stand by refusing to do what they are asked. If these predictions of dangerousness are in fact quite unreliable, it seems monstrous that on their basis people are sent to execution. And if psychiatrists know them to be unreliable, they should refuse to be the agents of such happenings. Such a refusal seems right in the center of the area of professional ethics.

MORAL OBJECTIONS TO THE DEATH PENALTY

So far, I have been asking whether there is an ethical (that is, moral) objection to psychiatrists' participation in capital trials, whether or not there is any ethical objection to capital punishment as such. That is to say that I have been considering matters of professional ethics, i.e., positive and negative duties that follow from the proper aims and standards of the psychiatric profession, or from what they in particular are asked to do in these legal proceedings. These are, we might say, matters that concern the consciences of members of *this* profession in relation to *their* professional activities and, moreover, have to do with duties and obligations that come from the nature of the profession. We often speak of these as ethical rather than moral questions; but I do not think that there is any particular significance in this. The terms "moral" and "ethical" are interchangeable in meaning, so far as I am concerned. If it seems more natural to speak of professional ethics rather than professional morals, that should not give the impression that there are two different concepts here. Where professional administrations have issued codes of ethics for a profession, this might just as well have been called a code of professional morality.

When I say that so far I have been considering one type of question and now want to go on to another, this does not, therefore, have to do with any supposed distinction between "ethics" and "morals," but rather with the source of obligations and restrictions on conduct that could equally well be called by either name. In what follows I shall use whichever term seems natural, and shall attach no significance to the choice of one or the other. What matters is that I am now going to discuss possible moral (or ethical) objections to the participation of psychiatrists in capital trials where these would spring from the possibly objectionable nature of the proceedings themselves. If there is a moral objection to capital punishment, then something will follow for anyone who has anything to do with it. If something special follows for psychiatrists, this will be because of the particular relation in which their work stands to the institution. If capital punishment is evil, we all have some duty to oppose it; but a special duty belongs, e.g., to educators, to politicians, to journalists, and to moral philosophers. A special duty will also belong to those actually asked to participate in the business, such as officials, lawyers, psychologists, and psychiatrists. Psychiatrists are asked to make significant contributions to legal proceedings involving the death penalty, and this is the reason that they, as psychiatrists, have a special obligation to consider the ethics of capital punishment. It is not that they have a special contribution to make to the debate about this moral question. They, like everyone else, must make their decision on the basis of considerations such as the evidence for and against the deterrent effect of the death penalty, the barbarity of the execution processes, and (above all, in my opinion) the horror of the fact that so long as capital punishment continues, mistakes will inevitably be made and innocent persons irremediably condemned. These facts are open to everyone; but not everyone has the same duty to give them careful scrutiny.

Should those psychiatrists who decide that capital punishment is an immoral institution refuse to participate in any way in capital penalty proceedings? In general, one supposes—it is a good principle—that if there is something bad going on there is a duty not to take any part in it. And it is, of course, immensely important that people should not suppose that their consciences have nothing to do with the things they do in some sort of official or "work" capacity. It is arguable that the absolutely critical factor in allowing the administration of the Nazi persecution of the Jews by ordinary decent German people was their readiness to substitute "conscientiousness" for conscience. Rainer Baum has argued this in his article "Holocaust: Moral Indifference as *the* Form of Modern Evil" in the collection *Echoes From the Holocaust* edited by Rosenberg and Myers.[14] Baum's thesis is that these things could not have taken place had there not been a readiness to resign morality to the "private" sphere, while merely being conscientious in their professional lives—that is, conscientiously and unquestioningly doing that which as professionals they were asked to do.

It is, therefore, of great importance that people of any profession question the work that as professionals they are asked to do and, in general, refusal seems the proper course when they are asked to be involved in any morally evil proceedings. Nor does the argument "If I do not do it someone else will" in itself have any force. In cases where this is true (which it often is not) that means that by nonparticipation one is not able to contribute directly to bringing the proceedings to a halt. This is not to say, however, that refusal will have no effect on public opinion, nor that *effect* is all that should concern one's conscience. Since, as I have argued elsewhere,[15] there is no reason to take it for granted that utilitarianism, which judges the rightness of actions solely by their consequences, is a true theory of morality there may be good nonutilitarian moral reason for refusing to participate in bad activities and institutions, *whether or not this will have any good effect.*

There is, therefore, a presumption on general moral grounds that if capital punishment is a moral evil, those asked to take part in procedures that can lead up to it should refuse to do so. This would, however, be a curious conclusion unless "taking part" is defined in a special way. For one of the ways in which lawyers, and others work *against* capital punishment is precisely by taking part in capital trials, and trying to get a lesser penalty applied. I do not know how often Tony Amsterdam and his group used to provide lawyers for the defense; I believe that more often they gave advice to defending attorneys who were often appointed by the courts without any regard for their lack of expert knowledge of the ways in which capital sentences could be challenged. If and when they did appear in court they could not possibly be accused of "participating in a morally evil institution," and the same is true, of course, of those who work for the Southern Poverty Law Center in Montgomery, Alabama, and by organizations such as the ACLU Capital Punishment Project and the NAACP Legal Defense Fund in New York. Margaret Cooke has described one such attempt to work against the death penalty from inside.

> An innovative approach to the utilization of expert testimony in capital cases has been the development of the team defense by the Southern Poverty Law Center. Attorneys, law students, paralegals and social scientists join in an effort to avoid the death penalty in every stage of the proceedings. The primary emphasis of this approach is on client participation; the defendant is encouraged to assist the defense, testifying, questioning witnesses, and making arguments to the jury. A standard battery of pretrial motions has been developed; community attitude surveys are utilized in jury selection and jury composition challenges; an offensive strategy of motions is utilized whereby relevant trial motions are injected to destroy the continuity of the prosecution's case; and a model penalty phase of trial has been developed wherein general arguments against capital punishment, e.g., nondeterrence, moral-religious questions, remorse, and rehabilitation, are introduced.[16]

Is it open to psychiatrists who oppose capital punishment thus to work against it from inside? The obvious difficulty is that psychiatrists are asked for a report, or for testimony, about the defendant's past, present, or future state of mind, not for arguments for the prosecution or the defense. That is to say that although a psychiatrist may have been called in by one side or the other, he is not supposed to be part of the adversarial lineup. It is not consistent with his professional integrity to tailor his evidence for the defense. What he can do, and apparently some psychiatrists do do, is to refuse to work except for defense attorneys. Then he will know that if his opinion as delivered to the attorney is unfavorable to the defendant, the defense will not call him to testify. It is true that this is the situation in which he is likely to be subpoenaed by the prosecution, when he will have to give his honest opinion in court; but nevertheless it seems to me a good course of action for a psychiatrist opposed to the death penalty. He cannot be sure that he will not have to give testimony that will have the opposite effect from the one he believes himself to have a duty to try to bring about; but this may happen to anyone, whatever good cause he is working for.

If this seems a reasonable course of action it does not, on the other hand, seem right that psychiatrists who oppose the death penalty should refuse to participate at all in capital cases in death penalty jurisdictions. One would imagine that were the courts left without this testimony, rather crude M'Naughten-type criteria would be used to determine fitness to stand trial and the relevant *mens rea* at the time of the crime. Psychiatrists can of course testify only in the light of criteria laid down by the courts. Nevertheless there must be some latitude in deciding how to apply these criteria. In particular there must be scope for a merciful emphasis on mitigating circumstances so far as these concern the state of mind of the accused or convicted, as also his psychological history. Defendants facing the death penalty need psychiatrists, and the worst thing that could happen from their point of view would be a general exodus of those psychiatrists who oppose the death penalty on moral grounds. It would seem to make more sense for these psychiatrists either to work against capital punishment from the inside, or else to make their protest against it in other ways, using any special knowledge that they may have to bring before the public and the legal profession the inhumanity of the punishment and the bizarre nature of particular cases in which people of pathetic mental and emotional capacities have been executed.

My conclusion to this chapter as a whole is, therefore, that certain reforms are necessary even on the assumption that there are no moral objections to capital punishment; in particular that psychiatrists should simply refuse to predict future dangerousness. The case against the morality of capital punishment changes the nature of the debate, and may strongly suggest to those who are convinced by it that they should refuse to have anything to do with capital cases. Nevertheless, for the reasons given, I do not myself think that the case against capital punishment is a compelling case against any participation by psychiatrists in capital trials.

ACKNOWLEDGMENT

I am very grateful for the help which I have been given by Michael Aglion, David Conney, and David Dolinko.

REFERENCES

1. *Furman v Georgia,* 408 U.S. 715 (1972).
2. *Gregg v Georgia,* 428 U.S. 153 (1976).
3. Current Opinions of the American Medical Association: Section 2.06.
4. *Tarasoff v Regents of the University of California,* 118 Cal. Rptr. 129, 529 P.2d 553 (1974); 17 Cal.3d 425 551 P.2d 334 (1976).
5. Appelbaum PE: The parable of the forensic psychiatrist: Ethics and the problem of doing harm. Forthcoming in *Int J Law Psychiatry.*
6. Lifton JL: *The Nazi doctors.* New York, Basic Books, 1986.
7. Ewing CP: "Dr Death" and the case for an ethical ban on psychiatric and psychological predictions of dangerousness in capital sentencing proceedings. *Am J Law Med* 1982/3; 8/4: 407–428.
8. Mossman D: Assessing and restoring competency to be executed: Should psychiatrists participate? *Behav Sci Law* 1987; 5/4: 397–409.
9. White LT: The mental illness defense in the capital penalty hearing. *Behav Sci Law* 1987; 5/4: 413.
10. Monahan J: *The Clinical Prediction of Violent Behavior.* Rockville, Md. (5600 Fishers Lane, Rockville, Md. 20857): US Dept of Health and Human Services, Public Health Service, Alcohol, Drug Abuse and Mental Health Administration, National Institute of Mental Health; Washington, D.C.: For sale by Supt. of Docs., US GPO, [1981] Series: Crime and delinquency issues; Series; DHHS publication; no. (ADM) 81–921.
11. Hughes G: Legal aspects of predicting dangerousness, in Rosner R (ed): *Critical Issues in American Psychiatry and the Law.* New York, Plenum Press, 1985, pp 57–90.
12. Halleck SL, Applebaum P, Rappeport J, *et al*: Report of the Task Force on the Role of Psychiatry in the Sentencing Process, in American Psychiatric Association, *Issues in Forensic Psychiatry.* Washington DC, American Psychiatric Press, 1984, p 207.
13. *People v Murtishaw,* 29 Cal.3d 733; 175 Cal. Rptr. 738, 631 P.2d 466 (1981).
14. Baum RC: Holocaust: Moral indifference as *the* form of modern evil, in Rosenberg A, Myers GE (eds): *Echoes from the Holocaust.* Philadelphia, Temple University Press, 1988.
15. Foot P: Utilitarianism and the virtues. *Proceedings and Addresses of the American Philosophical Association* 1983; 57:273–283.
16. Cooke M, Capital punishment, in Cooke G (ed): *The Role of the Forensic Psychiatrist.* Springfield Ill., Charles C. Thomas, 1980.

16

HIV Infections and AIDS

Neuropsychiatric, Psychosocial, and Legal Issues

HAROLD M. GINZBURG

INTRODUCTION

The human immunodeficiency virus[1,2] (HIV) was isolated and identified two years after patients were initially diagnosed with the acquired immunodeficiency syndrome (AIDS).[3] HIV infection results in the eventual development of AIDS.[4] HIV infection causes profound suppression of the immune system by depletion of T-lymphocytes, especially of the helper/inducer subset bearing the OK T4 surface marker.[5] The sequelae of HIV infection result from primary HIV infection and secondary life-threatening opportunistic infections of the gastrointestinal, pulmonary, and neurologic systems. The T-cell suppression also predisposes to Kaposi's sarcoma, and non-Hodgkin's lymphomas.

In less than a decade, this previously unidentified retrovirus is estimated by the World Health Organization to have killed many tens of thousands and infected between 5–10 million.[6] HIV infection has become the focus of a worldwide prevention, education, treatment, and research effort.

HIV-infected individuals may not present clinically with HIV-related diseases for many years after infection, but they may be immediately subject to a number of personal, social, cultural, and legal consequences. While the medical community primarily directs its efforts to the approximately 2% of those currently infected with HIV who are symptomatic, the general community and the media are becoming more concerned about the asymptomatic HIV carriers. Thus, it is not surprising that HIV testing, regardless of its perceived sensitivity and specificity, has taken on a separate identity and purpose. It has

HAROLD M. GINZBURG • Bureau of Health Care Delivery and Assistance, Health Resources and Services Administration, United States Public Health Service, 5600 Fishers Lane, Rockville, Maryland 20857.

been several decades since the fundamental dynamic tension between the constitutional rights of the individual and those of the community have been so carefully scrutinized. This chapter reviews the neuropsychiatric and psychosocial aspects of HIV infection with a detailed discussion of the ethical and legal issues surrounding HIV counseling and testing, and presents several areas where the misuse of medical information may lead to discrimination.

EPIDEMIOLOGY

Magnitude of the Problem

The presence of antibodies to HIV is not diagnostic of AIDS or any other clinical disorder. In fact, the great majority of the estimated 1.5 million seropositive individuals in the United States remain asymptomatic.[7] Disease progression estimates in 1986 were that approximately 32% of these individuals will develop AIDS within 5 years of seroconversion, and an additional number of individuals will be ill with other HIV-related illnesses.[8] More recent estimates indicate that 42% of HIV infected homosexual men will develop AIDS after a period of 11 years.[9] The risk of developing AIDS and other clinical manifestations, once infected with HIV, increases with time.

By December 1988, more than 80,000 cases of AIDS had been reported to the Centers for Disease Control, and more than half of these individuals have died.[10] The CDC estimates that within the United States by 1991 there will have been more than a quarter of a million patients diagnosed with AIDS; half will be alive at the end of that year.[11] Estimates presented in the final report of the Presidential Commission on the Human Immunodeficiency Virus suggest that almost 500,000 Americans will have died or progressed to the later stages of the disease by 1992.[12]

The consensus opinion from a June 1988 federal conference in Charlottesville, Virginia indicates that 450,000 individuals will be diagnosed with AIDS by 1993. Additional consensus findings from that conference include the observations that the average time from infection to diagnosis with AIDS appears to be approximately 8 years; the average time of survival after the diagnosis of AIDS is less than 18 months. Thus, on average, each infected individual may spread the disease for almost a decade before death intervenes.

HIV appears to be neurotropic[13]; glial cells have been found to be infected with HIV.[14] Estimates from the prospective Multicenter AIDS Cohort (MAC) Study of 5000 homosexual men strongly suggest that 60% of HIV patients will develop some evidence of dementia during their illness.[15]

Transmission Vectors

HIV predominantly is transmitted through sexual contact by exposure to infected semen or cervical/vaginal secretions, or parenteral exposure to infected blood or blood components. Only a few cases have been reported involving transmission from exposure to other body fluids and body tissues.[16] Persons at increased risk of developing AIDS include homosexual and bisexual men, intravenous drug users, individuals transfused with contaminated blood or blood products (especially those with hemophilia A), and heterosexual contacts of persons with HIV infection. HIV can also be passed from infected mothers to their offspring.

HIV Infection (and AIDS) Is a Chronic Disease

As more chemotherapeutic agents are identified, and found to be efficacious, the estimated life expectancy for patients with HIV-infection can be anticipated to increase. Thus, the increasing longevity of HIV-infected patients will result in the need to conceptualize HIV infection as a chronic disease, and develop and implement therapeutic modalities that are responsive to the needs of those infected with a chronic disease with acute exacerbations.[17]

NEUROPSYCHIATRIC COMPLICATIONS OF HIV INFECTION

Introduction

In her review of the literature on HIV infection, Petito indicates that at least 40–50% of adults and as many as 70–80% of children with AIDS have clinical neurological dysfunction; as many as 80% of patients with AIDS have evidence of CNS disease at postmortem examination.[14] Neurological disease secondary to HIV infection (cerebral atrophy) has been described in the newborn. More commonly the developmental milestones in the first year or two of life are delayed or lost, and the clinical course may be that of either a progressive or static encephalopathy.[18]

Price reports that AIDS dementia complex (ADC) is the most frequent and most important cause of neurological morbidity in patients with AIDS.[16] Levy reports that 37% of 1286 patients with AIDS who were treated in a large university hospital had significant neurological illness. One-third of these patients, or approximately 10% of the total AIDS patients treated, presented with neurological symptoms as their initial manifestations of AIDS.[19,20]

In response to these clinical observations, the Centers for Disease Control (CDC) classification system for HIV diseases was modified to include a subgroup for patients without systemic symptoms who have clinical evidence of dementia, myelopathy, or peripheral neuropathy *and* evidence of HIV infection.[21]

Neuropathology

The identification of HIV DNA[22] and HIV-infected giant cells[23] in the brains of patients with AIDS, and the detection of HIV antibodies[24] and antigens[25] in the cerebrospinal fluid (CSF) of HIV-infected individuals strongly suggest a primary role for HIV in the development of organic brain syndrome and peripheral neuropathies.

Secondary neurologic complications of HIV infection occur as a result of opportunistic infections in the central and peripheral nervous system. Toxoplasmosis is reported to be the most common cause of a cerebral mass lesion in a patient with AIDS. Therapy may initially be effective; however, recurrences are common when treatment is stopped. Fungal, mycobacterial, and herpes virus (particularly cytomegalovirus) infections are common. Progressive multifocal leukoencephalopathy, usually caused by the papovavirus JC, also occurs.[26]

Resnick[27] has demonstrated that there is early penetration of the blood-brain-barrier by HIV. He and his co-workers recovered HIV from the CSF of 5/29 (17%) patients with and 5/23 (22%) without neurologic signs and symptoms. McArthur and his colleagues have reported similar findings in their study of 38 homosexual men.[28] They also found a high rate of CSF abnormalities in men with neuropsychiatric findings (N = 22), including pleocytosis (41%) elevated IgG and IgG index (47%), and oligoclonal bands (18%). Even in the absence of neuropsychiatric findings, the asymptomatic HIV-seropositive subjects frequently had CSF abnormalities. CSF abnormalities were found in individuals who were known to be infected with HIV for between six months to two years.

De la Monte[29] found that subacute encephalitis characterized by demyelination, gliosis of the gray and white matter, focal necrosis, microglial nodules, atypical oligodendrocyte nuclei, and multinucleation of cells were present in 27/30 (90%) of his autopsy series. Eighty-two percent of these patients with mild subacute encephalitis, as determined at autopsy, had no clinically recognizable neurological disorder.

HIV Infection of the Central (CNS) and Peripheral Nervous System (PNS)

Central Nervous System. CNS HIV infection is a great masquerader; there is no classical presentation. Early cognitive (forgetfulness, poor concentration, confusion, slowed thinking) and motor symptoms (loss of balance, poor handwriting, leg weakness) may be observed.[14,20,30] HIV-related peripheral neuropathies also are noted.[31] Primary and secondary depression, behavioral signs of apathy, dysphoria, fatigue, paranoia, and hallucinations are also reported to occur.[32] In the later course of the illness frank dementia is apparent, with mutism, ataxia, hypertonia, moderate-to-severe paresis, incontinence, tremor, facial release signs, myoclonus, seizures, and psychosis.[32]

Price reports that the AIDS dementia complex (ADC) is the most frequent and most important cause of neurological morbidity in patients with AIDS.[19] The salient clinical feature of ADC is a progressive cognitive loss. Slow mentation with mild or no evidence of cognitive impairment has also been reported.[33] However, cognitive capacity deficits underlie the major neuropsychiatric symptoms and contribute most to the associated morbidity (inability to function at work or learn new material in a school setting).[34] The progressive deterioration of memory found in HIV dementia (more difficulty with immediate and recent than remote memory) and an associated impairment of higher-order associative functions, such as expressive aphasia, dysnomia, (misnaming of objects), anomia (failure to recall names of acquaintances), agnosia (perceptual misinterpretations), and apraxia (deficiencies in perceptual-motor activity) are similar to the findings in a patient with a cortical dementia.[14,32]

HIV disease may involve both the subcortical and cortical areas. As noted in Huntington's disease, Parkinson's disease, and other extrapyramidal disorders, the associated pathologic alterations in subcortical structure (lesions in the striatum, thalamus, and brainstem, essentially sparing the cortical areas) result in a deterioration in intellectual capacity.[35] Thus, it is not surprising that subcortical HIV disease may present as a dementia with a slowing of mental processes, progressive impairment of memory (difficulty in retrieval of stored material), and deficits in manipulating or using acquired information such as is necessary for problem solving (e.g., map reading, mental calculations).

Improved cognition, but no changes in affect, were noted in a double-blind placebo-controlled trial of the safety and efficacy of AZT (zidovudine) on more than 280 patients.[36] This collaborative study noted that over a 16-week period patients with AIDS who received AZT had better test scores than those receiving placebo for attention, memory, motor skills, and general mental speed. There was also a significant reduction of symptomatic distress. Those with AIDS-related complex showed, on average, less clinical improvement; however, they had, on average, a better initial baseline study. No patients with AIDS had AIDS-dementia at entry into the study.

Peripheral Nervous System. Peripheral sensory neuropathies affect 10–30% of patients with AIDS. In a series of 40 patients, Cornblath and McArthur determined that the peripheral neuropathies developed subsequent to the constitutional symptoms.[31] Electrophysiologic studies revealed abnormal sensory and motor conduction, suggesting a dying-back axonpathy. Thus, the sensory neuropathy appears to be secondary to a distal axonal degeneration. The peripheral neuropathies are generally progressive. Cornblath and McArthur also report that tricyclic antidepressants provide partial symptomatic relief. However, in their three patients receiving AZT, no clinical change in the severity of the neuropathy was demonstrable.

PSYCHIATRIC COMPLICATIONS OF HIV INFECTION

Community Mental Health

The presence of HIV infection in a community produces fear and anxiety.[37,38] The behavioral responses to HIV, whether it is considered socially appropriate behavior (decreasing the number of sexual partners or ceasing to share drug paraphernalia) or socially inappropriate behavior (burning out a family where hemophiliac children are infected; supporting or just condoning "gay bashing") reflect individual attitudes, values and beliefs, and community mores. The levels of fear and anger in the infected, susceptible, and perceived-to-be-vulnerable populations (not at high risk "worried-well") has been correlated with media coverage of AIDS.[39]

The general population has difficulty understanding that medical scientists make probabilistic rather than absolutist statements. Most Americans do not fully understand why an AIDS vaccine or therapeutic cure cannot be developed immediately and inexpensively. This perceptual difficulty has been translated into unrealistic theories about deliberate plots on the part of some government officials to allow HIV to continue to "kill off" undesirables, and only to intervene when "middle America" is about to be harmed.

Individual Mental Health

The spectrum of HIV-related psychiatric illness is the spectrum of DSM-IIIR. Chronic stress, in its many clinical manifestations, can arise as a result of social isolation and the fear of stigmatization and discrimination. There appears to be a greater sense of helplessness among those infected with HIV than among cancer patients and other groups who are informed they have a lethal condition. The stigmatization of having a malignancy in the 1950s melted in subsequent decades as medical science progressed, and palliative and definitive treatments greatly improved the quality of life and survival rate of patients with cancers. The acceptance of the presence of HIV disease within the community is just beginning. Most reports in nonsensationalistic lay publications are scientifically accurate and as current as recent medical publications. By publishing promising therapeutic advances, hope and optimism can be widely disseminated. However, the media is a two-edged sword which is also capable of raising community fears and concerns when data are presented out of context or in a distorted manner.

There are no unique functional psychiatric disorders associated with HIV infection. Reactive depression, situational disorders, anxiety reactions, and exacerbations of prior psychiatric illness are frequent findings.[13] Repeated exposure to fear and a growing sense of futility may lead to hopelessness, anger, depression, and an inability to cope with the stresses associated with the HIV epidemic. This breakdown of coping skills can result in irresponsible risk-taking behaviors which can amplify the real and fantasied risks of becoming infected with HIV.[37]

Prevention of HIV Infection

Behavioral changes have been demonstrated among sexually active homosexual men[40,41] and intravenous drug users.[42,43] Studies of homosexual men and intravenous drug users at risk are studies in economic, racial, and social contrast. The largest ongoing study of homosexual men is the Multicenter AIDS Cohort Study which involves the collection of self-report data from approximately 5000 almost exclusively white, well-educated men.[41,44] During the period April 1984 to March 1986, the study participants indicated a dramatic increase in celibacy (from 2 to 12%) and monogamy (12 to 27%) and an overall decrease in the total number of sexual partners. The proportion not practicing receptive anal intercourse increased from 26 to 49%. Use of condoms with either anal insertive or receptive sex doubled over the course of a two-year period. However, less than one-third reported using condoms for anal intercourse. The direction and magnitude of reported changes in activities were constant when stratified by age, city, education, or HIV-antibody status.

Studies of intravenous drug users in New York City[42] and Northern New Jersey[43] are primarily studies of less well-educated urban nonwhites. Their risk factors are the sharing of drug paraphernalia and multiple sexual partners. Women have similar rates of HIV infection when exposed to the same risk factors.[43] While knowledge of the routes of HIV transmissions are well-known among intravenous drug users, access to sterile drug paraphernalia is generally limited. The limitation is both economic and practical. In most Northeastern states possession of drug paraphernalia is a criminal offense. As of December 1988, there are two experimental and very limited needle exchange programs in the United States, one in New York City, the other in Portland, Oregon.

Overall, sexually active homosexual and heterosexual men and women and intravenous drug users are knowledgeable about the transmission of HIV, and the implications of infection. However, as long as the disease is perceived to be a threat only to drug users of specific ethnic or racial groups, or homosexual men, heterosexuals, especially young heterosexuals of high school and college age, will continue to deny their risk. Denial and rationalization are frequent defenses for not engaging in safer sex.[45]

The use of disinhibitors such as alcohol and marijuana may be associated with increased impulsive "unsafe" sexual activity. For example, the use of psychoactive stimulants, such as cocaine, by homosexual men was associated with an increased risk of becoming infected with HIV, especially if the stimulants were used at the time of sexual activity.[45] As drug users decrease their intravenous drug use, and use other forms of their substances of abuse, risk of infection may not decrease. Sexual favors are frequently traded for crack.[46]

The HIV epidemic will be with us for many years to come. A definitive vaccine or chemotherapeutic cure does not appear to be on the horizon. Continuous behavior modification, and careful, rational decision making about intimate (sexual and those sharing drug paraphernalia) partners need to be reinforced in the media and in primary prevention interventions. Unlike many other infections, HIV is a lifetime disease that severely decreases life expectancy.

ETHICAL AND LEGAL ISSUES RELATING TO HIV INFECTION

Ethical Duty to Treat

Health care decisions should be based on ethical considerations for the well-being of the patient and the society. The personal and professional obligations of health care providers to their patients include ensuring accessibility to medical care and an unbiased, appropriate decision-making process concerning commencement and termination of treatment for patients infected with HIV. These decisions have a direct effect on the patient and therefore require the active participation of the patient and his or her surrogates.

A number of professional health care organizations have promulgated statements of obligation concerning the treatment of HIV-infected individuals. The American Medical Association has stated that:

> A physician may not ethically refuse to treat a patient whose condition is within the physician's current realm of competence solely because the patient is infected with HIV-4.[7]

And the American Nurses' Association has stated that:

> The nurse provides services with respect for human dignity and the uniqueness of the client, unrestricted by considerations of social or economic status, personal attributes, or the nature of the health problem.[48]

These professional organizations, and others, including the American Psychiatric Association, will not tolerate the denial of health care services on the basis of a diagnosis of HIV infection.

How well will the individual clinician respond to these pronouncements? What social and legal sanction(s) will be made against those not willing to abide by these statements of ethical principle? Statements alone, without vigorous action, will not end the discussion; but they will provide expectations for physicians, their patients, and the community. Mental health providers need to be prepared to deal with their own fears, and those of their patients, medical colleagues, and community. Finally, mental health providers need to understand that their own families will not always be supportive; they too will express fear and concern.

Confidentiality

The Physician Has a Duty to Warn. Confidentiality, in the physician-patient relationship, is not absolute. The treating clinician needs carefully to articulate this concept to all patients. A clinician may find it useful to inform his or her patients that local and federal health policies and laws may preclude the withholding of certain medical information. This statement then may become part of the therapeutic contract, especially where the patient's life-style suggests the potential for HIV infection.

Patients should be advised of the potential consequences of being tested for the presence of antigen or antibodies to HIV. Patients also need to understand the potential consequences of voluntarily disclosing the results of those tests. The Presidential Commission, consistent with the guidelines issued by the Centers for Disease Control (CDC), recommends that a spouse or sexual partner be notified, even without the consent of the infected individual, when the infected individual appears not to be willing to notify the other party.[12] This recommendation includes informing the victim of a sexual assault. The legal weight of the Presidential Commission is not that of law. Rather, its opinions are treated as those of an expert treatise on the topic. The presidential commission's recommendations are advisory. The information may be used by a medical expert as the basis for his or her medical conclusions; CDC guidelines traditionally have been utilized in this manner.

The Presidential Commission states that adherence to the principle of confidentiality does not obviate the need to protect those who may be unknowingly in immediate danger of being exposed to HIV. If a health care provider knows that an infected patient has refused to inform a sexual partner and continues to engage in behaviors that place that individual at risk, the health care professional should have the ability to warn the unsuspecting sexual partner.

The commission acknowledges the limits of confidentiality. They recommend that notification of third parties, by the physician who ordered the test(s) for the presence of antigen or antibodies to HIV, without written informed consent of the patient, is permissible under certain circumstances. Notification may be provided to those health care providers who are a part of the individual's health care team, and

> any consulting physicians with special need to know or outpatient case manager; and/or health care workers accidentally "exposed to the blood or blood contaminated body fluids" of the individual.[12]

Thus, such knowledge should not be restricted by law, in the health care setting, as it has been in some states.

The Commission further recommends that

> the health care provider should not have a legal duty to warn a patient's sexual partner in these instances, as some court cases have held in other third party warning situations.[12]

The Commission concludes that notifying sexual partners is a legal responsibility, and therefore is inconsistent with a health care provider's role. The Commission does recommend that states should begin to require reporting of HIV positive tests and tracing possible unsuspecting contacts. However, in what is believed to be the first decision of its kind, the District Court of Johnson County, Kansas blocked a Kansas City health maintenance organization from notifying an ex-wife or anyone else that the defendant had tested positive for HIV. The court noted that the man had not had sexual intercourse with his ex-wife for two years, and she had twice tested negative for HIV. The judge, citing a Kansas law on physician-patient confidentiality, said the "infinitesimal risk" of the man's transmitting the virus, at this point in time, to his ex-wife or his two children did not justify the breach of confidentiality.[49]

The Presidential Commission determined that there is a considerable variance in the manner in which individual states provide for confidentiality of HIV information. They also noted that there is a perceived lack of confidence that the confidentiality of HIV-related information will be maintained, regardless of the law. They recommend that a clear and comprehensive policy be developed and issued by the federal government. At the present time there is no national policy or law concerning the reporting of asymptomatic HIV positive individuals or AIDS patients to a central registry. Issues of contact-tracing of possibly exposed individuals, notification of emergency medical personnel and other health care providers that their patients have been infected with HIV, and criminal penalties for willfully transmitting HIV to another person have not been definitively addressed.[50]

In an attempt to protect the individual's rights, California enacted a confidentiality law that was sufficiently stringent as to prohibit an obstetrician from notifying the pediatrician assisting him at a delivery that the mother was infected with HIV. Most states have no specific laws governing the sharing of HIV-related medical information; however, medical personnel are bound by the established hospital policies and state laws with regard to disclosure of medical information and the sharing of the contents of medical records. The established civil laws on slander and libel are clearly applicable to circumstances where there is an inappropriate disclosure of damaging information. Health care providers face the dilemma of not knowing when or if they should notify other health care providers, or even a spouse or sexual partner, of the serologic status of their patient. The CDC guidelines of August 14, 1987 state that persons who are HIV-antibody positive should be instructed how to notify their partners and to refer them (the partners) for counseling and testing:

> If they are unwilling to notify their partners or if it cannot be assured that their partners will seek counseling, physicians or health department personnel should use confidential procedures to assure that the partners are notified.[51]

The health care provider involved with direct patient care has been determined to have an affirmative "duty to warn" other individuals known to be at risk of infectious diseases.[52] In 1974, the California Supreme Court in *Tarasoff v Regents of the University of California* extended the concept of the "duty to warn" to those at risk for physical harm from a patient receiving psychotherapy.[53] In 1976, the *Tarasoff* case was reargued and the California Supreme Court then extended the concept of the "duty to warn" to the "duty to protect" readily known and identifiable individuals.[54] The duty-to-protect doctrine requires that the therapist must take an affirmative action, such as contacting the police and the intended victim(s), and explicitly informing them of the name of the potential assailant, and the nature of the potential assault. The Nebraska Supreme Court recently held that a class of individuals not readily available had the right to be warned.[55] The Delaware Supreme Court recently held that a five-month delay between termination from treatment and an assault did not alleviate the physician's duty to protect.[56]

Table I presents factors which might enter into consideration when a clinician is determining whether or not to attempt to notify a sexual partner. Regardless of what decision the clinician reaches, and what actions, if any, he or she initiates, the decision and the events that follow must be documented.

The Patient Has a Duty to Warn. An HIV-infected patient may also have a duty to warn those in danger of becoming infected. Failure to notify the sexual

TABLE I. Risks and Benefits of HIV Antibody Testing[a]

Benefits

(1) To protect the blood supply by testing individuals who are considering donating blood;
(2) To ensure that organ donations are safe from HIV contamination;
(3) To help support a medical diagnosis when individuals exhibit unexplained symptoms that their doctors think might be related to an HIV infection;
(4) To help women at high risk decide whether to become pregnant or give birth;
(5) To help women with a history of risk behavior decide whether to breastfeed an infant or have an infant inoculated with vaccine produced from live virus;
(6) To reduce anxiety in individuals who are at low risk for HIV infection yet who have extremely high anxiety about it;
(7) To motivate individuals who continue to practice high-risk behavior and who feel that a positive test result may help them reduce these behaviors;
(8) To help researchers design experimental treatment protocols and to help potential subjects determine whether or not to participate in the drug trials;
(9) To help scientists determine the extent of HIV infection in the population at large and, by following seropositive individuals, to understand the natural history of HIV infection.

Risks

(1) Severe psychological reactions, including anxiety, nightmares, sleep disturbance, depression, and suicidal behavior;
(2) Disrupted interpersonal relations, including potential for rage reactions and their extreme manifestations, such as homicidal behavior;
(3) Social ostracism and self-imposed social withdrawal;
(4) Relationship problems (blaming partners, sexual dysfunction, disrupted ability to make plans as a couple);
(5) Stigmatization and discrimination if a positive antibody status is made known to others outside of guarantees of confidentiality;
(6) Problems with employment or insurance;
(7) Preoccupations with bodily symptoms;
(8) A false sense of security and denial if the test proves negative (for example, believing one is immune to infection and thus continuing with risk behavior).

[a]From Goldblum P, Seymour N: Whether to take the test: Counseling guidelines. *Focus* 1987; *2*(5):1–3.

partner of the risk of infection, i.e., from herpes, may subject that individual to liability for any resultant physical or emotional injuries.[57] In prior years, husbands have been found liable for infecting their wives with a venereal disease.[58]

Litigation focusing on defendants accused of knowingly exposing others to HIV infection has occurred. Florida and Idaho have made it a crime willfully or knowingly to expose another person to HIV.[59] Similar statutes are now being considered in other states, along with legislation allowing forcible isolation of infected people who are believed to threaten public safety. The prosecutors in these cases will be required to establish, beyond a reasonable doubt, that the defendant knew he or she was infected with HIV, that there was a deliberate and willful attempt to transmit HIV, and that the "victim" did not know that the defendant was infected when he or she was "exposed."

An Army private faced a court-martial for an AIDS-related assault.[60] Private Morris was tested, found to be positive for antibodies to HIV, and counseled to have protected sexual relationships (use condoms during sexual intercourse). He knowingly and willfully disobeyed this advice. At his court-martial the results of his HIV antibody tests and the fact that he was subsequently counseled were admitted as evidence against him. He was convicted of misconduct for having unprotected sexual relations while knowing that he was infected with HIV.[59] Under the Uniform Code of Military Justice, aggravated assault is an unauthorized act of touching that can "produce death or grievous bodily harm." The harm does not actually have to occur for such a prosecution. In this case, on subsequent testing, none of the three sexual partners demonstrated antibodies to HIV. Charges were not brought against him for having unprotected sexual relations with his fiancee. The prosecution determined that she had knowledge of his infected status and freely engaged in the high-risk behavior. The fiancee apparently freely accepted the risk of infection.

Divorce Matters. In Brooklyn, in 1987, Jane Doe sued John Doe for divorce.[61] The court did not permit her to claim that she suffered anxiety, humiliation, embarrassment, and a possible threat from AIDS because husband had failed to disclose his homosexual activities. The court held that a cause of action for intentional infliction of emotional distress based upon the infliction of "AIDS-phobia" would not be permitted since the psychological claim was based on a fear, which in turn was based on attenuated probabilities, which in turn were not based on any medical fact or proof. There was no contemporaneous or consequential physical injury. The wife tested negative for the presence of antibodies to HIV. If she had tested positive, she most probably would have been able to have made a claim for real damages.

Record-Keeping Issues. In spite of assurances of confidentiality, HIV test results must be noted in the patient's medical record and, as such, may be subpoenaed in a number of different types of legal proceedings. Furthermore, depending on local regulations, test results may also be reported to public health authorities for the purposes of surveillance and identifying case contacts. Colorado became the first of approximately a dozen states to require the names and addresses of persons who test positive for the presence of HIV antibodies be reported to state health officials. Further, Colorado is one of five states that requests the infected individual to provide the names of their sexual partners who are then contacted by the health department. These identified sexual partners are confidentially informed that they may have been exposed to a known medical danger, HIV infection. This Colorado law imposes a fine on doctors who do not report the names of seropositive individuals to the State Department of Health, and imposes a more severe fine on any state official who breaches the confidentiality of this information. These records may not be examined in any hearing, nor be released upon subpoena, discovery proceeding, or search warrant.[62]

HIV TESTING

The Validity and Reliability of the HIV Test

Since HIV lies dormant in various tissues of the body, it is presumed that all exposed individuals are infected and capable of transmitting the virus for years, and possibly for life. Because a valid, reliable, and highly sensitive test for the detection of HIV antigen is not commercially available, serologic tests for antibodies directed against HIV have been widely used in screening for exposure to the virus.

ELISA (enzyme linked immunosorbent assay) and Western Blot (WB) tests are actually indirect or surrogate tests for HIV.[63] Both tests measure the response of the immune system to the presence of HIV. These tests do not indicate whether or not there is active virus actually present in the patient at the time of the test. The body's immune system usually requires 4–24 weeks, and in some instances more than a year, to produce a sufficiently high titer of antibodies to be detected by the HIV ELISA test.[64]

A negative ELISA antibody test does not absolutely rule out exposure to HIV. It generally takes a minimum of 6 weeks from the time of exposure (infection with the virus) to develop a measurable antibody response. However, Imagawa and his colleagues have reported prolonged periods of infectivity, up to 18 months, prior to seroconversion on both ELISA and Western Blot.[64] Furthermore, a few cases of antibody-negative and culture-positive individuals have been documented, as have cases of antibody-positive individuals who have later become seronegative. A significant subgroup of homosexual men develop HIV $_p24$ antigenemia relatively early after seroconversion. However, the majority of seroconverters do not exhibit an antigenemia (75%).[65]

Thus, if an individual cannot mount an immune response because of other illnesses, or if the immune response is not sufficiently intense to be measured, the result of the ELISA screening test will be negative. While there have been instances in research studies where a patient has been found to have a positive WB and a negative ELISA, in clinical practice it is uncommon for a clinician to request the confirmatory WB if the ELISA is reported as negative. A confirmatory test is generally only requested when the ELISA is reported as either equivocal or positive. An initial ELISA positive sample is repeated by the ELISA method before it is tested by the WB technique. A specimen is considered truly positive only when both ELISA tests and the WB are considered to be positive (see Table I).

While the sensitivity (that is, the ability correctly to identify individuals who are truly infected) and the specificity (the ability correctly to identify individuals who are truly not infected) of the ELISA are approximately 99% or greater, there are limits to the usefulness of these tests.[63] False positive ELISA tests can occur. Individuals may be perceived as demonstrating the presence of antibodies to HIV when nonspecific serologic reactions occur. Most commonly, these false positive ELISA tests occur among those with non-HIV based immunologic abnormalities, those who have received multiple transfusions of blood

TABLE II. Interpretation of ELISA and WB Results

	No identifiable risk factors	Risk factors present
ELISA + & WB + (confirmed result)	True positive	True positive
ELISA + & WB − (equivocal)[a]	Likely to be a false positive. Repeat in 8–12 weeks, or as clinically indicated; counsel as if seropositive until true status is clarified.	Possibly a true positive. Repeat in 8–12 weeks, or as clinically indicated; counsel as if seropositive.
ELISA + /WB equivocal or indeterminant[b]	Unlikely to be a false positive. Repeat in 8–12 weeks, or as clinically indicated; reexamine medical history with patient; counsel as if seropositive.	Same as above.

[a]The CDC defines an equivocal HIV antibody result as one in which the ELISA is positive and the WB is clearly negative.[19]
[b]The Maryland State Laboratories Administration defines an equivocal *or* indeterminate HIV antibody result as one in which the ELISA is positive, and the WB either is negative, indeterminate, or equivocal.[20]
Note: Reprinted from Ginzburg H: HIV-related diseases and the future of the delivery of psychiatric care, *Psychiatric Annals,* 18:563–570, 1988.

or blood products, or in multiparous females. False negative ELISA tests most commonly occur among individuals who are infected with HIV but who have not had the infection for a sufficiently long period of time to have developed a detectable level of antibody to HIV or who stop producing antibodies to HIV.[66]

Burke and his colleagues found one false positive diagnosis of HIV infection in a careful review of 15 recorded positive results obtained from 135,187 military applicants, aged 17–18, from low prevalence areas.[67] They estimate the false positive rate to be 0.0007% (1 in 135,177). They emphasize that, when screening is conducted in low-prevalence populations, specimen-processing and data-management errors are relatively more important issues than the validity and reliability of the tests utilized.

Table II presents the Centers for Disease Control and the State of Maryland interpretation of HIV antibody test results. Local and federal health departments do not have a total consensus in this matter. This lack of consensus reflects the evolving nature of knowledge in this field. However, it does make it more difficult for physicians whose practice is not entirely related to HIV infection to know how to explain the test findings to their patients. In the final analysis, the physician must indicate to his or her patient that life-style behaviors play a significant role in the spread of this disease, and a negative or equivocal result is not a license to continue to place one's self in harm's way. Conversely, a positive result does not mean that since one is infected, the nature of future activities is irrelevant, and therefore indiscriminate behavior can be engaged in. There is some evidence that an infected individual may decrease his or her relative risk for the more rapid onset of disease by moderating their life-style. Appealing to the social conscience of an individual who has recently become infected not to spread the disease further may be extremely difficult. Anger at an identifiable partner, or the world-at-large must be acknowledged and dealt with in a therapeutic manner.[17]

Administration of the Test

The Surgeon General of the United States Public Health Service has stated that testing for the presence of HIV infection should remain voluntary and confidential, that pre- and posttest counseling must be provided, and that informed consent for testing must be obtained. In many locations, *anonymous* testing may also be obtained using identification codes or aliases. Pretest counseling should include a summary of risks and benefits to the individual in the event of a negative or positive test (as noted in Table 2).

HIV antibody tests are routinely employed to screen blood and organ donors. The tests are also widely used as an adjunct to the counseling of individuals at risk for HIV infection. As noted above, HIV antibody testing is required of all military recruits and active duty service personnel. Seropositive personnel generally are not discharged unless they are unable to perform their military duties. HIV testing is also required for Foreign Service personnel and Peace Corps Volunteers. Civilian and military personnel infected with HIV are not permitted overseas assignments.

Other potential uses of the HIV test, such as screening job applicants, applicants for insurance policies or marriage licenses, and routine screening of hospitalized or surgical outpatients are currently the focus of an intense national debate. In June 1987, President Reagan recommended "routine" testing for such groups as federal prisoners, marriage license applicants, and patients at drug treatment programs and venereal disease clinics. It is not clear whether the word "routine" means that people who object strongly could refuse such tests. Proponents of testing claim that identifying HIV-positive individuals will help protect those who are not infected. Objections to this proposal are that routine testing might drive those most at risk underground, and that the considerable expense of widespread testing would identify few cases, while diverting monies from more productive measure, such as education and research.

HIV Testing Recommendations

On August 14, 1987, the Public Health Service issued guidelines for antibody testing and counseling to prevent HIV infection and AIDS.[51] These guidelines are an attempt to balance the potential personal, medical, and public health benefits of testing for HIV antibody, with the need to ensure that the use of counseling and testing facilities will not result in the unauthorized disclosure of personal information and the resultant possibility of social and legal discrimination.[68] Even individuals who are tested and are found to be negative for the presence of antibodies to HIV may be discriminated against on the basis that they would not have allowed themselves to be tested unless they were engaging in risk-taking behaviors.

The necessity for counseling is also dictated by the potentially emotionally devastating impact of a positive test result. Clinicians ordering tests for the determination of the presence of antigen or antibodies to HIV must be able to provide both pretest and posttest counseling. This requires an understanding of the tests themselves, their limitations, and the implications of a positive, negative, or equivocal result.

The United States Congress has already passed a measure requiring testing for all those seeking permanent immigration. Those who test positive would be denied resident status. Although not yet enacted, many bills are pending that would mandate HIV testing for various other groups. Proposals to require routine testing of hospitalized patients provoked strong objections by medical experts, who argue that such a policy would not curtail the spread of infection, but rather raise concern about informed consent procedures and patients' rights. However, as noted above, medical confidentiality rarely is absolute and patients need to be made more aware of this.

Routine HIV testing of ostensively healthy individuals represents an inefficient use of financial resources. Louisiana and Illinois passed legislation requiring premarital testing.[69] Louisiana quickly voted to repeal the law, after the lawmakers recognized that Louisiana couples were traveling to neighboring states to become married. Anecdotal evidence is that couples in Chicago, Illinois are unwilling to pay the approximately $300 for HIV testing and counseling, and therefore are obtaining marriage licenses in neighboring Wisconsin.[70] Also, there is no clear indication that the physician ordering the test is under any legal obligation to inform the partner (who may also be infected) of the results of the test. A positive test in either state does not result in the marriage license application being cancelled.

COUNSELING

Pretest and posttest counseling is required, regardless of the outcome of the HIV antibody test. Those who test positive for antibodies to HIV will need continued access to counseling.[17] Pretest counseling should include information on the prevention of exposure to HIV infection and should specifically include information about:[17]

1. Modes of transmission;
2. Behaviors that increase the risk of infection and disease transmission;
3. Meaning and limitations of the results of the tests;
4. Confidentiality statutes, as they exist in the local jurisdiction, local and state reporting requirements, as applicable to HIV infection;
5. Protection from discrimination; and
6. Availability of additional counseling for related psychosocial problems.

Posttest counseling should include information on the prevention of exposure to HIV infection and should specifically include information about:[17]

1. Meaning and limitations of the test results, regardless of whether the results are positive, negative, or equivocal.
2. Explanation of the various possible interpretations of the test results is presented in Table 1. If the test results are positive, as determined by a positive ELISA and a positive confirmatory Western Blot test, then further counseling about the prevention of transmission, and the opportunity for health, mental health, and social service referrals needs to be conducted.
3. Understanding of the necessity of informing sexual partners and drug-using contacts about the test results. The infected individual also needs to be informed about the availability of state services to inform those partners that the infected individual is unable or unwilling to notify.
4. Availability of additional counseling for related psychosocial problems.

DISCRIMINATION

In the Workplace

The Occupational Safety and Health Administration (OSHA) has announced a plan for establishing guidelines for protecting the nation's five million health care workers from infectious blood-borne disease, including infectious hepatitis B and HIV. The new program does not constitute a specific, enforceable occupational health standard. Its guidelines can be enforced under the Occupational Safety and Health Act's general duty clause which requires employers to maintain workplaces free from "recognized hazards." Reports from CDC and the National Institutes of Health (NIH) have documented that HIV can be transmitted by accidental needle punctures as well as direct contact of infected blood with mucosal membranes.[71,72]

In 1982, CDC issued voluntary guidelines for protecting health care workers from HIV.[73] Those guidelines called for infectious material to be placed in an impervious bag, and gave specific cleaning instructions for equipment, linen, reusable dishes, and utensils, etc. Specific instructions were stated for cleaning "blood spills." These guidelines instruct employees in the handling and disposal of needles and other sharp items (i.e., needles should not be recapped, purposely bent, broken, removed from disposable syringes, or otherwise manipulated.) Gloves, gowns, masks and eye coverings should be used when the possibility exists that an employee may be exposed to blood or other body fluids. Hands should be washed immediately if contaminated with blood. To avoid the need for mouth-to-mouth resuscitation, employees should use mouthpieces, resuscitation bags, or other ventilation devices. Guidelines for the protection of dental-care personnel and persons performing necropsies or providing mortician's services were published by the CDC in 1983.[74]

Despite CDC guidelines and scientific data to the contrary, fears of possible transmission of AIDS by casual contact in the workplace have led to numerous dismissals of individuals with AIDS, or those belonging to a high-risk group. Indeed, the number of reported cases of AIDS discrimination continues to increase. Most cases of discrimination, bias, and wrongful termination fall under existing civil rights statutes. Specific legislation forbidding discrimination on the basis of HIV infection has been adopted in several localities.[75]

In June 1986 the Justice Department ruled that employers receiving federal funds can discriminate against people with AIDS. However, in March 1987, the U.S. Supreme Court, in *Nassau County School Board, Florida v Arline*, ruled that employers who receive federal funds cannot discriminate against people who are physically or mentally impaired by contagious diseases, holding that they are handicapped within the meaning of section 504 of the 1973 Rehabilitation Act.[76] In the Fall of 1988, the Justice Department reversed itself, stating that those infected with HIV are covered by section 504.

Controversial decisions to restrict activities of health care workers who are infected with HIV are also being considered. The Board of Health in Chicago attempted to limit the privileges of a physician with AIDS to non-patient contact responsibilities. Their justification was that the public's fear of contracting AIDS would deter patients from seeking medical care. The Board also cited two potential legal issues. The first involves their belief that a wrongful injury (or death) suit could result if a health care worker transmitted AIDS to a patient. The second involves their liberal interpretation of the informed consent doctrine. They stated that they believe that patients could claim that they had been the victim of the tort of battery by unknowingly receiving treatment from an HIV-infected clinician; they could claim that they would have sought treatment from a different clinician if they had known that their clinician was infected with HIV.[77] The court ordered the Board of Health to reinstate the physician in question to full status as a practicing physician at Cook County hospital.[78] The Board of Health subsequently has decided that patients at Cook County Hospital would have the right to refuse to be treated by workers who carry the AIDS virus.[78] This would be the first such policy for an American hospital. According to the news report, the policy would cover all hospital workers who routinely provide direct patient care, including doctors and nurses. The hospital, however, has not yet indicated how it would identify workers infected with the virus.

Counter to the beliefs of the Chicago Board of Health, the majority of public health professionals believe that a physician practicing in accordance with established guidelines does not place patients at significant risk of infection, and that whether or not a physician or other health care provider is HIV antibody-positive is immaterial to the delivery of good medical care.

Availability of Medical Care

Fear of contracting AIDS has resulted in numerous instances of patients in high-risk groups being refused treatment by physicians and hospitals. Recent cases include orthopedic and general surgeons who refused to operate on carriers of HIV.[79] Although not specifically illegal, many feel that such actions are not in keeping with the physician's ethical responsibilities. Most current litigation is being argued with existing anti-discrimination and civil rights statutes.

Medical Quarantine

Thus far, only Colorado and Indiana have enacted laws permitting AIDS patients to be isolated. In a recent case in Florida, a 14 year-old-boy who was seropositive for HIV was quarantined in a hospital psychiatric ward because it was felt that his continued sexual activity represented a danger to public health.[80] In the face of growing public fear of contracting AIDS, it is likely that many local governments will adopt measures restricting the activities of patients with HIV infection who do not follow guidelines concerning prevention of the disease.

Availability of Insurance

HIV disease is increasing the medical care costs and the medical insurance costs in this country.[81] The enormous sums projected for health care of patients with HIV-related diseases has resulted in insurance companies wishing to require HIV testing for applicants for life or health insurance, and denying policies to those who test positive. They claim that the ability to assess risk is the basic foundation of insurance underwriting, and that denial of this ability will result in the economic ruin of the industry. Opponents of this position hold that insurance is integral to achieving quality health care, and that refusal to insure an individual on the basis of sexual preference or antibody status represents illegal discrimination. Most states have had to consider establishing laws governing the use of HIV antibody tests by insurers. California and Wisconsin have banned mandatory testing. The City Council of Washington D.C. also banned such testing in June 1986 and this action resulted in over 90% of insurance companies refusing to continue to write individual policies within the city. Washington D.C. and Massachusetts have recently reversed their earlier bans on testing. Numerous lawsuits by homosexuals, claiming discrimination by insurance carriers, are currently in litigation.

In many states, patients with medically diagnosed and confirmed AIDS are eligible for benefits from publicly financed health and social assistance programs. However, Supplemental Social Security Insurance (SSI) will be provided only to those who have a diagnosis of AIDS (having ARC or a disabling non-AIDS HIV-related infection is not sufficient). It is estimated that the recent expansion of the CDC surveillance definition of the AIDS to include individuals with HIV-related dementia and wasting syndrome (emaciation) will increase the number of HIV-infected patients eligible for these benefits by 20%. A diagnosis of AIDS also may permit preferential admission to drug abuse treatment centers, and a variety of housing and social services.

PRODUCT LIABILITY

Testing for the presence of HIV antibodies in donated blood has only been available since March 1985, when the FDA approved the ELISA screening tests for use in screening blood and blood products. Since that time essentially all blood and blood products are routinely screened for the presence of HIV; soon blood and blood products will also be routinely screened for the presence of HTLV-I. The federal government has commenced a look-back program which urges individuals who received blood or blood products prior to 1985 be screened for HIV infection. This program, coupled with the long latency between infection and the presentation of illness, suggests that a significant amount of additional litigation dealing with contaminated blood and blood products can be anticipated. There have been several suits filed against manufacturers of blood products. The claim is that they either knew or should have known that their product was contaminated and taken steps to protect the recipients of their products.[82]

Plaintiff-patient attempts to recover damages because of receiving contaminated blood transfusions or blood products has in the past, been based on a number of different legal theories. These various theories (strict liability in tort, breach of implied warranties, and negligence) provide the vehicle for pursuing their legal claim. However, as jurisdictions define the supply of blood and blood components as a service, and not as the marketing of a product, the theories of strict liability or implied warranties are not applicable to providers of services.

More recently, however, courts are beginning to alter their traditional interpretation that the provision of blood transfusions and blood products is a service, and conclude that the provision of blood and blood products is the sale of a product, even if the product is provided without cost to the patient. Such an interpretation would mean that the principles articulated in the Uniform Commercial Code would apply and defendant-vendors (blood banks and administering physicians) could be held to a standard of strict liability.[82]

The legal claims currently being considered by state and federal courts include issues of the use of surrogate testing (testing for the presence of diseases, such as hepatitis B, which have been highly correlated with HIV infection), which may have been available prior to 1985, the introduction of more stringent self-deferral guidelines prior to 1985, and the nature of the informed consent provided to patients prior to the use of the blood or blood product.[83]

SUMMARY

HIV infection is pandemic in the United States and parts of Africa and is still spreading; HIV-infected individuals are found in essentially every nation in the world. While each nation, culture, and community may have a different means of addressing HIV-related medical, psychological, legal, social, and economic issues, the basic focus of any treatment or treatment program must be the delivery of nonjudgmental disease-appropriate care.

HIV infection is a chronic disease with the lungs and central nervous system being most affected by HIV and the associated opportunistic infections. The psychiatric complications and the fears associated with this pandemic disease need to be addressed by health care professionals in community and individual service care delivery settings.

There are a number of unresolved legal issues relating to HIV diseased. HIV testing has become a major political issue. Testing has become associated with access to life and health insurance and employment opportunities. There is a medical utility to the HIV test. There is also the possibility of the test being misused in nonmedical settings. Housing, employment, and insurance discrimination has been documented. Therefore, it is not surprising that confidentiality of medical information, and in particular HIV test results, is also a concern of those infected with HIV. Individuals have rights, and so do the members of their community. When is one set of rights given priority over another?

REFERENCES

1. Gallo RC, Salahuddin SZ, Popovic M, *et al*: Frequent detection and isolation of cytopathic retroviruses (HTLV-III) from patients with AIDS and at risk for AIDS. *Science* 1984; 224:500–03.
2. Barre'-Sinoussi F, Chermann JC, Rey F, *et al*: Isolation of a T-lymphocytic retrovirus from a patient at risk for acquired immunodeficiency syndrome (AIDS). *Science* 1983; 220:868–71.
3. CDC. Human immunodeficiency virus infection in the United States. A review of current knowledge. *MMWR* 1987; 36:(suppl 6)1–48.
4. Pneumocystis pneumonia—Los Angeles. *MMWR* 1981; 30:250–52.
5. Gottlieb MS, Groopman JE, Weinstein WM, et al: The acquired immunodeficiency syndrome. *Ann Intern Med* 1983; 99:208–20.
6. Mann J: Global AIDS: Epidemiology, impact, projections, and the global strategy. Presented at the World Summit of Ministers of Health on Programs for AIDS Prevention, London, Jan 26–28, 1988.
7. Curran JW, Jaffe HW, Hardy AM, *et al*: Epidemiology of HIV infection and AIDS in the United States. *Science* 1988; 239:610–16.
8. Goedert JJ, Biggar RJ, Weiss SH, *et al*: Three-year incidence of AIDS among HTLV-III infected risk group members: A comparison of five cohorts. *Science* 1986; 231:992–95.
9. Hessol NA, Rutherford GW, Lifson AR, *et al*: The natural history of HIV infection in a cohort of homosexual and bisexual men: A decade of follow-up [abstract]. Fourth International Conference on AIDS. Stockholm, Book 1, 1988, p. 283.
10. CDC: AIDS weekly surveillance report. December 8, 1988.
11. Barnes DM: Grim projections for AIDS epidemic *Science* 1986; 232:1589–90.
12. The Final Report of the Presidential Commission on the Human Immunodeficiency Virus Epidemic. Washington, DC, 1988.
13. Holland JC, Tross S: The psychosocial and neuropsychiatric sequelae of the acquired immunodeficiency syndrome and related disorders. *Ann Intern Med* 1985; 103:760–64.
14. Petito CK: Review of central nervous system pathology in human immunodeficiency virus infection, *Ann Neurol* 1988; 23 Suppl:S54–S57.
15. Ginzburg HM, Macher A: Clinical-pathological correlates of human immunodeficiency virus (HIV) infection: A Conference Summary, *Modern Pathology* 1988; 1:316–22.

16. CDC: Recommendations for preventing transmission of infection with human T-lymphotrophic virus type III/lymphadenopathy-associated virus in the workplace. *MMWR* 1985; 34:682–86, 691–95.
17. Ginzburg HM: HIV related diseases and the future of the delivery of psychiatric care. *Psychiatr Ann* 1988; 18:563–70.
18. Epstein LG, Goudsmit J, Paul DA, *et al*: Expression of human immunodeficiency virus in cerebrospinal fluid of children with progressive encephalopathy. *Ann Neurol* 1987; 21:397–401.
19. Price RW, Sidtis J, Rosenblum M: The AIDS dementia complex: some current questions, *Ann Neurol* 1988; 23 Suppl:S27–S33.
20. Levy RM, Bredesen DE, Rosenblum ML: Neurological manifestations of the acquired immunodeficiency syndrome (AIDS): Experience at UCSF and review of the literature. *J Neurosurg* 1985; 62:475–95.
21. Centers for Disease Control: Classification system for HTLV-III/LAV infections. *MMWR* 1986; 35:334–39.
22. Shaw GM, Harper ME, Hahn BH, *et al*: HTLV-III infection in brains of children and adults with AIDS encephalopathy. *Science* 1985; 227:177–81.
23. Koenig S, Gendelman HE, Orenstein JM, *et al*: Detection of AIDS virus in macrophages in brain tissue from AIDS patients with encephalopathy. *Science* 1986; 233:1089–93.
24. McArthur JC. Neurologic manifestations of AIDS. *Medicine* 1987; 66:407–37.
25. Ho DD, Rota TR, Schooley TR, *et al*: Isolation of HTLV-III from cerebrospinal fluid and neural tissues of patients with neurologic syndromes related to the acquired immunodeficiency syndrome. *N Engl J Med* 1985; 313:1493–97.
26. Levy RM, Bredesen DE, Rosenblum ML, *et al*: Opportunistic central nervous system pathology in patients with AIDS. *Ann Neurol* 1988; 23 Suppl:S7–S12.
27. Resnick L, Berger JR, Shapshak P, *et al*: Early penetration of the blood-brain-barrier by HIV. *Neurology* 1988; 38:9–14.
28. McArthur JC, Cohen BA, Farzadegan H, *et al*: Cerebrospinal fluid abnormalities in homosexual men with and without neuropsychiatric findings. *Ann Neurol* 1988; 23 Suppl:S34–S37.
29. De la Monte SM, Ho DD, Schooley RT, *et al*: Subacute encephalomyelitis of AIDS and its relation to HTLV-III infection. *Neurology* 1987; 37:562–69.
30. Snider WD, Simpson DM, Nielsen S, *et al*: Neurological complications of acquired immunodeficiency syndrome: analysis of 50 patients. *Ann Neurol* 1983; 14:403–18.
31. Cornblath DR, McArthur JC: Predominantly sensory neuropathy in patients with AIDS and AIDS-related complex. *Neurology* 1988; 38:794–96.
32. Navia BA, Jordan BD, Price RW: The AIDS Dementia complex I. Clinical features. *Ann Neurol* 1986; 19:517–24.
33. Poser S, Luer W, Eichenlaub D, *et al*: Chronic HIV encephalitis—II. Clinical aspects. *Klin Wochenschr* 1988; 66:26–31.
34. Buhrich N, Cooper DA: Requests for psychiatric consultation concerning 22 patients with AIDS and ARC. *Aust N Z J Psychiatry* 1987; 21:346–53.
35. Huber SJ, Paulsen GW: The concept of subcortical dementia. *Am J Psychiatry* 1985; 142:1312–17.
36. Schmitt FA, Bigley JW, McKinnis R, *et al*: Neuropsychological outcome of zidovudine (AZT) treatment of patients with AIDS and AIDS-related complex. *N Engl J Med* 1989; 319:1573–78.
37. Ostrow DG: Models for understanding the psychiatric consequences of AIDS, in Bridge PT, Mirsky AF, Goodwin FK (eds): *Psychological, neuropsychiatric, and substance abuse aspects of AIDS*. New York, Raven Press, 1988, pp 85–94.
38. Chodoff P: Fear of AIDS. *Psychiatry* 1987; 50:184–91.
39. Ostrow DG, Eller M, Joseph JG: *Fear of quarantine: An emerging psychosocial issue*, in Proc Second International Conference on AIDS, Paris, Institute Pasteur, 1986, p 183.

40. Fox R, Ostrow D, Valdisseri R, *et al: Changes in sexual activities among participants in the Multicenter AIDS Cohort Study* [abstract]. Third International Conference on AIDS. Washington, DC, 1987, p 213.
41. Winkelstein W Jr, Samuel M, Padian NS, *et al*: The San Francisco Men's Health Study: III. Reduction in human immunodeficiency virus transmission among homosexual/bisexual men, 1982–86. *Am J Public Health* 1987; 77:685–89.
42. DesJarlais DC, Friedman SR, Hopkins W: Risk reduction of the acquired immunodeficiency syndrome among intravenous drug users, *Ann Intern Med* 1985; 103:755–59.
43. Ginzburg HM, French J, Jackson J, *et al*: Health education and knowledge assessment of HTLV-III diseases among intravenous drug abusers. *Health Ed Q* 1986; 13:373–82.
44. Polk BF, Fox R, Brookmeyer R, *et al*: Predictors of the acquired immunodeficiency syndrome developing in a cohort of seropositive homosexual men. *N Engl J Med* 1987; 316:61–66.
45. Ginzburg HM, Fleming PL, Miller KD: Review: Selected public health observations derived from the multicenter AIDS cohort study. *JAIDS* 1988; 1:2–7.
46. Sterk C. Cocaine and HIV seropositivity [letter]. *Lancet* 1988; 1:1052–53.
47. AMA (American Medical Association). Report of the Council on Ethical and Judicial Affairs: Ethical issues involved in the growing AIDS crisis. Chicago, American Medical Association, 1987.
48. American Nurses' Association, Committee on Ethics. Statement regarding risk versus responsibility in proving nursing care. Kansas City, Mo., American Nurses' Association, 1986.
49. *Washington Post*, October 19, 1988, p A10.
50. *Confronting AIDS: Update 1988*. Washington DC, National Academy of Sciences Press, 1988.
51. CDC. Public Health Service guidelines for counseling and antibody testing to prevent HIV infection and AIDS. *MMWR* 1987; 36:509–15.
52. *Davis v Rodman*, 147 Ark 385, 227 SW 612 (1921).
53. *Tarasoff v Regents of the University of California et al* 118 Cal Rptr 129, 529 P2d 553 (1974).
54. *Tarasoff v Regents of the University of California et al* 131 Cal Rptr 14, 551 P2d 334 (1976).
55. *Lipari v Sears, Roebuck & Co.*, 497 F.Supp. 185 (D. Neb. 1980).
56. *Naidu v Laird*, 539 A2d 1064 (Del 1988).
57. *Kathleen K. v Robert B.*, 150 Cal App 3d 992, 198 Cal Rptr 273 (1984).
58. *Crowell v Crowell*, 180 NC 516, 105 SE 206 (1920), reh den. *Crowell v Crowell*, 181 NC 66, 106 SE 149 (1921).
59. *The New York Times*, June 19, 1987, p 1.
60. *United States v Morris*, 25 MJ 579 (1987).
61. *Jane Doe v John Doe*, 136 Misc. 2d 1015; 519 N.Y.S.2d 595 (1987).
62. *Washington Post*, September 13, 1988, p A3.
63. Weiss SH, Goedert JJ, Sarngadharan MG, *et al*: Screening test for HTLV-III (AIDS agent) antibodies: Specificity, sensitivity, and applications. *JAMA* 1985; 253:221–25.
64. Imagawa DT, Lee M, Nishanian P, *et al*: Prospective study on isolation of HIV form homosexual men who seroconvert [abstract]. Fourth International Conference on AIDS, Stockholm. Book 2, 1988, p 90.
65. Rinaldo C, Kingsley L, Neumann J, *et al*: Association of HIV $_p$24 Antigenemia with early phase of HIV infection [abstract]. Fourth International Conference on AIDS, Stockholm. Book 2, 1988, p 368.
66. Farzadegan H, Polis MA, Wolinsky SM, *et al*: Loss of human immunodeficiency virus type 1 (HIV-1) antibodies with evidence of viral infection in asymptomatic homosexual men. A report from the Multicenter AIDS cohort study. *Ann Intern Med* 1988; 108:785–90.
67. Burke DS, Brundage JF, Redfield RR, *et al*: Measurement of the false positive rate in a screening program for human immunodeficiency virus infections, *N Engl J Med* 1988; 319:961–64.

68. Curran WJ, Clark ME, Gostin L: AIDS: Legal and policy implications of the application to traditional disease control measures. *Law Med Health Care* 1987; 15:27–35.
69. *Los Angeles Times*, October 14, 1988, p 18.
70. *Washington Post*, July 30, 1988, p A1.
71. McCary E: Occupational risk of the acquired immunodeficiency syndrome among health care workers, *N Engl J Med* 1986; 314:1127–31.
72. Henderson DK, Saah AJ, Zak BK, *et al*: Risk of nosocomial infection with human T-cell lymphotropic virus type II/lymphadenopathy-associated virus in a large cohort of intensively exposed health care workers. *Ann Intern Med* 1986; 104:644–47.
73. CDC: Acquired immune deficiency syndrome (AIDS) precautions for clinical and laboratory staffs. *MMWR* 1982; 31:577–80.
74. CDC: Acquired immunodeficiency syndrome (AIDS) precautions for health care workers and allied professionals. *MMWR* 1983; 32:450–51.
75. *National Law Journal*, August 1, 1988, p 1.
76. *School Board of Nassau County, Fla. v Arline*, 480 U.S. 273; 107 S. Ct. 1123 (1987).
77. *Los Angeles Times*, February 25, 1988, p 22.
78. *The New York Times*, September 16, 1988, B 7.
79. *The New York Times*, January 3, 1988, section 4, p 7.
80. *The New York Times*, June 26, 1987, p A 16.
81. *Wall Street Journal*, December 2, 1988, p C1.
82. Lipton KS: Blood donor services and liability issues related to acquired immune deficiency syndrome. *J Leg Med* 1986; 7:131–86.
83. *Wall Street Journal*, December 5, 1988, p B1.

17

The New Sexual Issues

Public Policy Implications

RUTH MACKLIN

What do AIDS, the new reproductive technologies, and the new controversial sexual diagnoses all have in common? A cautionary tale can serve to illustrate the ethical and public policy implications of these new sexual issues.

Larry Luste and Bonnie Barren, a couple in their late thirties who have been married for three years, have been trying unsuccessfully to conceive a child. After an infertility workup identifies the causes as blocked fallopian tubes, preventing conception, along with a problem in Ms. Barren's intrauterine lining, which prevents implantation of the fertilized ovum, the couple decides to seek adoption. The adoption agency requires a complete medical history, including psychiatric records. The couple consents to the release of those records to the agency. In the course of its inquiry, the adoption agency discovers that 15 years earlier, Mr. Luste had been in psychiatric treatment, with a diagnosis of paraphilia. Although he was pronounced "cured" after four years of therapy, and he experienced no return of paraphilic symptoms, Mr. Luste is judged by the agency as unfit to be an adoptive parent. The couple's application is denied.

They next decide to try their luck with one of the new reproductive technologies. Bonnie Barren is unable to conceive or to carry a pregnancy, but she is capable of producing eggs. So the couple decides to pursue the route of embryo transfer. This involves surgical removal of Bonnie's eggs, *in vitro* fertilization using Larry's sperm, and implantation of the resulting embryo into the womb of a surrogate. This form of embryo transfer is sometimes referred to as "surrogate embryo transfer."

The couple learns of a clinic, the Fecundity Center, which provides these

RUTH MACKLIN • Department of Epidemiology and Social Medicine, Albert Einstein College of Medicine, Yeshiva University, Bronx, New York 10461.

reproductive services. The Fecundity Center will either arrange for the services of a surrogate mother through a broker, for a fee, or else do the procedure with a surrogate of the couple's own choosing. In the latter case, there need be no additional fee paid to the surrogate, but the clinic gets paid for doing the *in vitro* fertilization and subsequent embryo transfer.

Wanting to save money, Bonnie and Larry decide to try to find a friend or relative willing to act as a surrogate mother. A coworker of Larry's, Frannie Fertile, says she always enjoyed being pregnant and wants to help the couple out. She has been divorced for years, with two teenage children from her marriage. Frannie has decided not to marry again, although she has had many boyfriends since her divorce.

Bonnie, Larry, and Frannie approach the administrator of the Fecundity Center with their plan, which is accepted, in principle, after some negotiations. When the clinic provides the surrogate, its policy is to use only married surrogates who have already borne children. But because Larry and Bonnie are bringing their own preselected surrogate, one who did already have children, the clinic does not insist that she be married at the present time.

Larry and Bonnie want to make certain that what they are doing is legal. Although they have no reason to suspect that the Fecundity Center is operating outside the law, they decide to consult an attorney. Finding one who knew the current status of laws governing the new reproductive technologies in their state wasn't easy, but they are finally referred to a law professor who has studied these issues. Professor Blackstein informs Larry and Bonnie that at present there are no laws pertaining to surrogacy in their state. However, two bills have been introduced into the state legislature. According to one bill, only unpaid surrogacy would be allowed. It specifically would allow payment of medical and maternity expenses, lost wages, and reasonable attorney's fees.[1] Under the other bill, either paid or unpaid surrogacy would be permitted. But it contains a requirement that the fee be "just,"[2] which may give a court the power to increase a fee it finds too small.

Professor Blackstein points out that the two neighboring states in the tri-state area also have pending legislation, but no current laws. He advises Larry and Bonnie to stay away from one of these states, since the legislature is considering a bill that would ban surrogate motherhood altogether.[3] As for the other state, its proposed statute would discourage people from entering into surrogacy arrangements, and attempts to do so by negating the surrogate contract. The bill would make any contract for surrogacy void and unenforceable. In addition, Professor Blackstein notes, the bill specifies who the legal parents are in a surrogacy arrangement: the surrogate and her husband.[4]

Larry and Bonnie agree that they are on the safest legal ground remaining in their own state, using the Fecundity Center, as planned. Although Frannie, their chosen surrogate mother, is unmarried, the bill introduced in their state says nothing about the marital status of surrogates. And since Frannie is to be paid only for her medical expenses, they would not be violating a proposed ban on paid surrogacy.

The trio is now ready to proceed. But before the egg retrieval, *in vitro* fertilization, and embryo transfer can take place, Frannie must undergo the standard screening procedures required by the clinic, which include a psychiatric evaluation and a blood test to rule out the presence of syphilis, hepatitis, and HIV infection. In two weeks the results of the blood tests come back, and to everyone's horror, Frannie is found to be HIV-positive. Bonnie and Larry are, of course, saddened for the sake of their friend, as well as upset about the delay in their own reproductive plans.

For her part, Frannie becomes hysterical and threatens to commit suicide. Although the clinic provides a psychiatric evaluation of potential surrogates, it has not been in the practice of providing pre- and posttest counseling regarding the human immunovirus. After all, the clinic's administrator reasons, "We're a fertility clinic, not an alternative testing site for AIDS."

The psychiatrist is afraid to let Frannie leave the clinic, in light of her threat, and convinces her to enter the hospital on a voluntary basis. He promises that her stay will only be temporary and that she will receive appropriate treatment on the psychiatric floor of Mercy Hospital. Frannie's mood is a mixture of anger and depression, and she keeps repeating: "I'll kill the guy that gave me AIDS."

Larry and Bonnie now decide they had better take the costly but less problematic step of purchasing the services of a surrogate through the clinic. This involves a $10,000 payment to the surrogate, the maximum permitted under the proposed statute that allows paid surrogacy,[5] and an additional $15,000 to the lawyer who conducts the brokering for the clinic. To afford this, they sell one of their cars and take out a short-term, high-interest loan. They worry about their future financial solvency, since Bonnie plans to quit her job and stay home to take care of the baby.

After a wait of several months, Patty Mae Smith, a potentially suitable surrogate, is screened by the clinic's psychiatrist. When examining the woman's employment history, however, the psychiatrist notes a significant absenteeism. Upon querying Patty Mae about her monthly absences from work, the psychiatrist begins to formulate a diagnosis of Late Luteal Phase Dysphoric Disorder. He is about to disqualify Patty Mae as a surrogate, when she objects: "Are you saying I have PMS? Well, I know all about that. But why should that matter now? I won't be having my period while I'm pregnant, will I?" Swayed by Patty Mae Smith's impeccable logic, the psychiatrist accepts her as a surrogate mother to carry a baby for Larry Luste and Bonnie Barren.

Patty Mae asks the psychiatrist for reassurance that he will not reveal her diagnosis of Late Luteal Phase Dysphoric Disorder to anyone, especially her employer. "I know you psychiatrists think you're doing people a favor when you make a diagnosis that can excuse their bad behavior.[6] But frankly, I'd rather my boss think I'm lazy or skipping work to go downtown shopping than have him think I've got a psychiatric disorder." The psychiatrist promises complete confidentiality.

The *in vitro* fertilization is conducted, and the embryo transfer performed. For the next two months, Larry and Bonnie agonize while awaiting the results of pregnancy tests. They know that even the best clinics boast little more than a

20% chance of success with each attempt at *in vitro* fertilization. Their worst fears are confirmed when they are informed that this attempt has failed. They undergo the same procedure again, with still no success. Larry and Bonnie have now spent $10,000 for the medical procedures alone, not counting the broker's fees and eventual payment to the surrogate. They didn't count on these extra expenses, nor did they anticipate the emotional toll the failed attempts would take.

Larry and Bonnie begin to blame each other for their biological contributions to the failure. And, of course, they blame Patty Mae, in whom pregnancy did not occur. The psychiatrist at the Fecundity Center at first suggests that they see a marriage counselor, but they reject that suggestion. "There's nothing wrong with our marriage," Larry snaps. "It's Bonnie's eggs that are the problem."

"My eggs!" Bonnie retorts. "How do you know it's not your sperm?" and she bursts into tears.

Bonnie lies awake at night, anxious and depressed. In the morning, she can barely drag herself out of bed to go to work. When the couple realizes that without Bonnie's salary they will be in even worse financial straits, they decide to get psychiatric help. The cost of Bonnie's therapy is another unexpected expense, but one the couple feels is necessary.

Luckily for Larry and Bonnie, the next attempt at *in vitro* fertilization and embryo transfer succeeds. Patty Mae's pregnancy proceeds uneventfully, and in the sixteenth week she undergoes amniocentesis, in accordance with the provisions of the surrogacy contract she had signed. The contract read, in part, as follows:

> Patty Mae Smith agrees that she will not abort the child once conceived except, if in the professional medical opinion of the inseminating physician, such action is necessary for the physical health of Patty Mae Smith or the child has been determined by said physician to be psychologically abnormal. Patty Mae Smith further agrees, upon the request of said physician to undergo amniocentesis or similar tests to detect genetic or congenital defects. In the event said test reveals that the fetus is genetically or congenitally abnormal, Patty Mae Smith, surrogate, agrees to abort the fetus upon demand of Larry Luste and Bonnie Barren, natural parents, in which event, the fee paid to the surrogate will be in accordance with paragraph 9 ($1000). If Patty Mae Smith refuses to abort the fetus upon demand of Larry Luste and Bonnie Barren, their obligations as stated in this agreement shall cease forthwith, except as to obligations of paternity or maternity as imposed by statute.[7]

All three parents anxiously await the results of the amniocentesis. Several weeks pass, and the clinic calls to inform them that they must appear in person to obtain the results. When they are ushered into the office, a genetic counselor is present. She informs them that the fetus is normal except for a minor genetic aberration. There is an extra Y chromosome on the 47th pair. Larry and Bonnie ask what that means, and the counselor is evasive. She tells them quite frankly that there is some dispute about the meaning of a chromosomal diagnosis of 47 XYY. On the one hand, an initial hypothesis that an extra Y chromosome was a "criminal chromosome" has largely been abandoned. Yet there is still some evidence that the child may have emotional difficulties, or even exhibit antisocial behavior in later life. But the child will undoubtedly appear normal until the age of 12.[8]

Larry reacts quickly: "I don't want any of that. Our contract provides for an abortion in case the fetus is abnormal. This baby is abnormal, so that's that."

Bonnie isn't so certain, however. She probes further, asking the genetic counselor: "Is this really an abnormality? Do you recommend an abortion?"

The counselor hedges again. "Well, you see, it is a genetic abnormality, but there isn't any physiologic abnormality. Experts in genetics disagree about the meaning of the extra Y chromosome, and many admit their uncertainty. And as for recommending an abortion, we genetic counselors don't really make recommendations to couples. We just like to give the facts."

At this point, Patty Mae enters the conversation. "I don't think this is any reason for abortion. Abortion is a serious matter, not to be done for frivolous reasons."

"Look, Patty Mae," Larry interrupts. "This isn't your decision. You signed a contract. The contract says if the fetus is genetically abnormal, you agree to abort the fetus on our demand. We demand it."

Patty Mae: "Well, I'm not going against my conscience. It's wrong to abort a fetus with this amount of uncertainty about whether there's really an abnormality. I'm in favor of an abortion if there's a serious defect, or mental retardation. I thought the results of this prenatal test would be clear, that's why I signed the contract."

Larry: "You have to. I don't want to raise a kid who's likely to become a criminal."

Patty Mae asserts herself. "I know my legal rights. I asked a lawyer about this. My lawyer told me I could not prospectively assign to another person the right to compel me to have an abortion. She said there's a limit to what can be in a contract. Under *Roe v Wade*, the state has no constitutional authority to enforce a contract that prohibits me from terminating this pregnancy or that requires me to do so."[9]

Unable to rebut this legal contention, Larry is silent. Bonnie enters the discussion. "There is another option, you know. The contract also contains a clause that if Patty Mae refuses to abort, our obligations cease except as to obligations of paternity or maternity as imposed by statute. I guess that means we'd have to pay child support, or something."

Patty Mae: "Pay child support to whom? For what? Not to me! I don't want to raise this child. I just don't want to abort it."

At this point, the genetic counselor sees she has little further role to play. She excuses herself and calls in the administrator of the Fecundity Center. Larry confronts the administrator: "I thought when this clinic provides a surrogate, a psychiatrist performs an evaluation. Did a shrink examine this bimbo? Or what?"

At this outburst, Bonnie becomes nervous. She's afraid the administrator may judge Larry to be unfit to be a parent and call off the whole arrangement. Recalling their earlier difficulty when the adoption agency uncovered a psychiatric diagnosis of paraphilia, she is now worried that her husband's volatile nature will lead someone to delve into his past once again. The couple had discovered that old diagnostic labels tend to stick.

The administrator succeeds in calming Larry down. He explains that a psychiatric evaluation was carried out, and that Patty Mae Smith was found suitable. Bonnie asks, politely, what the evaluation was supposed to evaluate. Patty Mae interjects: "That's none of your business. Psychiatric evaluations are supposed to be confidential."

Then she softens. "The psychiatrist asked me lots of questions about my children, my marriage, and my feelings. He spent a lot of time on how I would feel about giving up the baby. But you know, I don't remember him asking any questions about how I feel about abortion."

At this point, the clinic administrator suggests that the three parents consult a lawyer, a psychiatrist, or both. Patty Mae asks if an ethics consultant was available, and the administrator says he heard there was a new professional organization, called the "Society for Bioethics Consultations," but doesn't know how to contact anyone from that group. Larry, Bonnie, and Patty Mae then agree to think things over for five days, and arrange to meet again with their lawyers if they have not come to an agreement by that time.

Patty Mae goes home and discusses the matter with her husband. He's upset about the fact that they won't be getting the expected $10,000. And he certainly doesn't want to lose the fee of $1000 Patty Mae would get if she goes ahead with the abortion. He urges her to undergo the abortion, and to see if Larry and Bonnie would be willing to try again with her as a surrogate. Patty Mae begins to waver. Her husband strengthens his case: "Besides, if you can go through this again and get pregnant, you won't have to deal with PMS for another nine months. Remember how bad that was? You're forgetting now, because you've been pregnant for the past four and a half months."

Patty Mae is convinced. She consents to an abortion, and Larry and Bonnie informally agree to try surrogate embryo transfer again with her as a surrogate. They then learn that for medical reasons it will be a few months before Patty Mae can be ready for another attempt at surrogate embryo transfer. Recalling the anxiety and depression Bonnie experienced, they are reluctant to wait. In addition, after talking it over, Bonnie and Larry think it would be bad luck to try again with the same surrogate. So they ask the clinic to provide another woman.

In the meantime, Frannie Fertile is still on the psychiatric ward. Although she has agreed to enter the hospital on a voluntary basis, she soon learned that voluntary commitment does not imply voluntary discharge. Although her initial depression upon learning that she was HIV-positive seems to have abated, so that after three months she was no longer judged to be a danger to herself, her anger at her sexual partner has grown. She thinks she knows who infected her, and continues to assert that she'll kill him when she gets out of the hospital. Repeated psychiatric evaluations have found her to be an apparent "danger to others"—one other, in particular—but psychiatrists have tentatively decided that they might be able to release her if they fulfilled their "duty to warn" the potential victim.

But now a new problem has come to the attention of the psychiatrists at Mercy Hospital. The hospital is a large inner-city facility with staffing problems. Adequate supervision is not available for all patients on the psychiatric ward, and it is known to the staff that patients are having sex with one another. Frannie is as promiscuous—if not more so—in the hospital as she was on the outside. And she is HIV-positive, capable of transmitting the AIDS virus to other patients by sexual contact.

What is the obligation of the staff? Can Frannie be put in isolation? Should she be? Is it ethically and legally permissible to breach confidentiality, and disclose her diagnosis to other patients who are at risk? Even if permissible, would that step be effective? It is, after all, a psychiatric ward, and one of Frannie's sex partners is a paranoid schizophrenic patient, another has severely impaired cognitive functioning, and a third is out of control as a result of heavy use of crack.

The situation contains multiple conflicting obligations. The obligation to Frannie to preserve confidentiality regarding her HIV status conflicts with the obligation to warn persons that they are at risk for contracting a deadly infection.[10] This latter obligation is increased by the fact that the persons at risk are other hospital patients, to whom the caregivers owe a duty to provide a safe, therapeutic environment. But can that duty be met simply by issuing a verbal warning, one that necessarily involves breaching a patient's confidentiality? Some psychiatric patients may fail to comprehend the warning, others may choose not to act appropriately even given the warning, and others may actually experience a worsening of their psychiatric disorder.

The staff is further distressed by their sense that patients on the psychiatric ward are vulnerable to exploitation by other patients, and sex on the wards may not be in the best interests of such patients. But, short of placing patients in physical restraints or in isolation—steps for which legal authority is probably lacking—the staff is powerless to halt these activities.

At a staff meeting, a psychiatric resident proposes that they seek to determine whether any of Frannie's sex partners are HIV-positive. If they are already infected, he reasons, the damage is already done and they need not worry too much about either warning them or isolating Frannie. Furthermore, there might be no way of knowing for certain whether they contracted the virus from Frannie or whether they were already HIV-positive when they entered the hospital.

Another resident objects: "But then you'll have to inform these men about the fact that they're infected with the AIDS virus. They'll need to be counseled. Besides," he adds, "you'll have to get their consent to test their blood for the AIDS virus. What reason will you give them? And what if they lack the capacity to consent? Or what if they refuse? In any case, you'd have to be prepared to give pretest counseling."

The first resident is impatient. "Look, these are psych patients. We have to protect ourselves and the hospital. Let's find out the score first, then deal with these problems later. We can just draw the bloods, saying it's for some lab tests. These guys won't know any better. This is a psych ward, and we're the doctors.

If things don't work out right, no one will put too much credence in the word of a mental patient anyway."

The ward attending interrupted. "We have to do the right thing ethically. And legally, too. In this state it's against the law to test anyone's blood for HIV without their consent. And ethical guidelines urge pretest counseling, as well as posttest counseling for those found to be seropositive. I think we ought to determine whether these three patients have the capacity to grant consent, and then ask their permission to find out their HIV status."

That plan is adopted. The patients' capacity to give consent is evaluated, and two of the three are judged to be capable of consenting. They both agree to the test. As for the third, the patient with severe cognitive impairment, consent is obtained from his brother, who is discovered to be the legal guardian. The patients are counseled, ELISA and Western Blot tests are done, and in two weeks the results come back. Two are negative, but the crack user's blood tests positive.

When the news is disclosed to the patient, in a long counseling session, he denies having used needles on the street. When queried about his sexual practices, he is enraged at the implication that he may be a homosexual. But he can't be sure that none of the women he's slept with were not infected.

Now the psychiatrists are really in a quandary about whether to disclose to him that his most recent sexual partner is HIV-positive. The patient, or his family, could bring a civil suit against the physicians and the hospital for failing to take due care to protect the patient from a lethal disease. And if the county's zealous D.A. got wind of this, he'd be sure to institute criminal charges. The psychiatrists decide to preserve their duty of confidentiality to their other patient, Frannie Fertile. But some are uneasy about this decision, believing that it is really themselves they're seeking to protect, and that the duty of confidentiality is merely a veil behind which to hide.

Let's return now to Larry and Bonnie. They receive a call from Fecundity Clinic informing them that another surrogate mother is available. The woman, Gloria Goodbirth, has served as a surrogate once before with no problems. Nevertheless, she undergoes another psychiatric evaluation at the clinic, along with the other medical tests. Once again, eggs are extracted from Bonnie, fertilized in the laboratory with Larry's sperm, and the resulting embryo implanted in Gloria's womb. So far, so good. Pregnancy ensues, and when the time comes for the prenatal diagnosis, everyone is nervous. The amniocentesis is performed, and when the results come back, everything appears normal. Bonnie and Larry are elated, and Gloria is already counting her $10,000.

Sometime during the eighth month of Gloria's pregnancy, Larry's work calls for him to travel to a neighboring state. He and a colleague make the trip by car, and returning rather late, they decide to get a bite to eat on the way home. They stop at a roadside diner, about an hour's drive from the town in which they live. They are about to enter, when Larry glances through the glass doors at a long bar situated in front of the restaurant portion of the diner. Seated at the bar, with a cigarette in one hand and a drink in the other, is Gloria Goodbirth. Larry stops short and goes pale. His colleague asks, "What's the matter?" and Larry gasps in reply: "That's Gloria, the surrogate. She's carrying our baby. She's not supposed to drink or smoke. The contract prohibits that!"

Larry can't decide whether to go up to the bar and confront Gloria, or call her on the phone to discuss the matter, or call his lawyer. He decides to do nothing at the moment, but to go home and talk it over with Bonnie. When Larry informs her, Bonnie is outraged. They consider hiring a private detective to follow Gloria and find out if going to bars and smoking cigarettes is a habitual practice of hers. But they decide that the best course of action is to contact their lawyer, since there is a contractual agreement for the surrogacy arrangement. In addition to their concern for the health of the fetus Gloria is carrying for them, they now have an additional financial worry: the unexpected costs of retaining a lawyer to do whatever becomes necessary.

Although Larry and Bonnie had consulted Professor Blackstein, a legal scholar in the area of reproductive laws, before embarking on the first surrogacy arrangement, they decide now to use their regular lawyer, the one who drew up their will and represented them when they purchased their home. Together they go over the contract. Clause 12 requires the surrogate mother "...to adhere to all medical instructions given to her by her obstetrician. Gloria Goodbirth also agrees not to smoke cigarettes, drink alcoholic beverages, use illegal drugs, or take nonprescription medication or prescribed medications without written consent from her physician...."[11] Larry asks whether a single infraction of this prohibition is sufficient to show that Gloria violated the contract. The lawyer says it is.

"Well, what can we do about this?" Larry inquires. Does the contract say what's supposed to happen when the surrogate violates one of its provisions?" The lawyer seems puzzled, and replies "Apparently not. But the penalty for breaching a contract isn't always included in the contract itself. If we treat this like any other service contract, the person who breaches the contract should be required to pay damages."

"What do you mean, 'damages'?" Larry sputters. It's a damaged baby I'm worried about. Maybe we should urge Gloria to have an abortion."

"Larry, what are you saying!" Bonnie exclaims. "Our baby is seven and half months gestational age. It's illegal to have an abortion at that stage of pregnancy. What's more, it would be immoral. Wrong, wrong, wrong!"

"I guess you're right about that," Larry admits. "But look, maybe there's no real harm done yet. Even if we could get Gloria to pay money damages, that's not the point. The point is to make sure we have a healthy baby. I want to be certain that Gloria doesn't smoke another cigarette or take another drink during this pregnancy." He turns to the lawyer. "How can we do that?"

"Hmmm," the lawyer muses. "I suppose you could hire a private detective to tail her."

"But," Bonnie objects, "That would only tell us whether or not Gloria is smoking or drinking. It wouldn't stop her from doing these things. Besides, what if she does it in her bedroom? Or her bathroom?"

The lawyer brightens. "You know, I remember reading about a case in California last year. The woman was taking drugs and not following her doctor's orders, and they tried to put her in jail for the remainder of her pregnancy. I don't remember what happened, but maybe we have a precedent there."

"Have Gloria put in jail? Isn't that a little extreme?" Bonnie asks.

"It's our baby!" Larry retorts. "Don't you want her to be perfect?"

The lawyer tells Larry and Bonnie he'll have to research the case, and that he'll get back to them. When he does look up the case, he finds that Pamela Stewart Monson was the subject of what was probably the first criminal charge ever brought against a woman for acts and omissions during pregnancy. In October 1986, criminal charges were filed against her in California. She had received no prenatal care early in her pregnancy, and when she did seek medical attention, was found to have been taking amphetamines. Sometime very late in her pregnancy, Ms. Monson was advised by her physician not to take amphetamines, to stay off her feet, and to avoid sexual intercourse. In addition, because she was found to have a placenta previa, she was told to seek immediate medical treatment if she began to hemorrhage. She ignored all of this advice. She took some amphetamines, had intercourse with her husband, and failed to contact the doctor or go to the hospital once she began to bleed. Her baby was born that evening, with massive brain damage. He died about six weeks later.[12]

An attempt was made to prosecute Pamela Monson on criminal charges under a California child support statute. This move by the District Attorney was an effort to extend child support statutes to create a crime of "fetal neglect."[12] But the effort failed in this case. The charges against Ms. Monson were eventually dropped.[13] The lawyer concludes that this case lacked precedential value because of a number of dissimilarities with the situation involving Larry, Bonnie, and Gloria. In his research, the lawyer comes across another case in which a physician in Baltimore went to court in an effort to force a pregnant woman to stop taking drugs. But that case seemed sufficiently different, since the pregnant woman was taking substantial amounts of Quaalude, Valium, cocaine, and morphine.[14]

In any event, these cases involved a pregnant woman bearing her own child, not one under contract to bear a child for another couple. Larry and Bonnie's lawyer concludes that this is a truly novel situation, and that existing law does not seem to apply in any clear fashion. The only point that does seem applicable is the customary remedy for breach of contract: money damages to be paid by the party who fails to fulfill her contractual obligations.[15] Although less common, there might be a possibility of obtaining a judicial order for specific performance on the part of the contract violator.

When the lawyer contacts Larry and Bonnie with these conclusions, they are less than satisfied. Should they try to seek a court order that would require Gloria to abstain from tobacco and alcohol? If not, they are left with two alternatives: ignore the matter and hope for the best, or confront Gloria with their knowledge of her behavior and demand payment of damages. The latter alternative also opens the possibility of pleading with Gloria to desist.

The lawyer suggests that they might obtain some leverage in trying to get Gloria to stop smoking and drinking with the threat of a suit for damages. Those damages would likely be much higher if Gloria were confronted with the couple's knowledge that she smoked and drank and she persisted in that behavior, than if she stopped immediately. In this circumstance, as in an attempt to get a court order for specific performance, there is the practical difficulty of monitoring Gloria's behavior, and ascertaining that she doesn't sneak a drink or a cigarette in private.

"Couldn't we require that Gloria undergo a urine test or a breathalyzer test?" Larry asks. "After all, employers and sports teams are doing that, why can't we?"

"Look," Bonnie urges, "Let's just confront Gloria with what we've discovered, tell her we can take legal action because of the contract, and see what she says. I'd like to avoid legal hassles. And besides, we really don't want to upset Gloria too much. That might do as much harm to the baby as her taking an occasional drink or smoking cigarettes."

Larry agrees to that plan, and they call Gloria to arrange a meeting. At first, Gloria is defensive. She accuses Larry and Bonnie of invading her privacy.

"Privacy!" Larry exclaims. "What privacy? You're under contract to us. You're carrying our baby."

"I'm well aware of the contract," Gloria says calmly. "But I'm the real mother of this baby."

"What do you mean, the 'real' mother? This baby came from Bonnie's egg and my sperm. We're the biological parents," Larry insists.

"True enough," Gloria replies. "But I'm the gestational mother, and the gestational mother is the *real* mother."[16]

Larry feels panic welling up inside, as he recalls the "Baby M" case in New Jersey. What if Gloria decides she wants to keep the baby? He remembers reading newspaper accounts about all the surrogate mothers seeking to get their babies back. He also recalls the meeting he and Bonnie had with Professor Blackstein. Despite the absence of laws governing surrogacy, and uncertainty about how courts will decide such cases, Professor Blackstein had cautioned that not all future cases are likely to be decided the same way as the Baby M case. For example, if a surrogate mother decided sometime during her pregnancy that she wanted to keep the baby, or made a pronouncement to that effect at the time of delivery, a decision might go in her favor. Professor Blackstein had also pointed out that some legal scholars have argued that the gestational or birth mother should be considered the legal mother for all legal purposes, and should not be allowed to give up her parental rights or relinquish her child until a reasonable time after the birth of the child.[17]

Larry reflects also on the fact that Gloria had to undergo a psychiatric evaluation by a psychiatrist as part of the screening process for surrogacy. If the psychiatrist could fail to predict that Gloria would break the contract by smoking and drinking, couldn't he also be mistaken about her willingness to give up the baby after birth? Larry is aware that psychiatric evaluations are often fallible, and that the ability of psychiatrists to predict how people will act is shaky, at best.

He also recalls how the psychiatric "experts" disagreed when they testified in the Baby M case. One "expert" diagnosed Mary Beth Whitehead as having a mixed-personality disorder, while another "expert," who had written the description of this disorder for the official psychiatric manual, contradicted the diagnosis.[18] Larry becomes even more worried when he remembers that the way such disputes are likely to be handled is by turning them into legal battles for the custody of the child. At least that was the way it was done in the Baby M case. Perhaps, like Mary Beth Whitehead, he and Bonnie would fail the "patty-cake test."

Sobered by these reflections, Larry decides that the best strategy is to calm down and treat Gloria nicely. For her part, Gloria becomes contrite and apologizes to Larry and Bonnie. She says this was, indeed, a one-time occurrence. She doesn't regularly smoke or drink, but had gotten very upset over some trouble her brother found himself in. She explains that her brother had locked his secretary in the office after threatening to rape her, then stopped for a drink on the way home and got into a fight with another customer at the bar, and when he got home, he yelled at his wife and threw her collection of Japanese prints into the fire. This was the culmination of along series of incidents, which had gone on for years. Her brother's wife is now pressing criminal charges, which he is trying to avoid.

Feeling a bond with Bonnie and Larry because of their baby, Gloria pours out her heart to them. She admits that her brother has been in this sort of trouble before. Since he went through puberty, he has been a source of embarrassment to this family because of his unprovoked aggressive behavior and his cruelty to people around him. They have now learned that one possible way to avoid the criminal charge would be to enter a psychiatric plea, under a proposed new diagnostic category: sadistic personality disorder.

Gloria says the dilemma is whether her brother would be better off or worse off with the psychiatric plea. On the one hand, he would avoid having to go to jail. But the stigma of a psychiatric diagnosis might turn out to be just as bad—if not worse—than a criminal record. And if he ended up in a psychiatric hospital, it could take longer to be released than if he copped a plea and got a reduced prison sentence.

Larry and Bonnie are reasonably satisfied with Gloria's explanation and her promise that she would refrain from drinking or smoking for the duration of the pregnancy. They sympathize with her for her brother's plight, saying they hope it turns out for the best. Larry suggests they all go for coffee, and Gloria replies: "Coffee? I read that pregnant women should stay away from caffeine. I haven't touched the stuff since the embryo was implanted."

It is time now to leave Larry and Bonnie and Gloria and Frannie. In our next episode, we try to resolve the many ethical and legal dilemmas raised by their story. This cautionary tale was intended only to illustrate the many public policy implications.

REFERENCES

1. Andrews LB: The aftermath of Baby M: Proposed state laws on surrogate motherhood. *Hastings Cen Rep* 17, 1987, p 35.

2. Andrews, p 35.
3. Andrews, p 32.
4. Andrews, p 40.
5. Andrews, p 35.
6. Macklin R: The premenstrual syndrome (PMS) label: Benefit or burden?" in Ginsburg BE, Carter BF (eds): *Premenstrual Syndrome: Ethical and Legal Implications in a Biomedical Perspective*. New York, Plenum Press, 1987, pp 17–30.
7. Annas GJ: Baby M: babies (and justice) for sale. *Hastings Cen Rep* 17, 1987, p 14.
8. Fletcher JC: Ethical issues in genetic screening, prenatal diagnosis, and counseling, in Weil WB Jr., Benjamin M (eds): *Ethical Issues at the Outset of Life*. Boston, Blackwell Scientific Publications, 1987, p 77.
9. Annas, p 15.
10. Binder RL: AIDS antibody tests on inpatient psychiatric units. *Am J Psychiatry* 1987; 144:2.
11. Annas, p 14.
12. Annas GJ: Pregnant women as fetal containers. *Hastings Cen Rep* 16, 1986, p 13.
13. *The New York Times*, November 23, 1987, p B10.
14. Pregnant drug user taken to court, *The New York Times*, April 27, 1984.
15. Annas, Baby M: Babies (and justice) for sale, p 15.
16. Elias S, Annas GJ: Social policy considerations in noncoital reproduction. *JAMA* 1986; 255, 64–65.
17. Annas, Baby M: babies (and justice) for sale, p 15.
18. Gould RE: And what about Baby M's ruined life? *The New York Times*, March 26, 1987, Op-ed p.

18

Surrogate Parenting

Some Guiding Principles for a Legislative Response

JOAN G. WEXLER

Men and women can produce babies today in other than the old-fashioned way. Modern scientific technology permits the separation of the genetic from the gestational aspects of reproduction, and allows such alternative methods as these: One party can donate either sperm or eggs. A couple can use an *in-vitro* fertilization technique using their own sperm and eggs. An embryo can be transplanted into a woman for gestational purposes even if her egg was not involved in the fertilization process. Furthermore, these new technologies of birth allow a married couple to involve a third party in the creative process. For example, a female third party can, by means of artificial insemination, become pregnant, and give the baby after birth to the couple.

Once you can have different combinations of people involved in making a baby, it becomes necessary to think about rights, responsibilities, and roles in new ways. The status of the various people who theoretically could be labeled as a "parent" must be determined. Difficult as this may be, the task is not impossible.

The law has addressed similar issues in the past. For example, our adoption laws, shaped over the past 100 years by public policy considerations, explicitly address the status and rights of the biological and adoptive parents. The principle behind most adoption statutes is that once a child is adopted, from a legal perspective, the biological parents simply cease to exist.[1]

There also is a developed body of law concerning artificial insemination,

This chapter is adapted from a paper presented at a conference on The New Sexual Issues: Psychiatry and the Law, at an annual meeting of the Tri-State Chapter, American Academy of Psychiatry and the Law, January 16, 1988.

JOAN G. WEXLER • Brooklyn Law School, 250 Joralemon Street, Brooklyn, New York 11201.

the process whereby a woman is intravaginally or intrauterinely inseminated with semen by a syringe or similar means. A woman may be inseminated with the semen of her husband or mate, or another donor, almost always anonymous, may be involved.[2] Although artificial insemination is referred to in the Bible,[3] the use of a third party donor did not become widespread until the 1960s.[4] Overall, it is estimated that in the United States between 6000 and 10,000 babies are conceived each year using this reproductive technique.[5]

In 29 states, statutes legalize and make provision for artificial insemination. In those states, a child born in this manner is the legitimate child of the mother and her husband even if the semen was donated by a third party.[6] The statutes in these states address a number of issues as part of their regulatory framework. For example, the majority of states require the written consent of the wife and the husband. Some statutes specify a particular procedure that must be followed; for instance, the insemination must be done by a licensed physician who may be required to file consents with the Department of Health or some other state agency. Several states have an express provision that the sperm donor is not the child's natural father.[7]

A majority of states, therefore, have accepted what might be described as surrogate fathering, and they have done so without much controversy. On the other hand, debate about a somewhat analogous reproductive technique, surrogate mothers, has been heated. Sparked by the *Baby M* case,[8] which involved a surrogate parenting agreement between William Stern and Mary Beth Whitehead, emotionally packed debate has raged in scientific, legal, and ethical circles about the moral and social implications of this practice.

The *Baby M* agreement was typical of surrogate parenting arrangements. Mr. Stern and Mrs. Whitehead signed an agreement pursuant to which Mrs. Whitehead would be artificially inseminated with Mr. Stern's semen, would carry the child to term, and would then surrender her parental rights and the child to him. Mr. Stern's wife, Elizabeth, was then to adopt the baby. Mr. Stern agreed to pay necessarily incurred costs, such as medical expenses, and $10,000 to Mrs. Whitehead. In addition, he agreed in a separate contract to pay a $7500 fee to an infertility center that had made the arrangement between the parties.

The legal contest focused on whether to enforce this agreement when Mrs. Whitehead changed her mind after the child's birth, and decided not to give up the baby. The New Jersey Family Court awarded permanent custody to Mr. Stern, permitted Mrs. Stern to adopt the baby, and terminated Mrs. Whitehead's parental rights.[9] Upon appeal, the New Jersey Supreme Court, the state's highest court, unanimously affirmed the award of custody to Mr. Stern, but reversed the trial court's directions to terminate Mrs. Whitehead's parental rights and to permit Mrs. Stern's adoption of Baby M. It also remanded to the lower court for a determination of Mrs. Whitehead's visitation rights.[10]

The New Jersey Supreme Court held that the surrogate parenting agreement in the *Baby M* case was illegal and unenforceable under the existing New Jersey family law. It pointed out, however, that the legislature was free to address the issue itself.

Although legislative proposals for dealing with surrogate parenting agreements have been debated for a number of years, the amount of discussion in state legislatures increased dramatically after the *Baby M* decision.[11] From such an active discussion, various legislative proposals are bound to emerge. I think that the issue should be addressed directly, on its own merits, and not decided by default under existing law that was enacted without reference to this new phenomenon. Legislators should do for all of the new reproductive technologies what the majority of states have already done for adoption and artificial insemination—face the challenges and resolve the problems created by appropriate legislation.

My intention in writing this chapter is to participate in this discussion about surrogate parenting. I will first articulate several guiding principles that should be used in analyzing any legislative response to the practice of surrogate parenting. I will then test certain proposed solutions against these principles, and, finally, propose a model of my own.

GUIDING PRINCIPLES

Stability for the Child

During the *Baby M* controversy a great deal of attention was paid to the rights and interests of the adults involved. Far more important, however, is the interest of the child. Any child born as a result of a surrogate parenting arrangement is entitled to stability in this fundamental sense: The child must know who his or her parents are. Scientists may have given us the ability to separate the possible strands of parenthood—the gestational, the genetic, and the child-rearing aspects—but it is up to the state, by means of its laws, to confer the legal status of parent of a particular child on someone, and I think that is essential.

There is a relationship between the child and his parents in the traditional intact family that is different from the relationship that child has with all other adults. The parents and the child live together, and the parents have the right and obligation to supervise, care for, and educate the child. The child also has a right to parental care and support. In return, the child must respect the parents' supervision and pay over any earnings to them. Obviously, this relationship can change and the various strands of rights and obligations will be separated if the family becomes dysfunctional. Parents do divorce, one parent may die, both parents may abuse or abandon the child. But prior to that time, the child can expect some certainty in his relationship with the two adults who are legally labeled his parents. Moreover, this order in the rights and duties of the parties has come to be expected in our culture, and thus reinforces the child's sense of the importance of the certainty of his status.

Avoidance of Custody Litigation

My second guiding principle is that litigation to determine custody should be avoided if at all possible. This stems from my belief that custody battles, although possibly useful in some way for the adults involved, are almost never good for children. Custody litigation may provide a therapeutic outlet for parents that permits their day-to-day relationships with each other and with the child involved to be less hostile. Be that as it may, the litigation of custody signifies to the child just what it signifies to anyone else—that parents are in overt conflict with one another. Even if the child is an infant, this hostile environment may have serious deleterious effects on the child.[12]

Custody litigation can arise in a variety of situations. For example, in New York when a birth mother revokes her consent to the adoption of her child within the prescribed statutory period, she can force a custody hearing. But most custody litigation takes place when parents divorce, and they cannot decide the custody issue themselves. In almost all these contests, the custody standard that is used is the best interests of the child.

Let me pause briefly to review this standard. In determining what placement will best suit a child, judges in most states are requested by law to consider a whole range of factors, such as the strengths and weaknesses of each parent, the child's relationship with both parents, and the financial circumstances of the parties. Judges assign the weight to each parental trait, act, or capacity that seems to be called for in the particular situation. This sounds exceedingly flexible and fair, but it is just this flexibility that has caused the best interests standard to be greatly criticized for the enormous amount of discretion it gives judges.[13] In addition, because the standard is so vague, judges often impose their own values in reaching a decision, subjecting them to further criticism from those with differing perspectives.

Such a decision-making process is particularly ill-suited to a custody dispute that arises from a surrogacy arrangement. Many who favor the current system in a divorce situation believe that courts can make the necessary assessments if aided by skilled mental health professionals, who interview family members and observe each parent with the child. Even if these sorts of thorough psychiatric examinations were available in the divorce setting, which they often are not, I think they are impossible to achieve in the surrogacy setting where the child is a newborn. There may be somewhat reliable information about the parents, and there may be minimal information about the child and his or her particular needs, but there can be none about the crucial point—the parents' relationship with the child.

Privatization of Family Law Issues

Family law is in transition from close state regulation to the increasing autonomy of the family and the individual. Consider, for example, the revolution in divorce law. We have moved, over a relatively short period of time, from statutes requiring the commission of a marital fault by one spouse before a divorce could be granted, to statutes that merely require that one spouse decide that the marriage is irretrievably broken. Although courts have the power to decide property and support issues after divorce, parties are encouraged to make such arrangements themselves. As to custody, too, most commentators who have addressed the issue have concluded that parents, not courts, are better equipped to make child-custody decisions.[14]

In the area of procreation and child rearing, the United States Supreme Court has also protected private decision making.[15] Whether or not constitutional rights are at stake, clearly such decisions are intensely private matters and private agreements concerning these issues deserve considerable respect.

While some argue that surrogate parenting ought to be regarded as a totally private matter that should be decided solely by the parties themselves, that approach would present serious problems. Some state involvement may be necessary to protect the needs of the children involved, who of course have no input into any private ordering. And the clash of new scientific technology with deeply held values cries out for some societal response. In short, private decisions deserve respect, but should not be controlling. The best way of handling this matter is to draft legislation that provides a presumption for private decision making.

DIRECTIONS FOR PUBLIC POLICY

With these three basic principles in mind—certainty of status for children, avoidance of custody litigation, and a presumption in favor of private ordering—let us examine the ways the law could respond to the problem of surrogate parenting.

Use of Existing Law

First, we could do nothing. It is true, as some have argued, that some existing law gives us a basis for legal analysis of this issue.[16] Contract law, adoption law, and constitutional law do obliquely touch upon the subject, but these bodies of law do not fully or adequately address the legal issues raised by the practice of surrogate parenting. Because of such gaps and deficiencies, if we do nothing, the status of a child born as a result of a surrogate parenting arrangement, particularly if one party wishes to renege on the deal, will be uncertain. As in *Baby M*, custody litigation is then likely. And because certainty of status and avoidance of litigation are two of my guiding principles, this option is unsatisfactory.

Prohibition or Nonenforceability of the Agreement

A rather extreme approach would be to prohibit surrogate parenting arrangements and declare that anyone who had taken part in one had engaged in criminal activity. This policing of intimate conduct violates my third guiding principle of private family decision making to such a degree that it is clearly unacceptable.

We could also try to discourage the practice by legislating that such contracts are void as against public policy and will not be enforced. This would permit such arrangements only when all of the parties involved chose to comply with the terms of the agreement into which they had entered.[17] The message that such a policy would send is that if parties want to enter into surrogate parenting arrangements that the state does not approve of, then they run the risk of living with an unenforceable agreement.

Such a policy would leave in its wake a host of unanswered questions. Many things can go wrong with surrogate agreements. If the surrogate mother decided to keep the child, what would be the biological father's rights and obligations, if the law had already washed its hands of the entire matter? What if the surrogate mother did not want the child, and neither did the biological father? What if the biological father wanted custody, or the right to visit with the child? Leaving the parties "where you find them" is a head-in-the-sand response. It simply means that courts will be forced to deal with problems on an *ad hoc* basis, with essentially no direction from the legislature as to appropriate regulation.

More importantly, from my perspective, this approach would create just the kind of chaos to which my first two principles are opposed. Assume, for example, that the surrogate mother is married at the time of conception. She chooses to keep the child, but her husband, despite a strong presumption in the law that the child is his, refuses to support the child or provide any kind of parental care, including the emotional nurturing and guidance that every child needs. The biological father would like to prove his paternity in the hope of at least visiting with the child. What result? The child's status is uncertain and he or she is not receiving care and protection from one of the adults in the household to whom the child naturally turns to provide it. Litigation is likely, ranging from a support action by the mother to a custody/visitation action by the biological father. If a primary goal is to protect children born from these arrangements, and provide them with basic rights, then this type of policy fails.

In addition, any legislative approach that is premised on discouraging surrogate parenting arrangements and hopes to have a chilling effect on them, is unlikely to achieve that objective. The demand for access to the baby-making market by making use of surrogate parenting is simply too great and it is likely to increase. Whether or not the incidence of infertility has actually increased over time, the statistics today reflect a veritable epidemic. An estimated 10 to 15% of all married couples are involuntarily childless—defined as those who have failed to conceive after trying to do so for at least one year of not using contraceptives.[18] Put another way, as many as one in six American couples are considered infertile.[19] Moreover, people attach enormous social and psychological significance to having a child, particularly one that is genetically related to them, and, in order to achieve that emotionally charged objective, they are capable of behaving in ways that some members of society may find morally questionable, or even repugnant. Moral and policy objections to surrogate parenting must, in my view, be compelling before we embark on another kind of Prohibition.

Prohibiting surrogate parenting would not, therefore, make it go away. Instead, there would be less monitoring and regulation than there is now, and with more unfortunate results. Intermediary organizations, which at present may be providing some minimal protections, might disappear altogether because of the lack of a financial incentive. Or, if they chose to continue their work, and continued to charge fees, in spite of a prohibition to the contrary, the cost would undoubtedly increase to reflect the cost of getting caught. Even knowing that the agreements would be unenforceable would probably not stop people from entering into them, and I surmise not only noncommercial arrangements would exist. Instead, women who chose to become surrogates would charge more for their services because the men involved would be more desperate to have the woman fulfill their commitments. And because the activity would be "underground," there would be less protection for the participants—most importantly, for the child.

If doing nothing or prohibiting surrogate parenting in some manner will not work, we are left with only one choice—a form of regulation. I therefore turn to a discussion of some of the issues that ought to be considered in drafting such legislation.

REGULATORY FRAMEWORK

My intention here is to point out features that ought to be included in any legislative proposal, not to provide a detailed piece of legislation. These recommendations must, of course, conform to my three guiding principles: certainty of status for children, avoidance of litigation, and a presumption in favor of the private ordering of family matters.

The only way to assure the status, security, and well-being of a child born through a surrogate-parenting arrangement—at least to the extent we can do this for *any* child—is to accept surrogate parenting as a matter of public policy and provide a limited, carefully regulated procedure that parties must follow.[20]

Status of the Parties

Any statute that addresses the surrogate-parenting issue must be specific as to the parties' status vis-á-vis the child from the time of conception until birth. The intended parents of a child conceived by means of surrogate parenting should be the sperm donor biological father and his wife. The surrogacy agreement, which, as described below, must be consented to by all parties and approved by a court, must clearly state that upon the birth of the child these intended parents will file a notice with the court, so that it will order a new birth certificate naming the intended parents as parents. This parallels what courts do now in adoption cases.

To guarantee that the child will have a legally recognized father should there be any uncertainty about the identity of the father, there should be a presumption, which will operate prior to the time the new birth certificate is issued, that the husband of a married woman surrogate is the father of the child. He must consent to the procedure and should have an opportunity after the child's birth to show that he did not give such consent.

Informed and Voluntary Consent

It is most important that the parties give informed consent to the surrogate parenting process and that they understand their rights and obligations. There are three elements of informed consent that have been identified as critical in the medical context: (1) the possession of information sufficient to make an intelligent decision, (2) the ability to understand and appreciate one's decision, and (3) voluntariness or freedom from coercion.

I believe that the parties in a surrogate-parenting arrangement are capable of giving this kind of consent. As discussed earlier, the law already recognizes that women are capable of making decisions about childbearing and protects their right to do so. But a surrogacy arrangement is different from the decision to have a baby, or even to terminate a pregnancy, and the law should account for this distinction. Rather than prohibiting women from being able to make the choice to take part in a surrogacy arrangement, the right to private decision making in these matters should be modified only to the extent that various safeguards be provided to assure that the woman, and the other parties involved, have all the information necessary to make truly informed decisions.

The best way of meeting this goal is to have a policy that requires court supervision of surrogacy arrangements at an early stage and to mandate that certain requirements are met *before* the artificial insemination contemplated by the agreement takes place. The intended parents, the surrogate, and her husband, if she is married, must join in the petition presented to the court asking for approval of the surrogacy arrangement. The requirements for court approval should include the following:

1. The intended mother must be unable to bear a child or be unable to do so without unreasonable risk to herself or the baby. Such an assertion must be supported by medical evidence.

2. To respond to the concern that a surrogate mother may not have sufficient knowledge about the process to know in advance whether she is capable of giving up the baby, the law should provide that only women who are over the age of 21 and who have already had a child will be permitted to be surrogates. This may not fully answer that concern, but it would help.

3. The child welfare agency in the jurisdiction that ordinarily makes a home study regarding prospective adoptive parents must do so here for the intended parents as well as for the surrogate. The agency's role should be somewhat limited. It should not have the power to screen for parental fitness except in those few cases where neglect or abuse is an issue. We do not apply a standard or guideline for choosing whether a particular set of parents is "fit to be a parent" for those who have children by ordinary means and there is little evidence that such screening has resulted in "better" adoptive parents than where no screening is done.

4. A report must be filed with the court, written by a licensed psychiatrist or psychologist holding a doctoral degree, evaluating the suitability of all the parties for their roles in the surrogate-parenting arrangement. This report must attest that the parties are aware of the possible psychological consequences of participating in surrogate parenting. The professional's function is

to inform the parties about the advantages, disadvantages, and consequences of surrogate parenting as well as alternatives to this procedure.

5. The surrogate mother must have undergone medical examinations for pregnancy, fertility, and sexually transmitted and genetically detectable diseases. The intended father should also have undergone medical examinations for sexually transmitted and genetically detectable diseases. The results of such testing should be exchanged by the parties prior to the filing of their petition with the court.

6. Adequate provision must have been made for all reasonable health-care costs associated with the surrogacy until the child's birth or before birth, if the agreement is terminated earlier.

7. The court must review the terms of the agreement that the parties have negotiated to ensure that there has not been overreaching by any party and that the interests of all affected individuals are protected. The basic terms—that the surrogate mother agrees to be inseminated by the sperm of the intended father, to carry the child to term, and then to surrender all parental rights to the intended parents—are fixed, but other terms may be negotiated by the parties themselves. For example, the parties can determine whether term life or health insurance will be provided for the surrogate mother and whether any fees are to be paid to her.

8. The surrogate mother and the intended parents must have independent counsel. If the court deems it necessary, the husband of the surrogate should have counsel as well.

Termination of the Surrogacy Agreement

One of the most controversial issues regarding surrogacy is the surrogate's right to revoke her consent to the agreement. If the surrogate can trigger a best interests hearing after the birth of the child by revoking her consent at that time, my two principles of certainty of status and avoidance of litigation will not be met. Furthermore, the third principle of private decision making is relevant to this issue as well. In divorce-related child custody situations, we prefer and encourage private decisionmaking not only because we want to discourage litigation, but because we want to encourage parties to reach a decision themselves. This reasoning applies as well in surrogate parenting cases. The parties to a surrogate parenting agreement have entered into it specifically to produce a child. They intended a certain result, and the suggested legislative provisions already discussed try to ensure that these decisions are well informed ones. Once we are fairly confident that all parties have entered the agreement freely and with full information, the law should protect their expectations.

The opportunities to terminate the agreement should, therefore, be extremely limited. Of course, after the court has entered an order approving of the surrogacy arrangement, but prior to the time the surrogate becomes pregnant, any party should be able to terminate the agreement, and the court should vacate its order.

The surrogate should also have the right to terminate the agreement for

180 days after the date of the last insemination, even if she is in fact pregnant at the time. This provision can be seen as an intermediate position between two extreme views that have been voiced by others. Some would argue that once the agreement has been entered into with the court's approval, the expectation interests of the intended parents should not be frustrated by the surrogate's unilateral action. Those from an opposing camp would argue that the surrogate should always be able to change her mind, even after the child is born. The 180-day period is thus somewhat of a compromise.

In addition, the choice of an 180-day period recognizes several other important considerations. A surrogacy arrangement is not like an ordinary contract—a human life is being created, and the biological mother ought to have some time to decide if she would prefer to keep the child. A surrogacy arrangement is also not like an adoption situation in which a postbirth consent is required. In that case, the theory is that many women who have unplanned pregnancies are under emotional stress during pregnancy, and are unable to make rational decisions about their future. On the other hand, in the surrogacy arrangement contemplated here, the decision to give up the child has been made in an informed manner, prior to the pregnancy, by an adult woman who has already had a child. The court will have already evaluated whether undue stress has been placed on the surrogate during the hearing procedure. Moreover, the 180-day period roughly coincides with the time during which the surrogate has a constitutionally protected right to terminate the pregnancy. If a woman has the right to abort that cannot be affected by any contractual provision to do otherwise, it makes sense that she should also be able to decide to bear and keep the child during this same period.[21]

Finally, after conception, a woman should be permitted to petition the court to annul or modify the contract under an exceedingly limited standard. She must be able to prove a compelling change in circumstances unforeseen at the time of insemination. She would not be permitted to make such a petition if the change in circumstances were not compelling and pertained to facts that should reasonably have been foreseen earlier. For example, if at the time of birth, the surrogate mother is told that she could not have other children, this would be a reason to petition the court for modification. On the other hand, her petition would be denied if it were based on an assertion that her children would be upset if she were to give the baby to the intended parents.

CONCLUSION

There has been a great deal of debate about the pros and cons of surrogate parenting. In this chapter I have attempted to add to this debate, and it is hoped to stimulate it, by presenting recommendations that provide a framework for an effective legislative response to the practice. These recommendations were based on the application of three principles: certainty of status for the child, avoidance of custody litigation, and privatization of the issue. I believe that this type of regulation that provides for judicial supervision will benefit all of the parties involved, particularly the child that is produced by this reproductive means.

REFERENCES

1. *See e.g.*, N.Y. Dom. Rel. Law section 114 (McKinney 1988).
2. This procedure is known as "artificial insemination by donor" (AID). When a husband or mate is involved, the procedure is called "artificial insemination by husband" (AIH).
3. "Because his wife Sarah was barren, Abraham impregnated her handmaiden, Sarah." Genesis 16:2.
4. *See* Ethics Committee of the American Fertility Society, Ethical Considerations of the New Reproductive Technologies 36S (1986); Walter: *Psychological and legal aspects of artificial insemination (AID): An overview*, 36 *Amer J Psychother* 1982; 93.
5. Curie-Cohen M: Luttrell L: Shapiro S: *Current practice of artificial insemination by donor in the United States. N Engl J Med* 1979; 300:555, 558. Wadlington, *Artificial conception: The challenge for family law. Va. Law Rev.* 1983; 69:465, 476.
6. In all these states a woman must obtain her husband's consent to the procedure, except in Maryland, where such consent is presumed. The states that have such statutes are Alaska, Arkansas, California, Colorado, Connecticut, Florida, Georgia, Kansas, Louisiana, Maryland, Michigan, Montana, Nevada, New York, Oklahoma, Oregon, Tennessee, Texas, Virginia, Washington, Wisconsin, and Wyoming.
7. Freed D, Walker T: *Family law in the fifty states: An overview. Fam. Law Q.* 1988; 21:534.
8. *In re Baby M*, 217 N.J.Super. 313, 525 A.2d 1128 (Ch. Div. 1987), *aff'd in part, rev'd in part, remanded*, 109 N.J. 396, 537 A.2d 1227 (1988).
9. *In re Baby M*, 217 N.J.Super. at 408–09, 525 A.2d at 1175–79. (1987).
10. *In re Baby M*, 109 N.J. at 463, 537 A.2d at 1261 (1987).
11. Freed D, Brandes J: *Surrogate parenting; Alternative reproductive techniques, N.Y. Law J.* 1989; 201:3.
12. In another article, I have argued that custody modification after divorce should be difficult to obtain and that vigorous statutory criteria should firmly limit both the parents' ability to bring such litigation and the courts' discretion to make custodial changes. *See* Wexler: *Rethinking the modification of child custody decrees*, 94 *Yale Law J* 1985; 94:757.
13. *See, e.g.*, Elster: *Solomonic judgments: Against the best interests of the child*, 54 *U. Chi. Law Rev.* 1987; 54:1; Mnookin: *Child custody adjudication: Judicial functions in the face of indeterminacy. Law & Contemp Probs* 1975; 39:226; Oster: *Custody proceeding: A study of vague and indefinite standards. J Fam Law* 1965; 5:21.
14. *See, e.g.*, Bodenheimer: *The rights of children and the crisis in custody litigation: Modification of custody in and out of state. U Colo Law Rev* 1975; 6:495, 506; Trombetta: *Joint custody: Recent research and overloaded courtrooms inspire new solutions to custody disputes. J Fam Law* 1981; 19:213, 227.
15. *See e.g., Roe v Wade*, 10 U.S. 113, 153–64 (1973); *Eisenstadt v Baird*, 405 U.S. 438, 453–55 (1972); *Griswold v Connecticut*, 381 U.S. 479, 485–86 (1965).
16. Garrison M: *Surrogate parenting: What should legislatures do? Fam Law Q.* 1988; 23:149.
17. *See* N.Y.S. Task Force on Life and the Law: *Surrogate Parenting: Analysis & Recommendations for Public Policy*, May 1988.
18. *See In re Baby M*, 217 N.J.Super. at 331–32, 525 A.2d at 1136–37 (discussion of trial judge).
19. *See* Blakeslee: *Trying to Make Money Making 'Test-Tube' Babies, The New York Times*, May 17, 1987, at C6, col.1; Mosher: Pratt: *N.Y. Times*, May 17, 1987, at C6, col.1; Mosher: Pratt: *Fecundity and Infertility in the United States, 1965–82*, National Center for Health Statistics Advanced Data #10, Table 3; Feb. 11, 1985; *50% Success Rate in $1 Billion Infertility Fight. The New York Times*, May 18, 1988, A25, col 1.

20. In February 1989, the House of Delegates of the American Bar Association approved the Uniform Status of Children of Assisted Conception Act, which had been approved by the National Conference of Commissioners on Uniform State Laws on August 4, 1988. Although this Act addresses all form of assisted conception, its provisions can be analyzed in terms of procreation by surrogate parenting only. It provides two alternatives that states may choose: one permitting, but regulating, surrogate parenting, and one prohibiting it. Thus far, no jurisdiction has adopted it. The Act recommends a number of provisions that conform to my thinking, and some of what follows in text is based on them.
21. *See* Uniform Status of Children of Assisted Conception Act, Comment to section 7, National Conference of Commissioners on Uniform State Laws, 1988.

19

The Use of Psychiatric Expertise in Sex Offender Cases

SHELDON TRAVIN

The subject of psychiatric expertise in sex offender cases raises a multitude of questions which have profound ethical implications. Given the major uncertainties that exist about why an individual commits a sexual offense, whether or not the individual has a diagnosable mental disorder and, if so, whether or not a special kind of treatment modality should be recommended, sex offender cases necessarily present particular ethical dilemmas to the forensic psychiatrist. These dilemmas are made all the more difficult because any proffered psychiatric opinion about the sex offender may lead to drastic consequences, consequences that may include mislabeling, confinement, and/or coerced treatment.

Recognition of the potential abuse of psychiatric expertise regarding the sex offender was underscored in the 1977 Group for the Advancement of Psychiatry (GAP) publication, *Psychiatry and Sex Psychopath Legislation: The 30's and the 80's*.[1] GAP comments on the lack of clinical validity and the confusing nature of such terminology as "sexual psychopathy" and "dangerousness," and critically examines the problems of sex psychopath statutory criteria for the identification of sex psychopaths, the methodological problems in evaluating treatment efficacy, the doctrine of informed consent relevant to treating sex offenders, and the risk and limitations of specific treatments, as well as the guaranteeing of adequate treatment. GAP stresses that sex psychopaths and sex offenders are a heterogeneous group for whom the heterogeneous legal classification of "sex psychopath" is invalid to determine treatability; that stigmatization with the sex psychopath label merely serves the purpose of remov-

SHELDON TRAVIN • Department of Psychiatry, Bronx-Lebanon Hospital Center, 1285 Fulton Avenue, Bronx, New York 10456, and Department of Psychiatry, Albert Einstein College of Medicine, Bronx, New York 10461.

ing these people from society on an indeterminate sentence; that predictions about "sexual dangerousness" are debatable; and that the "proper role of the psychiatrist when dealing with sex offenders is first and foremost that of a clinician" (p 937). Clinicians are cautioned against making generalizations which are not based upon a careful examination of the data and an adequate diagnosis of the individual case. The fact that an individual violates a sexual law neither indicates that the person has a diagnosable mental illness, nor the nature of the psychiatric disturbance, if present. There may be a schizophrenic psychosis, organic brain syndrome, neurotic conflict, sexual perversion, or other condition underlying the symptomatic expression of the sexual offense. In regard to treatment recommendations, and the reality that treatment may not be available in many penal systems, GAP advises that it is "better either to state what is needed or offer no opinion at all" (p 939).

With the recognition that the label "sexual psychopath" lacks acceptable clinical validity and that proven treatments do not exist for sex offenders, the Task Panel on Legal and Ethical Issues of the President's Commission on Mental Health[2] and the American Bar Association Committee on Criminal Justice Mental Health Standards[3] have also urged the abolition of sexual psychopath laws[4] (also known, among other names, as "mentally disordered sex offender laws"—MDSO laws). In 1985, only 16 states and the District of Columbia still had MDSO laws; but these laws were actually enforced in only six states.[5] Oliver[6] points out that when MDSO legislation was enforced in California before its repeal in 1982, it resulted in a number of consequences that reflected negatively on the psychiatrist's role. These consequences were described under the following headings: faulty (scientific) premise, slandering the mentally ill, covert misuse of the medical system, subservience of psychiatry (to judicially controlled decisions), deficient state hospitals (for adequate treatment programs), psychiatrist as jailer (as the state hospitals were virtually run by the Department of Corrections), and the misuse of psychiatry for purposes of social control, this last, of course, representing the gravest risk to its moral and scientific status.

While the trend is therefore toward an increasing unwillingness to use psychiatric expertise to identify mentally disordered individuals supposedly predisposed to commit dangerous sexual offenses who can be categorized as sexual psychopaths, there have been attempts in recent years to identify appropriate uses of psychiatric expertise in the assessment and treatment of sexually deviant or paraphiliac disorders. The diagnostic criteria for paraphilia have undergone major revisions in recent editions of the Diagnostic and Statistical Manual of Mental Disorders (DSM), and will be discussed below. Additionally, current conceptualizations of countertransferential phenomena will be discussed, as well as new assessment techniques, such as erection measurements, and treatment approaches such as the behavioral and organic. As will be seen, all of these developments have a direct bearing on forensic assessments of sex offenders.

Because of the rapid developments in the assessment and treatment of sex offenders, the ethical dilemmas that occur generally in forensic evaluations are compounded in this area. Ethical issues have been described by Rogers[7] in regard to agency, forensic identification, attitudes towards defendants, and the professional's role in the courtroom. Of particular relevance to the forensic evaluation of the sex offenders is the potential bias of the evaluator due to countertransferential attitudes which may not only incline the clinician to claim psychiatric expertise beyond the limits of existing scientific data and knowledge, but may also prejudice/contaminate the psychiatrist's neutrality (in either a positive or negative stance).

SOME COUNTERTRANSFERENTIAL ISSUES

While systematic research in the area of countertransference issues in forensic practice is relatively in its infancy,[8] a number of authors have contributed to the general discussion. Rappeport[9] writes that "probably the greatest danger that personal bias and an exaggerated response to human behavior will motivate our judgments occurs in the examination of sex offenders accused of actions totally unacceptable to our moral standards" (p 269). Rappeport considers child sexual abuse cases particularly likely to induce such "countertransference reactions," and adds that, because psychiatrists tend to recommend individual psychotherapy for certain compulsive sex offenders who often leave treatment after their cases are settled, confidence of the law in the psychiatrists' professionalism suffers. Gutheil and Appelbaum[10] point out that the personal involvement of the evaluator with certain aspects of the case, whether positively or negatively, could contaminate the evaluator's objectivity. Zonana[11] advises the psychiatrist continually to appraise the transference and countertransference issues as in a psychotherapeutic situation in order not to provide biased opinions beyond the data. Schetky and Colbach[12] discuss potential positive and negative countertransference problems for the forensic expert in the courtroom. They stress that the forensic expert needs to maintain awareness of countertransference problems with their threat to "selfhood" and the potential resulting loss of objectivity. Rada[13] warns about the common countertransferential reactions in the courtroom: overadvocacy in the form of arrogance, reluctance to acknowledge the possibility of error, or histrionic pleading of the position.

Basically, the two principal approaches to conceptualizing countertransference have been elucidated by Kernberg[14] as the "classical" view and the "totalistic" one. The "classical" approach, mostly adhering to the original Freudian[15] concepts, views countertransference as the therapist's unconscious reaction (stemming from the therapist's neurotic conflicts) to the patient's transference. In contrast, the more contemporary "totalistic" approach views countertransference as the entire conscious and unconscious subjective responses of the therapist not merely to the transference, but also to the patient's existence as a real person. This "totalistic" response is not necessarily derived from the therapist's neurotic conflicts, but is a response that most reasonably emotionally adjusted therapists would experience with the same patient in that situation. Therefore, countertransference responses, if adequately understood, can serve as a helpful tool for diagnostic and treatment purposes.

Although Heimann[16,17] was the first psychoanalyst to point out that countertransference can be used as a tool to assist the analyst in understanding the patient,[18] Racker[19] is recognized as the one who wrote most in depth on the subject.[20] Of particular significance is Racker's division of countertransference reactions into two main categories: direct countertransference and indirect countertransference. Direct countertransference is viewed as arising exclusively from the dyadic interaction between patient and therapist. Indirect countertransference, on the other hand, refers to the therapist's emotional responses to a third party outside the dyadic patient-doctor relationship. This third party is often a senior colleague or supervisor, and enormously influences the therapist's reactions to the patient.[20]

In recent years the concept of "dyadic" and variable third party or "triadic" countertransferential responses affecting the assessment and treatment of criminal offenders has been undergoing continual refinement. Travin and Protter[21] have described various factors that contribute to some clinicians' misdiagnosing underlying schizophrenia when there is accompanying antisocial behavior. In particular, the antisocial presentation of the subject in the context of a court setting often evokes a countertransferential "response set," a response which can be understood as closely allied with the "totalistic" view of countertransference. The manipulativeness and exploitiveness of the subject especially elicits emotions of anger and withdrawal in the clinician, who may respond by overlooking or minimizing psychotic features, and retaliate by bestowing on the subject the antisocial label. Protter and Travin[22] then adapted the term "response set" to include four categories of countertransference reactions that may be evoked in the forensic clinician during the psychiatric diagnostic examination, each of which may lead in some cases to a faulty evaluation. First, a "mad-or-bad response set" is indicative of the complex interrelationship of "illness and criminality." As mentioned above, with an antisocial presentation, the examiner may misdiagnose severe underlying psychopathology, such as schizophrenia.[21] Second, a "moralistic-punitive response set" reflects the examiner's attitudes and values about crime and punishment. An extreme moralistic viewpoint may result in a misuse of the evaluator's role for punitive reasons. Third, an "aggression and violence response set" is related to the examiner's difficulty in coping with marked aggressive behavior or, more likely, to fear of such aggression. Fourth, a "periodic negative response set" consists of idiosyncratic negative responses to the subject's primitive mental operations such as splitting and paranoid projections. An awareness of these "response sets" would enable the examiner to exercise better judgment in these cases.

Although these countertransference "response sets" emphasized the reactions that can occur in the one-to-one doctor-patient interaction, the additional and broad range of various third-party or "triadic" factors inherent in the forensic setting, each of which could affect transference and countertransference, had to be carefully considered.[22] In a forensic setting, the subject is obviously not seen in a dyadic arrangement, but rather is examined in a far-from-ideal triadic system of conditions which impinge upon the transaction between examiner and examinee. In this necessarily triadic complex of patient, psychiatrist, and court, such third party influencing issues as confidentiality, double agency, court-ordered examinations, and coercive treatment affect the roles of both examiner and examinee, and shape the nature of the transference and countertransference transaction. Chrzanowski[23] views the transference-countertransference phenomenon in psychoanalytic therapy as a transactional process in which "transference and countertransference are reciprocal and interlocking" (p 458). He observes that transference-countertransference patterns are usually modified by life's circumstances, that is, by each individual's particular ecosystem, including the individual's specific social and economic class, culture, family, politics, religion, and life experience. Chrzanowski believes that the emerging transference-countertransference patterns demonstrate "triadic transactional occurrences...In this way the me-you pattern recedes, with alluded-to third parties complicating the communicative field...triadic interferences define the nature of the particular mental disorder as well as the emergence of undistorted relational aspects..." (p 466). Although "instantaneous transference," according to Chrzanowski, may indicate severe psychopathology in the patient, "instantaneous countertransference" should warn the therapist that he or she is coming into the particular system of the patient, which may adversely influence clinical judgment. The potential to develop immediate countertransference, negative or positive, has particular relevance in the evaluation of sex offenders in forensic settings, as this context is replete with a multitude of variables sufficient to evoke both "dyadic response sets" and what may be called "triadic response sets."[24]

"Triadic response sets" are conceptualized as countertransferential reactions to a multitude of third-party or triadic factors that exist in the forensic examination. In the contemporary understanding of countertransference, triadic factors are seen as containing realistic aspects which affect the transference-countertransference interaction, even if both examiner and examinee remain unaware of the influence such aspects are exerting on the examination. Clarification of these intrusive triadic factors serves to make the examiner more sensitive to how these factors can influence the decision-making process.[25] For heuristic purposes, triadic factors have been expanded to include the broad range of the contextual as well as more ideational variables. Triadic factors may be subsumed under three major headings: theory, sociopolitical, and values.

Earlier certainty about a theoretical approach has given way in recent years to a more pluralistic outlook on the etiology and treatment of mental disorders. Since the way one diagnoses and treats psychopathology is based upon one's theoretical orientation, if one believes in one and only one theoretical system, and therefore insists that the patient conform to the one theory alone, and denies other possible interpretive perspectives, this constructing feature comprises a kind of—and significant—triadic factor. Sociopolitical factors, in the context of a forensic setting, refer to the complex arrangement imposed upon examiner and examinee. As mentioned above, issues of confidentiality, double agency, court-ordered evaluations, and coerced treatment serve as intruding triadic factors. "Values" is probably the most inclusive (and elusive) term of the three categories of triadic factors, not only because one's values comprise a strong preferential stance, but also because the term "value" can be and has been used in so many different ways. Drane[26] writes that in a broad, generic sense, "values" refers to "all the phenomena traditionally discussed in ethical treatises: rightness, obligation, duty, virtue, ideals, goals and norms of behavior..." (p 46). Howard[27] describes the term "as a catchall category for an enormous array of very different judgments, decisions, preferences, and orientations" (p 255). Clearly the examiner's values can influence his or her decision making, and failure to become aware of this may be operative in an intrusive, triadic way. Certainly "dyadic" and "triadic response sets" are not discrete entities; rather, they overlap on a continuum of third-party involvement.[24] It bears repeating that although we have stressed "real" factors that are probably amenable to clarification, though not necessarily to resolution, the "unrealistic" neurotic aspects of countertransferential reactions are, of course, also in operation. Even though these neurotic aspects are not readily accessible, it surely behooves the forensic clinician to monitor his subjective reactions when evaluating sex offenders.

During the psychiatric interview of the sex offender, variable combinations of dyadic and triadic countertransferential response sets may be evoked in the examiner. Depending on the specific legal circumstances and the context of the interview, the sex offender will likely withhold what he believes could be damaging information. When the examiner asks probing questions, the subject may respond by vehemently denying or minimizing the deviant behavior, by claiming consideration because he or she was sexually abused as a child and is thus a victim, or by flatly rejecting responsibility for any wrongdoing or, indeed, the idea that any harm had been done to the putative victim. The subject's self-serving protestations have both conscious and unconscious derivatives. The subject's flat rejection of the possibility that he or she has done anything wrong, or that any harm has occurred, for example, may result from and reflect the subject's cognitive distortions. But such reactions, given the medicolegal context, also appear to have elements of malingering in the subject's denial of deviant behavior and feigning of normative behavior. Malingering and "malingering-like" phenomena have been reconceptualized by Travin and Protter[28] along a continuum of the subject's conscious self-awareness into three overlapping categories: "other-deceptive," "mixed-deceptive," and "self-deceptive."

The "other-deceptive" category refers to individuals who are substantially aware of deceiving; the mixed-deceivers category refers to individuals who have some awareness of deceiving others, but are also deceiving themselves; and the self-deceivers category refers to individuals who are almost completely deceiving themselves.

The examiner's "total" subjective reaction is evoked by the varying contributions of the dyadic and triadic factors in a number of ways. First, the examiner's response to the presentation of malingering may take the form of countertransferential reaction, such as the dyadic "mad-or-bad response set," or the "moralistic-punitive response set." In this situation, the examiner may angrily or punitively label the subject antisocial. Second, the examiner may respond to the subject's vehement denials and minimization in countertransferential dyadic/triadic response sets by beginning to question whether the documented behavior is really accurate. The examiner then may experience doubts as to his/her ability to provide a competent evaluation, and may withdraw from the case. Third, the examiner may respond to the gross cognitive distortions of the sex offender with a combination of dyadic/triadic response sets, so that, failing to recognize the extreme variations of cognitive distortions, the examiner may diagnose these faulty beliefs as irrational. Fourth, the examiner may respond in a countertransferential triadic response set by recommending a particular treatment approach according to his/her own theoretical biases. Fifth, the examiner's response to the sex offender's claim of personal victimization can take the form of a countertransferential reaction that taps into and stems from the examiner's own inner conflicts. This may lead the examiner to minimize the offender's risk of further sexual offense and stress the offender's need to receive treatment in the community.

Diagnostic Issues with Sex Offenders

The complexities of the issues involved in diagnosing sex offenders in a forensic setting serve to intensify the impact of congruent dyadic and triadic factors in the forensic examination. Because techniques for the assessment and treatment of sex offenders are in relatively underdeveloped stages, forensic evaluations necessarily reflect the personal biases and values of the examiner. The very vocabulary necessarily invoked in these evaluations is subject to extreme variations of meaning; such terms as "child molester" and "dangerousness" are inherently ambiguous, and this ambiguity has attended their use in this literature,[29] while the seemingly more "scientific" term "pedophilia" is used (both in the literature and in practice) idiosyncratically: it has been defined variously in the narrowest and in the most inclusive ways possible.[30] Even the diagnostic criteria for sexual deviation or "paraphilia" delineated in DSM-III-R pose some diagnostic dilemmas for the clinician which will be discussed below. In general, Reich[31] views psychiatric diagnoses as presenting ethical problems to the clinician because psychiatric diagnoses are susceptible to misuse. This misuse, in some instances, can be purposeful, but in most cases it is caused by three main nonpurposeful reasons: "the inherent limitations of the diagnostic process, the power of diagnostic theory to shape psychiatric vision, and the beauty of diagnosis as a solution to human problems," for "explanation, mitigation, and exculpation purposes," for "reassurance," for "humane transformation of social deviance into medical illness," for "exclusion and dehumanization," for "self-confirming hypothesis," and for "discreditation and punishment" (pp 63–82). These diagnostic perils become all the more problematic in a forensic setting where, as Ciccone and Barry[32] have pointed out, "diagnostic labels in and of themselves often have an effect on the decisions made by the legal system" (p 24).

The bestowal of the diagnostic label "paraphiliac" disorder, or, more specifically, "pedophilia" or other sexual deviancy, on someone who has committed an unlawful sexual offense, raises the question of whether, in fact, we are not medicalizing criminal behavior. Medical history offers many examples of this phenomenon in which socially condemned and/or morally reprehensible behavior has been transformed via value-laden diagnoses into a disease entity. Such was the case with masturbation in the 18th and 19th centuries.[33] In the evaluation and treatment of sex offenders, these problems of definition and labeling converge and complicate one another. For example, in 1987, in a multidisciplinary approach to rape investigation, Lanning[34] underscored the point that not all child molesters prefer children over adults as sex partners, although this preference was the key criterion for the diagnosis of pedophilia in the DSM-III[35] then in use. Lanning proposed a model of child molestation for use in law enforcement that distinguished between situational and preferential offenders, a model he based upon two different authorities, Groth[36] and Dietz.[37] Groth[36] had classified sex offenders into a pedophile-fixated type and a pedophile-regressed type, and defined the latter type as sex offenders who, under stressful situations, merely substituted children for adults. Dietz[37] had noted that some individuals engage in single acts of sexual crimes because of a variety of situational factors, such as intoxication or stressful circumstances. Dietz therefore differentiated between paraphiliac and nonparaphiliac offenders, a distinction that could fit in with Groth's categories of preferential and situational sex offenders. Dietz offers the example of "baby-sitters who molest the children in their care," and asserts that, while some of these baby-sitters "will have a lifelong preference for sexual contact with children (pedophilia)," other of these individuals have "no particular interest in such activity, [but] exploit the opportunity to do something different and forbidden" (p 1490).

The standardized criteria used to diagnose sexually deviant behavior has undergone a series of revisions through subsequent editions of the American Psychiatric Association's *Diagnostic and Statistical Manual of Mental Disorders*. In DSM-I,[38] sexual deviations were listed under "sociopathic personality disturbance"; in DSM-II[39] they were listed under "personality disorder and certain other nonpsychotic mental disorders" and were essentially described as symptomatic expressions of underlying personality pathology. In DSM-III,[35] the term "paraphilia is introduced and placed under the general category of "psychosexual disorders," independent of personality-disorder considerations. According to DSM-III, the essential feature of paraphiliac behavior is its repeated or preferred nature. Among the paraphiliac disorders, the diagnostic criteria for pedophilia is "the act or fantasy of engaging in sexual activity with prepubertal children is a repeatedly preferred or exclusive method of achieving sexual excitement" (p 271–272). In the most recent, revised edition of the DSM-III-R,[40] the emphasis on repetition as a diagnostic criterion has been buttressed by a criterion of duration: DSM-III-R cites the diagnostic criteria for pedophilia as follows: "Over a period of six months, recurrent intense sexual urges and sexually arousing fantasies involving sexual activity with a prepubescent child or children (generally age 13 or younger). The person has acted on these urges, or is markedly distressed by them" (p 285).

Despite the gradual development in the conceptualization and definition of paraphiliac disorder reflected in the DSM editions, the current DSM-III-R diagnostic criteria for paraphiliac disorder remain somewhat problematic for the mental health clinician. Especially troublesome are the references made to "recurrent intense sexual urges and sexually arousing fantasies," and the stricture that "the person has acted on these urges or is markedly distressed by them," since clinical experience has shown that sex offenders tend to deny or minimize the extent of their deviant sexual behavior. Moreover, as Abel *et al.*[41] have pointed out, denial is sex offenders' "most commonly used defense: conscious or unconscious" (p 298). So as to ensure their outpatient sex offenders of confidentiality, and thus enable their treatment, Abel *et al.*[41] obtained a Certificate of Confidentiality from the federal government ensuring the confidentiality of these patients.

Only then were these investigators able to elicit a true picture of the paraphiliacs' unlawful sexual behavior, which turned out to be considerably more than previously acknowledged. Based on the self-reports of 561 men who were assured of confidentiality under this federal certificate, Abel *et al.*[41] found that the majority could engage in sexual activities with adult partners without relying on deviant sexual fantasies, that paraphiliac and nonparaphiliac behavior occurred in most of the men, that multiple paraphilias existed in the same individual, and that the occurrence of only one paraphilia was rare. These investigators attributed their success in eliciting this information to three things: they concluded that: (1) the amount of time—up to five hours—spent per case, enhanced the possibility of establishing rapport; (2) the specificity of their questions pertaining to participating in each paraphiliac behavior resulted in usefully detailed answers; and (3) the assurance of maintaining confidentiality the Certificate provided their patients was crucial to their ability to obtain the information essential to their treatment and study of these patients.

In view of the difficulties inherent in obtaining information from sex offenders about their fantasies, it is worth noting that questions have been raised about the significance of deviant sexual fantasies. Conte,[42] for example, questions both the actual prevalence of such fantasies among sex offenders, and the significance of such fantasies; he challenges the assumption that these fantasies are more common among offenders than among "normals." Such questions can only be answered by further research; but the needed research will inevitably be bedeviled by the sex offenders' fundamental and undoubtedly complex resistance to acknowledging such fantasies. In five years of involvement in the assessment and treatment of sex offenders in a court clinic, we have found that, even in the postconviction stage, when the issue of innocence or guilt has already been settled, most offenders would not disclose the extent of their deviant fantasies or urges until well into the treatment phase. Therefore, in using DSM-III-R, most sex offenders seen on initial examination would not seem to meet the diagnostic criteria of paraphilia cited in the DSM-III-R. How, then, should we proceed with court-referred treatment cases when the individual has a documented history of repeated sexual offenses over an extended period of time, but initially denies or minimizes these deviant activities and does not admit to having any fantasies or urges whatsoever?

One strategy that has proved effective in bringing these patients to acknowledge having engaged in deviant sexual behavior—confronting these deniers with the results of their erection measurement studies—will be discussed below. For now, the significant point of such a confrontation lies in the fact that an admission of deviant sexual behavior is not necessarily an admission of its true extent or of its repetitive nature, much less of fantasies, urges, and preferences. Obviously, if the patient denies or minimizes the repetitive nature of his deviant sexual behavior, he will certainly not provide details of fantasies and urges. In our experience, these patients generally move slowly from an acknowledgement of behavior (frequently brought about by confronting the patient with their erection measurement studies), to an acknowledgement of repetitive behavior, and only later on in the course of treatment (if at all) acknowledge and provide details about fantasies and urges. This is probably because behavior, even repetitive behavior, can be subject to cognitive distortions ("I was drunk," "I was high," and so on), whereas fantasies and urges go beyond the patient's ability to mask or minimize via cognitive distortion. The admission of urges and fantasies constitutes the patient's confrontation with his own problems, and forces the patient to acknowledge some degree of responsibility for his behavior; this admission is essential to treatment; it is also, as has been pointed out, a criterion for diagnosis; and finally, neither this admission, nor, for that matter, an acknowledgement of the repetitive pattern of deviant sexual behavior, are likely to emerge in the initial examination during which the clinician must arrive at a diagnostic decision. Thus the psychiatrist is confronted with a dilemma that is at once medical, legal, and ethical, for these clinical appraisals, as can readily be appreciated, are subject to personal bias, a danger compounded by the enormous ethical implications inherent in recommending continuation of assessment and then treatment for an offender population, a population whose very ability to give informed consent is constrained by the circumstances of their legal status, and thus a population for whom denial makes legal as well as psychological sense.

A medical/psychiatric model does exist, however, for the assessment and treatment of repetitive behaviors (i.e., alcoholism) regardless of the patient's denial.[43] At present, this model seems to provide a workable approach to the assessment and treatment of sex offenders. If it is our best clinical judgment (based on the documented repetitive nature of the patient's deviant sexual acts) that this pattern of behavior exists, we regard these sex offenders as having a probable diagnosis of paraphilia that in our experience will likely be confirmed later on in the assessment and treatment phases. This treatment model enables us to assess the repetitive behavior of these patients as other repetitive behaviors (again, such as alcoholism) are assessed, and allows us to recommend and provide the treatment that alone can confirm the diagnosis as it enables the patient to move from denial to acknowledgment and confrontation, and potentially toward control of his deviant sexual impulses.

Typology Considerations for Sex Offenders

Although sex offenders are recognized as being a heterogeneous group, efforts to find certain common characteristics have been pursued.[44,45] The question of whether there are identifiable characterological traits has generated considerable discussion. Swanson[46] emphasized the need to consider contributory life events rather than concentrate on a particular personality structure. Quincey[29] wrote that "the selection of a child as a sexual object is not necessarily a reflection of some enduring character trait or disposition on the part of the offender" (p 205).

In a study of cases of paraphilia associated with mild character pathology, Schmidt *et al.*[47] concluded that (1) "sexually deviant behavior is performed by individuals of varied personality types"; (2) "the severity of the personality disorders (or character pathology) varies from one case to the next"; (3) "the frequency of sexually deviant acts is not a function of the severity of character pathology"; and (4) that "patients with very different personalities appear to use their deviant behaviors for a similar purpose" (p 285). Similarly, Conte[42] has argued that "there is no currently verified profile of the typical adult who sexually abuses children. Indeed, all available information suggests that there is considerable variation in the characteristics..." (p 345)

Recent reviews on the limitations of the Minnesota Multiphasic Personality Inventory (MMPI) in the assessment of sex offenders have appeared in the literature. Levin and Stava[48] argue that the MMPI seems better fitted to measure types of psychopathology than to be used as a personality test. Hall *et al.*,[49] in reexamining the utility of the MMPI to describe child molesters, found that "no single 2-point MMPI code type as predominant, and two-thirds of the sample had more than two MMPI scale elevations" (p 493). These findings indicated that sex offenders are an even more heterogeneous group than previously believed.[49] Furthermore, the MMPI is of limited value in differentiating patterns in this population. Interestingly, the Supreme Court of New Jersey affirmed a trial court's ruling that expert testimony claiming the defendant lacked the psychological traits of a rapist was scientifically unreliable and therefore inadmissible.[50]

Recently, attempts have been made to create taxonomic systems for classifying sex offenders, especially rapists and child molesters, using both rational and empirical strategies in complementary ways.[51] Much of this research is done at the Massachusetts Treatment Center for Sexually Dangerous Persons in Bridgewater, Massachusetts. Prentky *et al.*[52] stated that "the general purpose of this taxonomy is to reduce heterogeneity through the development of discrete, coherent subgroups" (p 43). The taxonomy of rapists is derived from Cohen *et al.*'s[53] original typology of four kinds of rapists that are differentiated by the relative motives of sexuality and aggression in the offender. They are the rapist-displaced-aggression type, the rapist-compensatory type, the rapist-sex-aggression-defusion type,and the rapist-impulse type. Prentky *et al.*[52] constructed a decision tree for subtyping rapists along three dimensions: (1) "meaning of the aggression in the offense"—instrumental (not more than necessary to force compliance) or expressive (to hurt or humiliate the victim);

(2) "meaning of sexuality in the offense"—compensatory, exploitative, displaced anger, and sadistic; and (3) "impulsivity in history and life-style"—high or low (p 46). The result was a breakdown of rapists into eight subtypes which "corresponded to offenders we had worked with who possessed the specific characteristics of the particular subtype" (p 45). However, this taxonomic system for rapists has been undergoing validation analyses and only tentative conclusions about a revised system are available.[54] Knight[55] has also started to construct a taxonomic scheme for child molesters and, citing Cohen *et al.*'s[56] model of four types of child molesters as his starting point—the fixated type, the regressed type, the exploitative type, and the aggressive or sadistic type, Knight[55] concludes that there is a "need to develop multiple typologies..." because "it is unlikely that any one typology is going to be adequate for all purposes—etiology, treatment, prognosis—and only a multitude of perspectives is going to help explain the extremely complex problem of child molesting" (p 19).

Brief Review of Specialized Assessment Techniques

Basically, specialized techniques for the assessment of sex offenders can be divided into two main categories: self-reports and physiological methods. Because self-reports depend upon the truthfulness of sex offenders, continuous efforts to develop physiological methods to obtain objective data are being made. Despite some progress, this goal has been difficult to attain. Essentially, both the self-report and physiological methods have such serious limitations that neither should be used as the sole instrument of assessment.

Self-reports, in addition to what the subject discloses to the examiner in the interview, essentially involve scales, questionnaires, and inventories to be completed by the individual and then scored by a rater. Conte[57] describes one class of self-reports as containing unidimensional scales that are short and restricted in the information obtained and another class of self-reports that consist of multidimensional inventories or questionnaires useful in the evaluation of sex offenders. Among the self-report instruments described by Conte were the Sex Inventory (SI)[58] used for the screening of sex offenders, the Clarke Sex History Questionnaire for Males (SHQ)[59] for the evaluation of deviant sexual behavior in males, and the Derogatis Sexual Functioning Inventory (DSFI)[60] that provides information in a number of sexual areas of functioning. Conte[57] believes that, despite some limitations in each of the reviewed scales and inventories, "a good beginning has been made in the development of instruments for assessing sexual functioning" (p 574). In the Bronx-Lebanon Hospital Sex Offender Treatment Program, the self-report instruments that we use include a Sexual Interest Card-sort to assess the individual's sexual arousal to specific categories and a Pedophile Cognition Scale to elicit the subject's cognitive distortions, both of which instruments were developed by Abel and Becker; an Assault Knowledge Inventory, which is comprised of seven different attitude scales, including the rape myth acceptance scale developed by Burt,[61,62] Adult Self-Expression Scale,[63] which is a measure of assertiveness, and the Minnesota Multiphasic Personality Inventory (MMPI).

Physiological methods for the assessment of sex offenders may also be considered to be at the beginning stages of development. Plasma testosterone levels were investigated in 52 rapists and 12 child molesters by Rada *et al.*,[64] who found that the testosterone levels of the rapists and child molesters were within normal ranges. Higher mean testosterone levels occurred among the violent rapists and the highest testosterone level (1236 ng/100 ml) was found in the only offender (a rapist) who had murdered his victim. In another study, Rada *et al.*[65] found that rapists had higher testosterone levels than child molesters and control subjects, that violent and nonviolent rapists had about the same testosterone levels, and that violent child molesters had the highest testosterone levels of the three groups. Rada[66] has concluded that "our knowledge of the effects of androgen hormones on the forms of sexual expression and on the commission of aggressive acts remains rudimentary" (p 463).

Physiological measures of sexual arousal in humans have been reviewed in great detail by Zuckerman,[67] who concluded that such physiological measures as heart rate, blood pressure, electrodermal measures, catecholamines, and pupillary dilation were not considered to be specific responses to sexual arousal. Only measurements of penile erection were found to be useful as specific indexes of male sexual arousal. Bancroft and Mathews[68] have also concluded that only penile measurements differentiated between sexual and nonsexual stimuli, and in a pattern specific to the individual.

In a comprehensive book in the field, entitled *Patterns of Sexual Arousal: Psychophysiological Processes and Clinical Applications*, Rosen and Beck[69] have pointed out that "the concept of a chain of sexual response components, leading up to and including genital arousal and overt behavior" (p 215) was first emphasized by Barlow.[70,71] Although Barlow's model includes three postulated components—"(1) deviant sexual arousal; (2) heterosexual skills deficits; and (3) deviations in gender role" (p 215)—the focus of laboratory studies has consistently been on the evaluation of deviant sexual arousal. A major criticism of this research has been directed at the assumption of a relationship between the finding of deviant sexual arousal in the laboratory and its generalizability to outside aberrant sexual behavior. Laws,[72] for example, has argued that deviant sexual arousal patterns can describe only the quality of the offending, but cannot be used in a quantitative manner to predict the probability of unlawful sexual behavior. Another weakness of the Barlow "chain" of deviant behavior, according to Rosen and Beck,[69] is the assumption that deviant sexual arousal is of equal importance in the diagnosis of all forms of paraphiliac disorder. But this does not appear to be true. For example, clinical studies have indicated that deviant sexual arousal is less of a critical factor in the motivation of exhibitionists than of child molesters.[73,74] Additionally, Langevin *et al.*[73] have found that the laboratory erection measurements of exhibitionists could not be distinguished from those of "normal" controls except for the exhibitionists' responses to peeping and outdoor masturbation. Importantly, Rosen and Beck[69] also point out that many normal males without a known history of paraphiliac behavior have shown positive erectile responses to deviant stimuli in the laboratory.[75,76]

The potential use and abuse of erection measurement studies in the legal context was the subject of research by Travin *et al.*[77] These investigators reviewed the results of erection measurements of 185 subjects who were referred to the Forensic Psychiatry Clinic by probation, parole, or child protective agencies for evaluation of their suitability for being treated for paraphiliac disorder. The evaluations were performed in the presentence or postconviction stage, when the question of innocence or guilt had already been decided. The results of the study could be categorized into six groupings: Group (1) consisted of 73 subjects (39.5% of the entire sample) who admitted to paraphiliac disorder and showed deviant arousal; group (2) consisted of only five subjects (2.5% who admitted to the paraphiliac disorder but showed no deviant arousal; group (3) consisted of 35 subjects (19%) who initially denied a paraphiliac disorder and continued to do so even after confrontation with their laboratory results; group (4) consisted of 12 subjects (6.5%) who denied a paraphiliac disorder throughout the assessment and showed no deviant arousal; group (5) consisted of 59 subjects (32%) who at first denied the deviant behavior, but when confronted with their positive laboratory findings acknowledged the deviant behavior. Group (6) consisted of only one subject who initially denied a paraphiliac disorder, did not show deviant arousal, but acknowledged the deviant behavior. The results of this study support the efficacy of erection measurements in the treatment context, but emphasize the care that must be exerted in using these measurements since "the occurrence of both false-positive and false-negative results in the data obtained at a time when secondary gain is greatly reduced suggests that there is a heightened potential for an increased number of false-positive and false-negative results, as well as incidence of response faking, in the critical trial phase. Thus the major potential for abuse of erection measurements would be its use as evidence for conclusionary purposes" (p 248). Finally, the authors reiterated their finding that a significant number of subjects continued to deny their deviant behavior, and only acknowledged it when confronted with their positive laboratory findings. This indicates the pitfall of accepting the initial denials of sex offenders.

SOME TREATMENT CONSIDERATIONS

In order to make appropriate treatment recommendations, the forensic psychiatrist should be informed about the various approaches to the treatment of paraphiliac disorders, about the recent data on treatment outcomes, and about the availability of treatment facilities. Although treatment may be conceptualized as falling into three main categories—the psychodynamic (including individual[78] and group[79]), the organic,[80] and the behavioral,[81]—the treatment of choice for any subject may involve varying combinations of these treatments; thus every treatment recommendation must have its origin in a careful evaluation of the patient. But treatment decisions must also be realistic; they must be informed by the availability of treatment facilities.

In a comprehensive survey of treatment programs for sex offenders in

North America, Borzecki and Wormith[82] found that in America the predominant theoretical orientation was toward psychodynamic rather than behavioral treatment, whereas in Canada the reverse is true.They also found that the dominant model of treatment was group psychotherapy in America. The treatment programs they examined in this study were generally located within correctional institutions, though the institutions offered both resident and outpatient services. Borzecki and Wormith were dismayed at the scarcity of treatment programs: of the 31 states that provided them with information, only 21 states had any sex offender programs, and no reliable outcome data was available for the existing programs.

In regard to group psychotherapy of sex offenders in the community, the original, optimistic results of a two-year outcome study by Peters and Roether[79] (of treated probationers, only 3% were rearrested (1% for sex crimes), in contrast to a 27% rearrest rate (8% for sex crimes) in a group of untreated probationers), were revised in a later study. In 1966, Peters found that the rearrest rates of probationed sex offenders in the two-to-three years following treatment was approximately 10%, which was about the same as that of a nontreated control group of probationers.[83] Similarly, in a 10-year follow-up study of convicted pedophiles, exhibitionists, and sexual assaulters randomly assigned either to psychotherapy or to intensive probation supervision, Romero and Williams[83] found that there was no difference in the recidivism rate between the two probationed groups, and that the best predictor for recidivism after treatment was the individual's arrest rate for sex offenses prior to treatment. Romero and Williams caution, however, that it is difficult to interpret these findings because it is possible that group psychotherapy may have a genuine and positive affect on the rate of subsequent sex offenses that is obscured by extensive undetected crimes. On the other hand, Giarretto *et al.*,[84] working only with the families and perpetrators of incest who are involved in the criminal justice system (including self-help programs), have reported no recidivism in their experiences with more than 600 families since 1971. It should be noted, however, that their results relied to a great extent on self-report.

Organic treatments for male sexual offenders have been divided by Bradford[80] into three main groups: antiandrogens or other hormonal agents, surgical castration, and stereotoxic neurosurgery. Since stereotoxic neurosurgery is only of academic interest, and surgical castration is important only because of its reference to the actions of the hormonal system, antiandrogens and other hormonal agents comprise the organic treatment of primary concern.

Because the Food and Drug Administration (FDA) did not approve cyproterone acetate (CPA) for behavioral research, Money, Migeon, and Rivarola began experimenting with medroxyprogesterone acetate (MPA, Depo-Provera).[85] DepoProvera, a synthetic progesterone manufactured by the Upjohn Pharmaceutical Company, has already been used for a variety of female disorders. MPA decreases the level of testosterone in the plasma, primarily by the induction of testosterone-A-reductase in the liver, but also by affecting its production rate, and accelerating its clearance rate. MPA also has an antigonadotropic effect, and competes with androgens at androgen receptors.[86] MPA has become the drug most frequently used for the experimental treatment of paraphiliac disorders in the United States.[87] Its side effects include weight gain, hypertension, mild lethargy, leg cramps, hyperglycemia, hypogonadism, and, in high doses, it has been shown to produce breast cancer in female beagle dogs. It must be administered intramuscularly in order to produce, usually within one to three weeks of treatment, the intended effect, which is to reduce the plasma testosterone level, which is correlated with a reduction in the sexual drive in general, but not in the alteration of the direction of the drive. The major drawback of MPA is that within seven to ten days after the cessation of the drug, libido, erectile, and ejaculatory capacity begin to return along with the same deviant urges. Also, in 1981, Berlin and Meinecke[87] reported that 15%, or 3 out of 20 paraphiliac patients, experienced a return of sexually deviant behavior *while* taking medication. One of these cases was connected to alcohol usage. Moreover, of the 11 patients who dropped out of the treatment program, 10 suffered relapses. Clearly, further research into the appropriate uses, and into both the short-term and long-term adverse effects of MDA is indicated.

Behavioral treatment of paraphiliac disorders have been developing despite the lack of satisfactory foundations. As Rosen and Beck[69] note, "although conditioning processes are seldom viewed as a sufficient explanation for the acquisition of paraphiliac arousal, both classical and instrumental conditioning procedures have been widely used in the application of behavioral approaches to treatment" (p 218). Earls and Quinsey[88] have also noted that the development of procedures to assess the individual's behavioral functioning in such areas as social skills and assertiveness skills, as well as in the measurement of certain attitudes or in the identification of cognitive distortions, has not been demonstrated empirically to be needed. There is no scientific basis for assuming that sex offenders have these kinds of behavioral, attitudinal, or cognitive deficits. Earls and Quinsey add that "it is possible that we have already identified the only distinguishing characteristic of sexual offenders, i.e., their inappropriate sexual arousal..." (p 380). Yet, in their comprehensive survey of research on the treatment of paraphiliacs and its outcome, Kilmann *et al*,[89] have concluded that, despite the fact that no single theory has emerged to explain adequately the development of paraphiliac disorder, and that no one type of treatment is clearly superior to another, "the overall findings offer tentative evidence for the efficacy of the behavioral treatment approaches to reduce or eliminate the occurrence of paraphiliac sexual behavior and to foster appropriate, non-variant sexual behavior when relevant.... A comprehensive, multimodal treatment program seemed to be essential in preventing or reducing recidivism" (p 218). Given this situation, many behaviorally oriented centers where sexual offenders are treated have essentially incorporated a variety of key elements into integrated treatment programs.[81,90,91] Abel *et al*,[91] in their treatment paradigm for sexual aggressors, have included such elements as decreasing deviant sexual arousal through covert sensitization and masturbatory satiation, developing adequate heterosexual arousal, heterosocial skills training, assertiveness skills training, empathy skills training, sexual knowledge, and treating sexual dysfunction. Each sex offender is assessed in these areas so as to determine treatment needs.

Abel and Becker have since refined the paradigm that they used at the Psychiatric Institute in New York. Their revised paradigm emphasizes six major components: (1) masturbatory satiation; (2) covert sensitization (both of which are self-control techniques); (3) cognitive restructuring to correct fault belief systems; (4) sex education; (5) social skills training; and (6) assertiveness training. This cognitive-behavioral paradigm is essentially the one we have adopted as the core component of the Sex Offender Treatment Program at the Forensic Psychiatry Clinic at Bronx-Lebanon Hospital Center.[92] In addition, we employ a focused psychodynamic component in selected cases, which is consistent with the current emphasis in psychiatric treatment on brief dynamic psychotherapy focussed on a particular symptomatology.[93]

Recently, two outcome studies on the treatment of child molesters in outpatient treatment programs have been published. Abel *et al.*,[94] in a study of 192 pedophiles in such treatment programs, have identified three significant factors that characterize the 67 pedophiles (34.9%) who dropped out of treatment: "(1) the [great] amount of pressure the subject was under to participate in treatment; (2) the diagnosis of an antisocial personality; and (3) the lack of discrimination in the choice of sexual victim or paraphiliac act" (p 226). In contrast to Abel *et al.*,[94] we have found that patients who stay in treatment tend to be those who have had both external (court-ordered) motives and internal motives, i.e., a personal commitment to receive the benefits of treatment.[95] Significantly, we also found that incest offenders who were internally motivated to be treated, but were not subject to external motivating factors—those, for example, who were not under the coercion or threat of criminal sanctions—dropped out of treatment at a higher rate than patients who had similar internal motivation to be treated but also had external (court-ordered) motivations. In regard to treatment outcome, Abel *et al.*[94] found that of 98 subjects who were evaluated one year after treatment, 12 had recidivated. The only demographic characteristic that distinguished these recidivists was that, in general, they were divorced or single rather than married or separated but not divorced, as were the nonrecidivists. Recidivists were also less likely to have approved of the treatment goals of the program, and were more likely to have had multiple pedophiliac behaviors and targets. In a compilation of data from multiple sources, Marshall and Barbaree[96] found that the overall recidivism rate among 64 treated child molesters after an average follow-up period of 44.31 months was 14%, whereas the recidivism among 53 untreated patients, after an average follow-up period of 42.13 months, was 32%.

CONCLUSION

In general, the forensic psychiatrist may evaluate a sex offender as he or she would evaluate any other criminal offender, in order to provide an expert opinion to a legal question such as whether or not an offender has the mental capacity to stand trial. In making decisions such as these, the countertransferential issues we have discussed may be of paramount importance, as they have the potential to interfere with the neutrality of the forensic examination. But it is in the context of making treatment recommendations, particularly in the presentence phase after the determination of innocence or guilt has been made, that the forensic psychiatrist must bring to bear all of his or her special expertise on sex offender cases. The forensic psychiatrist must be sensitive to the operation of dyadic and triadic countertransferential response sets, and must continually update his or her knowledge on the whole array of issues that pose particular dilemmas to forensic clinicians—issues including diagnostic criteria, typology, specialized assessment techniques, treatment methodologies, and outcome studies. The basic uncertainties that pervade the assessment and treatment of sexual offenders must be taken into consideration.

Currently, there are no standardized protocols for the assessment (as well as for the treatment) of sex offenders, which could form an irrefutable basis for making treatment recommendations. Generally, the various paradigms for the assessment of sex offenders combine a variety of techniques, both general and specialized. McGovern and Peters[97] have developed guidelines for evaluating child-molester offenders in Portland, Oregon. These guidelines instruct the clinician to review police and social service reports, to interview victims and witnesses, to obtain a complete psychosocial history and family background, to assess the offender's acknowledgment of responsibility, and psychological tests (such as the MMPI), and to perform penile plethysmograph and polygraph tests. Finally, there is a risk-assessment phase which uses their P and M scale. This involves the collection of the data in four categories which are then scored, and this score is used to predict the potential of these offenders for successful treatment in a community-based setting. This issue of predicting dangerousness is, of course, extremely pressing. Though erectile measurements should not be used as the sole assessment instrument, attempts have been made to use erectile measurements as an indicator that at least suggests the possibility of dangerous sexual behavior. Abel *et al.*[98] have developed a Pedophile Aggression Index (PAI) and Avery-Clark[99] *et al.* have devised a Dangerous Child Abuse Index (DCAI); both represent attempts to assist in the prediction of violent sexual behavior among child molesters. Basically, both these indexes involve dividing mean erectile responses to audiotaped cues by mean erectile responses to consenting cues to arrive at numerical values used to categorize levels of violence. These index computations have thus far not been consistently replicated.

In regard to the admissibility of scientific evidence into a courtroom, Curran[100] has highlighted some significant points. He writes that "the liberal and open acceptance of 'expert' testimony and opinion is in direct contrast to a very strict attitude toward accepting scientific proof based on tests and technical procedures" (p 1280), and goes on to note that "the liberality of the expert opinion rules escorts much scientific data into court on the coattails of the highly respected authority" (p 1281). Curran points out, however, that many innovative techniques used in forensic science may not be admitted as evidence, despite the prestige of the expert witness. The polygraph, which is one of the most frequently attacked specialized techniques, is a case in point. Because of the potential for faking, and of the still-unsubstantiated validity of the erection measurement technology, penile erection studies should never be used as the sole criteria for making treatment decisions to the court. In addition, the assessment of sex offenders by penile erection studies raises the issue of coercion. This is the reason why, even if the incarcerated offender is willing to undergo penile plethysmographic studies as part of his presentence evaluation, the Institutional Review Board (IRB) at our hospital center forbids its use for this purpose. Incarcerated offenders could not be expected to give voluntary consent.

The ethical dimensions in making treatment recommendations are enormous. This is not only because of the continuing uncertainties about the assessment and treatment technologies, but also due to the coercive ways in which they are carried out. Treatment as a condition of probation or parole is frequently mandated by the courts and parole boards. Halleck[101] has discussed some of the ethical problems in treating patients who consent to treatment under duress. Because treatment could benefit many patients in prisons or hospitals, Halleck doesn't categorically disapprove of consent under pressure. He does, however, recommend that certain rules be followed. "First, the patient should be given a clear explanation of the possible consequences of treatment. Second, the patient should be told what other treatments are available and he should be given an opportunity to choose among them...Third, no special punishment should be imposed on the patient if he refuses treatment...Fourth, the treatment to which the patient consents under direct threat of sanction, like treatment imposed upon a nonconsenting patient, should be reviewed and approved by a committee..." (p 384). Because of the uncertainties of these assessment and treatment technologies, and because of the coercion factor, one solution to the ethical dilemmas posed by court-ordered examination reports is for the clinician to outline the various approaches to treatment that are available in addition to recommending the specific treatment he or she believes most appropriate. The clinician should resist the countertransferential tendency to overadvocate by recommending that the patient be treated in a community-based setting; decision about treatment setting should be left to the court. Unfortunately, the reality is that there are very few treatment facilities in or out of prison; so the clinician is frequently faced with the fact that, if imprisoned, the offender will not receive appropriate treatment.

In cases in which the judicial decision has been made to release the prisoner to the community with the condition that he receive treatment for his unlawful sexual behavior, and the offender has been referred to us by the probation or parole board, we then do a complete assessment, including penile plethysmographic studies. Based upon our evaluation, we notify the parole or probation department of our acceptance or rejection of the patient into our Sex Offender Treatment Program. When we accept an offender for treatment, we provide the patient with a description of our methodology, but we also explain that other methodologies exist, but that we adhere to our methodology because we believe it can be helpful to the patient in maintaining his self-control over previously distressing urges and behaviors. We also stress that active treatment takes approximately one year, but that the graduate phase, which requires less frequent visits, will continue for many years.

REFERENCES

1. Group for the Advancement of Psychiatry: Psychiatry and Sex Psychopath Legislation: *The 30's to the 80's. Vol IX, Publication No. 98*, New York, Mental Health Materials Center Center, April 1977.
2. The Task Panel on Legal and Ethical Issues of the President's Commission on Mental Health. Washington, DC, US Government Printing Office, 1978.
3. American Bar Association Committee Criminal Justice Mental Health Standards. Part VIII. Special Dispositional Statutes, Standard 7-8.1 Repeal of psychopath statutes. Washington, DC, American Bar Association, July 1983.
4. Brakel SJ, Parry J, Weiner BA: Sexual psychopath laws, in *The Mentally Disabled and the Law*, 3, Chicago, Ill., American Bar Foundation, 1985, p 743.
5. Weiner BA: Legal issues raised in treating sex offenders. *Behav Sci Law* 1985; 3:325–340.
6. Oliver AD: The sex offender: Lessons from the California experience. *Int J Law Psychiatry* 1982; 5:403–411.
7. Rogers R: Ethical dilemmas in forensic evaluations. *Behav Sci Law* 1987; 5:149–160.
8. Gutheil TG: Clinical issues in forensic psychiatry, in Michels R, Cavenar Jr. O (eds): *Psychiatry*, vol 5, New York, Basic Books, 1986.
9. Rappeport JR: Ethics and forensic psychiatry, in Bloch, S, Chodoff P (eds): *Psychiatr Ethics*. Oxford, Oxford University Press, 1981.
10. Gutheil TG, Appelbaum PS: *Clinical Handbook of Psychiatry and the Law*. New York, McGraw-Hill, 1982.
11. Zonana HV: Forensic psychiatry: Critique of a critique. *Bull Am Acad Psychiatry Law* 1984; 12:237–241.
12. Schetky DH, Colbach EM; Countertransference on the witness stand: A flight from self. *Bull Am Acad Psychiatry Law* 1982; 10:115–121.
13. Rada RT:: The psychiatrist as expert witness, in Hofling CK (ed): *Law and Ethics in the Private Practice of Psychiatry*. New York, Brunner/Mazel, 1981.
14. Kernberg O: Notes on countertransference. *J Am Psychoanal Assoc* 1965; 13:38–56.
15. Freud S: The future prospects of psycho-analytic therapy. *Standard Edition*, 11:139–151, London, Hogarth Press, 1957.
16. Heimann P: On counter-transference. *Int J Psychoanal* 1950; 31:81–84.
17. Heimann P: Counter-transference. *Br J Med Psych* 1960; 33:9–15.
18. Sandler J: Countertransference and role-responsiveness. *Int Rev Psychoanal* 1976; 3:43–47.
19. Racker H: *Transference and Countertransference*. New York, International Universities Press, 1968.
20. Hunt W, Issacharoff A: Heinrich Racker and countertransference theory. *J Am Acad Psychoanal* 1977; 5:95–105.
21. Travin S, Protter B: Mad or bad? Some clinical considerations in the misdiagnosis of schizophrenia as antisocial personality disorder. *Am J Psychiatry* 1982; 139:1335–1338.
22. Protter B, Travin S: The significance of countertransference and related issues in a multiservice court clinic. *Bull Am Acad Psychiatry Law* 1983; 11:223–130.
23. Chrzanowski G: The transference-countertransference transaction. *Contemp Psychoanal* 1979; 15:458–471.
24. Protter B: The Role of Forensic Psychology. Presented at the Annual Meeting of the Eastern Psychological Association in New York, Spring 1983.

25. Travin S, Protter B: Triadic factors in the practice of forensic psychiatry. Presented at the 38th Annual Meeting of the American Academy of Forensic Sciences in New Orleans, La., Feb. 15, 1986.
26. Drane JF: Ethics and psychotherapy: A philosophical perspective, in Rosenbaum M (ed): *Ethics and Values in Psychotherapy*. New York, Free Press, 1982.
27. Howard GS: The role of values in the science of psychology. *Am Psychologist* 1985; 40:255–265.
28. Travin S, Protter B: Malingering and malingering-like behavior: Some clinical and conceptual issues. *Psychiatr Q* 1984; 56:189–197.
29. Quinsey VL: The assessment and treatment of child molesters. *Canad Psych Rev* 1977; 18:204–220.
30. Araji S, Finkelhor D: Explanations of pedophilia: Review of empirical research. *Bull Am Acad Psychiatry Law* 1985; 13:17–37.
31. Reich W: Psychiatric diagnosis as an ethical problem, in Bloch S, Chodoff P (eds): *Psychiatric Ethics*. Oxford, Oxford University Press, 1981.
32. Ciccone JR, Barry DJ; The experience of using DSM-III in a court clinical setting: I, basic changes in the methodology of psychiatric diagnosis. *Bull Am Acad Psychiatry Law* 1978; 6:23–30.
33. Engelhardt Jr HT: The disease of masturbation: Values and the concept of disease. *Bull Hist Med* 1974; 48:234–248.
34. Lanning KV: Child molesters—A behavioral analysis for law enforcement, in Hazelwood RR, Burgess Aw (eds): *Practical Aspects of Rape Investigation: A Multidisciplinary Approach*. New York, Elsevier, 1987.
35. American Psychiatric Association: *Diagnostic and Statistical Manual of Mental Disorders* (DSM-III), ed. 3, Washington, DC, American Psychiatric Association, 1980.
36. Groth AN: Patterns of sexual assault against children and adolescents, in Burges AW, Groth AN, Holmstrom LL, Sgroi SM (eds): *Sexual Assault of Children and Adolescents*. Lexington, MA, Lexington Books, 1978.
37. Dietz PE: Sex offenses: behavioral aspects, in Kadish SH (ed): *Encyclopedia of Crime and Justice*. New York, Free Press, 1983.
38. American Psychiatric Association: *Diagnostic and Statistical Manual of Mental Disorders* (DSM-I). Washington, DC, APA, 1952.
39. American Psychiatric Association: *Diagnostic and Statistical Manual of Mental Disorders* (DSM-II). ed 2, Washington, DC, APA, 1968.
40. American Psychiatric Association: *Diagnostic and Statistical Manual of Mental Disorders* (DSM-III-R). ed 3, revised, Washington, DC, APA, 1987.
41. Abel GG, Beck JV, Cunningham-Rathner J, Mittelman M, Rouleau JL: Multiple paraphilic diagnoses among sex offenders. *Bull Am Acad Psychiatry Law* 1988; 16:153–168.
42. Conte JR: Clinical dimensions of adult sexual abuse of children. *Behav Sci Law* 1985; 3:341–354.
43. Personal communication from Dr. Judith V. Becker. Sexual Behavior Clinic, New York State Psychiatric Institute, November 16, 1988.
44. Kopp SB: The character structure of sex offenders. *Am J Psychother* 1962; 16:64–70.
45. Gebhard PH, Gagnon JH, Pomeroy WB, Christenson CV: *Sex Offenders: An Analysis of Types*, New York, Harper & Row, 1965.
46. Swanson DW: Adult sexual abuse of children, the man and circumstances. *Dis Nerv Sys* 1968; 29:677–683.
47. Schmidt CW, Meyer JK, Lucas J: Paraphilias and personality disorders, in Lion JR (ed): *Personality Disorders: Diagnosis and Management* (revised for DSM-III), ed 2, Baltimore, Williams and Wilkins, 1981.
48. Levin SM, Stava L: Personality characteristics of sex offenders: A review. *Arch Sexual Behav* 1987; 16:57–79.
49. Hall GCN, Maiuro RD, Vitaliano PP, Proctor WC: The utility of the MMPI with men who have sexually assaulted children. *J Couns Clin Psych* 1986; 54:493–496.

50. *State v Cavallo*, 443A 2d 1020 (1982).
51. Knight RA, Rosenberg R, Schneider BA: Classification of sexual offenders; perspectives, methods, and validation, in Burgess AW (ed): *Rape and Sexual Assault: A Research Handbook*, New York, Garland Publishing, 1985.
52. Prentky R, Cohen M, Seghorn T: Development of a rational taxonomy for the classification of rapists: The Massachusetts Treatment Center. *Bull Am Acad Psychiatry Law* 1985; 13:39–70.
53. Cohen M, Seghorn T, Calmas W: Sociometric study of the sex offender. *J Abnorm Psych* 1969; 74:249–255.
54. Prentky RA, Knight RA, Rosenberg R: Validation analyses on a taxonomic system for rapists: Disconfirmation and reconceptualization, in Prentky RA, Quinsey VL (eds): *Human Sexual Aggression: Current Perspectives*, Ann NY Acad Sciences, vol 528. New York, The New York Academy of Sciences, 1988.
55. Knight RA: A taxonomic analysis of child molesters, in Prentky RA, Quinsey VL (eds): *Human Sexual Aggression: Current Perspectives*, Annals of the New York Academy of Sciences, Volume 528, New York, The New York Academy of Sciences, 1988.
56. Cohen M, Boucher RJ, Seghorn TK, Mehegan J: The Sexual Offender Against Children. Presented at a meeting of the Association for Professional Treatment of Offenders, Boston, Massachusetts, 1979.
57. Conte HR: Development and use of self-report techniques for assessing sexual functioning; a review and critique. *Arch Sexual Behav* 1983; 12:555–576.
58. Thorne FC: The sex inventory. *J Clin Psych* 1966; 22:367–374.
59. Paitich D, Langevin R, Freeman R, Mann K, Handy L: The Clarke SHQ: A clinical sex history questionnaire for males. *Arch Sexual Behav* 1977; 6:421–436.
60. Derogatis LR: Psychological assessment of psychosexual functioning. *The Psychiatric Clinics of North America*, vol. 3, no. 1. Philadelphia, WB Saunders Company, April 1980.
61. Burt MR: Cultural myths and supports for rape. *J Personality Soc Psych* 1980; 38:217–230.
62. Burt MR, Albin RS: Rape myths, rape definitions, and probability of conviction. *J Appl Soc Psych* 1981; 11:212–230.
63. Gay ML, Hollandsworth JG, Galassi JP: An assertiveness inventory for adults. *J Couns Psych* 1975; 22:340–344.
64. Rada RT, Laws DR, Kellner R: Plasma testosterone levels in the rapist. *Psychosom Med* 1976; 38:257–268.
65. Rada RT, Laws DR, Kellner R, Stivastava L, Peake G: Plasma androgens in violent and nonviolent sex offenders. *Bull Am Acad Psychiatry Law* 1983; 11:149–157.
66. Rada RT: Plasma androgens and the sex offenders. Bull *Am Acad Psychiatry Law* 1980; 8:456–464.
67. Zuckerman M: Physiological measures of sexual arousal in the human. *Psychol Bull* 1971; 75:297–329.
68. Bancroft J, Mathews A: Autonomic correlates of penile erection. *J Psychosom Res* 1971; 15:159–167.
69. Rosen RC, Beck JG: *Patterns of Sexual Arousal: Psychophysiological Processes and Clinical Applications*. New York, Guilford Press, 1988.
70. Barlow DH: The treatment of sexual deviation: Towards a comprehensive behavioral approach, in Calhoun KS, Adams HE (eds): *Innovative Treatment Methods in Psychopathology*. New York, Wiley, 1974.
71. Barlow DH: Assessment of sexual behavior, in Ciminero RA, Calhoun KS, Adams HE (eds): *Handbook of Behavioral Assessment*, New York, Wiley, 1977.
72. Laws DR: The assessment of dangerous sexual behavior in males. *Med Law* 1984; 3:127–140.
73. Langevin R, Paitich D, Ramsey G, Anderson C, Kamrad J, Pope S, Geller G, Pearl L, Newman S: Experimental studies of the etiology of general exhibitionism: *Arch Sexual Behav* 1979; 8:307–331.

74. Abel GG, Blanchard EB, Barlow DH: Measurement of sexual arousal in several paraphilias: The effects of stimulas modality, instructional set and stimulus content. *Behav, Res Ther* 1981; 19:25–33.
75. Malamuth NM, Check JVP: Sexual arousal to rape depictions: Individual differences. *J Abnorm Psych* 1983; 92:55–77.
76. Quinsey VL, Chaplin TC, Upfold D: Sexual arousal to nonsexual violence and sadomasochistic themes among rapists and non-sex offenders. *J Consult Clin Psych* 1984; 52:651–657.
77. Travin S, Cullen K, Melella JT: The use and abuse of erection measurements: a forensic perspective. *Bull Am Acad Psychiatry Law* 1988; 16:235–250.
78. Cox M: Dynamic psychotherapy with sex offenders, in Rosen I (ed): *Sexual Deviation*, ed 2. Oxford/New York, Oxford University Press, 1979.
79. Peters JJ, Roether HA: Group psychotherapy for probationed sex offenders, in Resnik HLP, Wolfgang ME (eds): *Sexual Behaviors: Some Clinical and Legal Aspects*. Boston, Little, Brown, 1972.
80. Bradford J MW: Organic treatments for the male sexual offender. *Behav Sci Law* 1985; 3:355–375.
81. Marshall WL, Earls CM, Segal Z, Darke J: A behavioral program for the assessment and treatment of sexual aggressors, in Craig KD, McMahon RJ (eds): *Advancement in Clinical Behavior Therapy*, New York, Brunner/Mazel, 1983.
82. Borzecki M, Wormith JS: A survey of treatment programs for sex offenders in North America. *Canad Psych* 1987; 28:30–44.
83. Romero JJ, Williams LM: Group psychotherapy and intensive probation supervision with sex offenders. *Fed Probation* 1983; 47:36–42.
84. Giarretto H, Giarretto A, Sgroi SM: Coordinated community treatment of incest, in Burgess AW, Groth AN, Holmstrom LL, Sgroi SM (eds): *Sexual Assault of children and Adolescents*. Lexington, Massachusetts, Lexington Books, 1978.
85. Money J: The therapeutic use of androgen-depleting hormone, in Resnick H LP, Wolfgang ME (eds): *Sexual Behaviors: Some Clinical and Legal Aspects*. Boston, Little, Brown, 1972.
86. Bradford J MW: Organic treatments for the male sexual offender, in Prentky RA, Quinsey VL (eds): *Human Sexual Aggression: Current Perspectives*. Annals of the New York Academy of Sciences, vol 528. New York, The New York Academy of Sciences, 1988.
87. Berlin FS, Meinecke CF: Treatment of sex offenders with antiandrogenic medication: Conceptualization, review of treatment modalities, and preliminary findings. *Am J Psychiatry* 1981; 138:601–607.
88. Earls CM, Quinsey VL: What is to be done? Future research on the assessment and behavioral treatment of sex offenders. *Behav Sci Law* 1985; 3:377–390.
89. Kilmann PR, Sabolis RF, Gearing ML, Bukstel LH, Scovern AW: The treatment of sexual paraphilias: A review of the outcome research. *J Sexual Res* 1982; 18:193–252.
90. Abel GG, Blanchard EB, Becker JV: An integrated treatment program for rapists, in Rada R (ed): *Clinical Aspects of the Rapist*. New York, Grune and Stratton, 1978.
91. Abel GG, Becker JV, Skinner LJ: Aggressive behavior and sex, in Meyer JK (ed): *Symposium on Sexuality. The Psychiatric Clinics of North America*, vol 3, No 1, Philadelphia, WB Saunders Company, April 1980.
92. Travin S, Bluestone H, Coleman E, Cullen K, Melella J: Pedophilia: An update on theory and practice. *Psychiatr Q* 1985; 57:89–103.
93. Protter B, Travin S: Sexual fantasies in the treatment of paraphiliac disorders: a bimodal approach. *Psychiatr Q* 1987; 58:279–297.
94. Abel GG, Mittelman M, Becker JV, Rathner J, Rouleau JL: Predicting child molesters' response to treatment, in Prentky RA, Quinsey VL (eds): *Human Sexual Aggression: Current Perspectives*, Annals of the New York Academy of Sciences, Volume 528, New York, The New York Academy of Sciences, 1988.

95. Travin S, Cullen K, Melella JT, Coleman E, Bluestone H: Profile of sex offenders seen in a court clinic. Presented at the 39th Annual Meeting of the American Academy of Forensic Sciences, San Diego, CA, February 21, 1987.
96. Marshall WL, Barbaree HE: An outpatient treatment program for child molesters, in Prentky RA, Quinsey VL (eds): *Human Sexual Aggression: Current Perspectives*, Annals of the New York Academy of Sciences, Volume 528. New York, The New York Academy of Sciences, 1988.
97. McGovern K, Peters J: Guidelines for assessing sex offenders, in Walker LEA (ed): *Handbook on Sexual Abuse of Children*. New York, Springer, 1988.
98. Abel GG, Becker JV, Murphy WD, Flanagan B: Identifying dangerous child molesters, in Stuart R (ed): *Violent Behavior—Social Learning Approaches to Prediction, Management and Treatment*, New York, Brunner/Mazel, 1981.
99. Avery-Clark CA, Laws DR: Differential erection response patterns of sexual child abusers to stimuli describing activities with children. *Behav Ther* 1984; 15:71–83.
100. Curran WJ: Courtroom presentation of forensic scientific evidence, in Curran WJ, McGarry AL, Petty CS (eds): *Modern Legal Medicine, Psychiatry, and Forensic Science*. Philadelphia, F.A. Davis Co, 1980.
101. Halleck SL: Legal and ethical aspects of behavior control. *Am J Psychiatry* 1974; 131:381–385.

20

Clinical Judgment and Value Judgment

Moral Foundations of Psychiatric and Legal Determinations of the Status of Homosexuality

ROBERT LLOYD GOLDSTEIN

In this chapter I will examine two truly momentous decisions about the status of homosexuality in our society, arrived at by the American Psychiatric Association 15 years ago and by the Supreme Court of the United States just two and one half years ago. The former decision relates to the *diagnostic* status of homosexuality; the latter to its *criminal* status. By juxtaposing these two epochal decisions, psychiatric and legal, I will attempt to demonstrate that within both systems value judgments and value-laden policy decisions played a major role and were decisive in reaching a resolution of the disputes over homosexuality. The two decisions which I will discuss are the 1973 decision of the APA's Board of Trustees to remove homosexuality *per se* from the diagnostic nomenclature (DSM-II[1] at the time) and the 1986 decision of the Supreme Court in *Bowers v Hardwick*,[2] which upheld the constitutionality of Georgia's sodomy law, thereby refusing to grant constitutional protection to private consensual homosexual acts. In discussing each of these landmark decisions, psychiatric and legal, I will review the process of how these decisions were arrived at, as well as the related scientific and legal conceptions of "Truth." I will attempt to demon-

Presented at the 14th annual conference of the Tri-State Chapter of the American Academy of Psychiatry and the Law, *Impartiality and Advocacy in Mental Health and the Law,* New York, NY, January 14, 1989.

ROBERT LLOYD GOLDSTEIN • Department of Psychiatry, College of Physicians and Surgeons of Columbia University, New York, New York 10032.

strate how, within each model of decision making, the "truth" arrived at was determined in large measure by the value judgments and moral sentiments of the decision makers, notwithstanding their ostensible reliance on more objective touchstones consistent with their respective professional methodologies. I will not attempt to deal with the *substance* of the controversies in any depth. I do not propose, for example, to argue the merits one way or the other as to whether homosexuality *should* have been removed from the DSM. Instead of rehashing those old arguments, I prefer to focus on the *process* of decision making that took place and the explanations advanced as the basis for the decisions.

THE PSYCHIATRIC DECISION

Let us examine the psychiatric decision first. In their book *A Philosophical Basis for Medical Practice*,[3] Pellegrino and Thomasma observed that "psychiatry like the rest of Medicine is a *tertium quid*, grounded in the clinical encounter, poised between art and science, the most scientific of the humanities and the most humanistic of the sciences."

Wallace[4] noted that, in part, the philosophy of psychiatry "comprises inquiry into the...relationship between psychiatric theory and practice on the one hand and cultural norms and moral values on the other...and assesses whether psychiatric theories and therapies themselves entail world views and moralities." Also in this regard, Stone[5] observed: "Psychiatry does not stand outside history or morality, but how do we decide which history and which morality to accept?...I am deeply suspicious of anyone who makes the contrary claim that history, morality and human values are all irrelevant to psychiatry."

Yet notwithstanding this perspective, the epistemological tradition of modern American psychiatry is radically pragmatic, inductive, empirical and operational.[6] The DSM approach epitomizes this tradition. It seeks to avoid a theoretical stance or speculative system-building about etiologies. It steers clear of theoretical preconceptions as well as reigning medical fashions. By utilizing the descriptive, phenomenological approach "to cleave to data potentially perceivable by *any* psychiatrist of whatever theoretical orientation," it emphasizes the possibility of theory-free observation and the attainability of uncontaminated scientific truth.[6] Pierce[7] defines such ideal scientific truth as "the ultimate conclusions of the ultimate scientific community." Such universalistic claims of scientific certainty view the truth about empirical reality as "univocal, ahistorical, and the property of 'the' scientific community," rather than truth as defined by a particular scientific community[8] at a particular time and place. A number of philosophical critiques have challenged such claims.[9,10] These are very interesting issues to consider, but are beyond the scope of this chapter.

A consideration of the homosexuality controversy allows us to examine the interface between the epistemological foundations of psychiatry and its cultural and moral dimension. The dispute over the diagnostic status of homosexuality challenged the profession's most fundamental assumptions about its philosophical underpinnings and its methodologies. Indeed, it was a major controversy of great depth and broad constituency that will surely go down as one of the most extraordinary episodes in the annals of psychiatry, if not in the entire history of science.[11] I cannot begin to convey to you the broad scope and richness of detail of all that transpired during that historic professional upheaval.

The definitive account of the protracted controversy and the Byzantine infighting that accompanied its uneasy closure can be found in Ronald Bayer's scholarly account of the subject, a fascinating study entitled "Homosexuality and American Psychiatry: The Politics of Diagnosis."[12] Also, the quintessential insider's perspective is provided by Robert Spitzer's many articles and letters reflecting on his pivotal role in the controversy.[13,14] As a leading guiding force behind the development of the DSMs, Spitzer assumed a dominant leadership role during the vicissitudes of the homosexuality dispute and its final closure. Drawing on these two main sources and others, I will attempt to recapitulate in broad outline form the highlights of the events as they unfolded on what Stone has referred to as "one of the first great battlefields in the attack on psychiatry's hidden values."[15]

For thousands of years, homosexuality had been viewed as evidence of sinfulness, criminality, or pathology. During millenia of theological disapprobation and state condemnation, dating back to biblical pedagogy and Judeo-Christian law, homosexual sodomy was punished by harsh ecclesiastical and secular sanctions.[16] The Anti-buggery statute of 1533 (during the reign of Henry VIII) served as the model for the sodomy statutes adopted by the original 13 colonies.[17] Sodomy statutes remained on the books as criminal offenses in all 50 states as recently as 30 years ago. Twenty-five states still prohibit such behavior, although enforcement is infrequent.[18]

The gradual decriminalization of homosexuality was largely a reflection of the trend towards its medicalization, which began in the 19th century. Homosexuals came to be viewed from a psychiatric perspective now, as "sick" rather than "sinful" or "criminal."[19] In our time, despite the findings of Kinsey,[20] Hooker,[21] Marmor[22] and others that challenged the conventional wisdom and demonstrated that the level of psychopathology and general social functioning of homosexuals did not differ significantly from that of heterosexuals, nonetheless, orthodox psychiatry continued to apply the sick label automatically to all homosexuals. Psychoanalysts viewed homosexuality as evidence of profound and pervasive psychopathology representing the end result of severe intrapsychic conflict.[23]

In DSM-I (1952),[24] homosexuality was characterized as a *sexual deviation* under the more general rubric of "Sociopathic Personality Disturbance." In DSM-II (1968),[25] homosexuality was again listed as a *sexual deviation*, but now classified under "Personality Disorders and Certain Other Non-Psychotic Mental Disorders." By the late 1960s, militant homosexual activist groups began to lobby and mount vigorous protests against the official psychiatric position. They argued that psychiatric labeling stigmatized them and was used as an ideological justification to perpetuate a broad range of discriminatory practices against them as a group. A crescendo of painfully disruptive public confrontations took the psychiatric establishment by surprise, arousing a melange of anger, consternation, bewilderment, guilt and, in some circles, concern and reappraisal. In 1968, homophile activists protested at the AMA convention in San Francisco, demanding an equal voice at the meeting for those who disagreed with the orthodox pathological view of homosexuality, including representatives from their own ranks. Similar protests took place at a panel discussion on homosexuality at Columbia's College of Physicians and Surgeons in the same year. In 1971, homophile groups continued to ventilate their wrath at the APA convention in Washington, DC. During the Convocation of Fellows, one gay activist leader commandeered the microphone to declare: "Psychiatry is the enemy incarnate. Psychiatry has waged a relentless war of extermination against us. You may take this as a declaration of war against you."[26] Not surprisingly, many psychiatrists felt confused and beleaguered. They had viewed themselves as professionals who sought to help those homosexuals who wanted treatment. Now they were dismayed to "hear their profession denounced as an instrument of oppression and torture."[27] The pressures brought to bear on organized psychiatry were not, however, exclusively at the level of "guerilla theater tactics." The campaign of disruption and intimidation by some elements was complemented by a rational and modulated professional discourse on the part of gay leaders in psychiatry and psychology, as well as others within the professions, who presented a sober and compelling argument against continuing to classify homosexuality as a psychiatric disorder. They were able to marshal the evidence of empirical studies that called into question the official position on homosexuality, which they viewed as scientifically unwarranted. During this difficult period, the APA Committee on Nomenclature was receptive to this professional input and became involved in a process of intellectual reassessment and professional soul-searching. This process ultimately led to a rethinking of the foundations of the psychiatric nosology in current usage. It is apparent, however, that this process of reappraisal and reformulation hardly took place in a climate of detached and dispassionate study within a remote ivory tower. It took place on the front lines, as it were, with the clamor of battle all around. Apparently there were many pressures to act quickly in order to resolve the dispute and prevent further "bloodshed." This was hardly the proper atmosphere conducive to the measured and methodical resolution of a serious scientific controversy.[28] Even if, as the proponents of the change in nosology maintained, it was primarily a decision based on scientific grounds (accelerated, perhaps, but not dictated by the external pressures and threats), there still remains a lingering impression of at least the *appearance* of capitulation to political forces. One cannot underestimate the importance of appearances. It would be no different, for example, if a jury while deliberating was surrounded by an unruly mob, howling for blood, just outside the courtroom. Any verdict delivered under such circumstances, no matter how just, that happened to coincide with the expectations of the mob, would always be suspect because of the appearance of coercion. Bayer puts it this way:

"The entire process...seemed to violate the most basic assumptions about how questions of science should be resolved. Instead of being engaged in a sober consideration of data, psychiatrists were swept up in a political controversy...The result was not a conclusion based on an approximation of the scientific truth as dictated by reason but an action demanded by the ideological temper of the times."[29]

Spearheaded by Spitzer's efforts, a compromise acceptable to all parties was hammered out within the Nomenclature Committee. An attempt was made to find a middle ground between those who maintained homosexuality was a variant of normal sexuality and those who maintained it was invariably pathological. A restricted definition of what constitutes a psychiatric disorder was the key to reaching a compromise formulation. The restricted definition of psychiatric disorder was two-pronged. It required the presence of subjective distress and/or "some generalized impairment in social effectiveness or functioning."[30] Homosexuality *per se* would no longer necessarily constitute a psychiatric disorder; nonetheless, it would not quite be viewed merely as a variant of normal sexuality, either. Under the new formulation, it was still clinically and ethically justified for psychiatrists to treat those homosexuals who desired to change their sexual orientation. By means of this "theoretical refinement," homosexuality was deleted from the official nosology and replaced by the compromise category of "Sexual Orientation Disturbance," which held that only *ego-dystonic* homosexuality is a disorder.[31] Critics attacked the new classification as "psychiatric nonsense," because it implied that the only disturbed homosexual is one who is disturbed because he is homosexual. He is considered ill only if he is unhappy with his condition and wishes to change.[32] Psychoanalysts emphasized that according to their theories, perversions are the negative of neuroses and therefore they are usually ego-syntonic. Motivation for treatment, they said, should not be a proper criterion by itself for judging someone to be ill.[33] Others charged that the committee had voted with its conscience to attempt to alleviate the social burden of homosexuality.[34] In the face of credible doubts as to the scientific validity of the orthodox psychiatric perspective, they assumed that the committee had decided "When in doubt, do not label."

In less than a year, the new proposal sailed through the various decision-making councils of the APA and homosexuality was deleted from the DSM-II by a unanimous vote of the Board of Trustees in December 1973. APA President Freeman emphasized that this action was not to be viewed as a pronouncement that homosexuality was either normal or preferable to heterosexuality.[35] Meanwhile, orthodox psychiatrists were stepping up their resistance to these developments. Embittered by the ideological rebuff and repudiating the compromise formulation in no uncertain terms, they mobilized for action against those they viewed as apostates who had taken over the APA's governing bodies and usurped the mantle of scientific leadership.[36] Just as the battle with gay militants appeared to be peacefully resolved, an ideological civil war between psychiatrists loomed on the horizon. An Ad Hoc Committee Against the Deletion of Homosexuality from DSM-II demanded a referendum of the general membership to ratify or reject the decision of the leadership, which they regarded as dangerously misguided.[37] Amid acrimonious debate, the referendum was held in April 1974. The profession was held up to a considerable amount of ridicule for attempting to resolve a scientific dispute by recourse to a democratic vote of the membership. Spiegel[38] charged that the controversy had deteriorated into a "popularity contest." Others had a field day mocking psychiatry's pretensions to be accepted as a clinical science like other branches of medicine.[39] One critic charged that "having forsaken the canons of science, psychiatry had revealed itself to be a subdivision of theology...having behaved like a Church council deciding matters of dogma."[40]

The referendum supported the change in the nomenclature, but revealed a profound split in the membership over the issue. Out of approximately 10,000 votes, 58% supported the change, while 37% opposed it. Procedural closure of the dispute had been achieved for the time being and homosexuality was no longer *officially* viewed as a disorder.[41] However, indications were that a sizable segment of the profession maintained its allegiance to the orthodox pathological perspective and would continue to practice accordingly.[42] The denouement was marked by further complications involving charges of fraud and collusion between gay activists and the psychiatric leadership, in attempting to sway voters to their side. An attempt to overturn the referendum was unsuccessful.[43] At last the dust cleared and the battle appeared to be over for the time being. Some of the wounds would never heal. It was clear to most that revising the official nomenclature would not really resolve all controversy regarding homosexuality. A further discussion of the later vicissitudes of diagnoses-related-to-homosexuality in the nosology (through DSM-III-R[44]) is beyond the scope of this paper. Suffice it to say that the very last vestige of the old pathological perspective on homosexuality—in fact, the last reference to the term "homosexuality"—has been totally expunged from DSM-III-R. The residual category of "Sexual Disorder Not Otherwise Specified" remains perhaps the only professional warrant for providing treatment to those homosexuals who wish to change their sexual orientation.

Spitzer's commitment to the DSM formulation has remained steadfast. He believes the best approach is the atheoretical, phenomenological model of mental disorders which holds that it is the *consequences* of a condition and not its putative *etiology* which determine whether or not it should be classified as a psychiatric disorder. Using the two-pronged restricted definition of psychiatric disorder (i.e., subjective distress and/or generalized impairment in social effectiveness or functioning), homosexuality does not qualify as a psychiatric disorder, provided that no subjective distress is present and that *heterosexual* functioning is *not* taken as the norm (so that inability to function heterosexually is *not* necessarily viewed as an impairment in functioning).[45] Spitzer observes that it is not possible at present to reach a consensus among psychiatrists whether or not heterosexual functioning represents an "important area of functioning," such that inability to function heterosexually because of an exclusive homosexual orientation would rise to the level of a psychiatric disorder.[46] Gays maintain that homosexuality does not represent a functional impairment because there is no impairment in *sexuality per se*. They refuse to accept *heterosexuality* as the norm. Are there guidelines to determine objectively what standards of functioning are to be employed? Spitzer has concluded that whether or not to use heterosexual functioning as the norm (so that inability to function heterosexually represents an impairment in a major area of functioning) is at heart a *value* judgment, and not a matter of scientific fact.[47] Thus it would appear that even under the DSM model, the concept of psychiatric disorder cannot always be value-free. A value judgment perforce comes into play in determining the boundaries of psychiatric disorder in the case of homosexuality. In the absence of any evidence that the range of general psychopathology seen in homosexuals differs at all from what is seen in heterosexuals, Spitzer concludes that where to draw the line is a *social* judgment, *not* a *scientific* one. In a 1981 article he acknowledged that the diagnosis of *Sexual Orientation Disorder*, which replaced *Homosexuality* in DSM-II, although scientifically sound, represented a nosological compromise between two opposing camps.[48] This gives further support to the conclusion that the new nosology was, to a significant extent, the product of politics. In that sense, at least in part, it must be viewed as a value-laden policy judgment.

After the fact, there were varying interpretations of the APA's closure of the controversy. Robitscher[49] criticized "the undisciplined antics of psychiatrists who change their diagnostic categories around to suit their needs and moods or in response to social pressure and who do not realize that they are arming their legal and sociological critics with all the ammunition they need to "prove" that psychiatric designations are arbitrary."

Spitzer maintained throughout that the change in nosology was *primarily* "motivated by a sincere intellectual assessment of what was best for the classification on *scientific* grounds"[50] and not as a response to social pressure or as a civil rights issue. If the decision to break with what were seen as conventional but scientifically unwarranted beliefs also served to improve the public perception of homosexuals by removing the stigma of psychiatric illness, so much the better. But such a potential benefit was seen as icing on the cake, a *secondary* effect that flowed from a decision reached *primarily* on scientific grounds. Stone[51] viewed the decision as consistent with the nature of psychiatry *both* as a moral and a scientific enterprise. He characterized it as "an act of moral compassion producing a small change in public perception...but a small change that in the long run can exert a powerful effect."

THE LEGAL DECISION

Let us now turn to a consideration of how the law dealt with a recent landmark determination of the status of homosexuality. It is certainly very much the business of the law to provide trustworthy procedures for the authoritative settlement of disputes and the resolution of conflicting social interests. Gutheil and Mills[52] have written about the epistemological problems that arise at the interface between psychiatry and the law. Legal "truth" lacks the aura of absolute certainty that often envelops scientific knowledge. As one legal scholar observed: "There are no correct or incorrect judicial decisions, only good or bad ones."[53] If scientific truth is the ultimate conclusions of the ultimate scientific community, then in the United States at least, the ultimate legal truth is what the Supreme Court decides when it speaks in a case. Such decisions are sometimes irreverently characterized as "the voices of infallibility...by a narrow majority."[54]

Such *infallible* judicial decisions "will often provide sustenance for armies of academic lawyers ruthlessly seeking material for the footnotes of a law review article that will conclusively show that the judge[s] made a mistake."[55]

So it was, in 1986, with *Bowers v Hardwick*, a bitterly divided five-four decision, in which the Court decided there is no constitutional right to engage in private homosexual sodomy. Hardwick had been charged with violating the Georgia statute criminalizing sodomy by committing the act with another adult male in his own bedroom. Although seldom enforced, nevertheless sodomy statutes impose a stigma of criminality. Hardwick challenged the constitutionality of the statute in Federal District Court. The court dismissed for failure to state a claim. The Court of Appeals for the 11th Circuit reversed and remanded, holding that the statute violated Hardwick's fundamental rights. The Supreme court reversed the judgment of the Court of Appeals. Justice White announced the Court's decision, which held that the Constitution does not confer a fundamental right on homosexuals to engage in sodomy. The decision was based on the following premises: first, that the privacy rights that had been articulated in a line of cases from *Griswold v Connecticut*[56] through *Roe v Wade*[57] do not extend to homosexual erotic conduct. *Griswold* and its progeny had "discovered" a zone of privacy rights protected by the penumbras of the Bill of Rights (and emanating from the 1st, 3rd, 4th, 5th, 9th and 14th amendments). This hierarchy of constitutional rights encompassed by the right to privacy included personal autonomy rights, freedom of individual choice of values, freedom of intimate associations, and others. It drew a circle around certain areas of conduct denoted as private, into which the law was not permitted to intrude in order to promote purely moral or religious standards. Having established a constitutional right to privacy in a number of areas, the outer boundaries of such a right in regard to consensual sexual conduct had remained unclear until *Bowers*. Justice White explained that the Privacy Doctrine did not extend to homosexual sodomy because such conduct had no relation to those areas traditionally protected, which were limited to family relationships, marriage, procreation, contraception, and abortion.[58] Secondly, homosexual sodomy failed to qualify as a "fundamental right," which would have required heightened judicial scrutiny to insure that the statute was necessary to promote a *compelling* state interest and was the least burdensome alternative available (i.e., a right deeply rooted in the nation's history and tradition or implicit in the concept of ordered liberty).[59] Thirdly, the Court was hesitant to recognize any additional rights not explicitly granted in the text of the Constitution.[60] And finally, the Court underscored the fundamental value-laden policy behind its decision: that is, affirmation of traditional majoritarian moral sentiments regarding homosexuality. The Court explicitly noted that considerations of morality may properly serve as a rational legal basis for the proscription of homosexual conduct.[61] In a concurring opinion, Chief Justice Burger was even more emphatic. In what has been characterized as a "primer on Judeo-Christian moral standards,"[62] he referred to the "ancient roots" of sodomy laws and the "millennia of moral teaching" against the evils of homosexuality, concluding that sodomy statutes are constitutionally based on legislative authority to regulate morality.[63]

By endorsing public morality as an acceptable basis to uphold governmental intrusion even into the "sacred precincts of...bedrooms,"[64] the Court appeared to follow Lord Devlin's doctrine,[65] namely, that the majority has a right to impose its moral views for the overall welfare of society, in order to protect public morals and preserve the social fabric. Devlin believed that the public interest in preserving a decent society subordinated the claims of personal autonomy.[66] This would appear to be a serious setback to those (like Hart)[67] who maintain that morality is not the law's business or that morality cannot be legislated. Along these lines, the dissenters argued that the Constitution was designed to protect the minority from the tyranny of majoritarian moral standards when individual rights are at stake. Justice Blackmun,[68] the author of *Roe v Wade*, argued in his dissent that morality is not an acceptable basis for upholding sodomy laws or intruding into the private lives of homosexuals to punish their alleged immorality. The decision in *Bowers* would foreclose millions of homosexual couples from free enjoyment of their exclusive mode of sexual enjoyment and sexual intimacy. According to Justice Blackmun, expressions of sexual intimacy should be regarded as the very essence of liberty and personal autonomy. He concluded that "the mere knowledge that other individuals do not adhere to one's value system cannot be a legally cognizable interest, let alone an interest that can justify invading the houses, hearts, and minds of citizens who choose to live their lives differently [citations omitted]."[69]

A survey of numerous law review articles commenting on *Bowers* reveals almost uniform criticism of the Court's reasoning and specifically of its reliance on majoritarian moral standards as a sufficient basis for its decision. One commentator regarded it as a judicial attempt to legitimize society's homophobic heritage.[70] Some of these articles reflect their position in dramatic titles, such as "*Bowers v Hardwick*: The Supreme Court Closes the Door on the Right to Privacy and Opens the Door to the Bedroom;"[71] "*Bowers v Hardwick* and the Legitimation of Homophobia in America;"[72] and "The Supreme Court as Super Legislature Emasculates the Right to Privacy."[73] The consensus of the critics is that "it is not the function of the criminal law in our governmental policy to provide either a medium for the articulation of or the apparatus for the intended enforcement of moral or theological values."[74] In calling for the Court to reconsider its analysis and reverse itself in the near future, Justice Blackmun concluded that "depriving individuals of the right to choose for themselves how to conduct their intimate relationships poses a far greater threat to...[our traditional] values...than tolerance of nonconformity could ever do."[75]

CONCLUSION

In conclusion, I would like to return to our original thesis that, within each model of decision making, "value judgments and value-laden policy decisions played a major role and were decisive in reaching a resolution of the disputes over homosexuality." This is notwithstanding the fact that the psychiatrists grounded their decision primarily in what they viewed as a scientifically based theoretical refinement of the nosology and that the Supreme Court based its opinion primarily on a constitutional analysis of the outer boundaries of the Privacy Doctrine. In regard to the APA decision to remove homosexuality from the DSM, it is clear that the entire process was to a significant extent shaped by political forces of an extrascientific nature. The new diagnostic category substituted for homosexuality, which was the "brainchild" of the Nomenclature Committee, was as much a tribute to Spitzer's excellent lawyering skills in negotiating and drafting an ingenious compromise as it was the product of his formidable scientific expertise. It reflected a fundamental value judgment that homosexuality was not a disorder, based on a calculated decision not to insist on *hetero*sexual functioning as the norm. I would agree with Bayer who concludes that there is no answer to the homosexuality question that is not ultimately "a political question, representing an historically rooted, socially determined choice, regarding the ends of human sexuality."[76] In other words, the question of whether or not homosexuality is a disorder, even apart from its historical ingredient, is not a purely scientific one...it cannot be resolved solely by reference to the learning of psychiatry. Value and policy considerations *must* come into play in reaching a decision.

The legal decision handed down in *Bowers* likewise represents a value judgment of the first magnitude. Any doubt on this issue can be laid to rest by referring to the explicit language of the written opinion itself. For example, Justice White stated: "The law, however, is constantly based on notions of morality, and if all laws representing essentially moral choices are to be invalidated...the courts will be very busy indeed."[77] Chief Justice Burger went even further in his concurring opinion: "Decisions of individuals relating to homosexual conduct have been subject to state intervention throughout the history of Western Civilization. Condemnation of these practices is firmly rooted in Judeo-Christian moral and ethical standards...To hold that the act of homosexual sodomy is somehow protected as a fundamental right would be to cast aside millennia of moral teaching."[78] Interestingly, the Court never mentions or takes note of psychiatry's radical change in perspective on homosexuality. It seems too preoccupied with the moral teaching of the past.

Finally, if I might be permitted to venture a value judgment of my own at this point, I would suggest the following:

As major institutions in our society, both psychiatry and the law must be kept responsive to the continuing processes of changing social conditions and attitudes. Heraclitus observed: "Nothing steadfastly is. Everything is becoming."[79] Institutions like psychiatry and the law have a reciprocal relationship to social change. They can have a molding effect on the processes of social change and development. Major decisions arrived at by these institutions carry the potential to "become a kind of self-fulfilling prophecy and create the social climate necessary for [their] acceptance."[80]

In today's society, homosexuals continue to make small gains in their struggle against an endemic cultural antipathy that has been amplified by concern over the AIDS epidemic. "The political, legal and social gains they have achieved in recent years are unlikely to be reversed."[81] But there is a long way to go in order to achieve anything like the full social legitimation which they seek. Within this context, the psychiatric decision is a forward-looking one, marked by a combination of rationality, sensitivity, and tolerance. It is fully in line with psychiatry's humanistic tradition. In contrast, the legal decision is a backward-looking one, reflecting the extent to which the law is reluctant to move more than a few millimeters ahead of public opinion.[82] The law dares not stray too far from the contemporary climate of opinion. Despite recent gains in the legal recognition and protection of homosexual rights in a variety of contexts, the Court is not yet ready to extend that recognition and protection to homosexual erotic practices. It seems no less true today than it did over 100 years ago when Holmes wrote:

"The life of the law has not been logic: it has been experience. The felt necessities of the time, the prevalent moral and political theories, intuitions of public policy, avowed or unconscious, even the prejudices which judges share with their fellow men."[83]

REFERENCES

1. American Psychiatric Association: *Diagnostic and Statistical Manual of Mental Disorders*, ed 2 (DSM-II). Washington, DC, American Psychiatric Association, 1968.
2. *Bowers v Hardwick*, 478 U.S. 186 (1986).
3. Pellegrino E, Thomasma D: *A Philosophical Basis for Medical Practice*. New York, Oxford University Press, 1981, p 59.
4. Wallace ER: What is "truth"? Some philosophical contributions to psychiatric issues. *Am J Psychiatry* 1988; 145:137–147.
5. Stone AA: Presidential address: Conceptual ambiguity and morality in modern psychiatry. *Am J Psychiatry* 1980; 137:887–891.
6. op cit, n 4.
7. Peirce, CS: Pragmatism and pragmaticism, in *Collected Papers*. Cambridge, Harvard University Press, 1965.
8. Engelhardt HG, Caplan, AL: Patterns of controversy and closure: The interplay of knowledge, values and political forces, in Engelhardt HT, Caplan AL (eds) *Scientific Controversies: Case Studies in the Resolution and Closure of Disputes in Science and Technology*. Cambridge, UK, Cambridge University Press, 1987.
9. Faust D, Miner RA: The empiricist and his new clothes: DSM-III in perspective. *Am J Psychiatry* 1986; 143:962–967.
10. op cit, n 4.
11. Bayer R: *Homosexuality and American Psychiatry: The Politics of Diagnosis*. New York, Basic Books, 1981.
12. *ibid.*
13. Spitzer RL: The diagnostic statutes of homosexuality in DSM-III: A reformulation of the

issues, in Engelhardt HT, Caplan AL (eds) Scientific Controversies: Case Studies in the Resolution and Closure of Disputes in Science and Technology. Cambridge, UK, Cambridge University Press, 1987.
14. Spitzer RL: A proposal about homosexuality and the APA nomenclature: Homosexuality as an irregular form of sexual behavior and sexual orientation disturbance as a psychiatric disorder. A symposium: should homosexuality be in the APA nomenclature? *Am J Psychiatry* 1973; 130:1207–1216.
15. op cit, n 5.
16. Slovenko R: Foreward, the homosexual and society: An historical perspective. *U Dayton Law Rev* 1985; 10:445–457.
17. *ibid.*
18. Weller CW: *Bowers v Hardwick*: Balancing the interests of the moral order and individual liberty. *Cumberland Law Rev* 1986; 16:555–592.
19. *op cit,* n 16.
20. Kinsey A, *et al.*: *Sexual Behavior in the Human Male*. Philadelphia, Saunders, 1948.
21. Hooker E: Male homosexuals and their "worlds," in Marmor J. (ed) Sexual Inversion. New York, Basic Books, 1965.
22. Marmor J: *Sexual Inversion*. New York, Basic Books, 1965.
23. Socarides C: *The Overt Homosexual*. New York, Grune and Stratton, 1968.
24. American Psychiatric Association: *Diagnostic and Statistical Manual of Mental Disorders*. Washington, D.C., American Psychiatric Association, 1952.
25. *op cit,* n 1.
26. *op cit,* n 11.
27. *op cit,* n 11.
28. *op cit,* n 11.
29. *op cit,* n 11.
30. *op cit,* n 13.
31. *op cit,* n 13.
32. Socarides CW, Volkan VD: Challenging the diagnostic status of homosexuality [letter to Editor]. *Am J Psychiatry* 1981; 138:1256–1257.
33. *ibid.*
34. Robitscher J: The uses and abuses of psychiatry [The 1976 Isaac Ray Award Lectures]. *J Psychiatry Law* 1977; 5:331–404.
35. *op cit,* n 11.
36. *op cit,* n 11.
37. *op cit,* n 11.
38. *op cit,* n 11.
39. *op cit,* n 11.
40. Goldstein RL: Homosexuality. [Letter to Editor] *Psychiatr News* 1974; 9:2.
41. *op cit,* n 11.
42. *op cit,* n 11.
43. *op cit,* n 11.
44. American Psychiatric Association: Diagnostic and Statistical Manual of Mental Disorders, ed 3—Revised [DSM-III-R]. Washington, DC, American Psychiatric Association, 1987.
45. Spitzer RL, Endicott J: Medical and mental disorder: proposed definition and criteria, in Spitzer RL, Klein D (eds) Critical Issues in Psychiatric Diagnosis. New York, Raven Press, 1978.
46. *ibid.*
47. *ibid.*
48. Spitzer RL: The diagnostic status of homosexuality in DSM-III: A reformulation of the issues. *Am J Psychiatry* 1981; 138:210–215.
49. *op cit,* n 34.

50. Spitzer RL: Open letter to Jonas Robitscher, J, MD *J Psychiatry Law* 1978; 6:595–601.
51. *op cit*, n 5
52. Gutheil TG, Mills MJ: Legal conceptualizations, legal fictions, and the manipulation of reality. *Bull Am Acad Psychiatry Law* 1982; 10:17–27.
53. Pannick D: *Judges*. Oxford, Oxford University Press, 1987.
54. *Salisbury v Gilmore*, 2 K.B. 38, 51 (1942) Lord Justice MacKinnon).
55. *op cit*, n 53.
56. *Griswold v Connecticut*, 381 U.S. 479 (1965).
57. *Roe v Wade*. 410 U.S. 113 (1973).
58. Ferree CW: *Bowers v Hardwick*: the Supreme Court closes the door on the right to privacy and opens the door to the bedroom. *Denver U Law Rev* 1988; 64:599–612.
59. *ibid.*
60. *ibid.*
61. *op cit*, n 18.
62. Tharpes YL: *Bowers v Hardwick* and the legitimization of homophobia in America. *Howard Law J* 1987; 30:537–549.
63. *Bowers v Hardwick*, 478 U.S. 186 (1986) (Burger CJ, concurrence).
64. *op cit*, n 56.
65. Devlin P: *The Enforcement of Morals*. London, Oxford University Press, 1965.
66. *ibid.*
67. Hart HLA: *Law, Liberty and Morality*. Stanford, Stanford University Press, 1963.
68. 478 U.S. 186 (Blackmun J, dissent).
69. *ibid.*
70. *op cit*, n 62.
71. *op cit*, n 58.
72. *op cit*, n 62.
73. Levitan SA: The Supreme Court as super legislature emasculates the right to privacy: *Bowers v Hardwick*, 106 S. Ct. 2841 (1986). *Suffolk U Law Rev* 1987; 21:853–876.
74. *People v Onofre*, 51 N.Y.2d 476, 488 (New York Court of Appeals 1980).
75. *op cit*, n 68.
76. *op cit*, n 11.
77. *op cit*, n 2.
78. *op cit*, n 63.
79. *op cit*, n 4.
80. Jones HW, Kernochan JM, Murphy AW: *Legal Method: Cases and Text Materials*. Mineola, NY, Foundation Press, 1980.
81. *op cit*, n 16.
82. *op cit*, n 80.
83. Holmes OW: *The Common Law*. Boston, Little Brown, 1881.

21

Protecting the Rights of the Elderly

STANLEY R. KERN

The State of California defines elder abuse as infliction of injury, intimidation, cruel punishment, or other treatment resulting in physical harm, pain or mental suffering. The California statute also encompasses the concept of neglect, that is, the deprivation by a caregiver of vital goods or services.[1] Other states have similar statutes.

It is a fact of life becoming more and more apparent to the general public that the elderly are frequently taken advantage of. There are more articles in professional journals and in the daily newspapers of elder abuse and every few months one reads of a nursing home that is closed down or fined for mistreating its residents.[2] At times nursing homes are described as "snakepits"[3] and do not meet the minimum standards for handling food in a sanitary manner or administering medicines properly.[4] Occasionally an owner of a nursing home is arrested for heinous crimes against the elderly.[5] Even children and other relatives, including spouses, have been accused of mistreating elderly members of their family.

In fact, a New Hampshire researcher found elder abuse by a spouse was more than twice as prevalent as abuse from an offspring living in the home. In this study, equal numbers of men and women were victims and economic status and age were not related to the risk of abuse. Abusers were more likely to be a spouse with Alzheimer's disease or another family member with drug, alcohol, or mental illness problems who is financially dependent on the victim.[6] If these grave situations receive such publicity, one can imagine the numerous instances where there are more subtle attempts to override the civil rights of the elderly. Fortunately, there are some social agencies, such as the Community Health Law Project in New Jersey, and organizations, such as the American Association of

STANLEY R. KERN • New Jersey Medical School, South Orange, New Jersey 07079.

Retired Persons, that attempt to prevent such situations from occurring. Also, governmental offices such as ombudsman for the elderly have been established to protect the elderly from abuse and to see that their civil rights have not been abridged. However, it is important for physicians and particularly psychiatrists to be alert to the more subtle situations where civil rights of the elderly are ignored or attempts are made to brush aside their rights and liberties.

I present five cases that illustrate such situations. Two situations occurred in a nursing home and in three situations the individual was living in the community.

> F.S. was 68 years old when he was admitted to the nursing home with the dual diagnosis of Parkinsonism and Alzheimer's. He was placed on Lanoxin for a heart condition, given Sinemet for his Parkinsonism and 5 to 10 mg. of Valium IM as necessary if he became upset. Of course he was confused and disoriented but shortly after entering the nursing home he became paranoid: "Make sure my door is locked because they're in there all the time." He hallucinated that young men with a gun were in his closet and coming after him. He was not bedridden and he would wander the halls, fearful of entering his room. On several occasions he was found kneeling on the floor and would not move. Once he attacked a nurse and he threatened other residents, so that they were fearful of him.
>
> An attempt was made to control some of his symptoms and behavior by replacing the Valium with Mellaril, first 10 mg. at bedtime and then 50 mg. three times a day. When the patient complained about the Mellaril and objected to it, the attending physician at the nursing home changed the medication to Thorazine Concentrate and had it put in his food or drink. This still did not control his behavior and 2 1/2 years after his entry into the nursing home he was transferred to a V.A. Hospital. At no time after prescribing the Thorazine was the purpose of the medication or its possible side effects explained to the patient and when he did object to the medication it was given to him anyway surreptitiously.

> L.L. is a 91-year-old widowed white female who has been in the nursing home for about 18 months. She is in remarkably good physical health for a woman her age and she wanders about the nursing home socializing with the other residents. Several months after entering the nursing home she began to verbalize paranoid ideation, complaining that someone was going into her room, cutting up the chair, and rearranging the clothing in her closet. A discussion with the staff and her family revealed that her son was bringing in bottles of liquor for her and if he was not available she would have the nursing home handyman go into town and buy a bottle or two for her. This was stopped immediately and she was placed on Mellaril tablets, 10 mg., three times a day. The underlying delusion continued, but she was not as disturbed by it. A month or so following the initiation of the Mellaril I asked the nurse if there was any problem with the patient in taking the medication. Her answer was: "No, I told her it was a vitamin to give her more energy." I objected to her lying to the patient and told her to answer honestly. On my next trip to the nursing home, again, I inquired

about the medication. This time the nurse stated, "I give the medication, tell her to take it and leave before she can ask me any questions." Some of the problems we have to face are not always with our patients.

P.L. is an 86-year-old single white female, living alone in a rental apartment. She has a lovely, well-kept home and walks everywhere in town to do banking, shopping, and receive medical care. She has lived in her apartment for over 35 years and pays less than $200.00 per month in a prime old area due to rent control. She receives a pension check and social security and had saved $80,000 in a local bank. Two months before being brought to the attention of a social agency she had an accident where a limb from a tree fell on her and she was hospitalized for 10 days. After discharge she became confused about her finances and started to search for and converse with deceased family members. Apart from this confusion, she continued to maintain her home and meet her daily needs. Her attorney, sensing her concern and confusion about her finances, referred her to the trust department of a local bank. They set up a trust agreement, handling all her bills and nonpersonal mail. One would think this would have lessened her anxiety, but having been bright and independent, she resented this arrangement and feared loss of control of her finances. Her confusion increased and, having no living relatives, she left her estate to the apartment manager and an elderly neighbor who was suffering from serious rheumatoid arthritis.

The landlady, the neighbor, and a social worker who was called in all thought she was incompetent. The Community Health Law Project was called in and arrangements were made to have the patient examined for competency. She expressed resentment about being talked down to by the social worker, the trust officer at the bank, her landlady, and neighbors. She described her accident and her confusion following the hospitalization. She stated that the members of her family are no longer living, but sometimes she feels as though they are, and even sets the table for all five of them for dinner. She talked of aging and her frustrations with the decline of her health and memory. Incidentally, she was dressed appropriately and her home was described by the worker from the Project as being clean and attractive. Though she manifested memory deficits, they were not severe, and it was felt that she was competent and could continue to live on her own.

A conversation with the neighbor revealed that the neighbor had no mobility due to her arthritis and she resented seeing the patient free to come and go so easily. She stated that it was not appropriate for an elderly women to feed the birds in the path and walk around so much. Counseling was instituted with the neighbor to improve her attitude.

A meeting with the landlady indicated that she wanted the patient to move out so that she could raise the rent which could be well over $600 per month. She was advised that the patient was quite capable of continuing to live in her apartment.

The trust officer was contacted and made to realize that the patient resented giving up her independence even though she needed help and that she needed to be treated as an adult.

Arrangements were made for regular medical checkups and her attorney was made aware of her situation and difficulties so that he could advocate for her if necessary.

A follow-up revealed that she is doing well and living independently. The trust officer has a good working relationship with P.L. and they have visited several residents for senior women. She saw one place that she liked and realizes the time may come when she may need residential care. Her confusion has stabilized and her functioning remains good.

P.E. is a 72-year-old widowed black female living in a 4th floor walk-up apartment in downtown Newark, New Jersey. She was referred by her landlord to the Division on Aging in Essex County with the statement, "The woman is crazy. Get her out of my building." P.E. had no phone, so a worker was sent to the superintendent's apartment first. The worker found that the building was in a neighborhood that was being rebuilt and suspected that the owner wanted her out so that he could raise the rent. The superintendent claimed that P.E. runs down the hall shouting and screaming and knocking on doors. The worker went to P.E.'s apartment and was let in with no problem. P.E. was appropriately dressed and was quite willing to talk to the worker.

She had broken a leg and it had not healed properly, only to be injured again on her bed frame, so that she had limited mobility. It was difficult to picture this woman running down the hallways and screaming. She left the building only to visit her physician at a nearby clinic. She had friends who brought her groceries and she appeared to be doing well. She needed to have her benefits increased and was eager to move to senior housing where she would have access to an elevator and thus would have greater mobility.

She was evaluated for the possibility of any psychiatric disability. She was noted to be an elderly black female who was appropriately attired in a clean and neat dress. No gross unusual mannerisms were noted. Her affect was adequate and appropriate and her speech was spontaneous and coherent. There was no evidence of any delusions or hallucinations. She was oriented as to time, place, and person, and her sensorium was clear. No psychiatric disability was noted, so an attempt was made to seek increased benefits based upon a physical disability.

She was placed on a senior housing list and arrangements were made for transportation so that she could see her physician regularly.

Follow-up revealed no behavior previously described by her landlord for some time. Then one day the landlord called, with P.E. shouting in the background. A worker went to the building immediately and found that she had been drinking, but that her behavior was not extreme. She was referred to the New Jersey Council on Alcoholism who arranged AA meetings for P.E.; and at present she seems to be getting a great deal from these meetings. She is due to move soon and she seems excited and looking forward to the move. Her benefits have been increased and she is not drinking. A follow-up psychiatric visit indicated that she was competent to manage her affairs.

S.W. is an elderly (approximately 90 years old), black female found sitting on a couch in the living room of the house where she lived. Her landlord had taken control of her finances for his benefit and it was alleged that he was using the house to sell drugs. During the time of my examination of S.W., numerous individuals came and left the house, passing through the living room. S.W. was attired in a clean print dress, a sweater, and slippers, and she exuded an odor of urine. Her white hair was neatly braided. During the examination she ate a chewy candy bar. Her affect was bland and her speech was low so that it was frequently hard to understand her. She was difficult to question but there was no evidence of any overt delusions or hallucinations. She was disoriented as to time, place, and person, and her memory was severely impaired. She could not be tested in other areas.

It was my opinion that S.W. manifested a dementia, senile-onset type, and that she was not competent to make decisions regarding her welfare in all respects. I recommended that a competency hearing be held and a guardian be appointed to make decisions regarding her finances and her welfare. A report was submitted regarding my findings, conclusions, and recommendations; but no competency hearing was held and the last I had heard was that no change had been made in her living arrangements or her finances. In effect, my examination and report was an exercise in futility.

I think that there are two main things that can be learned from the cases that I have presented. First, in facilities such as hospitals and nursing homes, forensic psychiatrists, being more conversant with the law, should alert physicians to the manner in which ancillary personnel and others are treating the residents and patients in these facilities. I believe that they have an obligation to advocate for the patient in situations where their legal rights are being threatened or are actually brushed aside. Physicians can be confused about various laws, and even when laws are instituted requiring the reporting of abuse, neglect, and exploitation of adults, physicians may be unclear as to their legal duty.[7]

Second, social agencies, governmental agencies, and various volunteer agencies can be extremely useful in taking care of patients and protecting their rights. It is important to be aware of what agencies are available in the community and even to make some casual contact with them so that you might be of mutual assistance to each other for the benefit of the community. Too many physicians, including psychiatrists, depend upon social workers and other ancillary personnel to be familiar with the type of social agencies that might be available in a particular area, rather than being knowledgeable themselves.

Those of us who work with an elderly population should realize that with good fortune we will one day be part of that population. Advocating for this group and changing the attitude of people toward this group may come back to reward us one day.

REFERENCES

1. Pies R: Elder Abuse: Clinical Detection and Intervention. *Ger Med Today* 1987; 6:1, 24, Jan.
2. Gapen P: Nursing home faces loss of license over patient deaths. *Am Med News*, January 17, 1986, p 10.
3. Carlova J: Are doctors to blame for nursing home snakepits? *Med Eco*, November 21, 1983, p 63.
4. Cohen R, Whitlow J: Jersey nursing homes faulted on standards. *The Star-Ledger*, December 2, 1981, p 1.
5. *The Star-Ledger*, November 15, 1988, p 63.
6. *The Star-Ledger*, February 9, 1989, p 1.
7. Daniels RS, Carl-Daniels CL: Abuse of elders: Physicians are confused. Letters to the Editor. *JAMA*, 1988; 260:22, 3276.

22

Ethical Issues in Mandatory Drug Testing

CYNTHIA B. COHEN

THE DEVELOPMENT OF THE DEMAND FOR DRUG TESTING

The idea seems remarkably practical: Since substance abuse can be a matter of life-and-death, not just to those who use drugs, but to all of us, we should identify illegal drug users and weed them out from positions of responsibility. If we find them in the workplace, we should discharge them; if we spot them on the playing fields, we should remove them. An apparently simple and objective form of technology is available for identifying these persons—urine testing. Mandatory urine testing of employees and athletes has increasingly been advocated as a means of identifying those whose drug use represents a significant threat to our society.

But what if a person does not use drugs, is a steady and able worker, and bristles at having to void under the gaze of a company monitor? Indeed, what if a worker does use drugs and exhibits these same characteristics? Should a young college athlete be subject to mandatory testing to deter him or her from starting on drugs? Should all high school students be tested for drug use? What if these tests are not as reliable as has been assumed? Should potential employers be told that a worker has been fired from a previous position because he tested positive for drugs? The apparent practicality and simplicity of the idea of mandatory drug testing vanishes in a morass of ethical and political confusions, scientific and social uncertainties.

In 1986, President Reagan ordered all federal agencies to introduce programs to achieve a "drug-free workplace."[1] All federal job applicants were required to undergo testing for illegal drug use. Federal employees who were in

---

CYNTHIA B. COHEN • Department of Philosophy, Villanova University, Villanova, Pennsylvania 19085, and the Hastings Center, 255 Elm Road, Briarcliff Manor, New York 10510.

sensitive positions," where danger to the public health and safety or national security...could result from failure of an employee adequately to discharge his or her position" were made subject to random testing. The president's order also invited private firms, which are not bound by fourth Amendment restrictions that affect state and federal governments, to require drug testing of all workers, whether or not their drug use might directly affect the public health and safety. By 1987, 50% of the *Fortune* 500 companies were testing all job applicants for drugs, and many other firms were joining their number.[2] The practice has grown so rapidly that the courts have had little time to develop a theory regarding its legal acceptability. The question whether mandatory drug testing can be justified in the workplace and, if so, under what conditions, had just reached the Supreme Court of the United States at the time of this writing.[3,4]

Why has there been an upsurge in the demand for drug testing in recent years? A major reason is that we have only recently become aware of the special danger to the public safety that can be presented by certain workers who are under the influence of drugs, such as air-traffic controllers, pilots, railroad employees, and bus drivers. Consider some of the facts in the transportation sector. Between 1972 and 1983 drugs or alcohol were involved in railroad industry accidents that resulted in 25 deaths, 61 injuries, and property damage totalling over $19,000,000.[4] The danger to public safety created by drug use among railroad employees was brought home forcefully in 1987, when a freight train ran through a series of stop signals near Baltimore and crashed into a passenger train that was travelling at more than 100 miles per hour.[5] Fifteen passengers and the passenger train engineer were killed; 158 others were injured. Drug tests revealed that the freight train engineer and brakeman had smoked marijuana before the crash. Such information has spurred demands to require government and private sector employees, as well as college and professional athletes, to submit to drug testing.

THE ACCURACY AND PREDICTIVE VALUE OF DRUG TESTS

Drug testing cannot be ethically justified if it does not produce reliable results. The scientific aura that currently surrounds drug testing leads people to assume that it is accurate. It seems similar to any routine medical testing in which a sample is sent to a laboratory and results are provided by trained personnel. Yet routine medical tests can give incorrect results; for this reason they are often performed in conjunction with other tests that are designed to provide corroboration. Testing for the presence of drugs in the body, however, is not often done in conjunction with other tests due to financial pressures; a single positive test is usually taken to provide conclusive evidence of the presence of drugs.[6] This means that those who test positive incorrectly are often left without the means to rectify the situation, for they are usually unable to afford more expensive testing to reveal the error.

And it is possible to test positive incorrectly. The accuracy of the most commonly used and vigorously promoted tests for drugs is under serious question. In 1985, for instance, the Centers for Disease Control conducted a study of 13 drug-testing laboratories and found wide ranges in their accuracy.[7] The laboratory error rate ranged from 11%–100% when blind samples were sent as though they had originated from a treatment program. False positive results of up to 66% were received from these randomly chosen laboratories. C.D.C. investigators concluded that laboratories are often unable to detect drugs at concentrations called for by their contracts. High error rates were caused by such factors as poor management, inadequate personnel, broken chains of custody, and faulty maintenance and transmission of reports and records. A 1988 study from the National Institute for Occupational Safety and Health pointed out that the estimated predictive values of positive urine tests was "surprisingly low;"[8] there was no reliable way to ascertain whether those who tested positive had taken drugs. Moreover, several over-the-counter medicines, as well as poppy seeds, can produce positive tests for certain drugs, leading to even greater error.[9]

It seems reasonable to expect that large-scale testing would use new and inexperienced laboratories whose accuracy would be even lower than that of established laboratories. Currently, there are no standardized laboratory procedures in place for drug testing to avoid this problem, and there is no accepted proficiency system for rating laboratories. The National Institute on Drug Abuse is in the process of drafting a set of standards for employee testing at the time of this writing that may help to alleviate some of these problems.[10]

Even if the administration of tests were extremely accurate across laboratories, there is a major hazard in screening large, unselected populations, for the practical value of the test varies with the composition of the group to which it is applied.[11] Groups in which it is unusual to find drug users show many false-positive results. When a test with 95% accuracy, which means that it gives the wrong answer once every 20 times that it is used, is applied to a large group of whom only 1% are drug users, five people will be wrongly charged with drug use for every correct finding. A useful test must have a small percentage of error compared with the percent of drug users in the group being screened. Some suggest that tests be applied only when there is at least a 50% chance that the subject is on drugs and that the test used should have an accuracy of at least 95%. Even then, five out of every 100 of those tested would be falsely accused. But if we knew that the chance an individual was a drug user was 50% from the start, it is unlikely that we would need to test that person. More standard personnel methods would, in all likelihood, have been adequate to reveal that fact.

When positive test results are accurate, this does not necessarily indicate that their subjects were under the influence of drugs at the time of testing. Urine tests only determine whether a drug has been taken recently. Subjects may have consumed drugs days or weeks earlier and these substances may have no effect on job performance at the time of discovery. Nor does the presence of traces of drugs in the urine indicate whether an individual has a long-term problem of use or addiction.

These problems of accuracy and error raise the basic question of how many false accusations are enough to outweigh the benefits derived from detecting a certain number of drug users. False positives and negatives can be costly in many ways. Employees may lose their jobs; athletes may have their careers and personal lives ruined by them. They may be stigmatized socially and professionally for the remainder of their lives because of erroneous test results. If it is ethically justifiable to engage in drug testing, this should only be done with methods that minimize the damage to individuals. It appears that we do not currently have tools that are sufficiently accurate to detect drug abuse with the potential for harm at a reasonable cost. This leaves us with tests that have an enormous capacity to coerce and intimidate without producing reliable results.

The application of mass screening programs for drugs promises to generate more problems that it will resolve. The use and interpretation of affordable drug testing is currently so ill defined that testing programs cannot be justified. Further, no urine-detection system, no matter how accurate, can determine whether the test correlated with behavior and whether the subject was drug-impaired at the time that the urine was collected. Testing of workers and athletes, therefore, seems serious folly.

THE GOALS OF TESTING FOR DRUGS

The ethical issues involved in programs of mandatory testing for drugs arise from the goals or intended purposes of these programs. At least four such purposes have been suggested: (1) ensuring the safety of others; (2) ensuring the safety of individuals who use drugs; (3) deterring potential drug users; (4) preserving the integrity of businesses. We will examine each of these purposes in an effort to ascertain whether there are morally justifiable reasons for instituting programs of mandatory drug testing in the workplace or on the athletic fields.

Ensuring the Safety of Others

Whether to use mandatory drug testing in an attempt to protect the public health and safety is at issue mainly in the workplace. What is at stake is how to weigh individual freedom and privacy against the needs of society. We place tremendous importance on the autonomy and privacy of individuals and maintain that they have the right to be free from unreasonable searches and seizures. We require special justification for interfering with these basic values. Is such justification provided by the right of the public to be free from the threat of serious injury and death and the right of coworkers to a safe working environment?

Privacy must be invaded in truly accurate urine-testing because surveillance is essential during the collection of urine. Deception by workers can readily be effected by substituting someone else's urine for one's own or purchasing mail order samples. To avoid this, parts of the anatomy that are private must be exposed to others by the worker and closely observed during testing. This is intrusive and degrading.

Privacy is in further danger of erosion since tests can reveal much more than whether illegal drugs are present in the body. They can provide information ranging from what prescription drugs the person uses, to whether the subject is pregnant, or being treated for schizophrenia, depression, or a heart condition. In order to minimize the impact of false-positive tests, employees are sometimes required to provide their employer with a list of medicines they are taking. This is itself an unwarranted intrusion into their privacy, and places them at risk of being fired when the employer learns of the conditions for which they are taking medication. This is the kind of information that individuals want to keep private because it is susceptible to misuse. Evaluation of job performance can be made to depend on the employer's desire to minimize future potential risk by excluding those with undesirable life-styles, health habits, or medical conditions from the workplace.

Further, the concept of testing can be expanded to include searching workers' lockers and cars for drugs, frisking them as they enter work, and viewing them constantly with hidden cameras. There is pervasive concern that surveillance of everyone in the workplace through repeated testing for drugs would not only diminish our adherence to the value of individual privacy, but would also add unwanted totalitarian features to the fabric of our society.

A related reason for objecting to mandatory testing of workers for the presence of illegal drugs is that this presents a challenge to the basic presumption in our society that persons are innocent until they have committed some wrong. The rationale behind mandatory testing is that all workers are to be treated as drug users who will endanger others until they prove otherwise. It is contrary to the basic moral and legal traditions of justice in our society to force people to prove they have not committed crimes with which they have not been charged. We do not penalize people *before* they have done something wrong. The threat to the principle of the presumption of innocence that is posed by blanket mandatory testing seems at least as great as that presented by drug abuse in the workplace itself.

Yet we do accept intervention into the lives of individuals when they place others at risk by their behavior, even though this means some sacrifice of their individual privacy, freedom, and right to be presumed innocent. When those in positions of public responsibility or in dangerous occupations engage in drug abuse and impair their job performance, they may pose a risk of serious harm to others. In such cases, we consider it justifiable to subordinate their privacy and liberty to the public good. But we allow this only when there is strong evidence that these persons do represent a threat to others. Before you search an individual, you have to have some evidence to justify your suspicions. There has to be a reasonable suspicion, not only that they are taking drugs, but that their actions may lead to the injury of others.

It may be maintained that *all* workers can pose a risk of serious harm to others, either directly or indirectly, regardless of the position that they hold, and that the only way to ensure public safety is to engage in blanket mandatory testing. It is arguable that this would not interfere with the liberty and privacy of individuals to any great extent, since workers would only have to contribute a small sample of urine if strict testing procedures were followed. This does not seem the moral equivalent of locking these workers in jail or invading the privacy of their bedrooms.

Yet some lines can be drawn between those who would pose a serious threat of harm to others if they were affected by drugs at work and those who would not. Mandatory blanket testing of workers would be overinclusive and underinclusive in several respects. Such testing would be overinclusive in that it would cover those who do not use drugs, those in positions without significant potential for causing serious accidents to others, and those who are in positions with significant potential for causing serious accidents to others whose drug intake does not in fact cause risk of harm to others. It would be underinclusive in that it would not cover those who represent a danger to others for reasons not related to the use of illegal drugs. It would not include, for instance, those who use legal drugs or who are prone to alcoholism. Indeed, it is arguable that the failure to call for testing employees for legal drugs indicates that the real goal of testing is not to assure the public safety, but to test for illegal drugs as a "backdoor" method of enforcing the law.

An additional factor weighing against massive drug-testing of all workers is that this seems unnecessary. Large segments of the employee population are already subject to extensive monitoring. The worst drug abusers who represent a danger to others can be detected on the job by less draconian measures than blanket mandatory testing. Random assessment of workers' job performance by employers can more effectively achieve the goal of ensuring the safety of fellow workers and the public.

If we do not test everyone in the workplace, whom should we select to test? All who have a past record of having used drugs at some time? All who can predictably be found to be susceptible to drug abuse in the future? All who are in public service or who have jobs related to public safety? Only those individuals who inadvertently provide evidence of drug abuse and resulting job impairment?

Mandatory testing of those in sensitive positions within and without the federal government is ethically supportable under certain conditions. It is arguable that those who deal with military and security matters, airline pilots, air traffic controllers, train engineers, and nuclear facility operators must be free of drug-related impairments in order to protect the public. They are in positions where diminution of their alertness or reaction time might result in severe injury or damage to others. There may not be time to wait for some reasonable basis for suspicion that the individual has used illegal drugs. One study of the effects of marijuana, for example, showed that airline pilots performed at potentially dangerous levels 20 hours after they had smoked marijuana, even though they had no overt signs of impairment.[12] Mandatory testing of all who are in positions that directly affect the public safety would prevent drug abusers among them from harming others before their impairment became noticeable. The need to ensure the public safety and security weighs heavily against full protection of the freedom and privacy of those who are in such critical positions.

The definition of "sensitive positions" used by the federal government includes jobs that are critical to "public health and safety or national security." The application of this definition by the government, however, seems overly broad in some instances. Those in "sensitive positions," for example, are deemed to include animal caretakers at the Department of Health and Human Services. Drug use by these employees, it is maintained, could jeopardize the results of research and the lives of animals.[13] Such attenuated examples make it difficult to fathom who among federal employees could be said not to have some effect on the public health and safety. There seem to be no limits to scope of the concept "sensitive position" as it is being applied. If we are to require testing of all who have such jobs, the meaning of "sensitive positions" must be more narrowly defined.

To justify drug testing of some who are not in "sensitive" positions for the purpose of ensuring the safety of others, it should be necessary to show that drug-use produces job-related physical or mental impairment in individuals, that this is dangerous to others, *and* that there is reason to believe that the individual to be tested uses these drugs in proximity to the workplace. There should be evidence of declining or erratic performance by an employee, evidence that this will lead to harm to fellow workers or consumers of the product or service that the employee provides, and evidence that these problems are related to drug use. Drug tests of workers in positions that are not sensitive should not be random, but should be limited to those who are reasonably suspected, on grounds that can be articulated, of using drugs in a way that impairs their job performance and that is detrimental to others. Such tests should not be initiated on the basis of chance or inarticulated hunches.

We must also recognize that those who are not in "sensitive" positions who test positive may not pose a threat to others. Correlations between the presence of drugs in the body and behavioral consequences cannot be made without some evidence of a causal connection between them. Illegal drug use in itself does not provide evidence that an individual worker will put in a deficient performance on the job that will endanger others. He or she may be able to fulfill the requirements of the job unimpeachably. There is considerable debate about whether intervention into the working lives of those with traces of drugs in their urine can be justified.

Ensuring the Safety of Individuals Who Use Drugs

Another kind of harm that drug abuse can create is to the users of drugs themselves. Individuals who experiment with drugs not only risk harming others, but place their own welfare in jeopardy. The chance that workers will injure themselves on the job or ruin their lives due to drug addiction raises serious questions about the obligation of employers and others to attempt to help them before it is too late. One justification of the federal government's proposed program of random testing of federal employees is to be able to identify and help those in the federal workplace who use drugs. This is clear from the fact that in this program, those who test positive are referred for treatment and counseling.

Concern about the well-being of drug users has been especially prominent in the college athletic setting where drug abuse can permanently injure those who have their whole lives ahead of them. Society, it is thought, owes them the measure of protection that is afforded by testing as they face the special challenges and stresses that college athletes encounter. This concern is backed by evidence that some young athletes have taken chances with their own lives by abusing drugs. After the death of a college basketball star in 1986, for instance, a task force at the University of Maryland recommended a widespread program of drug-testing among the college's students, staff, and faculty.[14] Some argue, because of such unfortunate deaths, that we should test all college athletes to ensure that we discover drug use before it ensnares them.

Testing individuals to protect them from themselves requires the same sort of invasion of their privacy and liberty that was entailed by testing to protect the safety of others. However, we require even more stringent justification of such incursions into individual privacy and freedom when the risk posed by an individual's behavior is to that person alone. This is as true for young adults as it is for those who are further on in years. Such justification is not available for blanket mandatory drug testing of employees and college athletes. This mode of testing would be overinclusive in that it would test those who do not use drugs, as well as those who do without placing their health in jeopardy, and it would be underinclusive in that it would not test for those who use alcohol, smoke cigarettes, or place themselves at risk by using other substances detrimental to their health. More fundamentally, the kind of coercive invasion into the privacy of individuals that testing would involve in order to protect them from themselves is alien to the ethical framework that informs our society.

The goal of providing for the safety of those who put themselves at risk by using drugs is laudatory, but can be reached through less intrusive and less coercive measures than mandatory urine testing. We can encourage youthful athletes and mature employees not to endanger their own lives with drug abuse through programs of education and prevention, rather than through programs of forced surveillance.

Deterring Potential Drug Users

Testing for drugs has also been heralded on grounds that it will deter drug use by those who are not currently users. Discovery through testing and the penalties that follow this, including loss of a job or a scholarship, can provide a significant deterrent to those who may consider experimenting with drugs. Businesses want to assure themselves that their employees will know that they can't use drugs and continue to work for their firm. Some who are responsible for the administration of sports believe that potential drug abusers who are thinking of emulating nationally recognized athletes will be discouraged when testing results in removing these athletes from the team.

When there is no evidence of widespread drug use, however, it is difficult to argue that mandatory drug testing will deter drug use, for there is no threat that such testing will avert. Surely more than unfounded fears must justify such an intrusive search. When drug testing is initiated in a workplace environment in which drugs are a significant factor, it may well serve as a deterrent to those who are not users. However, such testing seems no more justified than are random searches of the person and possessions of employees for money they may have embezzled in order to combat a wave of embezzlement on the job. There are other, less intrusive means available for deterring potential lawbreakers.

The deterrence argument has been used especially forcefully for testing star college athletes. Yet singling out college athletes for an invasion of privacy because they are admired by their peers cannot be justified. To do so is unjustifiably to press on them the role of special representatives of their institutions. Surely there are other students who also serve as role models on campus. If universities wish to diminish the influence of drugs by testing campus role models, they should also test those who are prominent in extracurricular activities, such as student government officers, and those who are elected to Phi Beta Kappa, as well as athletes. There is no reason why only athletes should receive this kind of scrutiny of their private lives. A less invasive form of deterrence would be to deemphasize the importance of college sports and to reduce the pressures that are placed on student athletes.

Those who become professional athletes, on the other hand, are in a different position from college athletes, for they are in a unique kind of business and must be held to a distinctive standard of behavior. They provide their customers with the enjoyment of watching games and the exercise of athletic talent, as well as the opportunity to identify with fantasy figures. Professional athletes become icons for fans in the special culture that surrounds professional sports. This contributes to the popularity of these sports and, in turn, to the economic health of these athletes' teams. Since drug abuse is one of the taboos of this special culture, athletes and owners of teams have reason to assure their fans that players do not take drugs. Mandatory random drug testing of professional athletes, therefore, can be justified as necessary for retaining their fantasy-laden images which, in turn, is essential for retaining their fantastically high incomes.

Preserving the Integrity of Businesses

Does the potential for generating economic harm to businesses justify mandatory testing of workers? Analysts have estimated that lost productivity, absenteeism, property damage, and the higher health-care expenses created by substance abuse cost American businesses tens of billions of dollars annually.[15] Some companies that have instituted urinalysis programs to test for drugs have reported increased job efficiency and significant declines in lost work time and accident rates.[16] Yet when we consider that it is estimated that 40,000,000 people smoke marijuana at least once a year and that 20,000,000 use it regularly,[17] we must ask whether it is economically prudent to try to ferret out these drug users.

Employers have a duty to protect workers. This is, at a minimum, part of their obligation to use their business' resources in the most efficient way. They have a responsibility to detect unfitness for work on the part of their employees and may be held legally responsible if employees who are under the influence of drugs cause accidents or create harm for others on the job. Employees using controlled substances may be more apt to produce defective products for which their employers will be liable. Employers, therefore, have a right to demand that workers who do not meet some basic minimum level of performance be removed from their positions.

Indiscriminate testing of employees is too intrusive to be justified by these arguments when other methods of detecting impaired job performance are available that respect the privacy, freedom, and dignity of the individual. Employers can control drug use on the job by supervising their work force adequately and testing only when there is reason to believe that an individual is having difficulties on the job that are related to drugs. Objective indications of drug use, such as deterioration of work habits and chronic absenteeism would adequately identify those eligible for testing. Further, while employers have a right to expect that their workers will not be under the influence of drugs when they report to work, there is serious question about whether urinalysis for drugs will prevent this.

The power relationship between the employer and employee in these circumstances must also be considered. Drug tests are ordered and paid for by the employer. There is no doctor-patient relationship between the tester and the employee and therefore, no control over the situation by the employee. The resulting information is apparently not his or hers. This means that the employee, unless he or she is a member of a union that has negotiated some protections for workers, is at risk of being summarily fired after having tested positive, and has no way to remedy the matter. Such workers are in a unique position of dependency in which they require some form of protection against intrusive drug testing.

Some argue that an employee who uses drugs poses a more indirect threat to the integrity of the workplace because one who is willing to flout the law with respect to one behavior will be willing to flout other laws.[17] An employee who is willing to use drugs might also be willing to embezzle company funds or to endanger the fiscal health of the employer in some other way. Workers who test positive should therefore be transferred, demoted, or fired. However, there is no convincing empirical evidence to support these claims.

Still others maintain that drug use can generate expensive addictions that will induce otherwise honest employees to enrich themselves at the employer's expense. A federal court of appeals argued that "the drug user's questionable integrity, as well as the high financial cost of obtaining illegal drugs may increase his susceptibility to bribery by criminal drug enterprises."[3] However, tests give no indication of the degree of expense of the employee's drug habit, and some drugs are inexpensive. This argument, therefore, is also wide of the mark.

Employers have a right to expect their employees to report to work in fit condition and not to become impaired while on the job. But they do not have the right to subject them to bodily searches if they have no reason to suspect them of drug use that impairs their job performance. Sound management practices, including appropriate supervision and counseling provide effective ways to detect drug-related problems on the job and to resolve them. Urine testing of demonstrated accuracy may be a useful part of an overall program if it is limited to those employees who are reasonably suspected of using drugs in a way that impairs their performance at work.

RESPONDING TO THOSE WHO ARE DRUG ABUSERS

How should employers deal with drug abuse on the job? What should college athletic coaches do with the information that they derive from drug tests? Should the goal of testing for drug abuse be deterrence and punishment or rehabilitation and treatment?

Some employers have discharged employees who have tested positive. The poor morale that mandatory firing creates is a special cost that employers must take into account. Employees who feel that they are not trusted may not work as well as they might. Turnover is expensive for employers, as is recruiting and training new employees (who may themselves become substance abusers). Some firms have decided against testing because of such human and economic costs. They would rather build a relationship with employees based on confidence and loyalty and help them when drug or other problems arise than ensure that they have caught every individual who has used drugs.

The argument that counseling and referral for treatment are more beneficial to the employee and to the employer in the long run was implicitly accepted in President Reagan's Executive Order of 1986 in which drug testing of federal workers was addressed. This Order established an employee-assistance program for assessment, counseling, and referral for treatment. It indicated that no employees could be discharged or disciplined for illegal drug use if they voluntarily sought counseling or treatment and refrained from illegal drug use thereafter. Employees in "sensitive positions," however, could be suspended from work while they underwent treatment.

Testing urine for the presence of drugs in the body will not prevent drug abuse or cure addiction. Education and voluntary rehabilitation are methods that bear promise of being effective for achieving these ends. Managers and coaches should be taught to spot the signs of drug dependency and to address the individual appropriately. Rehabilitation of drug abusers has been more effective than dismissal except in the most extreme cases.[18] A good assistance program for these employees returns five dollars for every dollar invested in it. Moreover, treatment should not be restricted to drug abusers. Those who are having difficulty in performing adequately at work for any reason should be given special attention and treatment.

THE LARGER ISSUE

Testing for illegal drugs seems to provide a quick cure for the complex social problems of drug abuse. It is a lot easier to test for drugs and to remove those who use them from the workplace or the playing fields than it is to curtail illegal drug use in other ways. Unfortunately, testing does little to address the social problem of drug use in our society, although it does reinforce the illusion that we are doing something about it. Surely we can try to mount educational programs and other ways of dealing with drug abuse that do not invade the privacy, liberty, and dignity of massive numbers of individuals, the vast majority of whom are not drug abusers.

REFERENCES

1. Executive Order No. 12,564, 5 U.S.C. s7301 at 175–76 (1986).
2. Rothstein L: Drug Testing in the Workplace: The challenge to employment relations and employment law. *Chi-Kent Law Rev* 1987; 63:683–704.
3. *National Treasury Employees Union v Von Raab*, 816 F.2d 170 (1987), *cert. granted*, no. 86-1879. This case was decided in *National Treasury Employees Union v von Raab*, 109 S. Ct. 1384 (1989), 103 L.Ed. 2nd 685 (1989), in which the Supreme Court upheld a program that required urinalysis for all customs officers who sought transfer or promotion to jobs directly involving drug interdiction or requiring that a firearm be carried. The Court found that special governmental needs other than law enforcement were involved and that the government's interest in apprehending drug users outweighed the privacy expectations of the customs officers. The Court, however, was not willing to uphold a drug-testing program for employees who handle sensitive information, observing that the Customs Service had defined this category, which included accountants, animal caretakers, and baggage clerks, more broadly than necessary. The dissent stressed that the record showed no need for drug tests of Customs Service employees nor any connection between the testing and any threatened harm to the national interest. It maintained that the real reason for the program was to show that the government is serious about its "war on drugs" and argued that the impairment of individual liberties cannot be the means of making a symbolic point, even for a worthy cause.
4. *Railway Labor Executives' Association v Burnley*, 839 F.2d 575 (1988), *cert. granted*, no. 87-1555. This case was decided in *Skinner v Railway Labor Executives Association*, 109 S. Ct. 1402 (1989), 103 L.Ed. 2nd 639 (1989), in which the Supreme Court sustained a federal regulation requiring blood and urine tests of railway employees involved in major accidents, arguing that the government's compelling interest in ensuring the safety of the travelling public by conducting such tests outweighed the employees' limited privacy expectations. The Court ruled that tests could be ordered for all employees on duty at the time of the accident, even when there was neither a warrant nor individualized suspicion of any employee. The dissent compared the sacrifice of civil liberties of railway employees in the war against drugs to the sacrifice of civil liberties by Japanese-Americans who were forcibly relocated during World War II, and challenged the Court's conclusion that the intrusion on personal privacy from drug testing was minimal.
5. *The New York Times*, February 19, 1987, p B-2, col 4.
6. Sexton T, Zilz U: On the wisdom of mandatory drug testing. *J Policy Analysis and Management* 1988; 7:542–547.
7. Hansen H, Caudill S, Boone J: Crisis in drug testing: Results of CDC blind study. *JAMA* 1985; 253:2382–2387.

8. Wells V, Halperin W, Thun M: The estimated predictive value of screening for illicit drugs in the workplace. *Am J Public Health* 1988; 78:817–819.
9. Morgan J: Problems of mass urine screening for misused drugs. *J Psychoactive Drugs* 1984; 16:305–317.
10. Wish E: Urine testing of criminals: What are we waiting for? *J Policy Analysis and Management* 1988; 7:542–564.
11. Anderson W: Too Many Bugs in Screening Measures. *The Wall Street Journal*, April 14, 1986.
12. Yesavage V, Leirer M, Denari A, Hollister J: Carry-over effects of marijuana intoxication on aircraft pilot performance: A preliminary report. *Am J Psychiatry* 1985; 142:1325–31.
13. Your boss is not a cop. *The New Republic*, June 6, 1988.
14. Vesey T: U-Maryland Drug Task Force backs expulsion, testing. *Washington Post*, October 23, 1986, p 81.
15. Smith D, Wesson D, Zerkin F, Novey J (eds): *Substance Abuse in the Workplace*, San Francisco, Haight-Ashbury Publishing, 1985.
16. Stille K: Drug testing: The scene is set for a dramatic legal collision between the rights of employers and workers. *National Law J*, April 7, 1986, p 22, col 1.
17. Reuter, P: Testing and deterrence. *J Policy Analysis and Management*, 1988; 7:554–557.
18. Murphy, B: How to protect employees who are tested for drug and alcohol abuse. *Practical Lawyer* 1987; 33:27–40.

Appendix: AAPL Ethical Guidelines for the Practice of Forensic Psychiatry

I. PREAMBLE

The American Academy of Psychiatry and the Law is dedicated to the highest standards of practice in forensic psychiatry. Recognizing the unique aspects of this practice which is at the interface of the professions of psychiatry and the law, the Academy presents these guidelines for the ethical practice of forensic psychiatry.

Commentary

Forensic psychiatry is a sub-specialty of psychiatry, a medical specialty. Membership in the American Psychiatric Association, or its equivalent, is a prerequisite for membership in the American Academy of Psychiatry and the Law. Hence, these guidelines supplement the Annotations Especially Applicable to Psychiatry of the American Psychiatric Association to the Principles of Medical Ethics of the American Medical Association.

The American Academy of Psychiatry and the Law endorses the definition of forensic psychiatry adopted by the American Board of Forensic Psychiatry, Inc.:

> Forensic psychiatry is a sub-specialty of psychiatry in which scientific and clinical expertise is applied to legal issues in legal contexts embracing civil, criminal, correctional or legislative matters; forensic psychiatry should be practiced in accordance with guidelines and ethical principles enunciated by the profession of psychiatry. (Adopted May 20, 1985.)

The forensic psychiatrist practices this subspecialty at the interface of two professions, each of which is concerned with human behavior and each of which has developed its own particular institutions, procedures, values and vocabulary. As a consequence, the practice of forensic psychiatry entails inherent potentials for complications, conflicts, misunderstandings and abuses.

In view of these concerns, the American Academy of Psychiatry and the Law provides these guidelines for the ethical practice of forensic psychiatry.

II. CONFIDENTIALITY

Respect for the individual's right of privacy and the maintenance of confidentiality are major concerns of the psychiatist performing forensic evaluations. The psychiatrist maintains confidentiality to the extent possible given the legal context. Special attention is paid to any limitations on the usual precepts of medical confidentiality. An evaluation for forensic purposes begins with notice to the evaluee of any limitations on confidentiality. Information or reports derived from the forensic evaluation are subject to the rules of confidentiality as apply to the evaluation and any disclosure is restricted accordingly.

Commentary

The forensic situation often presents significant problems in regard to confidentiality. The psychiatrist must be aware of and alert to those issues of privacy and confidentiality presented by the particular forensic situation. Notice should be given as to any limitations. For example, before beginning a forensic evaluation, the psychiatrist should inform the evaluee that although he is a psychiatrist, he is not the evaluee's "doctor." The psychiatrist should indicate for whom he is conducting the examination and what he will do with the information obtained as a result of the examination. There is a continuing obligation to be sensitive to the fact that although a warning has been given, there may be slippage and a treatment relationship may develop in the mind of the examinee.

The psychiatrist should take precautions to assure that none of the confidential information he receives falls into the hands of unauthorized persons.

The psychiatrist should clarify with a potentially retaining attorney whether an initial screening conversation prior to a formal agreement will interdict consultation with the opposing side if the psychiatrist decides not to accept the consultation.

In a treatment situation, whether in regard to an inpatient or to an outpatient in a parole, probation, or conditional release situation, the psychiatrist should be clear about any limitations on the usual principles of confidentiality in the treatment relationship and assure that these limitations are communicated to the patient. The psychiatrist should be familiar with the institutional policies in regard to confidentiality. Where no policy exists, the psychiarist should clarify these matters with the institutional authorities and develop working guidelines to define his role.

III. CONSENT

The informed consent of the subject of a forensic evaluation is obtained when possible. Where consent is not required, notice is given to the evaluee of the nature of the evaluation. If the evaluee is not competent to give consent, substituted consent is obtained in accordance with the laws of the jurisdiction.

Commentary

Consent is one of the core values of the ethical practice of medicine and psychiatry. It reflects respect for the person, a fundamental principle in the practices of medicine, psychiatry and forensic psychiatry. Obtaining informed consent is an expression of this respect.

It is important to appreciate that in particular situations, such as court ordered evaluations for competency to stand trial or involuntary commitment, consent is not required. In such a case, the psychiatrist should so inform the subject and explain that the evaluation is legally required and that if the subject refuses to participate in the evaluation, this fact will be included in any report or testimony.

With regard to any person charged with criminal acts, ethical considerations preclude forensic evaluation prior to access to, or availability of legal counsel. The only exception is an examination for the purpose of rendering emergency medical care and treatment.

Consent to treatment in a jail or prison or other criminal justice setting must be differentiated from consent to evaluation. The psychiatrists providing treatment in these settings should be familiar with the jurisdiction's rules in regard to the patient's right to refuse treatment.

IV. HONESTY AND STRIVING FOR OBJECTIVITY

The forensic psychiatrist functions as an expert within the legal process. Although he may be retained by one party to a dispute in a civil matter or the prosecution or defense in a criminal matter, he adheres to the principles of honesty and striving for objectivity. His clinical evaluation and the application of the data obtained to the legal criteria are performed in the spirit of such honesty and striving for objectivity. His opinion reflects this honesty and striving for objectivity.

Commentary

The adversarial nature of our Anglo-American legal process presents special hazards for the practicing forensic psychiatrist. Being retained by one side in a civil or criminal matter exposes the forensic psychiatrist to the potential for unintended bias and the danger of distortion of his opinion. It is the responsibility of the forensic psychiatrist to minimize such hazards by carrying out his responsibilities in an honest manner striving to reach an objective opinion. The practicing forensic psychiatrist enhances the honesty and striving for objectivity of his work by basing his forensic opinions, his forensic reports and his forensic testimony on all the data available to him. He communicates the honesty and striving for objectivity of his work and the soundness of his clinical opinion by distinguishing, to the extent possible, between verified and unverified information as well as between clinical "facts," "inferences" and "impressions."

While it is ethical to provide consultation to an adversary in a legal dispute as a testifying or reporting expert, honesty and striving for objectivity are required. The impression that a psychiatrist in a forensic situation might distort his opinion in the service of the party which retained him is especially detrimental to the profession and must be assiduously avoided.

Honesty, objectivity, and the adequacy of the clinical evaluation may be called into question when an expert opinion is offered without a personal examination. While there are authorities who would bar an expert opinion in regard to an individual who has not been personally examined, it is the position of the Academy that if, after earnest effort, it is not possible to conduct a personal examination, an opinion may be rendered on the basis of other information. However, under such circumstances, it is the responsibility of the forensic psychiatrist to assure that the statement of his opinion and any reports or testimony based on the opinion clearly indicate that there was no personal examination and that the opinion expressed is thereby limited.

In custody cases, honesty and striving for objectivity require that all parties be interviewed, if possible, before an opinion is rendered. When this is not possible, or, if for any reason not done, this fact should be clearly indicated in the forensic psychiatrist's report and testimony. Where one parent has not been seen, even after deliberate effort, it may be inappropriate to comment on that parent's fitness as a parent. Any comment on that parent's fitness should be qualified and the data for the opinion be clearly indicated.

Contingency fees, because of the problems that these create in regard to honesty and striving for objectivity, should not be accepted. On the other hand, retainer fees do not create problems in regard to honesty and striving for objectivity and, therefore, may be accepted.

A treating psychiatrist should generally avoid agreeing to be an expert witness or to perform an evaluation of his patient for legal purposes because a forensic evaluation usually requires that other people be interviewed and testimony may adversely affect the therapeutic relationship.

V. QUALIFICATIONS

Expertise in the practice of forensic psychiatry is claimed only in areas of actual knowledge and skills, training and experience.

Commentary

As regards expert opinions, reports and testimony, the expert's qualifications should be presented accurately and precisely. As a correlate of the principle that expertise may be appropriately claimed only in areas of actual knowledge, skill, training and experience, there are areas of special expertise, such as the evaulation of children or persons of foreign cultures, or prisoners, that may require special training and expertise.

VI. PROCEDURES FOR HANDLING COMPLAINTS OF UNETHICAL CONDUCT

The American Academy of Psychiatry and the Law does not adjudicate complaints of unethical conduct against members or others.

Complaints of unethical conduct against members of the Academy are referred to the attention of the appropriate committee of the American Psychiatric Association.

Members of the Academy or of the public wishing assistence in this regard may consult, in confidence, with the Chairperson of the Committee on Ethics of the Academy.

Commentary

It is the present policy of the American Academy of Psychiatry and the Law not to adjudicate complaints of unethical conduct against members or others.

General questions in regard to ethical practice in forensic psychiatry are welcomed by the Academy and should be submitted for consideration to the Committee on Ethics.

Should a specific complaint against a member be submitted to the Academy, it will be referred to the Chairman of the Ethics Committee. The Chairman will, in turn, direct the complainant to the member's local District Branch Ethics Committee.

The Academy, through its Committee on Ethics or in any other way suitable, will assist the local or national Committee on Ethics of the American Psychiatric Association in the adjudication of complaints of unethical conduct or the developing of guidelines of ethical conduct as they relate to forensic psychiatric issues.

Index

Abel, G.G., 277, 285, 286
Abortion
  Catholics and, 39, 48
  following surrogate embryo transfer, 246, 247, 248
  Hippocratic oath and, 47, 48
Accidents, drug use-related, 314
Accreditation Council on Fellowships in Forensic Psychiatary, 20, 21
Accreditation Council on Graduate Medical Education, 21
Acquired immune deficiency syndrome (AIDS). *See also* Human immunodeficiency virus infection
  dementia complex, 221, 222–223
  discrimination related to, 236, 237
  HIV infection relationship, 219, 220
  among homosexuals, 220, 221, 303
  prevalence, 220
Acquittal, insanity-related, 142. *See also* Insanity defense, not guilty by reason of insanity
Actus reus, 80
Adoption laws, 257
Adult Self-Expression Scale, 280
Adversarial system
  expert witnesses' role in, 12–13, 15–16, 28, 76, 86, 88, 329
  impartiality and, 117, 119, 122–124, 125–126, 128
  lack of understanding of, 22
  origin, 28
  process, 4
  psychiatrists' aversion to, 59–60
  purpose, 86–87
  therapeutic alliance and, 141
Advocacy
  of expert witness, 45, 60–64, 76, 78–79, 122
    vs. "hired gun" role, 44, 76–77
    impartiality and, 122
  in prison psychiatry, 68
Aesculapius, 37
Afflect v United States, 96
Ake v Oklahoma, 76, 101, 125, 144, 212
Alcoholism, 7, 225
Alienist, 5
Allen, Woody, 88, 108n.
Allen v Illinois, 157
Amendments
  Fifth, 151, 158
  Sixth, 158
American Academy of Forensic Sciences
  code of ethics, 66–67
  guiding principles, 67
  medical ethics survey, 31–32
  Psychiatry and Behavioral Science Section, 20
American Academy of Psychiatry and the Law, 20, 163
  adversarial system and, 22, 121
  ethical complaint adjudication, 171–174, 330–331
  Ethical Guidelines for the Practice of Forensic Psychiatry, 19, 32, 128, 130, 164–169, 171–172, 286, 327–331
    adversarial system, 121
    advocacy, 122
    confidentiality, 130, 164–165
    cross-examination, 122
    honesty and striving for objectivity, 164, 167–168, 329–330

American Academy of Psychiatry and the Law (*Cont.*)
Ethical Guidelines for the Practice of Forensic Psychiatry (*Cont.*)
impartiality and objectivity, 117, 119, 122–124, 125–126, 128
informed consent, 165–166
neutrality, 126–127
psychiatrist's qualifications, 168–169
Frye test and, 82
medical ethics survey of Tri-State Chapter, 31–32
American Association of Retired Persons, 307–308
American Bar Association, 20
ethical guidelines, 87
Criminal Justice Mental Health Standards, 97
impartiality, 87, 124–125
National Interprofessional Code for Physicians and Attorneys, 60, 69
American Board of Forensic Psychiatry, 19, 20, 21, 66, 67, 163, 327
American Board of Medical Specialties, 21
American Board of Psychiatry and Neurology, 20–21
American Civil Liberties Union, 77
Capital Punishment Project, 215
American Medical Association, 4, 14
Code of 1848, 36, 37
establishment of, 37
National Interprofessional Code for Physicians and Attorneys, 60, 69
Principles of Medical Ethics, 33, 39, 43
capital punishment, 46, 208–209
HIV-infected patient care, 226
American Nurses' Association, 226
American Psychiatric Association
ethical complaint adjudication by, 169, 171–174, 177, 180–181, 330–331
forensic psychiatry recognition by, 21, 22
Guidelines for Legislation on the Psychiatric Hospitalization of Adults, 187, 192
Guttmacher Award, 20
homosexuality diagnosis of, 293, 294, 295–299
Principles of Medical Ethics with Annotations Especially Applicable to Psychiatry, 14, 45, 171–172
capital punishment, 13, 46
American Psychiatric Association (*Cont.*)
Principles of Medical Ethics with Annotations Especially Applicable to Psychiatry (*Cont.*)
civil commitment, 45
dangerousness prediction, 27, 186–187
HIV-infected patient care, 226
sexual misconduct, 176, 178, 180
sexual misconduct charge adjudication by, 177, 180–181
geriatric psychiatry recognition by, 21–22
American Psychological Association, 137
Amicus curiae, 27
Antiandrogen therapy, 283–284
Anti-buggery statute of 1533, 295
Anti-Semitism, 9
Antisocial personality, 46
Appelbaum, Paul, 12, 13, 37–38, 43, 46, 69, 118–119, 161, 186, 211, 271
Army doctors, 64, 211. *See also* Military doctors
Arousal, sexual, 281, 284
Artificial insemination, 257–258
Assault
HIV exposure as, 229–230
by hospitalized patients, 187–191, 203
racial factors, 197
Assault Knowledge Inventory, 280
Association of Directors of Forensic Psychiatry Fellowships, 20
Attorney-client privilege, 144, 159
Auschwitz, 42
Autonomy
of family, 260
of patients, 47
in private practice, 130
as right, 63, 300
self-determination and, 199
Aversive conditioning, 137

Baby M case, 253–254, 258–259, 261
Barefoot v Estelle, 4, 13
Barry, Marion, 107n.
Battered spouse syndrome, 94, 95, 111n.
Battle of the experts, 87, 91, 119, 167. *See also* Expert witness, conflict between experts
Bazelon, David, 12–13, 41, 58, 75
Beauchamp, Tom, 40, 192
Beckley v People, 95
Binder, R., 187, 188, 190, 191

Beneficence, 15, 37, 40, 47
Bentham, Jeremy, 25
Bernard v United States, 98
Bertram v Wunning, 106n.
Best interests of the child, 27, 260
Bias 6, 15–16, 44
  inevitable, 15–16, 75–76, 87, 121–122
  responsibility for, 16
  therapeutic, 49, 61, 66, 88
  unintended, 329
Binder, R., 187, 188, 190, 191
Biographers, 87
Bisexuals, AIDS among, 221
Blackmun, Justice, 301
Blood transfusion, as AIDS risk factor, 220, 221, 231–232, 238
Bloom, J., 185
Bowers v Hardwick, 293, 300–301, 302
Bright v United States, 93
Brody, Baruch, 39–41, 46, 49
Bulletin of the American Academy of Psychiatry and the Law, 4, 20

Canadian Psychiatric Association, 202
Capital punishment
  competency to be executed evaluation, 144–145, 158–160
  dangerousness prediction in, 212–213
  defense testimony, 43, 45, 77
    honest advocacy for defense, 160
    insanity defense, 46, 212
  Miranda-type warnings, 158–160
  mitigating factors, 46, 207
  moral objections to, 208–209, 213–216
  personal examination, 45
  physicians' participation in, 45, 207–209
  primum nil nocere and, 210, 212
  professional ethics regarding, 45, 61, 208, 209–213
  prosecution testimony, 4, 11–12, 13–14, 61
  sentencing hearings, 145, 158–159, 207–208, 212
Capital trials, physicians' participation in, 43, 45, 46, 209–216
Care, continuity of, 141
Caring, morality vs., 48
Carrick, Paul, 34
CAT scan, 98
Causation, 90. *See also* Proximate cause
Caution, informal ethical sanction, 173
Center for Disease Control
  HIV antibody test interpretation, 232
  HIV guidelines, 226–227, 228, 235–236
Chakaka Samhita, 35
Chambers, Whittaker, 98
Character, evidence regarding, 90
Child abuse
  countertransference and, 271
  Miranda-type warnings and, 152
  model, 178
  reporting of, 138–139, 152
  sexual, 94–95, 111n.
Child custody, 43, 65, 132, 267n. *See also* Custody litigation
Child molester. *See* Pedophile
Children
  elder abuse by, 307
  legal rules regarding, 6–7
  sexual abuse. *See* Child abuse, sexual
  traumatic experiences of, 6–7
  as witnesses, 94–95, 111n.
Christensen v State, 108n.
Chromosomal abnormalities, 246–247
Ciccone, Richard, 63, 64, 275
Civil cases
  evidence, 22–23
  psychiatric testimony, 65
Civil commitment, 56, 136, 200–203
  American Psychiatric Association Guidelines, 45, 187, 192
  civil liberties and, 191–192
  criteria, 191–192
  for dangerousness, 187–195
    dangerousness prediction reliability and, 187–191
    therapeutic implications, 191–194
  justification, 201, 202
  Miranda-type warnings, 143, 152
  of not guilty by reason of insanity individuals, 156–157
personal examination, 45
  treater/evaluator dual role in 135, 136, 142
Civil practice, criminal practice vs., 132
Civil rights, of the elderly, 307–312
Claudius, Emperor, 35
Clear and convincing. *See* Evidence, clear and convincing
Clinical conditions, unusual, 140–141
Code of Ethics. *See* Ethical guidelines
Code of Hammurabi, 35
Code of Ishaq Ibn Ali Al-Ruhawi, 36

Colorado v Connelly, 97
Committee on Ethics, 45, 46, 120, 123, 172–173, 175, 178–180, 330–331
Common law, 47–48, 100, 199
Community Health Law Project, 307, 309
Community mental health, HIV infection and, 223–224
Competency decisions
  responsibility for, 82
  standard for, 199–200
Competency for execution
  evaluation of, 38, 45, 144–145, 159–160
  restoration of, 45, 145, 160, 207
Competency to give informed consent, 199–200
Competency to stand trial evaluation, 27, 132, 141, 144, 145, 154–155, 158
  pre-treatment, 135
  privacy in, 68
Competency to stand trial restoration, 141
Comprehensive Crime Control Act of 1984, 101–102
Concentration camps, 42, 47
Confession, involuntary, 97, 112n.
Confidentiality, 11, 129, 237
  betrayal of, 133
  in capital punishment cases, 212
  court-ordered testimony and, 131
  criminal cases, 152
  dangerousness and, 137–138
  duty-to-protect and, 203–205
  ethical guidelines, 130, 137, 164–165, 328
  in France, 36
  Hippocratic oath and, 203
  HIV antibody testing and, 226–227, 237
  HIV infection and, 226–230, 249–250
  Miranda-type warnings and, 152
  in prison psychiatry, 68
  prosecution of mental patients and, 140
  psychotherapists' sexual misconduct and, 177–178
  for sex offenders, 277
Confinement, involuntary, *See* Civil commitment
Conflict of interests, 11, 135, 142
Conflicting appeals, 40–41, 46, 49
Consent, 151–152, 165–166, 264–265, 328–329. *See also* Informed Consent
Consequentialism, 24–25, 26, 38
Contagious diseases, 47, 204
Contingency fees, 69, 131, 168, 330
Contracts, regarding surrogate embryo transfer, 245, 247, 251–254
Countertransference, 126–127
  classical view of, 271
  direct, 272
  dyadic, 272, 273, 274–275
  indirect, 272
  in prison psychiatry, 64
  "response sets" in, 272–273, 274–275
  totalistic, 271–272
  triadic, 272–275
Court martial, of HIV-infected individuals, 230–231
Credentialing, of forensic psychiatrists, 20, 21
Credibility, of witnesses
  children, 94–95, 111n.
  expert witness, 100
  eyewitness, 95–98
  mentally disabled witness, 97
Criminal cases
  Miranda-type warnings, 151–162, 166
    in capital punishment case evaluations, 154, 158–160
    in competency to stand trial evaluations, 154–155, 158
    confidentiality and, 152
    in dangerousness evaluations, 156–158
    in reconstructive evaluations, 155–156
  reasonable doubt and, 23
Criminal responsibility evaluation, 93, 144, 145. *See also* Insanity defense; Not guilty by reason of insanity defense
  treater/evaluator dual role regarding, 142
Critical Issues in American Psychiatry and the Law, 20
Cross-examination
  of expert witness, 61, 62, 88, 89, 100, 167–168
    avoidance of, 89
    honesty and, 167–168
    impartiality and, 122
  regarding eyewitness identification, 95, 96
Curran, William, 61, 65, 118, 286
Custody litigation, 259–260, 266, 330. *See also* Child custody
Cyproterone acetate, 283

Daileda v United States, 98–99
Dangerous Child Abuse Index, 286
Dangerousness, prediction of, 27, 43, 92, 141, 185–196
  in capital punishment cases, 77, 212–213
  civil commitment following. *See* Civil commitment, for dangerousness
  confidentialty and, 137–138
  contexts of, 109n., 185
  criteria, 202
  by Dr. James Grigson, 77
  legal vs. psychiatric purposes of, 63
  Miranda-type warning in, 156–158
  in not guilty by reason of insanity cases, 156–157
  preventive detention, 186
  psychiatrist's responsibility for, 210
  reliability, 92, 187–191
  for sexual offenders, 156–157, 269, 270, 286
  Supreme Court decision regarding, 27
  Tarasoff responsibility and, 137, 140, 152, 185–186, 203–205, 210, 228
  therapeutic implications, 191–194
  time factors, 190–191
Data
  clinical, 20, 58
  legal, 58
  organization of, 26–28
Data bank, 172
Death penalty. *See* Capital punishment
Deconstruction of self, 7
Defective delinquent, 109n., 136
Defendant
  psychiatric examination of, 166
  on witness stand, 80–81
Defense attorney, evidence restriction by, 79–80
Defense testimony
  in capital punishment cases, 43, 45, 160
  entrapment as, 103
  evidence, 98–99
  therapeutic bias in, 49, 61, 66, 88
Definition of forensic psychiatry. *See* Psychiatry, forensic definition
Dementia, AIDS/HIV-related, 220, 221, 222–223, 237
De Officiis (Cicero), 35
Deontology, 24–25, 26, 38–39, 40, 56–57, 62, 66, 67
De Placitus (Galen), 36
Depo-Provera, 283–284
Derdiarian v Long Island RR Co., 108n.
Determinism, 7, 8. *See also* Free will
Diagnosis, misuse of, 275
Diagnostic and Statistical Manual (DSM), diagnostic classifications, 10, 62, 91, 93, 140, 270, 276–277, 293–299, 302
  HIV-related psychiatric illness, 224
  homosexuality, 293, 294, 295–299
  paraphilia, 270, 275, 276, 277–278
  pedophilia, 140, 276–277
  personal examination, 14
  unusual clinical conditions, 140
Diamond, Bernard, 32, 38, 44, 48, 61, 66, 87, 89, 107n., 120, 121–122, 123, 124, 125, 126, 127, 146, 160
Dietz, Park, 276
Dilemma. *See* Ethical dilemma; Moral dilemma
Diminished capacity, 79
  reconstructive evaluations and, 155
Disability, 43. *See also* Social Security
Disciplinary sanctions, 142, 168, 173, 181
Disclosure, total, 80–81
Discoverability, 144
Discrimination, HIV infection-related, 235–237
Divorce, 65, 260
  HIV infection and, 227, 230
Doll, anatomically correct, 95, 111n.
Domestic-relations disputes, 168
Double agency, 11, 48, 63–64, 67–68, 140, 152. *See also* Dual agency
Dr. Death, *See* Grigson, James
Drane, J., 274
Drug abuse
  HIV infection and, 225
  mind-brain problem and, 7
Drug testing, mandatory, 313–325
  accuracy, 314–316
  demand for, 313–314
  goals, 316–323
Dual agency, 146. *See also* Double agency
Durham v United States, 75
Duty to warn or protect. *See also* Dangerousness, Tarasoff responsibility and
  third party protection as, 137–138, 311
Dyer, Allen, 33, 35, 37, 39, 48

Edelstein, Ludwig, 33–34
Edwards v United States, 105
Ego, 5, 7

Ego ideal, 48
Elder abuse, 204, 307
Elderly, rights of, 307–312
Electroconvulsive therapy, 137
Emergency medical care and treatment, 329
Entrapment, 103
Enzyme linked immunosorbent assay (ELISA), 231–232, 235, 238
Epidemics, 34
Erdelyi, Matthew, 97–98
Erection measurement studies, 278, 281, 282, 286–287
Esch v United States, 92
Estelle v Smith, 143, 154, 158
Ethical boundaries, 4, 11–12, 15, 16, 32–33
Ethical complaint adjudication, 169, 171–174, 177, 180–181, 330–331. *See also* Hearings on ethics complaints
Ethical dilemma, 16, 129, 197
  judgment approach, 40–41
  value-balancing in, 39–40, 53–55, 60, 64–70, 197
Ethical guidelines, 39–40, 49, 151
  of American Academy of Forensic Sciences, 66–67
  of American Academy of Psychiatry and the Law, 19, 32, 164–168, 171–172, 286, 327–331
    adversarial system, 121
    advocacy, 122
    confidentiality, 130, 164–165
    cross-examination, 122
    honesty and striving for objectivity, 164, 167–168, 329–330
    impartiality and objectivity, 87, 117, 119, 122–124, 125–126, 128
    informed consent, 165–166, 328–329
    neutrality, 126–127
    psychiatrist's qualifications, 168–169
  of American Bar Association, 60, 69, 87, 97, 124–125
  of American Board of Forensic Psychiatry, 32, 66, 171, 327
  of American Medical Association, 4, 14, 33, 39, 43
    capital punishment, 46, 208–209
    HIV-infected patient care, 226
    National Interprofessional Code of Physicians and Attorneys, 60, 69
  of American Psychiatric Association, 14, 45, 171–172
Ethical guidelines (*Cont.*)
  of American Psychiatric Association (*Cont.*)
    capital punishment, 13, 46
    civil commitment, 45
    dangerousness prediction, 27, 186–187
    HIV-infected patient care, 226
    sexual misconduct, 176, 178, 180
Ethics. *See also* Values
  Appeal Board, 180
  definition, 37
  functions, 48
  legal, 56
  personal vs. professional, 38, 131, 146
  medical, 31–51, 56
    Aristotelian, 48
    balancing approach, 39–40, 53–55, 60–70
    boundaries of, 32–33
    guidelines. *See* Ethical guidelines
    judgment approach to, 40–41
    origins, 31, 33–37
    problem resolution in, 43–49
    survey, 31–32, 44–47, 160
    traditional. *See* Hippocratic traditional ethics
Euthanasia, 48
Evaluation, informed consent, 165–166, 328–329. *See also* Informed consent
Evidence
  beyond a reasonable doubt, 23, 189, 229
  character, 90
  clear and convincing, 23, 80, 189, 201
  in civil cases, 22–23
  cumulative, 101
  hearsay as, 62, 70, 89, 107n., 178
  legal restrictions on, 79–80, 81, 89, 93, 98–99, 101
  preponderance of, 22, 58–59, 189
Execution, legally authorized participant in, 45, 46, 160
Exhibitionist, 281, 283
Expert witness, 27–28, 75–84
  adversarial role, 76
  advocacy of, 45, 60–64, 76, 78–79
    "hired gun" role vs., 44
    impartiality and, 75–76, 122
  bias of, 49, 61, 66, 87, 88
  choice of, 61
  conflict between experts, 87, 89, 91, 93, 101, 119. *See also* Battle of the experts
  credibility, 100

Expert witness (*Cont.*)
 cross-examination, 61, 62, 88, 89, 100, 122, 167–168
 definition, 77–78, 88, 107n.
 diagnostic classification and, 91–92
 disqualification, 83
 eyewitness testimony and, 95–98
 as "hired gun," 44, 76–77, 81–84, 87, 119, 123, 160
 honesty, 78–79, 329–330
  ethical guidelines, 164, 167–168, 329–330
 impartiality, 75, 87, 117–128
  adversarial system and, 75–76, 121
  advocacy and, 122
  cross-examination and, 122
  ethical guidelines, 67, 87, 117, 119, 122–126, 128
  loss of, 66
  neutrality and, 126–127
 lay witness and, 92
 in malpractice cases, 88
 need for, 86
 objectivity, 66, 69, 124, 164, 167–168, 329–330. *See also* Honesty; Impartiality
 partisan, 15–16
 private practitioner as, 130–131, 132
 qualifications, 82–83, 86, 88, 99–100
 total disclosure, 80–81
 treater/evaluator dual role, 129–150
  in civil vs. criminal practice, 132
  combination of roles, 140–142
  in competency for execution cases, 144–146
  confidentiality and, 68, 133, 137–138
  decision making, 135–137
  duty to warn or protect, 137–140
  Miranda-type warnings and, 143–144
  in private vs. public practice, 130–131, 132
  separation of roles, 142–143
  type of treatment involved and, 133–134
  warning regarding purpose of evaluation, 146
Eyewitness identification/testimony, 95–98, 111–112n.

Facts, values vs., 5–6
Family, autonomy of, 260
Family law, 26, 65
 privatization of, 260–261
Fantasy, sexual, 277–278
Faust, D., and Ziskin, J., 107n.
Federal employees
 drug testing of, 313–314, 319–320, 324n.
 HIV antibody testing of, 233
Federal Rules of Evidence
 regarding character evidence, 90
 regarding expert testimony
  Rule 403, 101
  Rule 405, 108n.
  Rule 702, 86, 87, 88, 95, 96, 98
  Rule 704, 100–105, 114n., 115n.
Fees, contingency, 69, 131, 168, 330
Fellowship training programs, 20, 21, 163
Fertilization, *in vitro,* 243, 245–246
Fiduciary relationship, 32, 37, 47
Fifty Admonitions to Physicians by Isaac Israeli, 36
Fink, Paul, 22
Fitzgerald v. Manning, 106n.
Foot, Philippa, 37, 48
Forensic hospitals, psychiatric practice in, 130, 131
Forensic psychiatry. *See* Psychiatry, forensic
Forensic Sciences Foundation, 20
France, confidentiality in, 36
Free will
 determinism vs., 7, 8
 legal view of, 62, 63, 68–69
Freud, Sigmund
 case histories of, 87
 childhood trauma theory of, 6
 on countertransference, 126, 127
 on metapsychological ego, 5, 7
 seduction theory of, 95
 on therapists' sexual misconduct, 175–176
Freudian concept, 271
Frye test, 82, 98, 112n
Frye v United States, 112n.
Furman v Georgia, 207
Future behavior, prediction of, 141. *See also* Dangerousness, prediction of

Galen, 33
Gall, Franz, 65
Gambling, pathological, 140
Gaylin, Willard, 53
Geriatrics, 21–22
Gilligan, Carol, 24, 48
Goals, ethical, 57

Goldwater, Barry, 14
Good clinical practice standard, 8–10, 12, 13
Gorman, W., 70
Green, Joyce Hens, 97–98
Greenson, R., 176
Gregg v Georgia, 207
Gregory, John, 36–37
Grigson, James, 13–14, 15, 43, 77, 109n., 213
Griswold v Connecticut, 300
Groth, A.N., 276
Group for the Advancement of Psychiatry, 269–270
Guidelines
  ethical. *See* Ethical guidelines for Legislation on the Psychiatric Hospitalization of Adults, 187, 192
  for protecting health workers from HIV, 235
Gutheil, Thomas, 58, 59, 69, 271, 299
Guttmacher, 59
  award, 20

Halleck, Seymour, 11, 104, 125, 136, 140, 143, 287
Harm, do no, 14, 15, 24, 31, 46, 211. *See also Primum nil nocere*
Harris, Jean, 91, 109n.
Hartmann, Heinz, 5, 6
Hawkins v. State, 98
Health care personnel
  AIDS among, 236
  HIV-infected patient exposure, 235–237
Health insurance, for HIV-infected individuals, 237
Hearings on ethics complaints, 169, 172–173, 175, 178–180, 330–331. *See also* Ethical complaint adjudication
Hearsay, as evidence, 62, 70, 89, 107n., 178
Hearst, Patricia, 103–104
Hegel, 211
Hepatitis B, 235, 238
Hill v United States, 103
Hinckley, John, 3
Hinckley case/trial, 8, 10, 98, 101, 113–114n.
Hippocrates, 31, 33
Hippocratic oath, 33–35, 36, 37, 44, 47, 65, 199, 209
  abortion and, 47, 48
Hippocratic oath (*Cont.*)
  confidentiality and, 203–205
  contemporary nonrelevance of, 47
  defense testimony and, 43
  primum nil noncere and, 11, 33, 160, 210
Hippocratic traditional ethics, 15, 32, 36–37, 44, 45, 46–49, 159
  Moslem and Jewish sources, 36
  primum nil nocere and, 11, 33, 160, 210
"Hired gun" role, 44, 69, 76–77, 81–84, 87, 117, 119, 123, 160
Hiss, Alger, 98
Hiss v United States, 98
Historians, 87
Hoge, S. 193–194
Holmes, Oliver Wendell, 58, 303
Homicide
  by battered spouse, 95
  by physician, 34–35
  rate, 197
  by schizophrenic, 202
Homophobia, 223–224, 301
Homosexuality, 293–305
  criminal status, 293, 299–301, 302
  diagnostic status, 293, 294–299, 302
Homosexuals
  AIDS among, 220, 221
  HIV infection among, 222
    discrimination related to, 237
    prevention, 224–225
Honesty, 78–79, 164, 167–168, 329–330. *See also* Objectivity
Hospitalized patients, *See also* Civil commitment; Forensic hospitals
  HIV antibody testing of, 233, 234, 249–250
  HIV-infected, 249–250
  violence by, 187–191, 203
Human experimentation, 211
Human immunodeficiency virus (HIV)
  asymptomatic carriers, 219, 220, 228
  epidemiology, 220–221
  isolation, 219
  transmission, 220–221, 231, 235
Human immunodeficiency virus antibody testing
  administration, 233
  benefits, 229
  confidentiality regarding, 226–227
  counseling regarding, 233, 234–235
  for health insurance coverage, 237
  of hospitalized patients, 233, 234, 249–250

Human immunodeficiency virus antibody testing (*Cont.*)
  informed consent for, 249–250
  recommendations regarding, 233–234
  risks, 229
  validity and reliability, 231–233
Human immunodeficiency virus infection. *See also* Acquired immune deficiency syndrome
  confidentiality regarding, 226–230
  discrimination, 235–237
  divorce and, 227, 230
  effects, 219
    AIDS development, 219, 220
    dementia, 220, 237
    neuropsychiatric complications, 221–223
    opportunistic infections, 222
    psychiatric complications, 223–225
  ethical issues, 225–230
  legal issues, 226–230
  prevention, 224–225
  quarantine, medical, 237
  surrogate embryo transfer and, 245, 248–250
Humanism, of the law, 67
Hume, David, 36–37
Hundert, Edward, 39–41, 46, 49
Hutcheson, Frances, 36–37
Hypothetical questions, 14
Hysteria, 95

Ibn-Tamas v United States, 111n.
Id, 7
Immigrants, HIV antibody testing, 234
Impairment of physician, 187
Impartiality
  adversarial system and, 122
  advocacy and, 122
  cross-examination and, 122
  ethical guidelines, 67, 87, 117, 119, 122–126, 128, 164
  impossibility of, 75, 87
  loss of, 66
  neutrality and, 126–127
In re Interest of D.L.S., 106n.
Incest offenders, treatment, 285
Incompetency to be executed evaluation. *See* Competency to be executed evaluation
Individuality, 199
Informed consent
  criteria, 151–152, 264

Informed consent (*Cont.*)
  ethical guidelines, 165–166, 328–329
  for forensic evaulation, 166, 328
  for HIV antibody testing, 234, 249–250
  patient autonomy and, 63
  right, 39
  for surrogate parenting, 264–265
  threatened violence and, 198–200
Inquisitional process, 4
Insanity
  legal test for, 102, 110n
  M'Naughten rule, 75, 155, 216
  reconstructive evaluations and, 155–156
Insanity acquittal, 132, 142
Insanity defense, 46, 67, 82, 105. *See also* Not guilty by reason of insanity, criminal responsibility
  in capital punishment cases, 46, 212
  conflicting expert testimony in, 101
  Rule 704(b) and, 105, 114n.
Integrity, 69
Intoxication, pathological, 140
Intravenous drug use, as AIDS/HIV risk factor, 221, 225
Isaac, Israeli, 36

Jews
  anti-Semitism toward, 9
  Nazi persecution of, 42, 211, 214
  sources of Hippocratic tradition, 36
Jones v State, 75
Journal(s), forensic psychiatric, 4. *See also* titles of specific journals
Journal of Forensic Sciences, 4, 20
Judge
  appellate, 3
  discretion, 105, 110n
  expert witness disqualification by, 83
  instruction, 16
  role, 58, 69, 91–93, 105
  trial, 3
Jury
  competency decisions, 82
  role, 69, 75, 91–93, 94, 101, 102
Justice, 56, 66
  as social value, 15

Kant, Immanuel, 5, 9, 10, 24
Kantor, Jay, 41–42
Katz, Jay, 39
Kennedy, Robert, 89
Kernberg, Otto, 271
Kohlberg, Lawrence, 48

Ladner v Higgins, 107n.
Lawyer
  choice of expert witness by, 61
  evidence restriction by, 79–80
Lectures on the Duties and Qualifications of a Physician (Gregory), 36–37
Legal system, humanism of, 67
Leo, Dr., 9–10, 11, 42
Liability. *See also* Malpractice
  for patients' violence, 185–186
Liberty as a value, 54
Life imprisonment without parole, 145
Lifton, Robert Jay, 42, 211
Lunacy commission, 82

MacDonald, Captain, 104, 114n.
MacDonald v United States, 108n., 114n.
Macklin, Ruth, 37
Malingering, 23, 107n., 145, 274
Malpractice
  under Code of Hammurabi, 35
  expert testimony regarding, 88, 99–100, 163
  legal, 88
  protection for members of ethics committee, 179
  sexual misconduct as, 176
Mandatory drug testing. *See* Drug testing, mandatory
Manslaughter, 109n.
Marijuana use
  as HIV infection risk factor, 225
  mandatory testing for, 314, 318, 321–322
Marriage license, HIV antibody testing for, 233, 234
McNaughten rule. *See* M'Naughten rule
Mead, Margaret, 35
Medical Ethics (Percival), 37
Medical ethics, 39–40, 56. *See also* Ethics; Hippocratic traditional ethics
Medical records, of HIV-infected individuals, 230
Medicine, as profession, 35–36
Medroxyprogesterone acetate, 283–284
Memory, expert testimony regarding, 95–98
Menninger, Karl, 64–65, 91
Mens rea, 67, 80, 109n., 155, 216
Mental disease or defect, 75, 110n.
Mental hospitals, psychiatric practice in, 129, 131
Mental illness. *See also* specific types of mental illness
  diagnostic classification, 91–92. *See also* *Diagnostic and Statistical Manual*
Mental and Physical Disability Law Reporter, 20
Mentally disabled
  as credible witnesses, 97
  prosecution of, 139–140
  violence by, 202–203
Mentally disordered sex offenders, 156–157, 270. *See also* Sexual psychopath laws; Sexually dangerous persons
Mental state, expert testimony regarding, 100–105. *See also* Competency decisions; Competency to be executed evaluation; Competency to stand trial evaluation; Insanity defense
  reconstructive evaluation, 155–156
Military doctors, 24, 48. *See also* Army doctors
Mill, John Stuart, 25
Miller, Robert, 45
Miller v People, 94
Mills, Mark, 58, 299
Mind-brain problem, 7–8
Minnesota Multiphasic Personality Inventory, sex offender applications, 279, 280
Minority opinions, 49
Miranda decision, 151
Miranda-type warnings, 68, 132, 143, 151–162, 166
  context of, 152–160
    capital punishment case evaluation, 154, 158–160
    during clinical practice, 144
    competency to stand trial evaluation, 154–155, 158
    competency to understand, 154
    confidentiality and, 152
    dangerousness evaluation, 156–158
    reconstructive evaluation, 155–156
  treater/evaluator dual role and, 142
Mirth Response Test, 10
M'Naughten rule, 75, 155, 216. *See also* Right and wrong test
Monahan, John, 187, 192–193
Moore, Michael, 8, 194–195
Moral adventure, 16
Moral dilemma, 39–40. *See also* Ethical dilemma

Moral minefield, 24
Morality, caring vs., 48
Morals, ethics and, 37–38
Multiple personality disorder, 97, 115n., 140, 142
Murder, 109n. *See also* Homicide
Murderer, testosterone levels, 281
Murtishaw v People, 213
Myerson, Bess, 94

NAACP, Legal Defense Fund, 215
Nassau County School Board, Florida v Arline, 236
National Federation of Societies for Clinical Social Work, 137
National Interprofessional Code for Physicians and Attorneys, 60, 69
National Medical Association, 145
National Treasury Employees Union v Von Raab, 324n.
Nazis, 42, 47, 211, 214
Negligence. *See* Malpractice
Neutrality, 121
  analytic, 126–127
  ethical, 31, 39
"New Hampshire" rule, 75
Newsletter of the American Academy of Psychiatry and the Law, 20
Non-maleficence, 37, 46, 211
Not guilty by reason of insanity, 13, 92, 145, 156–157. *See also* Insanity defense, criminal responsibility evaluation
Nursing homes, 307, 308–310

Oath-helping, 110n.
Objectivity, 66, 69, 124. *See also* Honesty; Impartiality
  advocacy vs., 60, 61
  definition, 125
  ethical guidelines, 167–168, 329–330
Occupational Safety and Health Administration, HIV infection guidelines, 235
Ophuls, Marcel, 87

Panel of experts, 82
Paraphilia, 243
  diagnostic classification, 270, 275, 277–278
  erection measurement studies, 278, 281, 282, 286–287
  treatment, 283–284
Parens patriae, 63, 201
Parents. *See also* Surrogate parenting
  adoptive, rights of, 257
  biological
    psychological vs., 6, 7
    rights of, 257
Partisanship, 15–16
Paternalism, medical, 47, 56, 194, 199
Pathological gambling. *See* Gambling, pathological
Patients
  autonomy, 47
  psychotherapist's sexual exploitation of, 175–182
    case example, 178–181
    confidentiality and, 177–178
    ethics committee hearings regarding, 178–181
    Freud on, 175–176
    incidence, 175, 176
    as malpractice, 176
    patients' complaints regarding, 177–178
Pedophile
  testosterone levels, 281
  treatment, 283, 285
Pedophile Aggression Index, 286
Pedophile Cognition Scale, 280
Pedophilia, 140, 275, 276
  diagnostic classification, 276–277
Pellegrino, Edmund, 47, 294
People v Beckley, 95
People v Izzo, 94
People v Miller, 94
People v Murtishaw, 213
People v Stricklin, 94
Perception, expert testimony regarding, 95–98
Percival, Thomas, 36, 37
Personal examination, 45, 168, 330
Pharmacological therapy, treater/evaluator role in, 133–134, 137
Philosophy, moral, 24–26, 211
Physician
  with AIDS, 236
  army, 211
  capital punishment participation by, 208–209
  "duty to warn", 228
  homicide by, 34–35
  Nazi, 42, 47, 211
  paternalism of, 47, 56, 194, 199

Physician-patient relationship
absence of, 161, 328
in Hippocratic tradition, 46
Piaget, Jean, 48
Pike v State, 75
Plato, 34
Pollack, Seymour, 12, 22, 31, 61, 64, 66, 67
Polygraph, 94, 286
Posttraumatic stress disorder, 107, 140
Pound, Ezra, 42
Pre-employment interview, 46–47
Premeditation, 109n., 114n.
Primum nil nocere, 11, 24, 31, 32, 160. *See also* Harm, do no
in capital pujnishment cases, 210, 212
origin, 33–34
Prisoners
HIV antibody testing of, 233
psychiatric treatment of, 63–64, 67–68, 129
Privacy as a value, 54
in mandatory drug testing, 316–319
Privacy, in mandatory drug testing, 316–319
Privacy Doctrine, 300, 302
Private practice, public practice vs., 129, 130–131, 132
Privilege, 144, 159. *See also* Confidentiality
Probability, 106n.
Product liability, 238
Profession, definition of, 33
Professional secrets, 36
Professionalization, 59
Proof, standard of. *See* Evidence, clear and convincing; preponderance of the; beyond a reasonable doubt
Prosecution
expert witness testimony for
before access by defendant to attorney, 166, 329
in capital punishment cases, 13–14, 61
ethics of, 4, 11–12
Miranda-type warnings and, 166
of mental patients, 139–140
Protect. *See* Duty to warn or protect
Proximate cause, 23, 90, 108n.
Psychiatrist. *See also* Psychotherapist
forensic. *See also* Expert witness
assessor role, 210, 211
definition, 211
double agent, 11, 48, 63–64, 67–68, 140, 146, 152
partisan, 15
Psychiatrist (*Cont.*)
private vs. public practice, 129, 130–131, 132
qualifications, 169, 330
roles, 32, 152
roles, understood by evaluee, slippage, 154, 158, 328
training, 20, 21, 69–70, 163
military, 24, 48, 64
prison, 63–64, 67–68, 129
Psychiatry
behavioral, 7
biological, 7, 62
definition, 163
geriatric, 21–22
political abuse of, 15
Psychiatry, forensic
certification, 21, 28. *See also* American Board of Forensic Psychiatry
definition, 3, 19, 22, 31–32, 66–67, 171, 327
ethical guidelines. *See* Ethical guidelines
ethics of, 3–17
ethical dialectic, 11–12, 32
ethical foundations, 4, 32
facts vs. values in, 5–7
issues in, 41–43
professional disagreements in, 23–24, 25–26
research, 28
scientific standard, 10–11, 12, 13
in Soviet Union, 15
special competence in, 21
as subspecialty, 4, 19–29, 69, 163
accreditation as, 20–22
training, 21, 28, 49, 69–70, 146
Psychotherapist, sexual misconduct by, 175–182
case example, 178–181
confidentiality and, 177–178
ethics committee hearings regarding, 178–181
Freud on, 175–176
incidence, 175, 176
as malpractice, 176
patients' complaints regarding, 177–178
reporting of, 138–139
Psychotherapy, 137
nonjudgmental nature of, 41
for sexual offenders, 283
treater/evaluator role in, 133
Punishment, moral philosophy of, 25

Qualifications, 168, 330
Quarantine, of AIDS patients, 237

Racism, 43
Rada, Richard, 271, 281
Railway Labor Executives' Association v Burnley, 324n.
Rape victim, as credible witness, 94
Rapist
  paraphilic, 140
  testosterone levels, 281
  types of, 279–280
Rappeport, Jonas, 10–11, 12, 120–121, 160, 271
Rashomon, 87
Rawls, John, 40
Ray, Isaac, 8, 75
Reagan, Ronald, 233, 313, 323
Reality, 87, 88
  medical vs. legal, 58–59
Reasonable doubt, 23
Reasonable medical certainty, 96, 106n.
Reasonable medical probability, 86, 158
Reasoning, moral, 7
Reconstructive evaluation, 155–156
Reductionism, biological, 6
Reed v State, 112n.
Reproductive technology, 257–258. *See also* Artificial insemination; Surrogate embryo transfer
Republic (Plato), 34
Res gestae witness, 106n.
Resnick, P., 145
Retribution, 153
Right and wrong test, 79. *See also* M'Naughten rule
Right to refuse treatment, 137, 142
Robertson v McCloskey, 97–98
Robitscher, Jonas, 119, 299
Roe v Wade, 247, 300, 301
Rofman, E., 187, 189, 191
Rogers, R., 271
Rooney, Andy, 113–114n.
Rosenhan, David, 107n.
Roth, Loren, 10, 11, 12, 13, 67, 160, 193

Sadistic personality disorder, 254
Sadoff, Robert, 114n.
Sanity, simulation of, 156
Saul, Leon, 176
Schizophrenia, homicide correlation, 202
Science, morality vs., 8
Scientific method, 58
Scientific standard, 10–11, 12, 13
Scribonius Largus, 35, 36
Sears, Roebuck & Co. v Haven Hill Farm, 100
Seduction theory, 95
Seelye v State, 113n.
Self, deconstruction of, 7
Self-determination, 63, 199
Self-reports, by sex offenders, 280
Sentencing hearing, expert testimony at, 76
  in capital punishment cases, 145, 207–208, 212
    Miranda-type warnings, 158–159
Sentencing statutes, dangerousness and, 185–189, 191
Separation, as trauma, 6, 7
Sex History Questionnaire for Males, 280
Sex Inventory, 280
Sex offenders. *See also* Child abuse, sexual
  confidentiality for, 277
  countertransferential issues, 217–282, 285–286
    assessment techniques, 280–282, 286
    diagnostic issues, 275–278
    typology of offenders, 279–280
  dangerousness assessment of, 156–157, 269, 270, 286
  treatment of, 138, 282–285
Sex psychopaths, 109n.
Sexual abuse
  of children, 94–95, 111n.
    countertransference and, 271
    reporting of, 138–139
  litigation, 111n.
  by psychotherapist. *See* Sexual misconduct, by psychotherapist
Sexual fantasies, 276–278
Sexual harassment, 180
Sexual Interest Card-sort, 280
Sexually abused child syndrome, 94–95
Sexually dangerous persons, 279. *See also* Mentally disordered sex offenders, Sexual psychopath laws
Sexual misconduct, by psychotherapist, 175–182
  case example, 178–181
  confidentiality and, 177–178
  ethics committee hearings regarding, 178–181
  former patients, 180
  Freud on, 175–176
  incidence, 175, 176

Sexual misconduct, by psychotherapist (*Cont.*)
as malpractice, 176
patients' complaints regarding, 177–178
reporting of, 138–139
Sexual partners, of HIV-infected individuals, 233, 235
confidentiality regarding, 226–228, 249–250
Sexual psychopath laws, 136, 145, 269–270
Sexual psychopath statutory criteria, 269–270
Shoplifting, 9–10
Simon, Robert, 176
Sirhan, Sirhan, 89
Slippage, 154, 158, 328
Social control, 43, 63, 65
Social Security, 24, 65
Sociopaths, 109n.
Socrates, 34
Sodomy
laws regarding, 293, 295, 300–301
Supreme Court decisions regarding, 300–301, 302
Southern Poverty Law Center, 215
Soviet Union, 15
Specific intent, reconstructive evaluations and, 155
Spitzer, Robert, 295, 297, 298–299, 302
Spouse
elder abuse by, 307
of HIV-infected patients, 226–227
Staggs v United States, 108n.
State v Christensen, 108n.
State v Gonzales, 108n.
State v Haseltine, 110n.
State v Hood, 108n.
State v Jensen, 110n.
State v Jones, 75
State v Lange, 82
State v Myers, 94–95
State v Pike, 75
Stern, William, 258
Stone, Alan, 24, 32–33, 41, 42–43, 55, 60, 177, 186, 187, 192, 193–194, 195
Strasburger, L., 141
Stricklin v United States, 94
Striving for Objectivity. *See* Honesty; Impartiality; Objectivity
Superego, 7, 48
lacunae, 66
Supervision after ethical misconduct, 181
Supreme Court decisions. *See also* specific decisions
disease-related discrimination, 236
family law, 261
homosexuality, 293, 300–301, 302
involuntary confessions, 97
mandatory drug testing, 314
prediction of future dangerousness, 27
psychiatric expert witnesses, 76
sodomy, 300–301, 302
Surrogate embryo transfer, 243–255
abortion following, 246, 247, 248
contracts regarding, 245, 247, 251–254
HIV infection and, 245, 248–250
Surrogate parenting, 257–268. *See also* Surrogate embryo transfer
principles of, 259–261
public policy regarding, 261–263
regulatory framework, 263–266
reproductive technology and, 257–258
Szasz, Thomas, 91

Tancredi, Lawrence, 15
Tarasoff v Regents of the University of California, 137, 140, 152, 185–186, 203–205, 210, 228
Tarnower, Herman, 91
Teleology, 57, 61, 62, 66, 67
Testamentary capacity, 14
Testosterone, 281
Therapeutic alliance
adversarial system and, 141, 142
treater/evaluator dual role in, 134, 135, 136
Therapeutic bias. *See* Bias, therapeutic
Therapeutic relationship, 180. *See also* Transference
Torsney case, 8
Tort cases, 85–86, 88, 100
Total disclosure, 80–81
Toulmin, Stephen, 39
Traditional medical ethics. *See* Hippocratic traditional ethics
Training, of forensic psychiatrists, 69–70
fellowships, 20, 21, 163
Transference. *See also* Therapeutic relationship
erotic, 176
factors affecting, 272, 273
negative, 135
Treater/evaluator dual role, 45, 118–119, 129–150, 330
in civil vs. criminal practice, 132

Treater/evaluator dual role (*Cont.*)
combination of roles, 140–142
in competency for execution cases, 144–145
confidentiality and, 68, 133, 137–138
decision making, 135–137
duty to warn or protect and, 137–140
Miranda-type warnings and, 143–144
in private vs. public practice, 130–131, 132
separation of roles, 142–143
type of treatment involved and, 133–134
Truth, 56, 59, 66
nature of, 87
psychiatry and, 5
scientific, 294
standard of, 12–13
whole, 79–80, 84
Tyson, Mike, 93

Ultimate issue rule, 69, 100–101, 102, 103, 104, 114n.
Uncertainty, 69
Unconsciousness, 62
reconstructive evaluations and, 155
Unethical conduct, 173–174, 175–182, 330–331
Uniform Code of Military Justice, 230
Uniform Commercial Code, 238
Union of Soviet Socialist Republics, forensic psychiatry in, 15
United States v Affleck, 96
United States v Alexander, 115n.
United States v Alvarez, 114n.
United States v Bernard, 98
United States v Brawner, 109n.
United States v Bright, 93
United States v Brodie, 114n.
United States v Buchbinder, 115n.
United States v Daileda, 98–99
United States v Davis, 115n.
United States v Dotson, 114n.
United States v Durham, 75
United States v Edwards, 105
United States v Esch, 92
United States v Hill, 103
United States v Hillsberg, 115n.
United States v Hiss, 98, 113n.
United States v MacDonald, 108n., 114n.
United States v Moore, 96
United States v Pohlot, 109n.
United States v Staggs, 108n.
United States v Washington, 103
United States v Webb, 108n.
United States v West, 108n.
United States v White, 109n.
Urine testing. *See* Drug testing, mandatory
Utilitarianism, 57, 215. *See also* Consequentialism

Values
balancing, 39–41, 55–57, 60–70
conflict of, 39–41, 43–46, 57
facts vs., 5–6
medical vs. legal, 53–72
processes of, 57–60
value-balancing problems of, 60–70
nonmedical, 15
traditional medical. *See* Hippocratic traditional ethics
Veatch, Robert, 33, 40
Victim, duty to. *See Tarasoff* case
Violence. *See also* Dangerousness, prediction of
management of, 197–206
case example, 198, 200
civil commitment and, 200–203
duty to protect and, 203–205
informed consent and, 198–200
psychiatrists' liability for, 185–186
mind-brain problem and, 7
Virtue, 48, 57
Voluntary consent. *See also* Informed consent
in surrogate parenting, 264–265

Warn. *See* Duty to warn or protect
Warning at onset of forensic evaluation, 143–144. *See also Miranda*-type warnings
Washington v United States, 103
Watson, Andrew, 8–10, 11, 12, 59
Webb v United States, 108n.
Western Blot test, 231, 232, 235
West v United States, 108n.
Whitehead, Mary Beth, 253–254, 258
Will, contesting of, 168
Wisconsin Sex Crimes Law, 136
Witness. *See also* Expert witness
children as, 94–95, 111n.
lay, 92
mentally disabled as, 97
res gestae, 106n.
Wold v State, 112n.

Workman's compensation, 65

Yesavage, J., 187, 188, 191

Zillboorg, Gregory, 57, 59

Ziskin, J., 107n.
Zitrin, A., 177
Zonana, Howard, 45, 271